The Hard Road
to Market

By the same author
(with John Moody)

The Priest Who Had to Die

The Hard Road
to Market

GORBACHEV, THE UNDERWORLD
AND THE REBIRTH OF CAPITALISM

ROGER BOYES

SECKER & WARBURG
LONDON

FOR FARIDA

First published in England 1990 by
Martin Secker & Warburg Limited
Michelin House, 81 Fulham Road, London SW3 6RB

Copyright © 1990 by Roger Boyes

A CIP catalogue record for this book is available
from the British Library

ISBN 0–436–05936–3

Set in 11/13 pt Linotron Electra by Deltatype Ltd, Ellesmere Port,
Printed in Great Britain by Clays Ltd, St Ives PLC

Contents

Introduction: The Post-Communist Age

This book probably began in Moscow on an early spring day in 1976. I was new then, and after years of study, new to working life. I felt safest in libraries and bookshops, and had struck up a sentimental attachment with a sales clerk in Dom Knigi, Moscow's largest bookshop. She had a sleepy freckled face, more Norman than Slavic. Her job was to make sure that not more than three people at a time browsed through the book stocks. We agreed to meet after work the following day and go for an ice-cream. It was a date of sorts and, happy with any kind of non-controlled contact with Russians, I strolled to the office. There was a grey slush on the ground and it sprayed like surf as a black Chaika limousine drew up outside Gosplan, the palace of statistics, of manipulated economics. 'Chaika' means seagull, but the car resembles rather the comic-strip Batmobile, finned in the style of the 1950s. An aide alighted from the back, the driver, built like a New York Irish cop, joined him and together they tugged out, bottom first, a Very Important Person. The numberplates suggested he was from the Central Committee; the manner of his exit indicated severe arthritis. Sure enough, he had a dark, smooth rubber-tipped cane that proved redundant because the two younger men – chosen perhaps for their muscles – hoisted him over the small atolls of melting snow onto the clean, defrosted steps of Gosplan. A few days later a particularly poor set of industrial production figures was due to be released but, on the anticipated date, the papers were full of more pressing business: a visiting theatre director, a report from a successful dairy farm in the provinces. When the figures eventually came out they were not so bad after all. Rather good, in fact.

The connection between the crippled Party man and the unexpected improvement in economic performance was, I suppose, an imaginary bond forged at a time of heightened sensibility. Perhaps the Western commercial attachés had merely been calling the wrong shots. Perhaps the Party man was visiting the planning institute to discuss personnel policy, or the interior design of the offices. But I like to think that the chance sighting was a legitimate piece of political ornithology; such is the vanity of the Kremlinologist. Whatever the case, I remember most clearly the expression on the bigwig's face as he was cradled over the puddles. It was a fixed, complacent gaze; a man so wrapped in privilege that he was unaware of his physical absurdity. The Emperor Tiberius, who would dispose of lives rather than pig-iron statistics, must have worn a similar mien.

Over a decade later, in Warsaw, I watched a member of the Polish Politburo visit a lightbulb factory that bears the name of an unsuccessful woman revolutionary. Making lightbulbs is not as glamorous as it sounds. It is dirty, sometimes dangerous, always noisy work. The workers from the morning shift were happy to crowd out of the assembly halls into a courtyard to drum up a welcome; they were mainly women, their hair tied back, some carefully manicured for a night out on the following day, a Saturday. They clucked and chattered. It was expected that at least one of the workers would complain to the Visitor about the poorly stocked department stores, about the absence of meat and the price of fish. This public grumbling was a normal procedure in Poland of the 1980s and did not denote a particularly fierce Solidarity stronghold or imminent revolt. Simply, people were no longer afraid to complain. The Party dignitary, with a cortege of managers and bodyguards, entered the factory premises, smiled (an innovation of the 1980s), waved and then held out his hand to be grasped by the masses.

Nobody took it. His features, which under better circumstances were blurred, as if distorted by a stocking mask, became a study in clinical anxiety. His eyelids fluttered rapidly; he looked like a rich fat boy in the bad part of town. The protocol of power had broken down.

The difference between these two slight observations is more than the difference between the Soviet Union and Poland, and more than the passage of time. The Communist Party, in the space of a decade, had grown old; to many, it seemed on the point of death. This book spans those years, from the time when the Party had the almost unquestioned right to determine the lives of a billion and a half people from Rostock to Shanghai, to the Gorbachev days of fear and experimentation, the 1990s admixture of recklessly improvised crisis management, the demolition of idols and the search for a new legitimacy. The revolutions of 1989, the snap revolutions, were made possible not so much because of the strength of democratic opposition but because of the fatal weakness of Party power. 'People power' as American news magazines insisted on calling the demonstrations that flooded the piazzas of the East, was important, but it was a symptom rather than the cause of Communist decline.

If there is a single reason for the collapse of Communist power then it must surely be the failure of the centrally planned economy to satisfy even the most basic of needs. The Party had built its power, its right to rule, on the basis of its control of the economy. Since the Party could not claim to be a competent managing class, since it could not distribute goods efficiently, it also had to yield its position as unchallenged arbiter of social justice. The market – black, grey and other shadings – crept into the crevices left by the Plan. Illegal markets flourished in even the most repressive of Communist countries – North Korea, say – and provided scarce goods at appropriately high prices. A black-money economy also sprang up, and its tentacles touch almost every citizen in the Communist world. There is barely a twelve-year-old child left in Poland or Romania who does not know the black-market exchange rates; it is dollars, not their local currencies, that can buy them Lego building blocks or Barbie dolls. Socialism accepted a second republic of True Economics, with its own rewards, punishments, imperatives and ideology. This market revolution is the key to understanding the accelerating events in Eastern Europe; the market that took hold of Soviet-Bloc societies in the 1970s and 1980s changed fundamentally the terms of reference. It undermined a dogma which still draws on egalitarianism, which is still emotionally opposed to private property. If there is a core message to the works of Marx and Engels, it is the persistent, almost obsessive attempt to show that men in a market society lose their human quality and that this quality can only be regained by suppressing exchange.

Marx, of course, was writing and thinking at a time of child labour, of naked early Capitalism, when the limitations of the market seemed all too obvious. Marxism failed as a predictive device, but not even the early apostles of free markets could really guess the resilience of Capitalism. Most assumed that the saturation of markets would set up frontiers. Instead Capitalism has shown itself remarkably capable of innovation, prospecting new markets and transforming workers from units of labour into savers and consumers with a fixed stake in the survival of the system. In centrally planned economies, by contrast, a high-suction market has been created and life is framed around permanent shortages. The bureaucratic apparatus is swollen to a point

where innovation is regarded as a threat. As in the West, the worker has
been remodelled into a consumer – but one doomed to frustration
within the official economy.

The black market, the Republic of Economics, was actively
encouraged by Communist authorities in the 1970s. It siphoned off the
savings of the workers, it provided a form of incentive and in its way
sustained the official economy. But it also widened the social gulf – the
great social divide is between those with and those without access to hard
currency – and exposed the cupidity of Party officials who, wanting to
play the money game, took bribes for political services. These are the
tensions that were unbottled by the 1989 uprisings, and that still bubble
away in the Soviet Union. It was primarily a consumer revolt that
tipped the scales in that year. Poland, after a decade of battle between
the Communist authorities and Solidarity, agreed to a power-sharing
deal that would, it was plain, phase out the Communists; by September,
the first non-Communist government of the region was sworn in. But
there was also a twin revolt in East Germany. On the streets there were
Solidarity-style demonstrations demanding a freer society while, across
the borders, there was a vast exodus of young East Germans to the West.
After some fifteen years of living in Central and Eastern Europe, I am
still prey to the romance of opposition. It was thus slightly shocking to
talk to the eighteen- and twenty-year-olds from Leipzig and Karl-
Marx-Stadt as they walked across the open Austro-Hungarian border.
They told banal stories about impoverished lives; they wanted jeans, a
good job, a car that did not squeak and growl like the Trabant. They
were the East German television generation, filled every night with
Western images of success – from hair-spray advertisements to 'Dallas' –
and had grown up with the idea that they were trapped in an economic
system that could not offer them a shadow of the lifestyle enjoyed by
their contemporaries in Essen and Munich. This generation was not
frightened off by the old propaganda about unemployment and
homelessness – indeed they were barely aware of the propaganda, since
they did not read official newspapers or watch East German television
news. Knocking holes in the Berlin Wall did not help this generation
come closer to its dreams. They filed through the new control points,
gaped, and returned. The volume of the East Berlin black market
quadrupled in six months: the rush was on to earn as many Western
marks as possible; plumbers, taxi drivers, tailors, builders abdicated
from the local currency and laboured only for hard currency. A
depressing sight of the times was the file of East German girls outside the

brothel in West Berlin's Savigny Platz, competing for business against the West German prostitutes. Most were trying to save enough money to do up a kitchen at home, over the Wall.

The East German uprising unlocked the others: the Czechs, the Bulgarians, the Lithuanians, even the Romanians. East Germany was the linchpin of the Soviet security system; if Moscow allowed the Germans to go then there were truly no obstacles left. Freedom was in the air. But freedom to do what?

This book is about the post-Communist era. It is a story-book, a reporter's notebook without academic pretensions, though academics have walk-on parts. I believe that the forces that sapped the authority of the Communist order are laying the foundations of the new. To talk of the post-Communist age is not to suggest that Communism is dead and buried, any more than Daniel Bell's expression 'post-industrial society' signified the demise of industry. Even in Poland where Communism seemed most alien – Stalin said it was like putting a saddle on a cow – the values of Socialism, only four decades old, are already deeply entrenched. The scale of Communist power is still vast but Communism is now only one of many forces at play in determining the future shape of East European societies. As political pluralism took root, long-neglected sectional interests began to recover their voice. Farmers revived pre-war agrarian parties, newly liberated newspapers began to jostle for attention, television satellite antennae sprouted on rooftops, economies were opened up to Western business. But the contours of these astonishing changes were marked out by the market revolution, and the post-Communist dilemma was how to strike a compromise between market and state. There are no entirely pure models of free markets or planned economies. Perhaps it is feasible to stake out a middle ground without abandoning the principles of Socialism. That certainly was the premise of the reform Socialist administrations in the Soviet Union, Bulgaria and elsewhere. To other societies, such as Poland and Hungary, reform Socialism had lost its charm: the drive was on to convert wholly to a free market. There is no solid answer and it is not helpful to view the problems of the disintegrating Soviet Bloc as a battlefield between Capitalism and Communism.

Instead, I have tried to look at the daily difficulties from birth to death, in the health service, education, in the purchase of a house or a car, to test how services currently in the hands of the black market could be channelled into legal, private enterprise. But market forces have to be understood; they do more than plug the supply gaps opened up by a deficient planning machine. Markets disperse authority, and make the centre seem vulnerable and weak to the periphery. Gorbachev cannot introduce an integrated nationwide market in a multinational empire. Freeing food prices throughout the Soviet Union would release a destructive genie. Markets that operate in authoritarian systems also make for a new form of geo-politics. Scale becomes important. A nationwide market might be feasible in the Baltic Republics, in Poland, in Hungary, but not in a territory that stretches from the eastern borders of Poland to the northern frontier of Mongolia. The Gorbachev puzzle is thus how to turn black markets into white without disrupting public order and without pulverising the foundations of Socialism. The East European societies, Gorbachev's neighbours, are not so constrained; they have no imperial obligations, no commitment to carry the flag of Socialism. But they, like Gorbachev, must solve the riddle of how to introduce Capitalism without capital, how to satisfy the constantly rising expectations of their peoples.

The spread of the black market in the Soviet Bloc of the 1970s effectively criminalised everyday life. To survive, it was usually necessary to break the law; to prosper, or even to fulfil the Plan, some kind of criminal transaction was compulsory. My search for the roots of the Capitalist revival in Eastern Europe thus took me into the criminal underworld. This book is peopled with prostitutes, pimps, smugglers and money-changers. During a decade or more of stagnation, they were the dynamic force in society. At times I have gone directly from a formal interview with a Party official to have a drink with a member of the Communist underworld in an expensive hotel bar. Although the black-marketeer might entertain fantasies about the West, his feet were always closer to the ground than those of the avowed Communist. The criminal made money out of weakness or shortage; the official made a career out of concealing weakness. The past decade has witnessed two parallel developments: the rise of entrepreneurs who perforce have to deal in black markets, who operate in and out of the legal dimension, whose role can never be clearly defined in a society shaped on Communist lines; and the shaping of a criminal class which is sometimes identical with, and always close to, the emerging entre-preneurial group.

The Hard Road to Market is an account not only of the markets that govern everyday life in late-Communism, but of those other markets that cater for human rather than systematic weakness: gambling, smuggling, prostitution and moonshine industries. There is some, but not much, scope for Gorbachev-style reform in these areas. Certainly, as Gorbachev is aiming for moral as well as economic perestroika – to rebuild Socialist man – the wild side has to be taken into consideration. The revival of the market is a criminal continuum, from the supplier of disposable nappies to the supplier of moonshine liquor.

My favourite bar in Eastern Europe is a late-night place, Na Trakcie, one of Warsaw's seediest spots. Foreigners are rare there, apart from the strange Libyan-Palestinians who seem to float so freely on the fringes of the black markets. Here, long after the conventional nightclubs have shut, late-night metropolitan low life gathers for a *wodka* or three. Waiters, taxi-drivers, drug-dealers, prostitutes, businessmen who sell furs and buy bathroom tiles, unbuttoned policemen, the Macheaths and Peachums, the entire *Threepenny Opera* of a Communist capital. Some of these characters were Party members (an alcoholic doctor, some of the policemen, one of the waiters) not out of conviction but because it paid to be in the network of power. Some doors were opened, some contacts forged. Nowadays there is nobody, not even the policemen (though they retain their cards) with an active party interest; it has become an irrelevancy. When a new (if short-lived) Polish industry minister, Mieczyslaw Wilczek, turned out to be a millionaire private industrialist, there was only a flutter of surprise. The party was only admitting what everybody in Na Trakcie had known for ages: that Communists were no longer equipped to run an economic strategy and that private business, legal or illegal, was now in the ascendant.

The criminalisation of ordinary existence, the ousting of the Party, the search for improvised solutions to economic or political dilemmas, the drift in values between gut egalitarianism and crass materialism: all this establishes a societal framework that calls for a new elite, for different forms of political management. It is an odd paradox that at a time when police states are being demolished, the police are growing in importance as the managers of the post-Communist society. They are already competing for control of perestroika and the outcome of the competition will determine the *socialist* quality of market reform. For that reason, this book discusses the market revolution in terms of both crime and punishment. The Republic of Economics, that segment liberated from Lenin, cannot be run by a business class alone. If black-market forces are to be washed white, if the market is to be expanded throughout society, then it is the police, and a group that I call judicial technicians, who will come to set the pace of change. Market

Socialism, as an ideal, is a kind of auction in which different groups, operating in a pluralistic framework, bid competitively for political or economic liberties. But who is to set the limits of change, to declare, so to speak, the reserve price in this auction? Not the Party, which has retreated almost completely from economic management in Eastern Europe. When the fashionable phrase was 'scientific and technical revolution' – a fancy way of saying modernisation – the leadership pool was drawn from engineers. Every Politburo member wanted his son to be an engineer, in electronics or missiles; few urged political careers on their children (with Nicolae Ceausescu, as ever, the dishonourable exception). Now there is still a need for rule by technicians, but technicians who can handle the rapidly changing social and economic ground-rules, experts at maintaining order. Martial law in Poland in 1981, the shooting of students in Peking in 1989, were auguries. Market Socialism demands either supervision or repression. For every one of Socialism's problems, from housing to food, from factory to parliamentary democracy, there are only two outcomes: a market solution or the battening down of expectations by a repressive apparatus. Both demand the different skills of police technicians. There is no 'Marxist' solution to the chronic shortage of cars in Eastern Europe. There is a market response: freeing prices, raising production incentives, allowing personal imports. That entails bringing the car black market above ground and only the police–judiciary complex is capable of such supervision. And there is the repressive response: Romania, under the Ceausescus, banned the use of private cars in winter. Plainly, that too endows the police with important powers.

I identify the managers of post-Communism as private entrepreneurs, policemen and a specific Westernised breed of new-look politicians. They are all transitional figures, because these are transitional times. The best this book can do is take snapshots, hold the events in freeze-frame. The more one experiments with market or semi-market solutions for the decaying Communist system, the more it becomes clear that there are successful and unsuccessful Capitalisms and so too there are failed and potentially successful variants of Socialism. *The Hard Road* is about the search for the appropriate formula, the right way through the maze. No claims to science, then; only an attempt to illustrate how, in the late twentieth century, an old order is giving painful birth to the new.

PART I

The End Of
The Old Order

1

Planned Shortages

THE PLAN

The secretary was frightened to open the door. From inside the office came explosive curses, invoking God, whores and mothers; September was not a good time to see the director of the Moscow factory named 'In Memory of the 1905 Revolution'. The plant makes electric coffee grinders and supplies them to most of the Soviet Union. The director, a man who wears his status on his lapels, is well-paid and highly regarded in the Party. It is said that he is one of the new breed, the educated technocrat who can get things done. But on a September morning, with production crippled and nobody returning his telephone calls, the director is a study in mental derangement. He slaps the blotter until the coffee cups spill their muddy contents; a proffered Western cigarette burns helplessly in the ashtray. There are no boxes to pack the grinders; the Plan is slipping. There is a shortage of the tiny electro-motors that drive the grinders, and neither metal nor moulds have been delivered.

In a few days, it will be October and the factory will lose its September bonus. Worse, even if by some miracle, the suppliers make good the shortfalls, it will be almost impossible to meet the October target. And then the winter starts, with its traditional bottlenecks.

'Call in the chief engineer,' he says on the intercom, a novelty (in the old days, last year actually, he had to walk the length of his long office, past the shiny wooden cabinet and the coffee table and green chairs for visitors, and the proud, gleaming grinder, to the secretary's alcove and ask her to make the call). The chief engineer arrived, the guest was parked with the secretary, and, behind the closed doors, the most powerful men in the factory decided to call in a *tolkach*.

Tolkachi are the quiet heroes of modern Russia. The name literally means 'pusher': their job is to travel around the Soviet Union prodding suppliers into coming up with the planned shipment, finding alternative factories or alternative goods. Nowadays, they are legally employed in the procurement division but they are regarded as shady figures, fixers with black- or grey-market connections. On stage and screen *tolkachi* are portrayed as rogues, careerists, sharks. But every major factory needs them; indeed a Gosplan (the Soviet State planning committee) survey of eighty-five supplying factories showed that they used sixty-eight thousand *tolkachi* over sixteen months. That is, several hundred *tolkachi* per factory.

The director of the 1905 Revolution Coffee Grinders needed three *tolkachi* to get him out of his squeeze. The first was a grizzled man who had been a career soldier but was pensioned out early because of a crushed hand. Like most *tolkachi*, he was an uncomfortable presence, not really fitting into the factory hierarchy, yet essential to its well-being. His task was to arrange for the cardboard boxes so that the hundreds of grinders lingering in the store-rooms could be sent off and a rough balance could be struck between the production and the sales figures. The *tolkach* travelled to the paper factory, part of a 'trust' – a group of factories and workshops that co-operate and are regarded as a single autonomous unit. The pusher found that almost nobody was aware of the problems of the coffee grinders. The packagers were running behind schedule for different reasons: absenteeism had been particularly high that summer because it was a good harvest and the workers were playing truant, the quality of paper had deteriorated and needed more processing, machines were breaking down. The coffee grinders would have to wait their turn. The *tolkach* knew the form: he threw up his arms in despair and invited the deputy chief engineer for a drink at his hotel. What the paper factory most needed, said the engineer, was a perforating machine. There was no provision for it in the Plan, but it must be possible to find somewhere. The *tolkach* took the hint and had the technical staff of his factory put together a makeshift machine. Suddenly, the cardboard boxes appeared.

The second and third *tolkachi* had similar experiences. One found it was impossible to obtain the promised electro-motors from an electrical engineering plant unless he came up with some copper wire. The *tolkach* bought the wire on the black market – it had presumably been stolen from a factory – and sent it by air freight to the electrical plant. Two days later he flew to the factory himself to press home the advantage. The third *tolkach* flew to Leningrad, to the Elektrosila factory, to arrange a new shipment of materials.

There is something both glamorous and squalid about *tolkachi*. Glamorous, because they can travel at will in an almost immobile society. They catch planes perhaps twice a week, know the Aeroflot schedule by heart, have mistresses in strange factory towns, live out of suitcases in provincial hotels. They dabble in the black market, know the barter value of everything from ski boots to robot arms. In the more advanced 'reforming' countries, in Hungary and Poland, the *tolkachi* travel to the West. Roman, a bespectacled sports fanatic, works for the Polish Academy of Sciences, technically as a research physicist. In fact, he spends several months abroad arranging computers for the engineering department, measuring equipment for the laboratories, desk-top photocopying machines. He is a licensed black-marketeer: millions of zloties are made available from the procurement budget and become, by means of the usual illicit alchemy, dollars or West German marks. In the West he bargains, pays wholesale prices; in the East, he is, on paper, a scientist of senior standing.

There is, though, a shabbiness about the whole process. *Tolkachi* wait in corridors for interviews, scramble like commerical travellers selling vacuum cleaners to bored housewives. They are necessary, vital, but not loved. *Tolkachi* are the stays of the economic Plan, that whalebone corset which struggles every month for five years to pull in the bulging stomachs of the Communist economies. The obvious failure of the Plan to match supply with demand has spawned the *tolkachi*, has introduced distortions and corruption into the industrial economy and has made the black market a necessary component in fulfilling basic needs. The Plan, once a remarkable scheme for generating growth and modernising peasant economies, is now an engine of shortage.

The first five-year Plan, initiated in 1928, was in fact completed in four years, running its course at the end of 1932 instead of the autumn of 1933. One has to be careful, though, when considering the Soviet planning system, in using the word 'fact'. Already it was plain that excessive optimism was to be a component feature of Plans. First, in the targets set, second, in the accounts of how the targets had been met and overtaken. In Russia, nothing exceeds like excess. Western economists balancing the elements of the Plan, taking into consideration that ballooning of statistics, came to the predictable conclusion that the first Plan in Soviet history was certainly not over-fulfilled. The point, though, was to educate, to change the mentality of the new Soviet man from that of a recently urbanised farmer's son into a striving industrial worker, setting records, beating them.

Stalin, in a speech in 1931 (4 February) made it clear that speed of production was a value in itself: 'It is sometimes asked whether it is possible to slow down the tempo somewhat, to put a check on the

movement. No, comrades, it is not possible. The tempo must not be
reduced! On the contrary we must increase it . . . We are fifty or a
hundred years behind the advanced countries. We must make good this
distance in ten years. Either we do so, or we shall go under.' And go
under they did: in 1941, the stunned Soviet Union was at war. Stalin's
speeches, read now, are full of such stumbling declarations. It is easy to
snigger ('Life has become better comrades, life has become more
joyous.' Stalin, 1932) but the use of central planning did indeed
industrialise a vast and primitive country; whole industries were
constructed. To visit Magnitogorsk in 1988 and comment on its
pollution and brown skies and its crude steel industry ('Pittsburgh twenty
years ago,' an American expert told the *Wall Stret Journal*, in August
1988) is to miss the point. Magnitogorsk was built in the 1930s
(admittedly in the wrong place) from nothing and is a symbol of how
central planning can concentrate resources and manpower and force
development. The same, in modern times, is true of the opening of
Siberia.

The Stalin-style economic plan was adopted by the East European
allies after the Second World War, when it served as a way of
reconstructing industry after the devastation wrought by the Germans.
Though it achieved some notable results (it was the Plan, after all, that
provided for the construction of thousands of apartments, scores of
hospitals) it was already viewed as an economic anachronism. There
was, of course, no choice. Nobody was proposing a private
Sozialmarkt–Wirtschaft, backed by external financial aid as in West
Germany. On the contrary, the East European economies (especially
the East German) were bled to help reconstruct the Soviet Union. By
the late 1950s the Plan, with its emphasis on all-out growth, was
beginning to resemble an athlete brought up on anabolic steroids, who
was now required to limbo-dance and rotate a hula-hoop. Moshe Lewin
(*Political Undercurrents in Soviet Economic Debates*, Princeton 1974)
rightly says that 'Stalin bequeathed to his heirs both a great industrial
power and an inefficient economy.'

After Stalin's death, a debate arose as to whether the existing problems
were the result of temporary deficiencies and abuses in the Planning
system, or whether the Planning system itself was producing shortages.
This was more than a minor doctrinal point. It was an attack on a whole
system of belief: was it necessary to believe in Planning in order to be a
Communist? How far could one tinker with mechanisms? What could
be thrown out? And, of course, the political question: how far could de-

Stalinisation go, could it extend to the great Mysteries of the Plan?

It was, understandably, an extremely quiet debate. After the various Communist take-overs in 1948, non-Marxist economists had been silenced. It took several years after the death of Stalin in 1953 for the economists to recover their confidence. Even then it seemed that a wholesale rejection of central planning was anathema; the defining statement appeared to be that of Friedrich Engels, who argued in *Anti-Dühring* that state control of the economy was an essential, penultimate step before the withering away of the state.

How brave then of Janos Kornai, the Budapest economist, to tackle this dogma head-on. His first detailed study, printed in 1959, was an investigation of the working of Hungarian light industry. It was drawn from personal observation and concluded that centralised planning resulted in extremely inefficient production, inflexible output, hoarding of stocks, reluctance to innovate, chronic shortages and pointless surpluses. More, the nature of the Plan was that partial reform – cutting the number of Plan indicators, improving factory incentives – would succeed, if at all, for only a short time. The problems that were becoming apparent in the Soviet-Bloc economies were not because of a temporary malfunctioning of the machine, but inherent in the whole centralised system. Later Kornai developed these observations into a coherent theory that set him apart not only from other Soviet-Bloc economists but also from the school of modellers who have tried to draw up rules for market 'equilibrium' in which supply seeks to meet demand. Central planning changes all these assumptions, he argues. For example, in neo-classical economic theory, firms maximise profits within their range of production possiblities, shifting prices up and down to match demand. Other theorists refine this model for the Soviet Bloc, adding constraints such as rationing of raw materials into the calculation. But Soviet-Bloc enterprises still, within their constraints, try to maximise profits and output while reducing cost. Nonsense, says Kornai (now at the Institute for World Economics in Budapest), the Plan always emphasises increasing output as rapidly as possible with little reliance on market signals. Communist industry is simply not driven by demand; all that counts is the availability of resources. The *Economics of Shortage* is now a basic text for an emerging generation of market economists (such as Jan Winiecki in Poland) in the Soviet Bloc; their ideas are still regarded as extremist but they are useful to the moderate, probably over-cautious reformist advisers to Gorbachev. Whenever the hard-liners object to an innovation and exclaim 'But

that's not socialism!', Aganbegyan (Gorbachev's economic adviser) and
his ilk can reply 'Maybe not, but there are far more radical ideas around
– think yourselves lucky!'

The Plan, as conceived and developed since the 1930s, is a
transaction between the factory and the central planning authorities.
The customer is excluded from the conversation. It works like this:
mid-way in the five-year Plan period, the Soviet state planning agency,
Gosplan, starts to look at the reported factory results. These are shown
on the basis of month-by-month, and year-by-year performance. On
the whole the factory managers can decide how to divide up the
production for the year; the main thing (indeed, until Gorbachev, the
only thing) was that the yearly target was met, or exceeded. On the basis
of these results, and of other information coming up through the Party
information network, Gosplan draws up a generalised picture of the
economy. Each enterprise is, by definition, supposed to be operating on
the basis of 'accountability' – *khozraschyot* – which is not, as popularly
believed in the West, an invention of Gorbachev (Lenin and others used
the term as early as 1921). They have at their disposal fixed and current
assets and an independent balance sheet. The quality of the information
supplied to Moscow can therefore be checked, but it rarely is. Gosplan
takes the figures and enters discussions with the regional and national
ministries. The broad priorities have been set by the Politburo – more
guns, less butter – but it is the horse-trading between Gosplan and the
ministries that really determines the eventual economic complexion. A
series of questions are exchanged; the impression is of a vast bee-hive.
How many rubber tyres do we need for the coming five years (asks
Gosplan). How many, given the initial returns from the relevant
factories, can we produce? What raw matrials are available? How much
must we import? How much foreign currency is available? Will there be
enough tyres to supply the scheduled increase in car production? Are
there enough specialist engineers to put two new rubber-processing
plants on stream? It takes only one flawed answer to throw the whole
production process out of kilter, to ensure a shortage of rubber tyres.
Gosplan is trying to keep track of millions of different goods, it allocates
the output of nearly 20,000 raw materials; it swells and swells. The new
five-year targets, pieced together, are submitted in draft to the factory
managements. The targets are seldom changed at this stage. Rather the
workers, through tame trade unions, are encouraged (that is, required)
to put up a Counter-Plan, a *vstrechny plan*, which commits them to
produce even more than the targets set by Moscow. The *vstrechny plan*

institutionalises an enthusiasm that is rearly, if ever, felt on the shop floor. Large red banners proclaim: 'We the workers of the Sverdlov liquorice factory commit ourselves to fulfil the Plan by 110 per cent!' Only Poland, whose workers have found alternative uses for banners, has stopped this kind of nonsense. There are cases of revising draft plans but usually because of changed circumstances at the centre: the Metallurgy Ministry may report a sudden shortfall in alloy needed for hubcaps or import possibilities might be restricted by a fall in world oil prices and a cutting back of Soviet hard-currency earnings. Gosplan has had a computer since 1966 (in full operation only since 1977) and tries its best to synchronise the changes. But Gosplan's vision of the Soviet economy is a static one; the trumpeted growth figures only barely camouflage the fact that the Soviet Union is not going anywhere in particular.

The obsession with growth is the core of the problem. Even when the growth rate slackened under Brezhnev, expansion and over-fulfilment remained the avowed aims of the Plan. Few Soviet-Bloc countries (Czechoslovakia in 1963, Poland in the early 1980s) have ever admitted to 'negative growth'. Gorbachev comes from the growth-school, though he has a slightly less mechanistic approach than Brezhnev. He has more concern with the quality of production than with the brute figures. In Murmansk in 1987, he altered a prepared speech to declare: 'I talked with dockers at the port today who said they received loaders that would not work – low quality. There are other instances. You buy a television and it breaks down in a few days, even hours. A farmer collects a tractor or a combine harvester and it needs another month to make them ready for use. Why do we bother to waste our time, our work, our raw materials and our energy to make sub-standard goods?' Fine. Yet one of his first acts after assuming power was to set detailed growth targets until the year 2000. That formed part of the economic programme for the Party Congress. Gorbachev used the old methods, followed the old logic by announcing a crash programme to boost the production of consumer goods. Because the official figures for the first six months of 1988 were encouraging, targets for the following two years could be beefed up, he declared: coats eleven per cent up, shoes ten per cent, ladies' tights one hundred and eighty per cent. Although that demonstrates political sensitivity – a shift of emphasis was needed if the pain of perestroika was to be cheerfully borne – it does not exactly advertise a passion for market forces. Gorbachev's reform of the planning system adds up to a slight unburdening of the central planners and freeing of initiative at the factory level; ministries assume a less dictatorial role, concentrate more on setting intelligent strategic goals. But this does not translate into market responsiveness. The information about shortages of tights does not come from any of the orthodox channels established by the planning machine; production figures for tights between 1980 and 1986 showed a steady, satisfactory increase. Bonuses all around. The leadership either has to guess about shortages or use personal observation (it is said in Moscow that much elementary consumer information reaches Gorbachev from his wife, who, in turn, hears it from her domestic staff; Czar Nicholas received rumblings from the Russian people by a similar route).

Suiting the production of millions of diverse products to demand is well-nigh impossible; it is as if China set up a state matrimonial agency to match all its unmarried males with all its unmarried females – a vast, unfeasible operation. Some attempts have been made to devise computer methods that could cope with all the simultaneous equations; Professor Scarf of Yale University has been using algorithms which solve a given demand-supply problem, and then repeats parts of the calculations to get better and widely applicable results. Gorbachev's advisers say that something similar could be applied to the Soviet Union (perfect competition, quips Peter Wiles, being replaced by perfect computation). But this is just a way of dodging market socialism and tackling the intractable problem of how to estimate demand. A reasonable guess can be hazarded on the demand of factories, since, when they are given their output targets, they then report back the necessary inputs: how many men they need, how much money in the wage fund, how much coal, how many trucks, how much metal. (As we shall see later, even these figures are liable to be faked.)

But what about the housewife in Irkutsk? Does anybody know how much lavatory paper she will need, how much cotton, how much soap, how many nappies? There is no channel of communication (though when shortages are desperate enough, the feedback will come through letters to newspapers, Party meetings, the unions, even shop-floor protests). Nor is the primitive Soviet-Bloc advertising industry able to mould demand or change consumption habits. It would, for example, be in the Planner's (and perhaps even the consumer's) interest if Poles and Russians ate less meat. Despite the shortages, Russian meat consumption is high, partly because it is a measure of material well-being. It would be shaming on a saint's name day, or a birthday, or at a normal dinner with guests, not to offer meat. The result: a big

demand for expensive feed grain to maintain large livestock herds and
the politicisation of the meat price (that is, it is difficult to cut subsidies
without risking political disturbances). A centrally planned economy
should be able to change these eating habits over time by offering
alternatives – fish, say. It could also offer more staples, since many
Russians are buying cheap meat in the absence of other satisfying
foodstuffs. But the Plan is incapable of achieving any of this. Apart from
main force, it cannot change consumption habits or behaviour.
(Romania has used a variant of 'force' by closing down many butcher's
shops and so severely restricting supplies that the population is now
almost vegetarian.)

Since it is difficult to calculate the demand, and since almost everybody
claims to be fulfilling their planned supply targets, the Soviet authorities
have had to look elsewhere for a comprehensive explanation of persistent
shortages. The Soviet Union has two major problems that can not be
regarded as 'systemic'. The first is a falling birthrate in the Russian
Federation and a resulting shortage of skilled manpower. The second is the
increasing geological difficulty of extracting raw materials in Siberia and
transporting them westwards. Soviet leaders are concentrating on these
problems, since neither represents a fundamental criticism of the workings
of the Plan. Brezhnev, especially, found these factors a sufficient
explanation for the slowdown. But real dilemmas are built into the Plan
and its failure to respond to the demands of a complex, modernised society.
And so the Kremlin must pursue at least some of the questions raised by the
breakdown of the Plan without admitting that a breakdown has occurred.
The vintage joke holds good. Stalin, Khrushchev and Brezhnev are
travelling in a train which abruptly stops. Stalin's solution: 'Shoot the
driver!' Khrushchev: 'Replace the driver with the guard, and the guard with
the driver.' Brezhnev: 'Pull the blinds down and let's pretend we're moving
again.' Had Gorbachev been in the same compartment he would have
rolled up his sleeves and started to bang the underside of the engine with a
spanner, while shouting at his three illustrious predecessors to push from
behind. The search for peripheral problems that actually strike at the heart
of the planning process brought first Andropov, then Gorbachev, to the
sadly deficient transport system. Ministers of rail and road have been
clearing their desks at an astonishing rate: none can please the Kremlin.
The logic is plain: deliveries from one factory to another are so slow that
most production is concentrated in the last 'decade' (ten days) of the month.
Then, using extra workers, the factory goes all out to meet the planned

targets and earn their bonuses. The quality, particularly of sophisticated products such as cars and televisions, is correspondingly abysmal. If one were to eliminate waste on the road and above all, if one were to speed up the transit of component parts, then production could be more evenly distributed throughout the month and the quality of Soviet-Bloc goods would improve. Bad habits – such as factory managers hoarding raw materials, or exaggerating the number of workers needed – would also be eliminated. Not a panacea, perhaps, but a real contribution to Plan efficiency.

In practice, the purge of the transport system is proving extremely difficult. Without destroying the whole fabric of the Plan, the only way to control transport abuses and deliver goods on time is through the police. But the patterns of corruption that have grown during seventy years of planning in the Soviet Union and forty-five years in Eastern Europe are too intricate to respond to police measures. The first offensive was against 'evaporating' cargoes and petrol tanks, that is, the sale of petrol coupons to petrol attendants on the black market (particularly common among Soviet troop units in Eastern Europe and Afghanistan), the forging of fuel coupons, siphoning off the sale of spare parts, and so on. But the war on 'phantom' deliveries has largely been abandoned. The stories are legion: in Poland, it was found that vodka bottles were sixty per cent more likely to 'break' in transit than bottles containing vinegar. Chemical analysts, cynics said, should look into this interesting scientific phenomenon. Even if goods are honestly registered when they leave the warehouse they have an uncanny habit of disappearing en route. To prevent drivers stealing glass window-panes – a rare product in Poland – the authorities ordained that if there were more than thirty per cent 'breakages' en route from the factory to the building site, the factory would be obliged to pay for a new shipment. The idea of this was to make the factory management put pressure on its drivers not only to stop stealing but also to drive carefully.

But construction workers quickly realised the economic advantages of this scheme. A friend of mine, obliged to put in a month on a building site before being allowed to study at university was told on his first day at work to smash the window panes for an entire apartment block – thirty per cent of that week's delivery. The builders then reported to the factory that all the panes had been broken in transit and claimed a new shipment. The remaining panes were sold off on the black market.

Drivers in East European countries – perhaps in the West too – are almost invariably members of a secret guild, an informal association with unspoken rules and bribe thresholds. According to what type of company they work for, their style of corruption differs. Fundamentally, however, there are three kinds of racket: black haulage, in which drivers use their company's empty trucks to transport goods for somebody else, straight theft, in which breakages are channelled to the black market, and petrol fraud.

Black haulage is common wherever houses can be built privately. That is, in Hungary, Poland and Czechoslovakia, but not, generally, in the Soviet Union. Sometimes it is just a matter of flagging down a driver before he approaches a quarry, have him load twenty per cent more rocks or sandbags and deliver them to your own building site, before he continues to his official construction project. In such a case, the loader also has to be bribed. In Hungary, truck and van drivers will also drive slowly around furniture shops trying to catch the eye of somebody who wants a new dining-suite delivered to his home. The key to controlling black haulage is to monitor properly the work sheets filled out by the drivers. A military report drawn up by the Polish army found widespread anomalies and evident corruption in the majority of depots checked by military inspection teams. 'Work sheets are open to fiction, falsification, unreliable data and fuel speculation as well as lies concerning working time and earnings . . . Work certificates are often given on blank sheets which encourages even the most honest drivers to make private routes and sell petrol. Out of ten depots checked in Warsaw, three had no lists of work sheets and another had issued several to one and the same driver. In several cases, the figures on the meters differed from the work sheet records, the differences sometimes amounting to several hundred kilometres . . .' A delivery of aluminium pipes will be replaced by a cargo of shoddy rusted iron and still meet the vague terms of reference stipulated in the work sheet. Because the building site has almost no contact with the factory, and because in any case builders have grown accustomed to the delivery of inadequate materials, nodody need be any the wiser. But that latter course entails some risk for the driver: were the factory to find out he would be put up on theft charges. As a rule however, truck depots are so enmired in faked returns and cooked books they prefer not to crack down even in the case of theft. That would entail bringing in the police, who might use the occasion to probe into inventories. If falsified work sheets are discovered, they are usually treated leniently and incur little more than the docking of wages. Truck driving is a grim job in Eastern Europe. Roads are poor, the hours have to be stretched to fulfil unrealistic plans and few people are prepared to put up with constant brickbats from all sides. To retain their drivers, most official depots put up with intricate rackets.

The same may well apply in the West, but the scale must be different if only because of the pervasive shortages in the East. Heavy lorries run on diesel oil and so does central heating. Result? Office blocks desperately short of heating fuel during the winter do deals with whole fleets of drivers. Lighter trucks working for smaller companies sell their coupons to garage attendants at a favourable market rate, a business that, if done sensibly, is almost undetectable, though it only works on a large scale during the summer when there are a large number of foreign tourists and private motorists in the Balkans and Hungary.

Corruption on the road is more apparent than corruption on the railroad track. It is obviously no simple matter to divert a trainload of vodka. There are stricter schedules and for some years the post of railway worker was a highly honoured one, a stationmaster ranking in status next to the regional postmaster in Czech and Slovak communities. In East Germany especially the statement '*Ich bin bei der Reichsbahn*' was enough to win over, in bars and at dances, the heart of any sensible far-sighted girl. To be a white-collar worker on the railways in those Communist countries which were part of the Austro-Hungarian or German empires was to be a civil servant with a guaranteed state pension, a uniform allowance, free travel and many other perks. But this was the Old World; in the New World even generous state pensions seem to have lost their value and salaries have not increased in line with the cost of living. Nowadays the railways recruit mainly those in the countryside who want to leave the ranks of the peasantry and can find no other route. The consequence of this was illustrated by a report in the Soviet labour newspaper *Trud* (1 November 1980). Vodka and brandy pilfered from railway freight cars guarded by conductors amounted to more than 4.6 million roubles (6.8 million dollars) each year. The conductors were obliged by law to guard every wagon containing an alcohol shipment, but in fact a survey showed that less vodka evaporated when there was a watchman on board: after a 2,000 kilometre journey, a ninety-wagon, eighty-proof train loaded with vodka was delivered without a single bottle stolen. 'It would seem that the results might convince the most stubborn of sceptics,' said the newspaper, though in fact the domestic trade, food and railway ministers have been meeting for many years without reaching any conclusion on vodka security. The railway ministry argued that to remove the conductors would break all the established rules, but what really concerned the officials was that the whole network of railway officials would be made redundant. There are 12,000 freight conductors in the Russian part of the Soviet Union alone. They earn well below the average income of urban factory workers. The cheapest vodka sells for five roubles a bottle so the temptation is constant.

The corrupt or fallible distribution network is only a fragment of the picture. The Plan militates against the consumer, actively works against him. Production figures are faked as a routine part of the planning process, and the goods that should theoretically be in the shops have actually never been made. The goods that are produced are likely to be old-fashioned and barely appropriate for their function because the Plan has squeezed out all incentives to innovation. Introducing new products entails risk, and risk carries no rewards.

The Magic Of Numbers

The quality controller is as welcome in a Soviet factory as the black plague; perhaps less so, since the plague would at least give the worker a few days off. Soviet workers are paid according to output, not quality; careful production takes time, reduces output and take-home pay. A factory that is run according to Plan rather than market principles has to devise a complex pattern of incentives for its managers. There are none of the rewards for good asset management that follow when the assets are privately owned. Instead, a Soviet manager's main interest must be in satisfying his superior rather than his customer. His financial stake is tied directly, and solely, to growth figures that please his superior in the hierarchical ladder. Managerial bonuses are traditionally linked to gross value of output. They are generally so large – 25–30% of the basic salary – that the incentive is not only to produce more goods, but also to conceal shortfalls, seek easy plan targets, disguise the real production possibilities of the factory, keep a secret reserve of workers, skimp on quality, choose expensive imports (since these will increase the output value) and, above all, to cook the books.

The workers, whose bonuses are derived from producing physical units (say, turning out 10 per cent more refrigerators than promised), enter the conspiracy. The bonuses and perks are quickly accepted as a normal, indeed indispensable, part of the wage packet. In some coal mines in the Soviet Union and Poland, even the government plays along with this idea. Coal-mining is valuable (in terms of dollar exports as well as domestic demand) and dangerous. Miners receive the most generous wages in the working community, enjoying early retirement, high pensions, special shops, and priority on the housing list and in the queue for cars. But it is still not enough: in a society that espouses egalitarian values, it is not done to create large differentials in basic pay. Miners can be top of the league – and have to be, if there is to be a constant intake of workers for this unpleasant job – but not so far ahead that they become a statistical embarassment. Instead, the management, with the nod from ministries, concoct plump bonuses. That is the secret contract that binds workers with management, officially sponsored trades unions with officially nominated bosses.

A landmark court case in Poland in 1981 exposed some of these motives for faking output. A factory director and two of his managers, running a service company, were found guilty of turning out false data in their annual reports and collecting the consequent bonuses. At the first hearing the director was given a year's jail, suspended from his job for two years and fined a small sum. One manager was jailed, the other acquitted. The defence lawyer appealed to the provincial court on the grounds that the crimes were not 'socially harmful'. The men were duly acquitted. The Prosecutor-General objected and the Supreme Court – saying that all faked statistics were socially harmful since they poisoned the economic picture of the government – upheld the original prison sentences. But most instructive were the detailed defence arguments of the factory director. First, he claimed, only faked *production* figures could really harm the state; service industries were not central to the Plan. Second, forging statistics was a 'collective' crime involving scores of employees and accountants, sometimes over years, and so no individual could be held responsible. There is some force to this argument: once the books have been altered it is difficult for subsequent honest book-keepers to blow the whistle. Forgery has become part of the operating premise. Finally, the factory director said that he had been acting 'out of concern for the earnings of my employees' and to enhance the standing of his enterprise. (A full account of the case is in *Przeglad Techniczny*, April 1981.)

A check of 323 Polish factories in 1980 showed that 72 per cent had made false reports. By the late 1980s the situation had hardly improved. The Supreme Chamber of Control found reporting irregularities in 80 to 90 per cent of a sample of 85 factories; some 60 per cent exaggerated the product quality. Of course, a substantial part of this false reporting is due to slipshod, rather than criminal, book-keeping. The controller said there was evidence of deliberate manipulation in about 25 per cent of

Polish factories. That proportion probably holds good for the Soviet Union too, though Soviet economists have yet to come up with an overall estimate.

There are two fundamental frauds: figures concerning storage, loss or quality are adjusted downwards, while figures reflecting output, the use of scarce materials, or sales of products not yet produced, are pushed ever upwards. At least part of this manipulation is encouraged by the flawed reporting procedures of the central authorities. Factories build up huge stocks of raw materials, not knowing when the next delivery will come. They tuck away machines and trucks, not knowing when a twist in the Plan will demand a spurt of activity and extra capacity. And they store goods they could not conceivably ever use in case a *tolkach* has to trade them for genuinely needed materials. In this, a Soviet factory resembles a Soviet housewife, an empty bag continually in her hand, an eye peeled for promising queues, a readiness to buy anything that might prove useful at some point in the future. A book-keeper from the Chelmek shoe factory exaggerated by 150 per cent his plant's use of coking coal. He knew that if he had disclosed the real figure, the factory's coal allocation for the next year would have been whittled away. The central authorities know about these fiddles and, in their questioning about stocks, leave many loopholes for false, half-true, or patchy reporting.

Distorted output figures are another matter. How can a customer publicly declare that it has received goods from a factory which has not even produced them yet? Quite often this is because the producer has a monopoly. If a factory needs a machine tool produced in only one plant in the Russian Federation, and refuses to sign a fake contract, then in the future it will get nothing. In the Silesian city of Wroclaw, the local building enterprise handed over to a co-operative, as complete, an empty shell of a building. It had to pretend it was complete in order to receive the year-end bonus – and the co-operative had no choice, since the building company was the only one in the city. Similar tricks are deployed throughout the whole centrally planned economy. Thus Warsaw Polytechnic claimed that between 1976 and 1978, some 441 of their inventions had been implemented in the economy. In fact, only 43 had been adopted.

The result is that the Plan is cheating the Planners; no Soviet-Bloc leader has a completely accurate picture of the economy. For a reformer like Gorbachev this is particularly bewildering. Even Nicolae Ceausescu, who inhabited a self-made world of distorting mirrors, complained that he was being fed wrong information. While distortion served some kind of purpose during the Brezhnev years by persuading workers and managers that they were successfully cheating the system, it only breeds confusion in a society on the brink of change. What, precisely, has to be reformed? Official statistics actually became more aberrant under Gorbachev. The Washington-based consultancy PlanEcon Inc. analysed the year-end Soviet statistical year-books, *Narkhoz*, and found significant divergences from already published Soviet figures. According to *Narkhoz*, national retail trade grew in real terms by 4.3 per cent in 1985 and by 6.4 per cent in 1986, but the figures developed from other Soviet sources are 1.6 per cent for 1985 and 0.5 per cent in 1986 – a drop of 3 per cent compared to 1981–4. The pessimistic figures are the more probable since retail trade was badly hit by Gorbachev's anti-alcohol sales campaign (revenue from alcohol sales accounted for almost 17 per cent of total retail revenue in 1984, dropping sharply thereafter; tax revenue from alcohol, before Gorbachev, covered about half of the total defence budget). These distortions carried over into the growth figures. The official growth for 1985 was 3.1 per cent, and 3.6 per cent in 1986. The Soviet growth index is the National Material Product which, unlike Western GNP estimates, excludes most services. But according to PlanEcon, Brookings and other Western specialists, the growth figure came out closer to 0.8 per cent for both years. Production figures were also adjusted upwards. Similar discrepancies crept in when it came to assessing, retroactively, the growth rate in the Brezhnev years. The Gorbachev team gave a much bleaker account of growth pre-1985 than those derived by the Western specialists.

The Plan, in other words was being manipulated, but by whom, for whom? Plainly, Gorbachev benefits from figures that show perestroika to be making a quick, substantial improvement on the Brezhnev era. But such falsification also neutralises his calls for further, more radical, reform. Massaging figures may be a long Russian tradition (see Gogol's *Dead Souls*) but it does not fit in with what is known about Gorbachev. A second possibility is that there is a conspiracy among statisticians to mislead the leadership; both Gosplan and the Central Statistical Administration (TTSU) are under great pressure to create a reform environment, yet an honest appraisal would overthrow everything, make a nonsense of their mathematical architecture. Finally, it may be that the measures are changing their statistical bases, that they are, for the moment, in a position of half-truth, half-lie, and are unwilling to announce that they are in transition. The Western economists who have built their image of the Soviet economy on a mendacious base (supplied, of course, by the Soviet press) are now unsure where to turn. Is Russia doing well, or not?

Abel Aganbegyan, who describes himself as Gorbachev's chief economic adviser, concedes some statistical distortion, and deplores it. But he is referring mainly to the meanings attached to brute figures.

For example: the Soviet Union proudly announced that it was smelting twice as much steel as the US. Yet it was turning out only a fraction as many steel products; the rest was lost or languishing in storage.

The Soviet Union produces 4.5 times more tractors than the US, although it has less tillable land. The tractors were sold to collective farms who found it easier to buy anew rather than repair the old. The farms paid with state-subsidised loans.

The Soviet Union produces almost 800 million pairs of shoes a year – 3.2 pairs per person – yet many remain unsold and queues, as usual, spring up whenever more expensive imported footwear appears in the shops.

Aganbegyan's point, made at a session of the Royal Institute for International Affairs in London, was about the blind use of statistics. Growth is not an unambiguously positive target. The steel has to serve a purpose; if it does not the smelter should be shut down, the workers re-deployed. And the tractors are effectively being dumped on the domestic market. The shoes are of such poor quality and design that they are un-buyable. Somehow, argue Aganbegyan and his friends, production has to be tied in with quality and with demand, and planned growth has to recover its meaning. That is a rather big 'somehow'. Poor quality leads directly to shortage: Polish lightbulbs that have lives 60 per cent shorter than those made in the West generate a constant, but ultimately pointless, demand. Yet the banners inside the Roza Luksemburg bulb factory in Warsaw are full of the usual slogans and Butlins-style encouragement: the Plan has been fulfilled 110 per cent; we can do even better this year; let's start the New Year with a new record; more and more bulbs, more and more light, radiant futures. *Ex oriente luxemburg.*

Innovation

Perestroika came to Ivanovo twenty years ago; Vladimir Kaibadzhe, the shrewd Georgian director of a machine-tool factory, devised a multi-functional workbench that would revolutionise the factory's working habits. There was some international interest at the Hanover and Leipzig fairs, but when it came to introducing the workbench into his own factory, Kaibadzhe had problems. Production would drop, at least until enough workbenches were ready; the workforce would have to be retrained, perhaps even trimmed a bit. Kaibaidzhe was handed an official reprimand by the Ministry; he should mind his own business, stop tinkering. Perestroika went away again, a fugitive idea for two decades.

The central Plan discriminates against innovation. There is no shortage of skills. The Soviet Bloc spends as much, probably more, on Research and Development (as a share of GDP) than does the West. Only outdated figures are available but roughly 3.4 per cent of the Soviet GDP is devoted to R and D, compared to 2.4 per cent in the US. The Soviet Bloc employs more R and D workers, turns out more scientists and engineers than any Western country (as a percentage of total employment) apart from Japan.

The problem comes in translating these skills, inventors and inventions, into a form that can be absorbed and used intelligently by the economy. There is no incentive to save material input, the delay is too long, the risk too great for a Soviet-Bloc factory management. As there is neither the threat of competition, nor the threat of financial failure, to spur managers into action, there is a clear structural bias towards inaction.

Ivanovo is 250 kilometres north-east of Moscow, an industrial centre full of engineering high schools grinding out potential innovators. The enterprise AutoKran has been producing cranes here since 1954 when it turned out its first 5-tonne model; nowadays it makes just under 5,000 a year. The same model. All special requirements, cited by over-optimistic customers, are ruled out. 'Our problem is perhaps that we have to think in thousands of units,' admits a top manager. 'The customer cannot pick and choose.' AutoKran, with five other similar factories scattered throughout the Soviet Union, is part of a Producers' Association. Ivanovo draws up all the models and then each factory produces its one variant; there is no competition. That is one reason, clearly, why only 5 per cent of the cranes can be exported (and these to Comecon countries). There has been an attempt to 'correct' the basic crane and the directors pored over a successful Japanese design; here, came the reformist cry, was a way of becoming competitive in world markets. State controllers were brought in to watch over the quality; production dropped, so did wages. The workers were restless. Over 100 new technicians had to be hired to copy the Japanese design; suddenly output had become much more expensive.

And now, for all this Western-style thinking (that is how they talk about it in Ivanovo) to bear fruit, the factory has to be modernised, automated. About 400 of the 6,000 workforce have been dropped through early retirement. Modernisation will cost about 4 million roubles a year for the next few years, but there is only 2 million available. The enterprise has a turnover of 160 million roubles a year, a profit on paper of 13 million roubles. The innovation costs should not be hard to find — but they are. The profits are skimmed off by the Ministry in Moscow to subsidise other engineering companies that are on the brink of collapse. From every rouble of profit, AutoKran retains only 42 kopeks. To finance its modernisation it would need 60 kopeks, at least.

The Gorbachev revolution is supposed to change this by encouraging *khozraschyot*, or cost-accounting. This means simply that Soviet industry is expected to fund all operations from its own resources; supplies and materials, investment and innovation are supposed to be financed from profits. The Soviet Union, of course, has been here before. On 29 August 1921 a Soviet decree declared that all factories would adopt *khozraschyot* as their guiding principle. Gorbachev's *khozraschyot*, introduced formally on 1 January 1989, may be declared with more feeling, may develop more teeth (via a bankruptcy law) but it contains all the weaknesses of the Leninist precedent. In AutoKran's case self-financing sounds good — at least they get to keep their profits. But the Plan ties the management into accepting over-priced and poor-quality supplies that will drag down its own profitability. It is obliged to accept chassis made by other enterprises, some of whom have not been subjected to quality controls. These parts frequently have to be returned. The delivery contracts last for several years and there are considerable political pressures against shifting from one supplier to another.

The Plan's clogged arteries are particularly evident in Czechoslovakia. Before the war, the country was regarded as one of the top European producers of engineering goods. A company like Skoda, founded in 1859, helped to make a capitalist Czechoslovakia highly competitive in world markets. In 1989 the car producer Skoda was declared technically insolvent. In the mid-1970s the Czech leadership gave the go-ahead to Skoda to produce a new model. By 1979 the prototype of a new front-wheel drive Skoda was ready, with engines of up to 1600 cc. But the Prague government then told Skoda that it had agreed with Moscow not to produce car engines of more than 1200 cc, so as to not to compete with the Soviet Lada on world markets. An interim Skoda car was devised, while the front-wheel drive car was hastily re-designed around a smaller engine. Meanwhile the authorities discovered that they were not producing the correct components for the new model and faced the choice of building new facilities or importing Western parts. This forced up the price – accepted by the Czechs, because the demand for cars is virtually limitless and production so small. By 1989, 14 years after the decision was made to produce a new car, Czechoslovakia was still turning out only 250 a day (compared to 400 of the old, outdated Skoda). It is one of many, many dismal stories. The obvious question is why a country as small as Czechoslovakia is producing cars at all; the answer is that Skoda's engineering traditions were ready-made for low-cost and efficient automobile manufacture. The Plan unhinged this tradition, built in commercial miscalculation and slowed down all attempts to innovate and automate. Market economics do not just whittle away the incompetent and shoot down lame ducks, they can also bring out traditional strengths in the manufacturing sector. Skoda was a strong company made weak by planned insensitivity. Again, the result is a shortage; in the cold February of 1989, hundreds of Czechs were camping in the open near the Skoda salespoint at Mlada Boleslav, anxious to put their names on the waiting list for the new car. The car, the blissfully named 'Favorit' cost just over £5,000; a place on the waiting list was being traded, by the more enterprising campers, for £600.

Gorbachev stumbled against these problems in the late 1980s when he tried to accelerate the introduction of computers in Soviet economic and social life. In theory, central planning was the ideal vehicle for a forced computerisation of the Soviet Union. Just as the Plan had industrialised a primitive agrarian country, so too it could close the technology gap with the West. But the Soviet system has never resolved the problem of how science should serve the economy. The need for computers was recognised in the 1950s, and the skills, as ever, were there in abundance, in the form of sophisticated cybernetic scientists. But the original needs, vaguely set out, were barely accommodated when it came to designing the mainframe in the 1960s. By the time the Soviet Union was producing computers in the early 1970s, they had no clear function and were hopelessly out of date. Western computers were imported (the more advanced were smuggled in by 'techno-bandits', Western businessmen who specialise in avoiding the Comecon restrictions) but more often than not they lay idle. A tour of Soviet factories yields similar images: a vast French computer in a petro-chemicals complex in, say, Plock, that is used only by the accounts department for processing wage slips; many more are cobwebbed because the service contract has expired and the domestic technicians cannot tackle the breakdown.

In December 1985 Gorbachev established a Scientific-Technical complex that would co-ordinate the development and production of different micro-computers and software. But this complex, under the control of the Academy of Sciences, actually has no administrative authority; its purpose is 'intellectual leadership'. The key players are four ministries – for the electronics industry, the radio industry, communications technology and machine building – and a state Committee for Information Technology. The computer components are made by factories under the supervision of 32 separate ministries. The complex is the co-ordinator of this jungle of bureaucracy, but has no design bureau of its own, no laboratories. Its scientists are housed in 17 different buildings in Moscow.

The fact is that this great innovatory thought has to be expressed through an antiquated economic machine whose main characteristics are avoidance of risk, delay-through-committee, and the lover-production of bureaucrats. The complex, headed by an exceptionally bright academician, Dr Boris Nauman, has come to the conclusion that it cannot modernise the Soviet economy within the normal trappings of the Soviet system. Instead, it is now trying to sidestep the bureaucracy by developing joint-venture companies with the West which will help design and, in part, build the Soviet microcomputer industry.

Every technical or economic innovation entails some changes in management and labour. Decisions taken quickly to respond to the market cannot become the subject of endless committees. Yet the function of these committees is to cement Communist control over the economy. Managers with market mentality are thus regarded as a direct threat to the old order, the web of power that connects the Party and the Planners. The 1980s was the decade when the Party fought to retain its hold on the economy; in 1989, in Eastern Europe at least, it lost that battle.

2

Party Games

There was a dull unease to the Communist Party of the 1970s. The brightest had a fugitive sense of the end of things, but in the main there was just a heavy pulse, a thud-thud of anxiety, as power slipped away. The party was intimately connected with the economy; central planners and political commanders were partners in a marriage that was both solid and intricate, a revolutionary fusion that had gained institutional bulk. Party reformers might flirt occasionally with market forces, yet to divorce communism from the Plan was unthinkable. But as the Western recession began to trickle through the frontiers, the planned economy looked sick indeed. Markets, primarily black but also grey, pink and brown (according to the colour spectrum devised by Aron Katsenelinbogen who adds a shade for every element of illegality), flourished and flowered. Nowadays, Poles queue to enter Skra, the largest open-air private market in Eastern Europe, a vast stadium-cum-bazaar that trades in Western clothes, records, kitchenware, in pets and car spare parts, in caviar and microchips. The streets of Warsaw, Budapest and, gradually, Moscow, boast, in between the bare bread shops, Pierre Cardin, Benetton and Austrian ski equipment. Twenty years ago such goods could only be bought on the black market, usually with dirty or hot money. But the black economy was at least tolerated, even if it was not, as now, dragged into the sunlight. While Krushchev stamped on black marketeers, put them in front of firing squads, Brezhnev encouraged them. It was as if the Royal Horticultural Society had suddenly declared that traditional weeds – hedge parsley, comfrey, meadow cranesbill – were actually rather beautiful and should be part of any self-respecting allotment.

The fact was that the second economy was deemed to be *supportive* of the communist system. The low consumer priorities of the five-year plan, the shortages generated by the system, could be borne in times when ideological or patriotic sentiment was strong – during the war, or the post-war reconstruction period – and, of course, at a time of terror.

(Few Soviet housewives complained about shortages in 1937.) But during less arduous periods, the shortages have to be explained away (Western sanctions, incompetent ministers, corrupt shop assistants) or plugged. Poland, rather than face reform, imported large quantities of consumer goods from the West in the early 1970s but this proved both politically and financially expensive. It was the black market, with its 'realistic' prices, that stabilised the system. Rather than develop a modern services sector, or shift industrial priorities – which would have upset the political coalitions that brought Gierek and Brezhnev to power – the frustrated consumer was offered more money. The Kosygin wage reforms gave the worker new status. He was richer than university staff and began, for the first time since the war, to feel like a consumer. His needs could only be met by the black market and the worker, from this point on, became a regular client of the second economy. Those who had services to offer – plumbers, repairmen – charged inflated rates, and by the end of the decade a substantial slice of the working class had gained access to privileges that had been the preserve of the elite. Once a week, there was a good chunk of roast meat, society became more mobile, buying cars and travelling abroad; by 1978 over a million Poles a year were visiting the West. Whereas black markets in the West tend to be a temporary solution to distribution problems – as in the destroyed West German cities after the war – in the East, they became a permanent feature. Gierek, Brezhnev, Honecker (more precisely: early Gierek, mid-Brezhnev, late-middle Honecker) are remembered with some affection by the middle-aged. Theirs was an era of personal enrichment, of embourgeoised workers.

It was also the beginning of the end of ideology, and of unquestioned Party control. The black market may have helped to stabilise an unreformed system, but it also sowed dragons' teeth. The existence of a second economy is a constant rebuke to the mis-managers of the first. The black economy may satisfy consumer appetites, but there is nothing that more thoroughly saps belief in the system. There is real friction between those who can afford black-market prices, and those who cannot. Both segments are disillusioned with the authorities, who have failed. Tolerating the second economy is an ideological retreat; moves to legalise it represent lasting defeat for an egalitarian-based dogma.

The 1970s thus became a time of concealment. The Party hid behind high fences, gobbling their privileges greedily, and in private, like Billy Bunter with a tuck parcel. The economy was put in the hands of

information managers, whose brief was to package the plan as
attractively as possible; the television screens spewed success. The
combination of Party complacency and official mendacity acted like
rising damp in an old building. First, there was a strange smell, then
ugly peeling (promptly painted over), a constantly spreading decay. By
the late 1980s, the house was declared uninhabitable.

The Party had lost control over the most dynamic and vital, the only
spontaneous, part of the economy. At the same time it bore responsibility for the crumbling of the planned economy, the permanent
shortages. What to do? It responded in the same way as incompetent
African regimes when they finally grasp the scope of everyday problems:
the Party withdrew from reality, drew down the shutters, sealed the
windows. In a gauche, off-hand comment after Martial Law was
imposed, the Polish spokesman Jerzy Urban told reporters: 'Don't
worry, the government will feed itself.' He meant to say something else,
but everybody took his words at face value: the Party elite, with its luxury
villas, special food supplies, its reserved beaches, its chauffeured
limousines and hidden petrol supplies, the Party could take care of itself,
thank you very much. This privileged isolation sometimes had fatal
results. In October 1977, Vera Husak (wife of Gustav, the then Party
leader) slipped and broke her leg while holidaying in Bardejeve, East
Slovakia. A specialist was summoned and recommended an immediate
transfer to the local hospital. Mrs Husak, however, refused to be treated
in an ordinary hospital – the party elite has its own network of SANOPS
clinics with Western medicine and equipment – and rang her husband.
Husak promptly ordered a helicopter to transport his wife to Prague. The
pilot refused to take off because of dense fog. The mountain rescue
helicopter team from the Tatras was then mobilised. The helicopter
flew first to Bratislava to pick up a SANOPS consultant, and on to
Bardejeve where Mrs Husak, a nurse and a bodyguard were taken on
board. But there was still a thick ground mist. When the helicopter's
faulty altimeter indicated an altitude of 400 metres, the aircraft was in
fact only a few yards from ground. It smacked into the earth and all the
passengers, apart from the SANOPS doctor, were killed.

There are many such fables about the arrogance of power. The most
graphic illustration of Party was the villa and dacha colonies of that era.
Small villages near lakes, surrounded by fir trees, were suddenly
transformed. Telephone lines were installed, water pipes – many of the
chosen sites were still drawing their water from wells – good access
roads, high wire fences, a police garrison whose dogs would terrorise the

mongrels of the local farmers. Wandlitz outside East Berlin, Zalesie and Magdalenka, outside Warsaw, Usovo and Zhukova on the fringes of Moscow, and countless such colonies were sprinkled around seaside resorts or on the margins of regional capitals: the Party put a premium on fresh air, away from the masses. In the Gorbachev era, these colonies were gradually broken up, to save money and to make a symbolic point about new-look socialism. Some villas became orphanages, some became government property for staging delicate negotiations or seminars. But most of the incumbents gave up their property only grudgingly. Indeed, as the Gorbachev-men – the Modrows and the Urbaneks – moved in for the kill, it emerged that the *nomenklatura*, that protected list of party-nominated jobs, had arrogated property rights for themselves.

Nowadays, when the heads tumble in Eastern Europe, the old Party elite can hang on to their pensions (half or two-thirds of salary) medical privileges and their apartments. Unless, of course, it can be shown that the ousted minister used illegal methods – army recruits as free builders, or materials stolen from construction sites – they sit firm in their villas, or sell up at a big profit. Lev Zaitsev, who was for a while Number 3 in the Gorbachev Politburo, was one of the many defenders of privilege. 'It is a question of freeing decision-makers from the everyday time-consuming business of buying food or whatever. And it is important that the Party hierarchy does not award itself fat salaries – that means we must have assistance in other spheres.' Gorbachev too is not exactly a leveller, though he insists that some of the subsidies in the Central Committee canteen should be cut. In Poland General Jaruzelski, surely the most Spartan of figures in the political class, bought his four-bedroom villa in Icarus Street at a heavy discount – just over 300,000 zloties (about $30 at 1990 exchange rates). Now, the 350 square metres villa is worth in excess of $100,000. General Czeslaw Kiszczak, the modest-living, Interior Minister, drives a red Peugeot bought at a closed Interior Ministry auction at a fraction of its real value. All this sits uncomfortably. But the Gorbachev philosophy seems to be that privilege contributes to the professionalism of the political class. The *nomenklatura* only becomes a liability, in this view, when it is not selected on merit.

That begs too many questions. The most abused word of the Gorbachev period was 'mafia' – there were, in the warmed-up rhetoric, Brezhnev mafias, Tbilisi, Alma-Ata and Novosibirsk mafias, mafias under the bed. One point was to show the connection between an ideologically bankrupt leadership and organised crime. But chiefly the word was being used in the sense of E. J. Hobsbawm (*Primitive Rebels*, New York 1959) – the 'mafia' as a general code of behaviour towards the state in a weakly governed society, a system of relationship that substitutes for strong state power, a secret society. The Party had lost its ideological mission and was substituting a network of personal allegiance for commitment to Marxism. The dynastic impulse had taken over, not only in Ceausescu's Romania (where until the Christmas 1989 revolution 50 relatives were positioned throughout the governing machinery), not only in the Balkan socialism of Zhivkov's Bulgaria, in Poland with its eccentric road to communism, but also in the Soviet Union, motherland of the Revolution. The Galina Brezhnev affair was, for Andropov, who exposed it as part of a succession struggle, and later for Gorbachev, a model of what happens to a Party that loses direction. The Brezhnev scandals interlock into one another: the illicit diamond and gold deals, the alliances that spanned the *nouveau riche* world of Moscow with its web of love affairs and political intrigues, and the subterranean world of fixers and black marketeers. At the centre of it all was Galina.

Galina Brezhnev inherited many features from her father, most noticeably the bushy black eyebrows, the slight sway in the gait, the slow-burning temperament that would quite unexpectedly ignite, a fierce loyalty to her friends. She was not a pretty woman but was attractive to men, a phenomenon that her friends attributed variously to her darkness, her passion, her good complexion and expensive manicures, and, more cynically, to her way with money and influence. As a student at the Moscow Teachers Training college, she was known as quite bright but restless, with a tendency to flirt heavily with her lecturers. 'I don't really know what I want,' she told one of her friends at the time, 'except that I would like to work with children, get around a bit, have people accept me for who I am.'

In those days her father was still some way from becoming General Secretary of the Soviet Communist party and her influence was limited. Her love affairs increased as her father's career progressed. She herself worked for a while at the Academy of Pedagogical Sciences – her ambition to work with children abandoned because of the pressures of marriage – and she subsequently found a niche in the Foreign Contacts department (Capitalist countries) of the Foreign Ministry in Moscow's Smolensk Square. This is the unit responsible for organising trips made by Western diplomats within the Soviet Union and official receptions for foreign dignitaries.

Her third and last marriage was to Yuri Churbanov, a men ten years her junior (she is now in her early sixties) and, eventually, deputy Interior Minister. Churbanov's network of contacts, of friends of friends, was extensive and wholly typical of the New Class. Their friends included two prominent Soviet journalists, film-makers, one prominent KGB man (Galina's uncle General Semyon Tsvigun, deputy chairman of the agency) the wives of senior officials in the Interior Ministry, a few members of the Foreign Trade Ministry (through her brother Yuri, deputy foreign trade minister), actors and actresses, a gypsy soothsayer who told her and her friends' fortunes, an underworld banker who was ready to float a loan at an hour's notice, a dentist who drilled the teeth of the elite. The cast was not unlike that of a typical Hollywood star; the friendship circle was drawn from those whose major profession appeared to be befriending or catering to the needs of stars. In that firmament there was little scope for the kind of warmth Galina craved: she looked outside and found kindred spirits in the unlikely shape of the director of the Soviet national circus, Anatoly Kolevatov, and his wife. They were a relatively sophisticated couple who had travelled widely in the West and shared Galina's love for the sunshine and seaside resorts. At a number of parties, usually given in the absence of her husband, Galina came to know not only the circus community – its young girl acrobats had long been prized by members of the New Class – but also those who were not quite in the circus world and inhabited a middle world between musical theatre and circus.

One of these was Boris Buriata, who was also known to the soothsayer Marusia Shevchenko. Buriata, often called Boris the Gypsy, was a singer, initially with the Moscow Gypsy Theatre. He is – or was until his arrest – a handsome man in the manner of 1930s cinema idols, a moustache somewhat thicker than that of Clark Gable, the flair of Errol Flynn. His sexual reputation marched before him and he immediately impressed Galina. They became lovers, probably in 1981 but perhaps earlier. Boris was drawn into the new circles, the children of the elite and those who were rising in the Party hierarchy through no effort of their own. The patronage of the Brezhnev family was enough to ensure a relentless rise irrespective of a lack of talent; indeed in many cases, a talent for politics or administration or running the national economy was seen as something of a millstone, an embarrassing burden best discarded or disguised.

What counted in the Brezhnev era, especially in the latter half of the 1970s, was unquestioned loyalty to the *Vozhd*, the Chief. He formed a small group around him, the secretariat of the General Secretary, which wrote his speeches and effectively ran his life. As he grew weaker, the group became more arrogant, refusing Republican party chiefs or Ministers the right to see him. Only a close relationship with the Secretariat, good standing in the Politburo, a membership of the larger Brezhnev faction known as the Dnepropetrovsk mafia, or the immediate family gained access to the leader as his mind commuted from astonishing clarity to a clouded world of memories.

Galina's importance grew; Brezhnev was impatient with his wayward daughter but would at least see her, listen to her. Usually it was unnecessary for Galina to seek an audience with her father; rather her request to a Minister or a senior Party official would be honoured automatically, assumed from the outset to have the backing of her father. Not without justification, Galina regarded herself as above the law because, after all, it was papa who said what was what. The Kolevatovs' began to exploit their frienship. It had always been the practice under Kolevatov to demand large bribes from those who wanted to join the circus – a thousand dollars was not an unusual request in return for a position with the State troupe. The logic was simple enough: the frequent tours abroad allowed every performer to carry out currency deals and smuggling rackets and become rich within a few years, quite independent of their artistic careers. Kolevatov, and above all his wife, knew that there were thousands of jugglers, bareback riders, fire-eaters and acrobats to choose from within the Soviet Union and they were all of more or less the same standard. The criterion of selection thus became bribes, not only for entrance to the troupe but also on a commission basis on deals done abroad or on return to Moscow. The friendship with Galina encouraged the couple to believe that even if anything was discovered at the customs point or even if they were discovered illegally buying and dealing diamonds or gold or dollars, then the aura of the Brezhnev family would protect them.

Indeed Galina began to receive the most extravagantly jewelled presents from the circus directors. Boris too was involved in the bribery racket. At first his relationship with Galina merely cemented the liaison with the Kolevatovs, who were in mortal fear of being dropped by her. For the simple act of being her lover, Boris received valuable presents from the circus managers. At the same time he used Galina's influence to leave the obscure Gypsy theatre and take a singing part in the Bolshoi company. Boris had a pleasant baritone which in a small room captivated the female audience, 'like hypnosis' one girl explained to me.

But in a large theatre, the lack of proper training and the clumsy guitar or balalaika strumming was less impressive. Even so he was accepted in the spirit of all socialist artistic enterprises – as a performer whose services were more in the realm of political protection than enhancing the creative *niveau*. To the relatives of Galina, Boris was something of an embarrassment; he gambled heavily and successfully, he borrowed and lent huge sums of money, he behaved like a flashy playboy, running a string of girlfriends along with his love affair with Galina. Galina was besotted. They had fights that would become the talk of the Moscow artistic community: chests of drawers would be hurled down stairs and the daughter of Leonid Brezhnev would scream, howl and rip up Boris's wardrobe. The police were never called.

Slowly, some of the family began to accept that this was more than a transient affair; Boris was invited to the home of Semyon Tsvigun who had married Vera, the sister of Viktoria, Brezhnev's wife. Tsvigun was an old Chekist who had met his wife in the early days of the secret police; she was by most accounts more intelligent than him. Some Soviet film sources say that she wrote many of the screenplays that appear under Tsvigun's name, telling stories of wartime bravery, invariably starring dashing secret policemen and women saving Mother Russia from the German Fascists. Other ghost writers, including quite prominent figures such as Alexei Kondratovich, former deputy editor of the influential literary journal *Novy Mir*, helped to write novels that were published under Tsvigun's name. All of this gives some idea of Tsvigun's vanity and his love of money, for each novel and film brought in several thousand roubles to augment his KGB salary. Tsvigun was part of the Dnepropetrovsk mafia: that is, he had known Brezhnev from the early post-war years in that bleak Ukrainian town where Leonid Ilyich had been first party secretary from 1945 to 1950. It was a period of making-do, of pushing socialism against the odds, of living under Stalinism and at the same time trying to solve complex social problems, above all building houses, shops and factories.

At first glance Tsvigun was a complete contrast to Boris, the aimless drifter who had battened on to Galina. But there were more similarities than differences: both loved young women but were technically and politically tied to older ones, both loved money, hard drinking and playing cards. In the end they both owed their good fortune to the same thing – the patronage of the Brezhnevs. So they began to meet regularly even without – especially without – Galina.

By the end of 1981, Galina's affair with Boris had become so

ostentatious and so tainted with corruption, that the KGB decided to
act. Rather than refer the case to the Procurator's office where
Brezhnev's advisers could quietly have killed it, Andropov presented the
dossier to Mikhail Suslov, the chief ideologue and a man of modest
lifestyle. Sometimes described as the 'conscience of the Party', Suslov
had missed his chance to become Party leader on a number of
occasions, pushing and prodding and eventually, from battle fatigue,
accepting the Brezhnev style of leadership as the least likely to cause
international complications. But the corruption of the era and the
incapacity of the leader disgusted him. On being presented the dossier,
he called in General Tsvigun, who as head of the internal affairs section
of the KGB should have acted against this and many other instances of
corruption. The conversation that ensued was the subject of intense
speculation: the strongest rumours say that there was a row, that Suslov
accused Tsvigun of acting out of family rather than Party loyalty, that he
had no business consorting with criminals like Boris the Gypsy and that
he would be held personally and politically responsible. Soon after,
Tsvigun committed suicide. The official communiqué said that he had
died after 'a grave and prolonged illness', but the statement, which
concentrated on his wartime exploits rather than his activities as KGB
chairman, was not signed by any of the Politburo – not even Brezhnev's
brother-in-law – apart from Andropov. Tsvigun had died in disgrace,
and gradually it was becoming clear that Brezhnev himself could not
escape the mud that was flying so thick through the atmosphere. The
KGB searched the Kolevatov's flat and found over 100,000 dollars in
hard cash and a fortune in diamonds; a search of Boris's apartment also
revealed a cache of diamonds and furs.

Meanwhile, Suslov, apparently because of his argument with
Tsvigun, had weakened and died. The Galina–Boris–Circus case was
put on ice for a few days and then, on the day of the Suslov funeral, the
KGB moved in to arrest the gypsy singer (when Boris was arrested he was
wearing an ermine cape, boots covered in mink and an Orthodox cross
made of diamonds), the circus-director couple and a string of others
connected with the diamond trade in Moscow. It was a clever move
because Galina could have tried to use her influence first to locate then
to free her lover; in the event, *le tout Moscou* was at the funeral, out of
their offices for the whole day.

Boris, the investigator discovered, had become Moscow's main
diamond broker, apart from the circus smuggling (Boris put the gems in
the lion's cage) he had supervised the theft of several major collections

including that of his circus colleague (and former lover) Irina Bugrimova, the legendary tiger dominatrix. These burglaries seemed to have gone undetected by the police – perhaps because of Churbanov's police connections. Galina and Sholokov's wife meanwhile were insider trading; as soon as they heard that the Council of Ministers or Politburo had decided to raise the price of gold or gems, the women would send their agents out to buy up jewellery in bulk. Usually they would buy on credit, or on the nod. And, when the price rises were announced they would sell on the diamond black market, usually through Boris.

Churbanov sat in the high-ceilinged courtroom on Ulitsa Varovskoya, looking almost dignified; trimmer than in the good years because of pre-trial imprisonment. He had been handsome, always tanned, with a muscular build. Only the stomach was flabby because of his love of good cognac. His lawyers, faced with a hopelessly politicised and therefore pre-determined case, made the best of a bad job. The Soviet press had already condemned Churbanov, presenting chunks of the indictment and investigative records that should have stayed secret – that was the line of the defence lawyer Andrei Makarov. 'The man Churbanov should not be harshly judged: he is the product and not the creator of the system.' What chance does a defence lawyer have in a show trial? None. He distinguishes himself only by his energy. His audience is no longer the judge's bench, nor the prosecutor (least of all, him), but his colleagues at the Soviet bar, the *advokaty*, who will say in years to come, 'Ah, that Makarov, what a fine job he made of the Churbanov case.'

Arrested in January 1987, Churbanov had spent 21 months in prison before entering the courtroom. He had already confessed to 'abuse of office'. At the beginning of the investigation, when the arrested Uzbek mafia confessed that Churbanov was part of a conspiracy to fake cotton statistics, he claimed that he had passed on about half the bribes to his wife Galina. That is, some 300,000 roubles out of the 656,838 he was accused of pocketing. But that was just a primitive sprint for refuge, an attempt to scare off the investigators. Soon it became clear that Galina was better placed at his side. So, yes, he received all the roubles. Two hundred witnesses appeared, mainly testifying to the evils of Rashidov, the Uzbek party leader. Rashidov too was dead, so the buck could safely be passed upwards. 'If somone in Uzbekistan tried to protect himself from the epidemic of corruption, they annihilated him,' declared one witness. And another: 'If you weren't bribeable, they destroyed you.'

Churbanov, portrayed in the Soviet press as a mediocrity, 'a vain man thirsty for power' (*Pravda*), 'a dissolute dandy' (*Ogonyok*), played his cards accordingly. Very well, if the Soviet media thought that he was a numbskull, then he would testify accordingly. Here he is describing how a member of the Uzbek Central Committee handed him his money: 'Umarov came into my hotel room with a briefcase and said "This is a present from Rashidov." He put the case down next to the bed and left. When I opened it I found 100,000 or 130,000 roubles. I wanted to give the money back – but to whom? Umarov had gone, and it would have been tactless to contact Rashidov.'

So because of these 'objective' factors, he decided the best thing was to keep the cash. 'They told me it was a present and that is how I regarded it.' As for other parcels, envelopes and briefcases that arrived in his office – he had no idea they contained money.

And yet Churbanov was not a fool. He was simply following the political practice of the times; in every society in the world, those in power were also given opportunities to become rich. Only in the Soviet Bloc was there a notional frontier between Party power and private wealth. His father-in-law had recognised this as a failing. At a time when ideological commitment was not enough to drive the Party, when people legitimately joined the Party because it would advance their career, some kind of financial incentives had to be provided as well as the *nomenklatura* perks.

Who unearths such scandals? The KGB. Perhaps because it allows professionalism – the pursuit of 'socialist legality' – to override its allegiance to the Party leadership. More likely, the KGB became a willing instrument in the Kremlin brawling that brought Andropov to power. Now the KGB, and other police and control agencies, have moved on and are establishing themselves as managers of reform socialism in Romania and Bulgaria. It was hardly surprising that Honecker's successor in East Germany was Egon Krenz, in charge of security policy, nor that Secret Police Chief Markus Wolf emerged strongly in the post-Krenz years. When the Party is under popular pressure to change, and when it has no ideological backbone to define the direction of that change, then policemen, or politicians associated with policemen, are favourably placed. It was Egon Krenz's decision not to shoot at demonstrators – despite the panic-stricken orders of Honecker in the troubled autumn of 1989 – and, in so doing, he admitted the possibility of talking to them.

Gorbachev put Churbanov on trial to demonstrate that the Party was a different animal. Khrushchev had to exorcise Stalin and the effort burnt him out. Gorbachev was more pragmatic, more effective about the ghost of Brezhnev. It was enough to emphasise the corruption, the bribes, the arrogance, the incompetence and then present a studied contrast to the new era. The trial, in 1988, served this function well enough. It was, of course, more show than trial. Here, implied the newspaper photographs (in which all the defendants apart from Churbanov hid their faces), are the relics of the 1970s.

The inclination to convert power into wealth, to match the living standards of the rising Money Class, was rampant in the 1970s, and early 1980s. But it was not a Brezhnevian aberration. Rather, it supplied an answer to the simple question: for what purpose are we here? Gorbachev, who has accelerated the demise of ideology, who admits the possibility of competition to communist power (and even accepts non-communist Governments among his allies), who has distanced the Party from the running of the economy, has not been able to provide a suitably new answer. And so he is obliged to maintain lines of continuity with the Brezhnev *apparat*. The Andropov and Gorbachev purges were admittedly dramatic. In Andropov's short 15-month reign as Party leader, 19 out of 84 government ministers were fired. But more significant was the large number of officials who were retained by Andropov. Many of them had dug into the honeypot in the Brezhnev years, yet they became the executive of Andropov. Gorbachev too did not launch a bold crusade against the Party.

Middle-level party cadres were only trimmed – 10 per cent under Andropov, about the same under Gorbachev. This was more than a quest for stability. Nor did it indicate political impotence on the part of Gorbachev. The obstructions of the party *apparat* in the reform process is much over-stated. It is constant purging rather than grand market-orientated reform plans that paralyse the Party machine; fear immobilises. Gorbachev's speeches intended for popular consumption were far brasher than those intended for the Party. Especially in 1988 and 1989, Gorbachev tended to caress the *apparat*, much as one soothes a hound before the hunt.

There is, though, a difference between Gorbachev accepting a measure of corruption or privilege within the Party, and the self-delusion of the 1970s. The Brezhnev, Gierek and Honecker elites built their own world of luxury and comfort, and believed – really believed – that they were building the same world for the rest of the nation. State laws were their laws to be changed, or broken, at will – the Gierek parliament managed to pass a law that exempted (or rather discounted by 90 per cent) the elite from 'luxury tax'. To help their children into sinecures was to help the young generation, to accept honorary doctorates or the vice-chancellorship of universities (complete with salaries) was a sign of trust in the educational system, to loot museums for 18-century furniture for their own salons was to exhibit a genuine commitment to national tradition and culture. Now the pictures and commodes have been returned to the museums, the children have been sacked, Gierek lost some of his fake degrees. But the self- righteousness remained.

After martial law was declared in 1981, the Poles waited for the show trials, Jaruzelski's reckoning with the Gierek decade. It did not come. Instead there was the sad, hopeless trial of Maciej Szczepanski, head of television. The logic was sound, if not overwhelming. Party rule under Gierek was a play of mirrors: fake statistics, production records that were broken with suspicious regularity, a picture of public well-being that was supposed to legitimise the leadership, the successful managers of the economy. It was impossible to put every economist, every factory manager on trial and it was extremely difficult to pin criminal charges on those with overall responsibility for the economy. And to put Gierek on trial, that would seriously challenge the authority of communist rule: from 1970 to 1980, Gierek *was* communism in Poland. Szczepanski, by contrast, did not appear to be a model communist. He was unpopular, even within the television organisation. Criminal, or at least negligence, charges could be brought against him. Politically, he was the perfect target – the manipulator of television screens that had made Poles believe in a false version of socialism. Had not Solidarity activists daubed 'TV lies' in huge white letters outside Szczepanski's office? Like the trial of Churbanov, the Szczepanski trial could make its point without dividing the nation.

Szczepanski argued that he had been merely serving Poland to the best of his abilities, side-stepping laws that were antiquated or impractical. He was a reformer, an innovator suffocated by the legislation of a past age. The indictment, though, showed that he had mismanaged the television budget, thrown away thousands of dollars on doomed or mediocre co-productions with the West, such as 'The New Adventures of Sherlock Holmes'. But, most intriguing of all, Szczepanski was said to have an exclusive yacht, a private helicopter, a ski lodge, several country houses, several cars and a hideaway with a jacuzzi bath, a library of porno videos and two coloured girls who massaged away the stress of watching so much television. Not much of this was true, but it was interesting, especially to the women queueing for meat. And the fact, or factoid, that the girls were 'coloured' was particularly titallating since it suggested that, like so much of Gierek's New Poland, they had been imported.

Szczepanski was arrested in October 1980, but years ground by before he appeared in the dock. It was a frustrating trial since not all the most lurid aspects of his life fell into the criminal realm. It was not actually against the law to be massaged. The questioning was thus mainly about accounting procedures within television, a subject of great intricacy. I went to Courtroom 242 several times in the 1980s. Szczepanski did not look much of a playboy any more. His skin had yellowed from too much artificial light. He was sharp, challenging witnesses like a terrier. After a short whispered conversation with his lawyers, he realised there was a journalist present. That had become unusual: halfway through the trial, the authorities had lost heart in making Szczepanski a political scapegoat but it was too late to abort. Instead the show trial lost its show and Polish journalists were even discouraged from attending. Szczepanski looked at me meaningfully and, handcuffed, shepherded by two militiamen, he was taken to the lavatory. The guards, young boys a bit overawed by this former member of the establishment, took off his manacles and left him in peace. I joined him in the lavatory.

'Do you want an interview?' he whispered.

'What, here?'

'No, written questions – give them to my lawyer.'

'OK.' This sounded fishy.

'But I must see everything before you print.'

'Well . . .' There was a standard journalistic formula for this kind of request, but I had forgotten what it was.

'And it must be printed in full, and . . .' Szczepanski was still dictating conditions when the policemen came to take him back to the court. Later it became clear that this was Szczepanski's manner, always had been – he was an over-bearing manager, with legions of enemies. The other members of the Gierek establishment had sufficient protection, even at the most dangerous times, to keep them out of court. I began to feel sorry for him. For a start, it was obvious that most of the stories were false or extravagantly embellished. His yacht was really quite small. The helicopter, cars and villas belonged to Polish television; Szczepanski had unrestricted access to them, but that was a slightly different matter. When he went abroad for conferences or negotiations, he was restricted, like all Polish officials, to a per diem allowance of £8. That did not go far in London even in the 1970s. So he took money from the television accounts, and, yes, some of it was changed on the black market. But he also modernised Polish Television, authorising new equipment, new studios: he played the political game, but not solely for himself.

After months and years of investigative arrest, Szczepanski became embittered. Why should he, of all people, be the fall-guy for the Gierek regime? The answer, he decided, was the shadowy figure of Mieczyslaw Moczar, a wartime partisan, the instigator of the 1968 anti-semitic campaigns and a constant challenger for the Party leadership. Moczar had been pushed into the chairmanship of the Supreme Chamber of Control (NIK), a body that was supposed to monitor government malpractice. But Gierek had taken away most of NIK's teeth and hoped that he would muzzle Moczar. The wily partisan general had spent his time preparing dossiers on mismanagement, corruption and the personal foibles of the Gierek leadership. He was biding his time for another leadership bid. And Szczepanski presented himself as a natural target.

Szczepanski made this into his defence. 'All the 35 charges levelled against me are without justification. Why was I arrested, indicted and tried? In my opinion this is not an economic but a political trial. All accusations which the indictment contained were meant to serve as an instrument of Party and political squabbling . . . I have been used in this trial as a substitute for all the rest of prominent people holding power in the 1970s . . .'

At this stage, Szczepanski was being repeatedly interrupted by the judge. 'Stick to the point,' he would say, 'answer the charges before you.'

As soon as Solidarity had established itself, as soon as the strikes of summer 1980 had shown themselves to be a real challenge to Gierek, NIK began to leak information to those in the Party leadership who decided it was time to topple Gierek. Then, to ensure that old Gierek cronies would not survive even after the toppling of their master, information was leaked to Solidarity. This was an extraordinary turn, even in such an oddball Socialist country as Poland. A former security police general with a reputation for compaigning against Jews and liberals leaked the contents of his reports to a revolutionary workers' movement which was at least partly populated with people who wanted to dismantle Communism and introduce a kind of Christian Democracy. The only element that connected the two was a contempt for the high lifestyles, abuses of power and privilege practised by the Gierek mafia. Strange coalitions form in the pursuit of power.

After a while the judge decided to call a halt: it was all getting too political – or rather politically dangerous. Certainly no word was going to be printed in the Polish press; still, Szczepanski was going too far.

'Enough, now,' said the judge.

'And one more thing,' said Szczepanski. 'Moczar and his propaganda wanted to show me as a debauchee, having sex with coloured girls, throwing away state money, and at the same time being part of the Gierek team. Don't you see? It was a plot: Moczar was trying to blacken Gierek's image and brighten his own. Don't you see. . . ?'

Nobody was listening.

Later, a kind of justice was done. Eight years jail. But Szczepanski was allowed out more or less immediately since he had served so long in investigative arrest.

Later still, he joined a private company, to become rich legally. Now he is a member of the Rising Class, an entrepreneur in a system that is only just coming to terms with money. Like many within the political establishment, he has been depoliticised. Communist values, never very pressing during his political career, have been discarded entirely. The system has run out of steam, but one man at least has found happiness.

3

Currency Apartheid

In the so far unwritten history of mediocre films, *Sparrows Are Birds Too* deserves at least a passing mention. Made in 1968 by Gyorgy Hinsch, it is a satirical portrait of Hungarian society or, more precisely, the Hungarian lust for dollars and all things Western. The hero is a small red-haired man who, having defected from Hungary fifteen years earlier, returns to his home country as a naturalised American, and a rich one to boot. His wad of dollars and his largely incomprehensible credit cards extract a high pitch of subservience from hotel and restaurant staff, allow him to steal his brother's girlfriend and make him into a Capitalist prodigal. At a striptease show in an expensive hotel on the sandy shores of Lake Balaton, the pecking order is clearly defined. The show opens with a traditional drum roll, then languid orchestral music. The girl (who has a Polish name since Polish girls are the staple supply for louche clubs and cabarets in Western Europe and the Middle East) removes her long white gloves. The lights go up. The manager kindly requests all guests paying Hungarian forints to leave the room. The band stops playing, the girl freezes in her pose. All those guests paying Bulgarian leva, Romanian lei and Czech crowns are kindly requested . . . The music resumes, the girl, unpeeling, reaches a fairly crucial stage – and out go a complaining Russian trade delegation and a solitary East German. The climax is witnessed only by the hero, safe in the knowledge that his American credit card will buy him even the secret of the seven veils.

Later scenes show the hero, a stubby underacting figure, picking his way across a beach crowded, body to body, with Russians, Hungarians and East Germans to a special compound whose entrance is usefully marked in German – '*Nur Für Dollarzahler*' ('Only Dollar Payers Permitted'). The beach is deserted apart from a few loose-limbed women and a white-coated waiter who wades out to sea to deliver yet another glamorously pink cocktail on a silver tray to a wealthy client on an undulating air bed. The final shot of this hugely popular film has the hero talking directly to the audience and reminding them to treat fellow Hungarians with courtesy and respect even though they may not have hard currency because, 'sparrows are birds too'.

Dollar up, dollar down, dollar in, dollar out, Western currencies have become a crucial quasi-legal element in the everyday economy of the East. There was probably no greater betrayal of Communism by ruling Communist parties than the decision to allow a kind of currency apartheid in their societies. Of course the vague idea that Communism should somehow strive to be a moneyless society was grounded in Bolshevik times. But the failure of Communist planners to provide sufficiently interesting or attractive goods for the increasingly discriminating consumers of Eastern Europe pushed the system not towards a moneyless condition but the quite different state of 'low moneyness' (the phrase of economist Gregory Grossman). In the West, money was a measure of worth, determining the size and appearance of your house, the speed at which you travel to work, the quality of your child's health and education and your access to information. In the East, local currencies do not convey such complex signals; connections, the exchange of favours, are more important to daily survival and, because of explicit decisions by party leaderships in the 1970s, the money that weighed most heavily, that had real significance, was foreign: above all the dollar.

It was this dual currency system, allowing a privileged but large group of people to buy luxury goods and essentials like toothpaste or contraceptives for dollars, that rotted the legitimacy of the Party authorities. The tensions between dollar-holders and earners on the one hand, and a swelling underclass of the undollared erupted again and again: in wage negotiations, in rows between farmers and food consumers, in the desertion of the social services for more lucrative work, in the resentment of heavy industrial workers against private or relatively independent craftsmen. The ubiquity of the dollar was a standing testimony day by day to the incompetence of the Party in running the official economy; 'low moneyness' was also a measure of low confidence.

Did the parties deliberately set out to destroy their native currencies? That would be a reckless claim even though the dual currency system played an essential part in the enrichment of the political class. Perhaps, though, there was a trace of early Bolshevism in it all, an ideological distaste for a strong currency that could one day translate into a strong opposition.

The Money-less Society

The collapse of the rouble after the Bolshevik Revolution was complete. Not even the galloping inflation, crippled production and organisational chaos of post-World War II central Europe could match the crash of the Russian economy. A prominent economic historian, Alec Nove, recalls as a child in the streets of Bolshevik Russia handing high-denomination bank-notes to beggars: the beggars would return them as worthless. Money ceased to have any kind of function; factories effectively bartered with each other for supplies; the central budget gave factories what they needed and everything was paid back to the state. By 1919–20, workers were getting most of their wages in kind. Those in the state sector were not charged for food or clothes; they travelled free on the trains, paid no rent. The pressure of the Civil War accelerated the moves toward a money-less economy. But even after the Bolsheviks had won, the idea persisted. Simply, the crisis that had forced a collapse in the rouble was to be exploited for ideological reasons. Bukharin argued that the abolition of the marketplace and complete state ownership would realise the full Socialism of Marx and Engels; money had no place in this picture. Even Lenin, architect in the 1920s of the New Economic Policy which encouraged profit-making, was talking in 1919 of organising the whole country into producers' and consumers' communes and 'carrying out the most radical measures, preparing the abolition of money'.

Outside, on the streets, there was semi-organised chaos worthy of Dante. Factory workers, unable to produce because supplies had dried up, scrambled in rubbish dumps for scraps of metal that could be made into cigarette lighters or toys and then exchanged for food. Wooden houses were pulled down, railway tracks pulled up for fuel. Coal production fell from twenty-nine million tonnes in 1913 to nine million tonnes in 1921.

Inside the noblemen's palaces that now functioned as revolutionary headquarters, there was great excitement. At last! The devastation of the country had created the perfect conditions for true Socialism. Frenzied work began, in mid-1920, on a budget plan that would completely eliminate money. The accounting was an elaborate balance between monies-in-kind; the value of steel against the value of bricks, cherries against bolts, pig-iron against sugar. This was strictly Through The Looking Glass. Bukharin deemed the study of economics to be defunct, since it referred to money, commodity exchange and private property in the means of production.

The idealism, of course, crumbled, and all the Bolsheviks changed their minds. But the core idea lingered on that money in some way perpetrated social injustice, that it was an obstacle to Socialism and was, ultimately, unnecessary.

Inflation, open or hidden (in the form of goods disappearing from shops), reinforced the view. By the same token, generations of Soviet and East European citizens have grown up accepting, as given, cheap or free social services. A seventeen-year-old in Sofia, though openly dismissing Socialism over a coffee and a doughnut, is offended and bewildered by the idea that he should pay for hospital services, or a market-price rent.

When the formula 'better work = more money = more goods/status' breaks down, the result is a strange mixture of superstition and black magic. Money, of local denomination, does not buy what one truly desires. Yet one works and one is paid in this money (old pre-Gorbachev joke: I pretend to work and they pretend to pay); it is not to be completely dismissed. Current Gorbachev-era inflation is not, despite the astronomical levels touched by Poland, so critical that one would want to plaster the walls with bank-notes or burn them in a stove. Moscow is not Weimar. But still it is proving nearly impossible to restore the meaning of money. And if money does not communicate correctly then what is one to make of, say, debt, or credit? The Soviet Bloc is heavy with debt. In the case of Poland, there is no conceivable way that it could be paid off before the middle of the twenty-first century. Debt frightened the Romanian President Nicolae Ceausescu so thoroughly that he strangled domestic production and domestic energy consumption. He feared that international indebtness would give the West some form of leverage, erode his absolute power. The same anxiety, less hysterical in its expression, steered Czechoslovakia and other Soviet-Bloc states. International debt is a daily fact of political decision-making, yet in individual lives, it is a marginal factor. The overdraft is virtually unknown and though Moscow has its share of crooked money-lenders – with their own back-up boys to get debtors to cough up – there is not a 'debt culture'. A form of hire purchase exists; some department stores specialising in televisions, radio and electronic gear have a desk marked *Kredit*. The bored woman will interrupt her nail-filing to set out the terms: 20% on a big colour television set, six months to repay at a rate of two per cent. But as money has depleted value, so too does personal money management; the *Kredit* desk is under-employed. Few Russians could plan their saving so far ahead.

While abroad, Raisa Gorbachev uses her American Express Gold Card, and other members of the travelling Politburo have access to credit cards (usually issued in the name, and on the account, of the local Soviet Embassy). To introduce credit cards to the broad Russian masses is a different matter altogether. First, the organisation of shopping would have to change. Many shops still use an abacus to calculate bills. Second, there would have to be something to buy. And, of course, the Russians would have to learn about a form of money that is not lumpy and carried around in bulging briefcases. The first attempts to introduce personal credit have therefore been confined to hard-currency accounts. An extraordinary commercial war broke out in 1988, symptomatic of the problems facing all financial reform in the Gorbachev era. Intourist, the Soviet travel agency, struck a deal with savings banks and the Moscow City Council to develop a credit card, called Sovcard, that would ease the Soviet Union into the world of automated banking. A deal was signed with Visa International providing for an internationally valid credit card – an ostentatious mark of privilege as long as foreign travel is restricted to such a tight minority. The first proud card-holder was Yuri Titov, chairman of the Soviet Olympic team. So far, so good, at least for the elite. But the Soviet monopoly on hard-currency deposits has always been held by Vnesheconombank (Bank of Foreign Affairs), which reacted furiously at the competition. It quickly signed up with Eurocard and Mastercard for an international link-up, and brought in furniture for a new domestic credit-card office. As ordinary Soviet savings banks are now encouraged to open hard-currency sections, the pressure is on the old monopolies. But how is one to spend hard-currency credit in Moscow? It is possible, of course, in the special stores for diplomats and the privileged. Indeed, since there are so few outlets, it should be easier to run than a Western credit company. It might absorb some of the hard-currency black market: if banks offer better services then it makes more sense to deposit money with them rather than keep it under a mattress. Transferring the credit idea to roubles requires a huge imaginative leap. First, roubles have to be able to buy more than the bare essentials; few people in the West buy their daily groceries with a credit card. Production has to increase – even Bukharin understood that eventually – the quality of goods has to improve and the concept of recreational spending has to be introduced. Those days are far ahead.

Doubling Up

The rise of a second currency to fill the money vacuum began in earnest in the late 1960s and 1970s. Its origins, though, were rooted in the chaos of the Second World War. In German-occupied Warsaw, for example, there were dozens of trading variants, from the legal Reichsmark to the zloty, the omnipresent dollar, gold, straightforward commodity bartering, cigarettes and ration coupons. The post-war Communist zloty had to replace all these currencies, had to pick up the long, fascinating tradition of the pre-war zloty and win credibility at a time when the shops were barren. The zloty was not up to the task and a new black market, orientated towards the shortages generated by central planning, was born. Even where the fear of illicit currency trading was strongest – in Soviet-occupied East Germany – a form of money market was in operation, tolerated in part because it serviced the garrisoned Soviet officers. A few days after the West German currency reform on 20 June 1948, the East Germans (or rather the Soviet Military Administration) introduced their own currency, the Deutsche Ostmark. The first one hundred Reichsmark, Hitler's currency, could be exchanged 1:1 for one hundred East Marks, one thousand Reichsmark bought two hundred East Marks and thereafter the curve dipped dramatically. Anybody with over five thousand Reichsmark had to prove that it was legally acquired, a virtual impossibility. The savings of most Germans had been eaten up in three years of purchasing on the post-war black market and all savings accounts had been dissolved when the Russians marched into Berlin. After the 1948 currency reform, the big black marketeers fled Westwards, but an illegal currency market persisted because, even with reformed money, there was nothing to buy. Eventually butter and other staples reached the shelves, priced at black-market levels. But to dodge the heavy jail sentences for currency trading, the black market functioned on ration cards.

Nowadays most of the Soviet Bloc is on a two- or multiple-currency system. In East Germany, the West German Mark makes the world go round. From July 1990, it became the official currency. The Polish black market can deal with any currency (even soft ones like the Bulgarian leva and the Hungarian forint for prospective holidaymakers) but prefers dollars. The Czechoslovak and Hungarian traders handle the Deutschmark and the dollar, but accept sterling at a pinch, the Bulgarians have a healthy business in Turkish lira. In Moscow, however, there is a flourishing business in 'certificate roubles' (paper coupons, representing real buying power in special shops, that are issued to legitimate dollar-earners) and the police enforcement of illegal currency exchange is haphazard. In Ceausescu's Romania, there was no elasticity. A tradition of police informers (largely cast off in other Soviet-Bloc countries because the rewards of betrayal were so poor) survived longest in Romania, and every transaction, every conversation with a foreigner, was regarded as suspect. As in post-War East Germany, a substitute was found for incriminating bank notes: Kent cigarettes. It is impossible, even in California, to punish a citizen for the mere possession of cigarettes. As Kent are of Western origin and can be bought legally only at hard-currency shops, they have a real exchange value. The rate fluctuated but before the 1989 revolution, it could be reckoned that a pack of Kents costing $1.40 in the West would go for one hundred lei, which in turn was the equivalent of $10 at the official rate of exchange. Nobody in their right mind smoked them. Five cartons would buy you a made-to-measure suit providing you supplied the fabric, a packet could get you to the front of the queue and an extra kilo of meat above your ration. In the grim winters when Romanians were ordered to use only one 40-watt light bulb a night, three packs of Kent persuaded the official meter-reader to juggle the numbers. A packet got you a seat reservation on a train, two hundred repaired your car. Why Kent? It was not really clear, though one theory was that this was the brand airlifted to Romania after the 1977 earthquake; others say Kent-as-currency existed long before, in the late 1960s.

The two-currency system began in earnest in the age of détente. Tourism from the West was increasing, the effects of Western credit were beginning to trickle into society. Consumers, after two decades of austerity, were more sophisticated in their demands and wanted more from their economy – not only higher wages, but all the trappings of the New Consumerism, good food, refrigerators and televisions. But the centrally planned economies, though they started to shift their focus away from the development of heavy industry towards services and the light and consumer industries, were unable to keep up with the rising expectations.

In Poland some of the new Western money was used to buy in consumer goods (hence the lingering popularity of Edward Gierek) in the early 1970s. The point was to secure a level of consumer satisfaction (it was after all the repression of a wage revolt that brought Gierek to power in 1970) while at the same time building up ambitious investment projects that would guarantee Poland's long-term future as an exporter of industrial goods. Elsewhere the credit was used more sensibly but ultimately – except in Hungary, which seized the reform nettle – it was used everywhere to put off the inevitable, an overhaul of the central planning system.

The collapse of confidence in the 1980s, accompanying colder times in East-West relations, dried up the hard currency. That meant not only that it was more difficult to pay for imported cigarettes, coffee, chocolates and clothes – all of which promptly became major black-market items – but also to pay for feed grain and spare parts and raw materials. The victims were the consumers. Scarce feed meant the slaughtering of livestock and less meat, few spare parts meant that without bribes cars and tractors often lay idle for months, the absence of raw materials caused shortages of items as diverse as rubber Wellingtons and fertiliser.

As the goods disappeared from the shops in the 1970s, so money lost its worth. Worker discontent in Poland and Romania was bought off with higher wages, but there was nothing to buy. For selected workers, such as coal miners, special shops were opened, creating a fool's paradise. The logic was simple: Poland needs to export coal to earn hard currency, coal mining is nasty work, so, to maintain productivity, we must pay coal miners more than other workers, but to make this pay meaningful, we must produce goods on which they can spend their cash. Other workers were not so lucky, and saw no point in working harder.

The introduction of hard-currency stores – variously called Pewex, Tuwex, Inter-shops – in the Soviet Bloc was supposed to answer two of these problems. Goods of high quality, that would normally have been exported, were redirected for 'internal export'. This dubious idiom conveys some of the double-think behind the Pewex system. Shops set up in East Bloc capitals, and later in every provincial outpost, offered consumer riches from the occident. You can still see children in Warsaw and Prague with their noses pushed against the window to view the Johnny Walker bottles, the Mars Bars, the Lego sets and the Italian cashmere jumpers. Outside in the streets, in the normal state-run shops, there were perhaps Cuban citrus fruit but nothing more exotic; a grim parade of unwashed root vegetables, tinned preserves, hard cheese, meat shops that boast only fatty sausage, toyshops with crude plastic cars, a world of aromas but no flavour . . . Inside, for dollars, there were no shortages. This then was a ready solution to one dilemma: how to encourage people to work harder without having to reorganise the economic system, a painless sustitute. Workers would want to earn more, to buy dollars on the black market and thus gain entry to the world of the hard-currency shop. Once there, they usually bought Polish export vodka, which was cleverly priced to be cheaper than vodka from a state-run zloty shop. Instead of constructing a proper wage incentive scheme and restoring the value of money, the East Bloc governments chose to legitimise the black market. Nobody admits to this, of course. In an interview, Tadeusz Bielski, general manager of Polish Pewex, skirted around the issue of the black market. His customers, he said, were those 'who continuously received hard-currency transfers from their families abroad, those Poles who are sent abroad to work, and foreign tourists, and foreigners living in our country.' Well, yes, up to a point.

In fact the second specific aim of the hard-currency market was to sponge up the dollars in the second economy: most published estimates reckon that there are two billion dollars in private circulation at any one time in Poland. The figure is lower elsewhere in the Bloc but the point is the same. The East European debt crisis has forced governments to scrape for every available dollar within the country. The hard-currency stores are not the only ploy – artificially high tourist exchange rates and compulsory exchange quotas are a uniform device – but they are the most efficient. Pewex, whose figures are the most readily accessible of the East European hard-currency stores, gives some twenty per cent of its revenues to the Treasury, and a further thirty-five per cent to the Ministry of Distribution and Services. Since the 1970s, Pewex has been trawling in two hundred and fifty million dollars a year, and edged up to about three hundred and sixty million dollars in the late 1980s. Other licensed hard-currency dealers also offered rare or unavailable goods for dollars: Pol-mot sold cars at a hefty profit to Poles reluctant to wait out the year-long queues. Typically, you encounter black-market hard-currency dealers inside or just outside a Pewex shop. They buy and sell dollars, accompany the client to a discreet staircase but are not notably scared of the police. If they express any fear it is usually intended to extract a more favourable price.

The rise of the hard-currency store has been extraordinary. A purely pragmatic move – to pick up surplus dollars and make the people a little more happy – has had a lasting economic and ideological impact. The black-currency market has effectively been declared a permanent and necessary feature of a domestic Communist economy. Privately, finance ministry officials in both Poland and Czechoslovakia admit this, shrug their shoulders and say something to the effect of, 'It exists, we can't get rid of it now, so let's get the maximum profit out of it.'

In Poland, long before the hard-currency market was whitewashed, it was quite legal to buy or sell Pewex coupons. These are simple dollar- substitutes, slips of Monopoly-like paper marked twenty cents, fifty cents or one dollar. Black marketeers advertised openly in the newspapers – 'Coupons For Sale, Best Price Offered.' The customer brought his zloties to the trader and at a rate akin to the black market exchange for real dollars was offered dollar coupons, or the customer sold his coupons for zloties; or coupons and zloties were put together to buy authentic greenback dollars. The government was thus under-writing the black market. By the mid-1980s, the authorities grew weary with the whole pretence. Warsaw needed dollars by hook or by crook. Anti-black-market laws were unenforceable; tolerating some forms of market exchange (trading in Pewex coupons) while banning others was both pointless and costly. From November 1987, the Polish Foreign Trade Bank (PKO) started to buy dollars from Poles at a price competetive with the black market. That in turn forced up the price offered by the crooked street changers. Within the week, the dollar could be sold at three different rates: almost one thousand zloty at the PKO bank, two hundred and fifty zloties at the official tourist rate, one thousand two hundred zloties at the black-market rate. There was thus a twenty-five per cent bonus for those willing to break the law. By March 1989, the Polish authorities had discarded even these minimal restrictions. Anybody willing to get a licence and employ a cashier can now change hard currency at market rates. Exchange booths have sprung up throughout Poland. The move in effect allowed the state to participate in the free hard-currency market and influence the exchange rate. State banks and official tourist companies set up their stalls alongside the reformed black marketeers. The black market did not entirely disappear: there were always Poles who wanted to avoid the queues at the licenced booths and make a quick transaction. As hyperinflation took off during 1989, Polish steelworkers and clerks could be seen on payday sprinting to change their zloties into dollars. The zloty could buy little while the dollar was the only safe hedge against inflation. A worker would change his whole pay packet into dollars and then, week by week, change some of the hard currency back into zloties to buy food and pay the bills. In one particularly troubled fortnight, in August 1989, the free market rose from six thousand to twelve thousand zloties per dollar. No wage increases, no indexation could keep up with such a rapid erosion of the zloty. By knocking down the legal barriers dividing those with access to dollars and those without, the Solidarity government struck a blow against senseless privilege, against 'currency apartheid', and took a step towards a more rational economy. By 1990, there was only one rate of exchange and money at last began to take on meaning. But it was also an act of desperation. The whole working class, not just pensioners and others on fixed incomes, would be pushed below the poverty belt if they were denied the possibility of buying and selling hard currency. And while currency liberalisation eased the life of high zloty-earning workers with industrial muscle, it did nothing to ease the plight of those working in the social services. At a party celebrating the newly awarded professorship to a Polish surgeon of world repute, he raised his arms out wide in despair: 'I still get only one hundred and fifty thousand zloties a month. You know how much that is on the black market today? Eighty pounds!'

This reshuffling of values – who is rich, who is poor, who deserves to be rich – characterised all the mobile East European states as they entered the 1990s. In Poland, soup kitchens were springing up everywhere. I met Zosia at one such Red Cross canteen in Warsaw's Mokotoska Street. She was the widow of a doctor and, to survive, was selling her husband's library, volume by volume, to a second-hand bookshop. A Handbook of Practical Neurology, published in 1959, yielded enough to buy meat for a week, but by early 1990 a similar textbook only bought two pork chops. She ate her free soup quickly, did not talk to her neighbours; she admitted her poverty but did not like to wallow in it.

The new rich, meanwhile, operated under camouflage. The free-market ethos of the Solidarity government should have encouraged a display of wealth – certainly 1990 New Year parties were remarkable for their opulence – but out of self-protection, the *nouveaux riches* kept their heads down in a society still committed to egalitarian values. They avoided the hard-currency casinos (six in Poland, three in Hungary, one in Bulgaria) which were packed with foolhardy farmers, Middle Eastern businessmen or professional Western gamblers.

To study the new rich of Eastern Europe at play in their natural habitat, the place to go was the Architects Club at the bottom of Warsaw's Foksal Street. A beautifully reconstructed nineteenth-century building, the Club provided the usual backing for a profession: organising lectures, running a cheap café, acting as an informal information bourse. At night, though, the Club changed character. At a time of the evening when the cleaners start work on the street debris (yellowed newspapers, broken bottles – rarely food or string or cigarette ends, the cleaning-ladies will tell you) and the homeward-bound buses flash past the stops and the drunks sprawl into lighted doorways, at about that time the private entrepreneurs come out to play. The Mercedes and Saab turbos line up outside the Club and out of the bucket seats spill the fast set of post-communism, the befurred and the bejewelled.

Poland and Hungary have 'seasons' as tightly defined as the British. It begins earlier, with the Carnival Ball, usually held at the Club, but takes off only really in the spring when the last snows have melted. I felt some sadness at one such spring ball. Gucci leather was beating a tattoo on the floor, cognac flowed like vodka and the wealth, with its natural accessories talent and beauty, was paraded as subtly as missiles on Red Square. Wowo Bielicki, a greying playboy (organiser of the Miss Poland contest before the formidable Mrs Julia Morley brought some order in the house) kicked off the evening by dervish-whirling a girl around the room. Then everybody joined in: the boutique owners, the Western computer representatives, the greenhouse proprietors (whose fortunes derive from selling flowers rather than time-consuming and tedious vegetables), car dealers, even a few architects. Talent was represented by a sprinkling of actors, designers and two satirists, Jan Pietrzak and Witold Filler. Beauty was represented by models from the stable of Grazyna Hase, now an exclusive fashion designer and a former companion of Bielicki.

Somebody began to drink Soviet champagne from a shoe and this evoked a small explosion of laughter. Somebody else cracked a joke about Russia. A drunken flower dealer slipped to the floor, and there was more laughter and merriment. A plate of salmon crashed between tables. Estimated cost: two weeks' wages for a steelworker, three weeks' for a university lecturer. Everybody was having fun.

Follow the revellers from the Architect's Club around the various stations of the *nouveaux riches* and one begins to wonder how the private businessman ever work enough to become millionaires. Certainly my tailor, a private craftsman beset with daily bureaucratic difficulties and minor persecutions, was as resentful as any state-employed dockworker at the flashy lifestyle of the Warsaw and Cracow *chiceria*. Summer sees them – the actresses, the waiters, the lawyers, the gynaecologists, the boutiquistes – at fashionable resorts like Deby. (A forester's son offered to take me through the woods to a point where one can view the

Communist world's most glamorous starlets bathing naked. The fee was modest.) Others are renting dachas in the Mazurian lake district, but so too are the not-so-rich: the truly wealthy can afford to travel abroad and do so, frequently combining a buying mission with pleasure. Winter takes the 'banana youth' – as even the middle-aged are known, reflecting the price and unavailability of the fruit – to Zakopane, Bukowina or Szczyrk near the Czechoslovakian border. There are many ordinary East Europeans in the same resorts, but the privately rich distinguish themselves by hiring private helicopter taxis from Cracow, by bribing their way to the front of their queue for the ski lift and hiring restaurants for the night in lieu of a good night club. In truth Zakopane is less of a ski resort, more of a catwalk. Stroll down the main street of this charming mountain village (where even the goatherds are now corrupt) and take in the afternoon spectacle. The Swiss skis (barely used), the Polaroid sunglasses, the French zip-up suits, the Italian boots. Even the tan comes from Helena Rubenstein.

These mimic lives are not dangerous to the system. They may even be comforting. These butterfly careers show plainly that money and power can be separated. The merit of the new rich is that they are essentially unproductive, traders rather than makers. But the entrepreneurial class is moving closer to the power centres, challenging state monopolies and showing themselves to be the true managers of Post-Communism.

Typical in this respect, is Lech Grobelny. A plump man in his mid forties, with a personal fortune of about two million dollars, he is the New Man of disintegrating Eastern Europe. He started out by opening automatic booths to take passport photographs, used the profit to play the black-currency markets, and when money trading became legal in Poland, promptly converted scores of his photo-booths into money-exchange kiosks. 'I freely admit,' he says, sitting in a string vest in the muggy atmosphere of one of his caravans, 'that I am one of the controllers of the hard-currency market.' He started the BKO – the Safe Savings Bank – offering interest rates far higher than the state-run banks: one hundred and eighty per cent on a year deposit, one hundred and twenty per cent on six months. Because there is no legal provision for this kind of individual bank – and no state guarantees – deposits are described as 'loans'. The Pole 'lends' his money to Grobelny and gets it back with interest a bit later. Perfectly legal. 'I wanted to show that there is no need to wait for a change of regulations, to wait for a sluggish government.' His next step was to open a chain of gold and jewellery shops as well as a network of pawnbrokers, to profit from the desperation of the newly impoverished. 'Hyperinflation has paralysed thirty per cent of private business in this country and so a group of colleagues and I decided to take matters into our own hands. A lower rate of the dollar is an important factor in the fight against inflation, so we are trying to keep it low. But the state-run banks are of no help at all. The government must be forced to limit the amounts of newly printed money and the monopoly of state banks must be broken, taxes should be promptly paid – all that would help end inflation.' The first phone rings, then the second, then the third. It is time for a bit of market rigging; the stranger must leave. One bodyguard escorts me down the street, the other stays near the trading caravan. 'People want to kill the boss,' says my guard. 'Lots, nuts mainly. Always carry my piece,' he pats his waist. 'Boss doesn't like it, but I mean what can you do? No law and order nowadays, bloody anarchy.'

Nobody else in Eastern Europe has gone quite so far. In Hungary the forint has a uniform exchange rate, as in Poland, but there have been no free-wheeling attempts to challenge the state monopoly of the banks by reformed black marketeers. In Romania, after the Christmas Revolution, the black market started to move out of Kents into dollars; the first step on a long road. And even in Russia, the currency black market is becoming whiter. There is not the same gaping need to soak up illegally circulating dollars, since the mere possession of dollars is a criminal offence. The restrictions on travel and working abroad put a clamp on the influx of private dollars. But, in the 1970s, the Brezhnev era, the system of control had been relaxed somewhat and a wide variety of dollar-substitutes were used by the privileged. That was a typically Brezhnevian policy of extending the frontiers of privilege, giving more and more people on the fringes of the political elite a stake in his political survival. Nowadays this is called corruption but then it seemed like good management, at least to the beneficiaries. Many Russians, not just crooked ministers and provincial party barons, became rich under Brezhnev. The money corruption at the top had a trickle-down effect and helped create a largely unproductive class of *nouveau riche* metropolitan society. Excited by my first meeting with a Jewish dissident in Moscow in 1976, I rapidly found myself out of my depth. 'You like Adidas,' said the human rights campaigner with something like pity, 'Adidas finished. Nike are the best, for running, walking. Look.' He gave a short demonstration. How to edge the conversation to Sakharov? Did Sakharov perhaps have a preference? 'Everybody has to have Nike nowadays,' said Tolya. 'Come here.' We moved to the bathroom out of range of the notional KGB microphones. The taps were turned on. A shrieking whisper. 'Do you know, do you know how much they cost. . . ?'

The main substitute currency in those days was the Certificate Rouble which was broken down into several categories, including the valuable D- coupon. The D-coupon was used by Westerners to pay for rare goods – cheap liquor, meat, fruit juices – in specially closed shops. It was also a way of paying Soviet employees who traded coupons at twenty times the official exchange rate of the dollar. The purchasers were either coupon-dealers or the staff of African and Far Eastern diplomats. North Korean diplomats ran a remarkable operation buying up D-coupons, purchasing wholesale cheaply priced hi-fi equipment and Scotch, exporting the booty under diplomatic seal and selling at great profit in West Berlin. The racket was wound up in the Andropov era but persists in many East European outposts – notably the North Korean embassy in Bulgaria, which channels low- priced goods out to the bazaars of Istanbul – and appears even to be sanctioned by the Pyongyang leadership as a way of subsidising necessary but costly embassies. D-coupons were only part of the story. Honoured ballerinas, theatre directors, officially recognised writers earning royalties overseas, tennis, football and chess players received wads of Certificate Roubles. The pounds earned by the competent Soviet players at Wimbledon were never seen by the players. Instead a larger percentage was deducted by the Soviet Tennis Federation (which assumes responsibility for training and hotel costs) and apart from small daily pocket money during the tournament, the rest became Certificate Roubles which allow the players to make purchases in restricted shops when they return to the Soviet Union. When a Soviet citizen acquires the star status of World Chess Champion Gary Kasparov, or his main rival Anatoly Karpov, they are given greater dicretionary power over their money. Karpov's wish to buy a BMW with car phone presented no problems; the ballerina, Maya Plisetskaya, at first cheated out of much of her Western fees, now has almost free access to her earnings and drives, lethally, a Ranger Rover.

The alchemy of turning soft into hard, or harder, currency is a matter of a few simple, but finely balanced, formulae. Take the price of chocolate. In East Germany, relative to the average wage, it is cheap. Good, milky slabs. In Poland, compared to the average wage, it is expensive. Queues snake around blocks outside Warsaw's premier sweet shop, Wedel, in Szpitalna Street. The black-market value of chocolate has stayed consistently high over the past decade: supply is patchy because domestic production is poor and cocoa beans have to be paid for in dollars; demand is acute because it is one of the few indulgences available to children. Here, then, is the reason why there are several *de facto* rates for the East German mark to the Polish zloty. Its value in zloties is anything between twelve and three hundred – twelve if you sell it to a bank. Nobody does. There are several thousand Polish workers employed in East Germany and to understand the relative value of money in the Soviet Bloc, it is instructive to take the Berlin–Warsaw–Moscow train, which for part of its route is known as the Chocolate Express. The Polish workers, on steel, building and mining projects, travel home at the weekend, or perhaps once a month after payday, with their earnings – about one thousand East Mark a month – and dump it on the black market where the rate is between sixty and eighty zloties per East Mark. In Poznan and points further West, the East Mark black market is quite strong since Poles can cross the border and shop for food. Better by far to bring shoes. East German shoes, some of them made under West German licence, are both stylish and robust. In Poland there is a chronic shortage of children's shoes; indeed some sizes can be bought only in the open-air black market in Bazar Rozyckiego at prices equivalent to a month's salary. The return on an East Mark, by trading in shoes, is between one hundred and fifty and two hundred zloties. There are problems though. Shoes are bulky. East German shoe-shop assistants are on the alert for bulk buyers with Slav accents. The shape of a shoe is easy for customs officers to feel through a bag. And so most Poles convert their earnings into chocolate, buying up hundreds of bars, selling them to dealers at a modest price that brings them an exchange rate of one East Mark= three hundred zloties, and then in turn, buy dollars with their illicit income supplement.

In practice, it works like this. The compartments are occupied from Berlin by rather raucous passengers with bulging cases, the returning workers. They drink West German beer or peel oranges, ostentatiously announcing their status. Over the border (a short distance from Berlin) in Kunowice or Rzepin, the dealers get on with empty suitcases or, more professionally, big plastic bags concealed under their coats. Eyes meet, and a few minutes later the first deal is struck near the lavatory. Past Rzepin, with the Polish customs safely off the train, business flourishes. The black-market dealers then either pitch their bags out of the window or pull the communication cord, and alight to meet cars that have been driving parallel to the train. The emergency brake is used often on the Berlin–Warsaw–Moscow express than on any other train in operation.

But if the conductor complains he is either bribed (very rarely) or, more commonly, threatened with violence. Quite a few conductors have fallen out of trains for this reason. The waiting cars immediately carry their loads to provincial black markets – in Lodz, Kielce, a central, semi-industrialised Poland starved of chocolate. The chocolate is untraceable, the dealers never existed.

Somewhere along the line the chocolates will become dollars. There are a thousand such stratagems that keep the second economy alive within the Bloc. Even if Gorbachev were to falter and were replaced by a leader of the blackest reaction, a young heir to Stalin, the dollar market would survive since it is impossible to have a uniform ban on travel. When martial law was declared in Poland in December 1981, perhaps the most drastic device now available to a regime in panic (with the exception of 'requesting' Soviet military help), the currency dealers burrowed more deeply underground for a month, but soon emerged sunnily confident. No regime can close its frontiers for very long and in the meantime, the only impact on the black market was the rise in the value of the dollar, and the erosion of the zloty's buying power.

There is a serious point to be made about cross-border trafficking. The Comecon summit of July 1988 drew up proposals for an integrated Socialist market as an obvious response to the deeper integration of the European Community envisaged for 1992. The countries, true, had an integrated trading unit, the Transferable Rouble, and more or less synchronised passport rules. But the Bloc also had to organise production in such a way that acute national shortages could be solved legally, according to market principles, rather than by the rough and ready practices of men on the Chocolate Express. It should be feasible, if economic reform is to mean anything, for individual factories in East Germany or Czechoslovakia to strike deals on their own initiative with Polish or Romanian distributors and overcome shortages.

The Chocolate Express and other smuggling networks have become a form of shadow market, functioning in the absence of common market forces. Indeed there is nothing as thoroughly anti-market as the structure of common trade which still seems to operate along the pattern attempted by the early money-is-bourgeois Bolsheviks. An important step towards restoring the significance of money in Eastern Europe is to put intra-Soviet Bloc trade on a money base. The mythical Transferable Rouble, with its absurd book-keeping, is holding back innovation and reform at home, and any intelligent foreign trade policy with the West. If Czech shoes continue to be paid for in Polish herring and Soviet cars in Bulgarian strawberry jam, then money will steadily lose meaning. The Hungarians are the most irritated by this ramshackle device; Budapest long ago understood that it must move towards a currency that is convertible with Western currencies, that responds to real changes in the marketplace. And though hard currency held by individuals must still be exchanged through the National Bank, factories and co-operatives do not need the approval of the authorities before buying dollars to import supplies. That is a small step towards convertibility. But trying to invigorate the Comecon currency system is a far larger task. The cultural differences are extraordinary. 'We simply do not understand the same thing when we are discussing such key concepts as Price, Convertibility, Bank and Market,' commented Dr Miklos Nemeth, the last communist Hungarian Prime Minister. The Hungarians believe that all Comecon trade should be processed by bilateral trading accounts and settled in local currencies. Trade surpluses would be counted in Transferable Roubles, part of which could be converted into hard currency. Everybody in the Soviet trading Bloc is reluctant to supply anything to their Eastern neighbours that could fetch real money, dollars, from the West. Stagnation is built into the system. Probably the only way out of the impasse is to promote black-market barons as Ministers of Finance and conduct all Soviet Bloc business in dollars. Despite the unstoppable rise of the greenback, there seems no immediate prospect of this.

PART II

Markets In
Everyday Life

4

From Cradle to Grave

EVERYDAY LIFE

It never pays to mock journalists. Even so, as correspondents from Communist newspapers arrived in Moscow, bright-eyed and bouncing with conviction, it became impossible to resist some *Schadenfreude*. Even the Euro-Communist heretics, the man from *L'Unita*, say, came equipped for a pilgrimage. Soon enough, they realised they were in for a safari. The *Morning Star* apartment was not very comfortable, to put it mildly. Cockroaches? Well, of course, they exist everywhere: London, worst of all, New York. Have you ever seen New York cockroaches? Big as rats. Slowly, the fortifications crumble. No fruit juice except for dollars? A ten-rouble bribe for a simple spare part? Tailing by the KGB? – surely the comrades trust us! No washing powder, no pork chops, no typewriter ribbons, no sugar, no lavatory paper; even the most robust faith falters under the avalanche of shortages, bureaucracy and bribes. Sooner or later, faced with the reality of a system that cannot satisfy the most basic of everyday needs, the True Believing Foreigner has to choose between cynical accommodation (even a limited amount of hard currency buys some privileges and, with an amiable Russian wife, life can be made tolerable) or a passage home to become Motor Industry correspondent in a country where workers are exploited, where racism is rife and where shops are full. The vision fades.

Perestroika, says the conventional wisdom, is better read than lived. The Soviet newspapers nowadays are frothy, abrim with scandal. As in the Polish solidarity era of 1980–81, when open season was declared on the Gierek leadership, the Soviet papers often get things wrong, scent malice in stupidity, conspiracy wherever the curtains are closed. But they do so with refreshing enthusiasm. In this sense, the Soviet press is far away from Soviet reality: there is no enthusiasm in the streets or the living-rooms. There is a feeling in Moscow and the provinces, even before the inevitable price reform, of prices running out of control. The difference between the existential minimum – one hundred roubles a month – and the average salary of two hundred roubles is not large. How

will reform help the run-down apartment blocks, bars and people in
Moscow's Prolyetarski district? Prolyetarski is where the two largest car
factories, Moskvitch and Zil, are sited, along with a constellation of
smaller plants. Nicotine-coloured smoke invades the sky. It is, as the
name suggests, a traditional worker's district. Long courtyards, battered
façades, the movement determined by shift changes. Visiting the
streets again after five years of perestroika, the surface changes are
minimal. Many bars, some of them with real charm, have closed
down, discouraged by the Gorbachev anti-alcohol campaign. A
German colleague recalls a bar on the Simonowski-Wall where a
splendid lady with high cheekbones and a touch of henna in her hair
used to sell vodka and 'buterbrody' for half a rouble. Now it is a food
shop with dirty windows. The big beer hall where workers could buy a
glass of thin beer from a machine for twenty kopeks, is closed too, for
'Remont', renovation; that is, in all likelihood, forever. Things look a
bit better in the Zdano-Universal Magazin, a four-floor department
store where the lifts do not work. There were Adidas shoes for sale, at
forty roubles a pair, and the crowd around the counter was thick. On
Saturday morning it was impossible to penetrate the people: coaches
from the provinces had brought in Russians from the villages to
ransack the shelves. The shoe shops, a constant butt of official
criticism under Brezhnev, appear to be better stocked. In the
household shops there were pots and pans, clumsy-looking electronic
equipment; prices were high, but not unreasonable. In the Gastronom
food shop on Volgograd Prospekt, you can sense a change in attitude.
In the Brezhnev years, if you loaded up your shopping basket with
butter, a stern assistant (not the cashier, that was the next hurdle)
would have sent you back with a flea in your ear. Now butter is more
expensive (three and a half roubles a kilo) and not always available in
the afternoon, but the shop assistant simply raises an eyebrow when
you pack the basket. If the customers can afford to hoard, then let
them. Old women are less in evidence, except as proxies in the
queues. The minimum pension for a woman who was a housewife is
now twenty-eight roubles a month. The price of lemons is three
roubles a kilo, grapefruit two roubles. The arithmetic is plain: the first
effect of economic reform is to make life more expensive. Those who
were traditionally protected from higher prices are now exposed.

  Somehow Gorbachev has to deliver the benefit of reform quickly to
the consumer and thus build up a natural, popular constituency for
change. Instead, partly because of obstruction, partly because of the

mechanics of implementing reform, the order of the day is sacrifice, many years of it, with only a vague promise of improvement at the end of the line. And the promise *is* vague. There are no Krushchevian pledges to overtake America in a decade or two. Economic reform can make factories more productive and profitable; it can make them more independent and, ultimately, more sensitive to the marketplace. It can introduce market forces in other spheres, enhance competition, expand the role of the private sector. It can, under optimal conditions, contribute to a recovery in manufacturing industry.

But the clockwork apparatus of daily life does not necessarily benefit from these changes. The 'suppressed inflation' that results from too much money chasing too few and underpriced goods, can be tackled by soaking up money (partly with higher prices, Western-style taxation and by the skilful manipulation of the black market) and by bringing more desirable commodities onto the shelves. That has happened in Hungary, but though life is certainly easier there than in the Soviet Union, or anywhere else in the Bloc, it has not provided a completely satisfactory answer to ordinary people. There are few queues but Hungarians are having to work extremely hard; many have second jobs to earn enough to keep ahead of inflation. And the shops of Vaci Utca, with their shining windows, have full shelves because they are so expensive; the goods have become unbuyable to all apart from a small group of New Rich Hungarians. If this is true for the most advanced of the reforming Communist economies, how much more dismal and dangerous is the prospect for the Soviet Union. The chosen route, in the Soviet Union, Poland and Hungary, is to liberalise the political system to make sacrifice palatable, to involve the people rather than to make them hapless victims of a reform inspired from above. The simple lessons of post-war history, especially but not exclusively in Poland, show glasnost to be a commonsense accompaniment to economic reform. But 'glasnost' and democratisation also create the impression that leaders are reforming out of weakness, forced into the corner by an outraged public opinion. That is, glasnost *simulates* a public commitment to reform. Glasnost thus covers up more than it reveals, camouflaging above all the uncertainty of the leadership's conviction. The police opponents to political reform in the USSR, Poland and Hungary sense the dangers of linking glasnost with perestroika. The East European secret police lobbies have modernised over the past decade and can no longer be fairly depicted as unreconstructed Stalinists; they have become one of the thinking wings of Party management and seem generally in favour of economic reform. Perhaps they see the situation more lucidly than the reform idealists: they realise that glasnost will not make the pain of reform go away and may indeed seriously debilitate national leadership. The police logic, self-serving but not necessarily false, is that reform-from-above in an authoritarian system requires the stifling of discontent rather than its open expression.

The impact of reform on ordinary existence is crucial to its success or failure. A national referendum on Polish reform in November 1987 demonstrated essentially that the people did not want the kind of change that made life worse in the short term in order to achieve a better-functioning economy in the future. First, short-term sacrifices have a remarkable tendency towards the infinite. Second, there was no real trust in the managers and administrators of the reform. Third, it was difficult to believe that a better-functioning economy would benefit not only the exporting factories, the trade balance and the debt-service ratio, but also Jan and Sergei and Jagoda.

How, to address the last point, can reform help? To grasp the scope of the problem, one has to study the details of survival in a world of short supply. The (black) market is already a major element in the distribution of scarce consumer goods. How can these market forces be brought above ground – and is there any point in doing so? Would privatisation help in key sectors of the consumer economy? What is the interest of bureaucracy in an inefficient economy? Can the economy, streamlined but still centralised, ever satisfy the consumer?

Birth, Sickness And The Investment Crisis

These questions begin at birth, but do not end with death. The hospital services of the Soviet Bloc are stuck in a deep crisis akin to that of the West; they are the victim of a decade of under-investment and the shrivelling of the 'social welfare' lobby in the Politburos and Central Committees. The imported growth of the 1970s and the resulting debt crisis of the 1980s, with its crippling interest rates, imposed intolerable strains on state budgets. The main victim in the past decade has been 'infrastructural' investment – road-building, waste disposal, ecological protection, schools and hospitals. The fabric of the social welfare state, built up in the 1950s, is coming apart at the seams and the results can be seen by the simple expedient of breaking a leg in Minsk, trying to swim in the Oder, or driving from Bucharest to Cluj. On the one hand there is an economy set to modernise and march into the twenty-first century, on the other there is a welfare network that can no longer cope with a normal, growing, ageing society. The hospitals of Poland, Romania and the Soviet Union, once proud monuments, are flaking, the lack of money complemented by and contributing to poor management, manpower and medicine shortages. Even Czechoslovakia, which had the most sophisticated health service in the Bloc, is suffering critical supply problems and is witnessing the erosion of the morale of its medical staff. Each country boasts its top clinics, reserved largely for the elite or professional groups, but in the average provincial hospital in the Soviet Union or Poland it is now common to find beds parked in corridors, damp patches on the walls, makeshift diagnostics, rationing of medicine and anaesthetic, the multiple use of one-use-only syringes. Some of this occurred in the late 1980s in British and Italian hospitals. But there are qualitative differences. The shortage of detergents, for example, means that Polish hospital floors are cleaned only with a mop and water, that uniforms are not properly laundered, that sheets are not washed frequently enough, that bed-frames are not sterilised between patients. Cross-infection is a serious problem and many patients leave hospital cured of one disease but infected with another.

Free medical care was a top priority of the Soviet Revolution, and the same principle was applied to the East European states after their Communist takeover. Although some of the East European countries had already moved towards free hospitals before Socialism, it was universally agreed that the process should be accelerated, partly as a way of dismantling privilege. Sickness was a great equaliser (though the demands of privilege for Party leaders soon buried the ideal). It was also viewed, in the initial stages, as an instrument of tacit Party education, much like service in the Army. Unlike factories, where simple workers can, if they master the correct rituals and responses, rise to become heads of Party cells and figures to be reckoned with, in a hospital the senior doctors, those who run the clinics and institutes, are invariably the senior Party representatives. It would be uncomfortable for all concerned if the Party Secretary of a hospital was an unskilled orderly in the laundry division – how could he give Party reprimands to senior surgeons, men bristling with professorships and degrees? One consequence of this hierarchical structure is that there is no rigid Party discipline at the level of the hospital ward. If the only people to hold responsible Party posts are in the senior administration, it follows that the wards are being run by largely unpolitical people. Medical staff at the sharp edge, those who operate regularly or tend the patients day by day, have three main concerns: they worry about the scarce resources available to the health sector, they worry about their own economic situation, and they worry about the quality of treatment that they can offer. In Poland in 1980, these concerns drove some eighty per cent of the employees in the health service to join the Solidarity union. Only Solidarity was expressing concern – and putting effective pressure on the government – about the huge slabs of investment for hospitals that were being mismanaged and steered in wrong directions. And only Solidarity acted to secure wage increases for medical staff.

By 1990, the situation had not improved: the wage differential between industrial workers and doctors had actually grown. At the bottom of the hospital hierarchy, life was almost impossible; so few Poles wanted to be orderlies that nurses (already in short supply) were forced to clean the floors and laundry, while doctors took over nursing jobs. Dr Zofia Kuratowska, a medical adviser to Solidarity (and Parliamentary Speaker) considered ways in which this *Teufelskreis* could be broken, including the use of religious orders in state hospitals. Medical staff threatened to strike – by, for example, refusing to sign birth, death or work absentee certificates – unless the health service received a bigger chunk of the budget.

The wage *misère* in Soviet-Bloc hospitals has had several lasting effects. First it has institutionalised bribery. *Izvestia* recorded the case of a man from Odessa who entered hospital to have his appendix removed. He brought with him over a hundred one-rouble notes. The roubles provided the necessary balm. He was taken quickly to the operating theatre (two roubles to the attendants), had a curtain around his bed (a rouble a day), his sheets were changed (a rouble a time), his wound was cleanly dressed, his bedpan emptied, he had easy access to the public telephone at the end of the corridor, and he was given a sleeping dose when required. Then the roubles ran out. Nobody bothered to take his temperature, the sheets became grimy, the curtain disappeared and the convalescence grew harder. Only an emergency infusion of fresh roubles brought the medical care back to a decent level.

The low pay has two other effects: it ensures that most doctors (some seventy per cent in the Soviet Union) are women, usually married. Their salary has become a useful supplement to the family income, no more. The Soviet Health Ministry sees no problem with this: women make good doctors, it demonstrates the educational opportunities for women under Socialism (in the West, women are still sometimes discouraged from entering medical school lest they become pregnant or otherwise 'waste' the training) and, in time of war, it makes good sense to have a female-based medical service. There is thus no great pressure to raise salaries. Apart from certain key areas, such as surgery, women doctors often move quickly into administration since this gives power and prestige; the top jobs in Soviet medicine are male-dominated.

For several decades that has remained the stable state. But the pressure on wages and manpower has opened up new ideologically alien possibilities. Private medical practice has always been legal or semi-legal in the Soviet Bloc. In Poland and Hungary, medical co-operatives in which doctors use their free time to offer medical advice for legally fixed fees are a popular outlet. There is no general practitioner system as in Britain, and the Soviet patient, for example, is obliged to go for a diagnosis to his or her local polyclinic and see the first available doctor. The good part of this approach is that if an appointment is made before 10.00 a.m., the doctor is obliged to see you the same day. Soviet doctors also make home visits without demur. But co-operatives give a more human face to diagnosis and make for GP-style continuity. The Soviet polyclinic doctor has, on average, six minutes per patient, and that includes dressing and undressing. The expansion of co-operatives and private practice is now on the Gorbachev agenda. A number of specialist private clinics were established in the Soviet Union after the Second World War, accounting for less than half a per cent of the whole health service. But this should double by 1995, and by the year 2000 private medicine will provide a real alternative. Private patients can choose their physician and pay about £3.50 to see a specialist.

Dr Yevgeny Chazov, formerly the medical adviser to Leonid Brezhnev, and Gorbachev's Minister of Health, wants more than this. He has pushed the idea of Moscow's first full-scale private hospital that will offer, apart from normal services, acupuncture and homeopathy at about ten roubles a day. His encouragement of co-operatives meant that about one thousand four hundred Moscow doctors had registered by 1988 to offer private treatment. Privatisation is a big step for a big country: the Soviet Union has the largest state health service in the world, one million doctors, three million hospital cancer clinics, and some top hospitals – such as Professor Svyatoslav Feyodorov's Institute for Eye Surgery – with world-class results. And yet, the simple facts are that the nation's health is deteriorating. Professor Feyodorov complained to *Pravda* (28 September 1987) that life expectation for men was now sixty-five, for women sixty-seven. By contrast, in the United States, men live on average to seventy-three, and women to seventy-seven. Heart disease was, as in the West, the main killer but in the Soviet Union the number of heart attacks that lead to death is twice as high as in the West. Dr Chazov shares these fears: 'We must bitterly accept the truth that many Moscow women are prepared to go anywhere to give birth to avoid Moscow's maternity rooms. Our medical equipment is unsatisfactory. Even basic items such as scalpels are so badly made that our surgeons must themselves re-sharpen the things after a couple of operations.'

Allowing private medicine to pick up some of the work is financial common sense: it rewards the better doctors who run their co-operatives after hours, and reduces the queues in the state hospitals. In the field of gynaecology it also makes the whole experience of giving birth more personal. But the Soviet-Bloc gynaecologist is often functioning on the fringes of legality. There is no more sensitive area than birth and birth control, partly because of the continuing social stigma of pregnancy out of wedlock, but also because giving birth is such a dominant experience for the mother that it demands individual personalised treatment. In Romania in the summer of 1983, a classic scandal was that of a gynaecologist from the Steaua Maternity Hospital who demanded one thousand two hundred lei from a husband whose wife was in childbirth in return for her 'personal care'. As an advance payment, the husband was required to hand over two hundred Kent cigarettes, the black-market currency. The transaction was overheard by an informer and because grudges were held against the woman doctor, the case was brought to court. The only unusual feature of the case was that it was discovered in the first place.

Giving birth lends itself to corruption for at least two reasons. The first is the combination of the unpredictability of birth with the inflexibility of hospital beds. A doctor will advise that a baby might be born prematurely and so the mother-to-be will book herself into a clinic that specialises in such births. By the eighth month, the situation may look more complicated and the mother will try – in vain, unless she oils her way – to transfer her booking into a different clinic. The second element encouraging corruption is the nine-month pregnancy period – at least half a year during which the matrons of the hospitals, sisters and gynaecologists can be bombarded with gifts to provide for a smooth birth. This need not take the form of explicit bribes, as in the case of the Romanian gynaecologist. The Prague weekly *Tribuna* cited a doctor who gave priority treatment to the wife of a plumber and another who bartered special medical treatment for a pregnant woman in return for the supply of building materials for his country cottage. The frequency of bribes in gynaecology wards has become so much a part of folklore in Czechoslovakia that matrons have actually charged nurses the equivalent of one thousand six hundred dollars in return for allocating them to maternity wards.

However, the gynaecologist comes into his own in the business of abortion rather than birth. Official figures indicate that Soviet women have on average six abortions in their lives: the true figure may be even higher. As a termination in a Soviet hospital is complex and painful, most women seek out a private doctor who can at least provide some form of anaesthetic. Since the overthrow of Ceausescu and the repeal of his most-hated laws, abortion is now legal throughout Eastern Europe. Stalin, encouraging Soviet motherhood, outlawed it in 1936 (two years jail for the abortionists), but the 'right' to abort is now regarded as fundamental. There are, however, social obstacles. In Poland, Slovakia and rural Hungary, the role of the priest is still strong; weddings with the bride four months pregnant are a standard feature of country life. In the Soviet Union, Party committees are particularly sensitive to directives about the flagging birth rate in the Russian Federation and do their best to discourage women from aborting out of convenience. In a state clinic an abortion can cost only five roubles but the initial procedures are so daunting that most women prefer to go for the much more expensive private operations. For a state-subsidised termination, the woman first has to apply to the factory union for permission to be sent to a hospital. This involves a talk with the secretary of the women's organisation who has to submit a written recommendation. The pregnant woman has to explain the circumstances: her limited housing space, her limited salary, the disappearance of the father. The personnel section of the union then talks to the woman and tries, more often than not, to dissuade her from an abortion. The next hurdle is the medical delegate from the woman's organisation, the Party (if the worker is a Party member), the trade union, the Komsomol and a bureaucrat from the Health Department. Each part of the submission has to be accompanied by written testimony – proof of the earnings of the girl's father (or husband), evidence from the local housing committee about the amount of space she occupies, plus other testimonies. The commission then decides whether the woman is physically and psychologically fit for an abortion and depending on the year – in 1965, 1970–71 and 1978, there was great anxiety about the birth rate – tries with measured zeal to change the woman's mind. The bureaucratic delays of these procedures – it can take several weeks before the woman even gets permission to be referred to hospital where she in turn has to wait for a bed – are nerve-wracking. In the late 1950s, Party members seeking an abortion were also reprimanded – a low-level but significant punishment – after the operation, presumably for weak morals. It is hardly surprising that private abortionists in a Soviet city can cost fifty roubles – that is ten times the official rate, but it is infinitely preferable to many women because it avoids the humiliation of the official procedures and guarantees some measure of secrecy.

Poor sex education, grisly operations and the sometimes expensive abortions have also led to an increase in illegitimate births in the Soviet Union. Slowly, doctors are beginning to speak openly about this problem in the official press. In the autumn of 1983, for example, Professor Mikhail Bedny, chief of Moscow's scientific research laboratory in medical demography, appealed for a detailed study, admitting that illegitimate births account for twenty per cent of the total.

Under Ceausescu, Romania banned abortion more or less outright and the result was a thriving illicit high-risk abortion business, a crooked adoption trade and extraordinary practices that were supposed to paper over the absurdities of the dictator's demographic policies. Romania has always had a robust birth rate – six new births per thousand in 1965, compared to 2.4 in Hungary and three in East Germany. Yet from 1965, the Ceasescu regime introduced a series of humiliating policies to boost the population still further. At most factories women had to submit themselves to monthly examination to determine whether they were pregnant. If they were, they had to have the baby or risk a jail sentence. 'Spontaneous' abortions were allowed, but only if an official of the Ministry of Justice was present. Even if the woman was having a haemorrhage, the doctor could not act alone; sometimes he had a choice between letting the woman die, and a jail sentence. The average birth rate before these measures were introduced was about two hundred and fifty thousand. Now it is close to five hundred thousand. Yet the number of gynaecologists, paediatricians, nurses and the quantity of available powdered milk and medical supplies did not increase proportionately. The whole Romanian medical service regarded the rules as nonsense. The lack of care partly explained the rise in infant mortality (1966–67: live births up to 92.8 per cent, infant mortality up 145.6 per cent). Because of a child's poor survival chances, the official registry offices did not register a birth until he or she was at least a month old. The point was to bring down the ratio of mortality to live births. Infant mortality is an acutely sensitive area since it is a direct comment on the quality of health care. That may explain why the Soviet Union stopped issuing mortality rates in 1974 (they had risen by one-third in the preceding three years); the current rate is somewhere between twenty-nine deaths and forty per thousand.

The private gynaecologists thus have considerable influence in the Soviet Bloc, out of all proportion to their numbers. It is not just a question of providing a personally supervised birth or a relatively painless abortion; the international standing of the health system, as measured by birth and infant mortality, is at stake. In Romania, gynaecologists – watched closely by the police and informers – risked and charged a great deal for performing terminations. More often they assumed, after the birth, a semi-legal and high-paying function: that of a baby broker. As in the back streets of Rio and Naples, there is an active black market in babies. Western couples, desperate for children and low on the adoption waiting list at home, travel to Bucharest and buy a selected child for hard currency. The Romanian gynaecologist, with contracts in West Germany and Austria, was the middle-man. He could either pretend to deliver the child to a foreigner holidaying in Romania, or more commonly, the child was entered on the passport in advance and simply left with the adoptive parents. It was a sordid business, that was not completely wound up even after the overthrow of Ceausescu.

Private or 'co-operative' medicine in the Soviet Bloc opens up a new grey-market territory. The problem is that, at this initial stage, private medicine is not fully-fledged competition. Instead, it has a parasitical mien, growing rich on the deficiencies of the state hospital service rather than urging it to ever-better standards.

It is, for example, almost impossible to obtain a body-scan unless you are a patient in one of the few Moscow clinics that have scanners. But go to your private doctor at the co-operative and, for one hundred and seven roubles, he will authorise a scan at the Oncology Institute. The money is split, legally it seems, between the co-operative and the body-scanners. In the pre-Gorbachev days, that would have been called a bribe. Certainly many ordinary Russians seem to regard it as such. The same outrage expressed by Britons about 'private beds' in NHS hospitals and queue-jumping for operations, is being vented now. 'You are not fighting to improve the medical service,' wrote one enraged *Izvestia* reader, 'you are fighting for added privileges for people with fat purses.'

Plainly the right balance between private and state service has to be struck. If the Soviet conservatives succeed, private medicine will be tightly circumscribed by law and strangled at birth. To stand a chance of success, it has to be allowed to function in a legal no-man's-land; private doctors should be free to use their fees to order medicines from the West without running the risk (as at present) of arrest for black-market speculation. The stifling of private medicine would be of benefit to the state sector, and would not even serve the cause of justice: instead there would be a boom time for bribes.

Whether one calls it bribery, or private enterprise, the point of payment is to sustain a level of service. The payment also buys the patient a special feeling of protection, a sense of being singled out, in his suffering, from the collective. A fascinating round-table discussion at the offices of the Polish Consumer Federation Magazine, V*eto*, highlighted the issues. These are the doctors speaking:

'The primary purpose of people coming to state-run dispensaries is to get sick leave, a prescription or a certificate entitling them to be admitted to hospital. One of the very last reasons that they come is to get actual treatment – but in those cases they are convinced that they have to grease our palms . . . (Another doctor speaks.) There's quite a number of patients who are absolutely convinced that they cannot get appropriate medical assistance without giving bribes and "gifts". Some time ago a group of patients were asked their opinions about so-called "envelope money" for doctors. Most of them claimed there was nothing wrong with that procedure, that they do it of their own accord and are glad that they are getting proper treatment for their own money. I used to work in the country and when I told a patient that he owed me nothing for my medical assistance, he became suspicious that not everything had been done properly . . . (Another doctor joins the discussion). People try to pay doctors and lower medical staff because they do not want to be treated mechanically like pieces of wood. Why for example has Nardelli (a faith healer) become so popular? After all, his methods have little if anything to do with medicine. The answer is that he treats every patient in a truly decent and humane way.'

A few patients begrudge the bribes. But the question is do the doctors readily take them? The V*eto* article is quite frank about this too, though it makes sure that the doctors, anonymous, but traceable, do not themselves confess to corruption.

'We've heard that there are doctors, particularly those in general hospitals, who do not refuse to accept dollars as a means of payment . . . In Katowice, normally one has to wait three months before being accepted by a hospital. If, however, you go for a private "chat" to the head of a given ward, you are admitted immediately. Doctors working in

the hospitals also have "private patients", even professors accept them
. . . (Another doctor speaks.) Doctors want to make money so that they
could gain more patients, and patients-to-be want to be treated by good
doctors. And then, a "good doctor" for some people becomes someone
who can boast fashionable clothes or a fast car – he must have access to
money, so he must be good, that is the way they think!'

Once the principle of payment has been accepted, there can be
serious discussion of 'privatisation'. The Solidarity government of
Tadeusz Mazowiecki anticipated serious resistance when it first openly
mulled over health-service reform. But the initial proposals, though
radical, were digested quickly enough by all apart from hospital
administrators who were set to lose their jobs under any serious
privatisation. The Solidarity idea was that hospitals should be paid for
every service, from an injection to a heart operation, and that the
earnings would be used to pay decent salaries and modernise buildings.
The central administration would thus become irrelevant – and so
would the Communist party bias of hospital management. Treatment
fees would be covered by a comprehensive medical insurance, adjusted
according to the salary of the patient, and employers would also be
encouraged to operate their own health-insurance schemes. Dispensaries and chemists would also go private, patients would pay for
medicine. In short, a Western-style system, with Western iniquities and
anomalies. Not everybody in Solidarity was pleased with the free-market
approach since it seemed an abdication from the fundamentals of social
justice that the union had once fought for. It was, they argued, only a
matter of time before the rich received priority on the waiting list for
operations or bought themselves better treatment; the point of privitisa-
tion was to improve health care for the whole nation, not for a privileged
segment. Otherwise, there was only a thin line between legal fees and
illegal bribes. The debate, with its echoes of the reforming British
National Health System, remained unresolved, part of the schizoid
divide between Solidarity-as-union and Solidarity-as-government,
between the reform-Socialist and market-liberal wings of Lech Walesa's
movement.

The Bribing Society

Bribes – concealed in small, discreet manilla envelopes, rolled-up
newspapers or bulging briefcases – smooth the passage from birth to
death. The combination of consumer shortages, a congealed

bureaucracy and social divisions conspired to make bribery a fixed element of the Soviet system since the 1920s. Indeed, many of the old bribery traditions of the Czarist civil service were carried over to Soviet Russia, and subsequently exported to allies like Czechoslavakia and Hungary which, under the Hapsburgs, had always maintained a well-trained civil service of high integrity. In the 1970s, the practice of bribery expanded and took root to the extent that some offices had fixed prices for certain services, such as planning permission to build a block of flats. There were three main reasons for this: the rapid growth in worker and managerial incomes under Brezhnev (and the relative decline of professional or intelligence salaries), a 'new consumerism' that encouraged high-spending habits, and a sense of class mobility, of personal improvement. Under the limited reforms of Alexei Kosygin, prime minister under Brezhnev, factories were offered money incentives for more efficient production, while at the same time industry was encouraged to turn out more consumer durables such as television sets and refrigerators. Other Soviet-Bloc countries introduced similar schemes, though Poland imported many of its consumer incentives. The reform did not have a major effect: rather it illustrated the remarkable possibilities of manipulating the Plan. However, money incomes rose steeply. Over sixty per cent of Russians bought their first television sets in the Brezhnev era, eighty per cent bought their first refrigerator then. Russians spent more on their food and drink (especially drink) in the 1970s than at any other time in history. But much money was simply not spent. Personal savings rose from about fifty-one roubles per person in 1970 to about nine hundred roubles in 1982. Most surplus money though was sucked into the second economy; the worker who had been thought to abhor the black market became, in the Brezhnev era, an active customer. In a sense, this was a form of democratisation through wealth, a pooling of privilege. Those at the top of the ladder were rewarded for their loyalty rather than efficiency and, since fidelity is easier to simulate than competence, became richer. At the bottom, the worker was able to afford several bottles of vodka a week – not just on payday – and, for special guests, exotic liqueurs. For the first time, Western goods entered his living-room, courtesy of the black market. But the consumer drive was matched by a drive towards self-betterment; education was increasingly acknowleged as a route to social improvement. The Soviet worker, relatively wealthy, watching television and enjoying a broader social life, now wanted his son to take up a 'respectable' job (typically, engineer). The

privileged access previously acquired only by those with *blat* – a network
of influential contacts – could now be bought with money (that is,
bribes). It seems that none of the physically imposing anecdotal books
about Russia is complete without a chapter about *blat*. Yet *blat* –
string-pulling, influence – is in decline. As Soviet society becomes more
sophisticated in its demands, so the old weave of useful family contacts
and friendships yields few rewards. In a state of chronic short supply,
such as Poland, exchange of information and personal recommendation is still important, whether it be a tip-off about a delivery of oranges
or exempting one's son from military service. But the 1970s and 1980s
swung the balance towards the bribe. The wage differential between a
coal miner – well-rewarded in all the Soviet-Bloc countries – and a
university lecturer (some of whom live close to the existential
minimum) or a bank clerk or librarian or a doctor, is now so vast that
bribery appears to many as a kind of social justice, an informal
redistribution of wealth. What could a miner want from these people? A
doctor is the most valuable since he can sign a sickness chitty, thus
preserving the miner's productivity bonus. A teacher or a lecturer can
give private tuition to his children, a bank clerk knows safe ways of
buying dollars. But the interesting element in these relationships is that
both partners are new to the bribing business and the etiquette has to be
more or less re-invented. The classical bribery partnerships – private
businessman and town clerk, truck driver and policeman, factory
manager and factory inspector, corrupt enterprise directors and corrupt
politicians – have their form book. But for the newcomers, it is a strange
shuffle in the dark. Wladyslaw Markiewicz, writer of muscular
reportage for the Polish weekly *Polityka*, saw the gap and published (30
August 1986) a guide to the new bribe-givers. It is written in simple,
teach-yourself language; I quote at length:

'Every decision to show "our gratitude" – that is, bribe – should be
preceded by careful analysis. We must find out who should be bribed
and analyse the level of difficulty of our problem. Thus, if we intend to
approach a clerk and get permission for building a house in an area
where contstruction is banned, we must be prepared for big costs. A bar
of chocolate or a nice pen is not enough. After all, what we are trying to
do is to persuade "an employee of the state administration" to break the
law. The principle is: the more risky and difficult the decision, the more
gratitude should be shown, and a larger amount has to be offered.

'We must investigate the personality of the "gratitude taker". We
must try to learn about his habits, weaknesses, hobbies. With this

knowledge we will not commit a fatal mistake. For example, we can avoid a grave error committed by a certain student who found out that his professor "likes to have a drink". He came to the oral exam, brought three bottles of vodka and put them on the professor's desk together with his student book, saying: "Please, confirm the receipt of three." Three is a pass mark. The professor thought for a moment, took the student book and wrote: "I'm confirming the receipt of two," (failed), and proceeded to throw the student out of the room together with his vodka.

'The first part of the reconnaissance done by the student was probably right. The young man showed a lot of ingenuity supported by a youthful sense of humour. But it was the same qualities that made the student forget that there are still some tactful, sensitive and morally pure people who may feel offended by our techniques. It is our task to detect this sensitivity and show our gratitude in such a way as to convince the recipients that they haven't actually accepted a bribe and make them think we believe that, despite everything, they are honest, decent people.

'Sometimes we can forget these niceties, when the price of a bribe is fixed in advance. For example, renting a shop or a boutique in a good street in the centre of Warsaw – five million zloties. Or having a phone installed – up to five hundred dollars. Or getting a room in one of the Warsaw hotels – five dollars. Bribes are mainly money. It's simply most convenient and the safest for both the parties involved. In the past, smaller problems were arranged with the help of nice boxes of chocolates. Today, we have a paradoxical situation when in order to arrange a box of chocolates that is to serve as a bribe, we must give another bribe. What we are dealing with then is a bribe raised to the second power.'

Because bribery is so widespread, it is virtually unpunishable. Professor Tadeusz Chrustowski, deputy rector of the Interior Ministry Academy in Warsaw, says that there is an almost constant figure for bribery-detection: some 3,084 in 1980, 2,460 in 1983, 2,928 in 1984, 3,389 in 1985 – less than one per cent of all crimes committed in a year. These figures distort the picture. First, bribery is obviously a nationwide phenomenon. Second, the number, of detected bribery cases that actually lead to conviction is small indeed. In 1972, for example, the statistical yearbook reported 1,100 cases of bribes accepted by civil servants. But police records show that there were only 594 suspects and that only 378 were ever sentenced. There is a similar disparity in detected bribe-givers – 1,584 reported, but only 781 convictions. Not surprisingly, the statistical yearbook stopped publishing such data in 1975.

A civil servant in Poland who demands bribes can be jailed for ten years, a more passive bribe-taker can get up to five years. Bribe-givers are also punished with jail. Similar regulations exist throughout the Soviet Bloc apart from the Soviet Union which so far only acknowledges the crime of taking bribes.

The police complain that it is extremely difficult to enforce anti-bribery legislation. The main method is to persuade bribe-givers, in return for immunity, to denounce the bribe-taker. The logical consequence of this is entrapment: that is, a police stooge pretending to offer a bribe to a civil servant and slapping on the handcuffs when he agrees. Professor Chrutowski is against dirty tricks. 'There are those in favour of using milita provocations – plain-clothes policemen would offer bribes and all those corrupted would be caught red-handed, or at least frightened. But illegal methods must not be used in the struggle for law and order.'

There is not a great deal of popular trust in such statements. Entrapment or 'provocation' is a standard practice of the criminal investigation and political wings of the Soviet-Bloc police forces. An elementary precaution is to avoid witnesses, as Markeiewicz writes:

'The best way to show gratitude is face to face with no one watching. We must take good care of our contact so that he can be sure we won't put him to any trouble.

'Money is best given in an envelope, accompanied by an exclamation like: "Look, you forgot this envelope – it was somewhere among the documents." Bigger objects should be brought in bags – preferably made of solid fabric – so that before entering the office and on leaving it the shape of the bag is the same. Bottles are best given wrapped in paper and upside down so that they look like bouquets of flowers.

'A perfect example of bribe-giving can be presented on the basis of what happened in a big city in Northern Poland some time ago. Evening-class students (teachers, by the way) treated their professor to a home-made cake during a break in the exams. He liked it, so they gave him a generous slice for his way back home. When he unwrapped it on the train, he was surprised by the weight of the slice. On closer inspection it turned out that a set of silver spoons was cleverly baked into the cake.'

It is noticeable that many bribery cases, successful in the sense that they came to court, involve teachers. That is partly because of the relative shift in earning power and status between the skilled worker and the teacher, partly because of the workers' new aspirations for their children. But is also reflects the growth of private education in the Soviet Bloc. Private tuition has been legal in Eastern Europe, even in Romania, since the Communist take-over. At first, the justification was that tuition could plug the gaps left by the educational disruption of the war. Since then, private tutors have become a symbol of social improvement. Sometimes it is a matter of catching up with classmates in a difficult subject like mathematics. If even twelve-year-olds get an unsatisfactory end-of-year grade (below 3 in a scale of 1 to 5) they have to repeat a class and effectively lose a year. There is thus great pressure to succeed, or at least to scrape through. Most private tuition, though, is in subjects associated with social climbing, above all, English. Many teachers have stories of being approached by fairly simple parents with the request that their child is prepared for university entrance; the rewards are considerable, perhaps five hundred roubles for tuition during the summer holidays. Some of the Moscow teaching co-operatives that sprang up in the Gorbachev era went further; they guaranteed good results in school exams and a place in one of the special lycées in the Soviet capital. There is intense competition for the top grammar schools in the Soviet Bloc – the Stefan Batory school, say, in Warsaw – and naturally enough, bribery comes into play. Most of the teachers convicted in recent years were denounced either by jealous parents, who saw more stupid children receiving better marks, or because the teachers had failed to keep their part of the bargain. A denunciation for bribery thus comes to resemble a breach of contract case in the West. The interplay of *blat* and bribery is best observed in the schoolroom.

Bribes can make the difference between a passing and a failing grade, but they cannot buy excellence, a grade 5. What they can do however is buy advantage: the university staff in charge of admissions have discretionary powers. Pupils with passing but less-than-brilliant grades may suddenly develop other qualities that make them strong candidates. And victims of national discrimination can square the odds with a meaty bribe: one young Jew paid a bribe of three thousand roubles to gain admission to a pharmaceutical institute in a Ukrainian city, but told the police when he found that he was expected to fork out a further fifty roubles for every subsequent examination in his college career. Bribery can get you in the door, but it cannot necessarily keep you inside. *Blat*, with its unstated political clout, can get you in and keep you in. The Rector (or vice-chancellor) of a university has, in all Soviet-Bloc countries, the power to waive normal admission procedures for promising candidates. He exercises this right mainly on behalf of the politically advantaged – the son, say of a former minister who would otherwise lose his deferment from military service. The Rector can advise the candidate to change his course (from history to journalism, from medicine to biology) and find him a niche. But the university staff cannot allow the boy to fail or drop out during the coming years since that would reflect on the Rector's judgement. And so, one deployment of *blat* guarantees political protection for some time, at least in education. Bribery, the common man's equaliser, is risky, expensive, and usually humiliating.

Shopping By The Light Of The Moon

The front line of corruption is the shop counter. Here an extraordinarily intricate network of tributes, bribes and political pay-offs combine: in the case of a food shop, the average day's business resembles the inter-family negotiations for a dowry in the Ottoman Empire. The director of a food shop has not only to sell food but to cover a large number of overheads, not included in the plan or the official accounts book, from his own pocket. He has to arrange regular payments – protection money in all but name – to the local police, the tax inspectors, the state auditors, as well as a regular tribute that gets passed up the line and ends up contributing to the private fortunes of senior officials in the Ministry of Domestic Trade. In all Socialist countries, above all in Romania and Bulgaria, this is viewed as a normal business practice.

At the same time, the manager has to cover the cost of meat stolen by the sales assistants (actually given as a perk). In a large department store this can add up to a vast monthly sum. Other payments have to be made to the supplying factories or farms – otherwise an unusually large quantity of merchandise or produce is liable to go astray en route – and to the workers unloading the delivery trucks. The manager gets his money back with the help of fraudulent book-keeping, the sale of lower-quality goods at high-quality prices, and a close relationship with black marketeers. In the Soviet Union the director of a good food store can rake off profits, even after making his *ex gratia* contributions, of several thousands of roubles a month. Above all, such managers value their friendships with senior party officials and KGB officers that often spring up as a result of contacts between the wives. The wife of a food-store manager is as much in demand on the Communist Party social circuit as a film starlet in the West; she alone can ensure the prompt delivery of cocktail snacks for two guests or the lamb, professionally diced, for a barbecue at the dacha. Yet the food manager leads a high-risk life; to offend a local party dignitary is almost certain destruction. Managers are replaceable and are all too obviously, too probably, up to their necks in serious economic crime.

Thus the director of Moscow's main food shop, Gastronom Number One in Gorki Street (still known by its pre-revolutionary name of Yelisevski's to Muscovites) fell an easy victim to the Andropov anti-corruption campaign. The Kremlin leadership, determined to make a clean break with the Brezhnev era and its tolerance for the soft life, put pressure on regional Party headquarters throughout the Soviet Union, but above all in Moscow, to crack down on bribery and *blat*. The Gastronom manager, Yuri Sokolov, had been refusing special food shipments to a number of dignitaries in the Moscow Party apparatus – that is, he was not corrupt enough – and so he was made a scapegoat. Police surrounded the shop, which still retains the wood panelling and chandelier of Czarist days, took away the account books and hidden food ready for shipment to the black market. Sokolov's five deputies were also arrested.

In some ways, then, the life of a sales clerk is more comfortable than that of the director: the smaller risk undertaken by a skilled shop assistant can nonetheless almost treble her income. Publicly, the inspection agencies, the police, and the prosecutors express indignation. Privately, many members of inspection teams take sweeteners and even economists realise that no great harm is being done. All that is happening is that higher (and often more realistic) prices are being paid for scarce goods, and that a small number of people, rather than the state budget, is earning money.

To the shopper these crimes rank above blackmail and only a little way below statutory rape. Those without political connections or money to bribe are condemned to queue, sometimes for days, for inadequate goods that may never appear. When, in the late 1970s, the Soviet authorities announced the sale of Yugoslav furniture – prized for its high quality – the queues began on 7 March. Standing, sitting and sleeping in deep snow in front of Dom Mebeli on the Lenin Prospect, the queue had reached five thousand by the crucial date of 25 March. On that day the queuers were allowed to submit a postcard with their own address and their number in the queue. Eventually, perhaps in the same year, the fortunate would be able to buy their wardrobes and dining-tables. The sight was astonishing: many borrowed cars from their offices or from friends to have somewhere warm to sleep during the night (with temperatures dropping to minus fifteen Centigrade) and whole families were mobilised. As in Poland, Rent-A-Grandmother services were set up; old-age pensioners with time on their hands would earn a sizeable sum to stand in line until the customer returned from his workplace. But over these weeks the mood changed in a way which must have made it clear to the Soviet leadership that queues are the equivalent of the mobs in revolutionary Paris. Easily angered, at once sycophantic and fiercely abusive towards the authorities, long queues in Eastern Europe are a kind of demonstration against decrepit economic management. At first the queuers were jealous of each other; after hours, rather than days, they established a collective cameraderie. Food and hot drink was too scarce to share, but the talk was more relaxed than is normal in a public place. As the check-in day approached, so did the revolutionary fervour of the queue. In the event there was not a storming of the Bastille, or its equivalent in the furniture business, but the anger spilled over in the middle reaches. Number 500 – he had painstakingly established over the previous three weeks exactly how many people were standing in front of him – was enraged to find that he had been allocated Number 800. Three hundred relatives of shop assistants and otherwise privileged names had managed to be put on top of the list without having to stand for a minute in front of Dom Mebeli. The shouting, the screeching and the venom was the nearest Moscow came to a popular uprising in the enforced calm of the Brezhnev era.

In Poland the crowd is an even more volatile instrument: it is above all political. The groundswell of discontent that eventually exploded in the Cegielski engine factory in Poznan in 1965 – the so-called Bread and Freedom Riots – and in the Baltic shipyards in 1970 and 1980, was clearly observable in the queues six months before. Just months before General Jaruzelski declared martial law in the winter of 1981, the queues were once again a barometer of serious discontent. Corruption behind the shop counter, or even an ill-founded suspicion of it, converts easily into political upsurge. Annoyed by the relative ineffectiveness of the official control teams, Solidarity unionists began to organise three- or four-man monitoring brigades to raid shops for hidden goods destined for the black market. Witold Pawlowski of the *Polityka* weekly described the scene in Lodz, a textile town in central Poland where, as he says, 'People used to go as if to Paris.' By 1981, as now, the shopping area was desolate: the choice of men's shirts began with the extra-large size of 44, there were no shoes available in any of the stores, most shelves carried only dust and out of the corner of one's eye there always seemed to be a crowd of women furiously tearing into a bale of just-delivered linen.

'The queue lives through several stages. When there is nothing in the shops, it stands quietly, recharges its batteries. When the goods are put on the shelves, it will undulate slightly. Then a few routine rackets spring up – people try to squeeze into the privileged queue for pregnant mothers and disabled, somebody tries to borrow a baby to jump the line – but in general everything proceeds quietly. But the queue really explodes when the shelves start becoming empty again and it is evident that there will not be enough for all . . .

'In this state of passion, the queue begins to circulate various rumours and speculative guesses as to the morals of the shopkeepers, the likelihood of there being goods in the store. The road from there to action is a short one. In Lodz the idea of a telephone hot line has been conceived as a kind of therapy, a safety valve. While the customers in the middle and at the end of the queue get hot and bothered and prepare to storm the shop, a cooler queuer can ring the number and call a (Solidarity) brigade.

'The queues then reach a higher level of political consciousness, get themselves organised, shout at the shop managers to show them the invoices, creep up from behind the shop to surprise the assistants, organise evening watches at the shop window to make sure that nothing gets removed.'

A brigade checks a rumour that twenty kilos of fillet steak was delivered to the delicatessen in Lodz's Dlugosza Street but has somehow disappeared. One of the team goes into the shop via the storeroom and blocks all escape routes, the rest go into the shop and ask what is available. '*Nie ma,*' nothing. Then to the storeroom where the find is: three and a half kilos of fillet, some chickens, some baby food, cheese, cigarettes stashed away behind the lavatory cistern, tomato paste. All goods that have presumably been bartered with other assistants from other shops in return for the fillet.

A shop assistant has three basic stratagems available to her. The first: a shop expects the delivery of new mattresses, so the assistant arranges through friends and contacts to have a group of would-be purchasers ready, tips them off the day before and they queue in the shop as if they were normal customers. Beforehand they give the assistant – always in a private place, never in the shop – a commission (usually about twenty-five per cent for furniture), and pay for the product normally over the counter; all that the assistant has sold is information, but that is the most precious commodity of all in a land of scarcity. In the Soviet Union, Poland and Czechoslovakia it is usually the store manager who finds the would-be purchasers rather than the assistants, but in this case the assistant is given a slice of the manager's commission to ensure that she serves only the chosen customers. Unless the customers are caught handing over the bribes, the transaction is virtually undetectable. The assistant pretends to operate on a first-come, first-served basis. If a customer, not in the general arrangement, joins the end of the queue, the assistant raises her hands in mock despair and declares: 'We have just at this moment sold out, try again next month.' The most efficient variant of this strategem is to have a regular closed group of customers who pay a 'retainer' to the manager or assistant every month in return for the tip-off.

The second stratagem, also designed to defeat the inspection teams who sporadically raid the stores, is for the assistants, perhaps in co-ordination with other colleagues, to buy scarce products on their own account. The money is put through the cash till and receipted, the shampoo or the radio set or the children's shoes are put under the counter to await a customer. This method is particularly favoured when goods are delivered without warning, without the vital week or ten days needed to recruit interested clients. In this case, if a wealthy-looking customer arrives enquiring after radio sets he is told that the store unfortunately has sold out but that the assistant would be willing to part with her own for a fifty per cent mark-up. This method at least ensures that some radio sets actually end up on sale: the assistant simply does not have the resources to take aside large quantities of scarce goods. In Poland the exception to this rule is stockings: a new, unexpected delivery of good-quality stockings is invariably sold out by noon before the majority of normal customers even realise that they have arrived. Stockings can be easily stored, are cheap to buy and can be readily smuggled out of the shop during the lunch break to hand over to a black-market contact.

Many goods, however, require the use of a third stratagem. This is the riskiest, for it involves a whole chain of people from the warehouse to the shop counter. The store manager is in steady contact with the foreman of the main warehouse – 'a friendship cemented with vodka,' it was explained to me in a dubious metaphor – who supplies several shops in a region. A regular customer approaches the shop assistant and asks for a certain brand of washing machine. The assistant is given a bribe and approaches the store manager. The manager asks the customer how much he is willing to pay and then contacts the warehouse foreman. An extra washing machine is then miraculously supplied within the week, the major part of the supplement given by the customer being split 40/60 between the shop manager and the warehouse foreman, who out of his share has to pay a small sum – two or three bottles of vodka – to the truck driver who transports it directly to the home of the customer. Even in orderly societies like East Germany such arrangementss are common, though the shop assistant prefers to avoid direct contract with the managerial class. In a case reported by the local Erfurt newspaper (November 1983), a sales assistant reached a deal with two delivery drivers who simply ensured that one additional refrigerator a month was supplied to her shop. This was sold for a one hundred per cent profit to a pre-arranged customer.

The imposition of martial law in Poland tried to put order into the queues, abolished the brigades and the so-called Queue Committees in the hope that this would also put an end to the public, spontaneous discontent. The idea of a Queue Committee is that the queuers themselves organise a rota scheme to ensure fair play. Every day, before or after going to work, the member of the queue has to make his presence known to the Committee. Two absences will deprive the customer of his place in the queue but it is possible to compensate for an absence by doing a four-hour stint in front of the shop registering new names on the list, checking who else is present and making sure that a competitive queue has not formed. If that seems complicated, it is little wonder: the amount of time spent telephoning other colleagues on the queue, arranging stand-ins, is equivalent to two full days work a week. Little wonder too that the Polish authorities view the committees as somehow sinister: at a time when the Solidarity trade union was banned, it was a perfect way of organising discontent on the street and in some circumstances a good way for a circle of black-market speculators to get the goods that they want. For something like refrigerators or washing machines, the queue stretches into the several hundreds with no certainty about when the appliances will be delivered. Queue Committees, symbolised by earnest men with clipboards perched on shop windowsills, at least saved many people the pain of queueing throughout the night for weeks on end. But some potential customers suspected the committees of being in league with the shop staff to salt away the choicest goods, and formed rival queues.

It needs only the faintest whiff of corruption to spark off minor riots in Poland. Thus in the autumn of 1982, almost a year after the banning of such Queue Committees, they were still thriving in Warsaw. In front of the kitchen supplies shop in Mazowiecka Street there was one queue committee of about twenty people (representing a true queue of three hundred) and a rival queue which did not accept the authority of the Committee. Insults were exchanged, panic set in, and the two queues started to beat each other up. Two people were seriously injured before the militia arrived: that day only four people from the Queue Committee managed to buy anything, and six from the rival queue. The biggest fight occurred that winter in front of the large furniture shop in Emilia Plater Street, where dozens of housewives were pushed through shop windows. Little, if any, of this is reported by the Polish or foreign press, because it is simply assumed that the behaviour of crowds is of only scant significance, subject to anthropological rules and best understood in terms of Konrad Lorenz and his goslings. In fact, a perceptive government pays close attention to the mood of queues, for they often show a nation's threshold of tolerance of corruption and social injustice.

Governments in Moscow, Warsaw and Bucharest are particularly worried about the loss of working time implicit in the queues. They are all concerned with raising labour productivity and controlling hidden inflation, two important prerequisites for successful reform of the economy, but their inability to supply enough goods to meet demand constantly saps their resolve. The head of the Polish Supreme Chamber of Control, General Tadeusz Hupaloswski, told parliament that economic plans for the following year were unrealistic: they were all calculated on the basis of a fully effective forty- two hours working week. In fact the average worker put in no more than thirty-four hours of which only twenty-seven were productive. Even that seemed on the generous side.

The people are constantly stealing time from their employers, not as in the West to increase leisure time (and thus perhaps making them more effective workers or more willing workers during the actual working hours) but to acquire scarce goods. Professor Peter Wiles (1982, *Crisis in the East European Economy*, ed. J. Drewnowski., Croom Helm) has pointed out that the relationship between longer time in the queues at a time of superficially improving living standards fosters discontent. If the volume of consumer goods increases by ten per cent, he writes, we are in effect seven per cent better off (because the marginal utility of income drops). But if the Russians originally put in forty-two hours a week plus five hours of queuing, and scarcity increases the amount of queuing to 9.7 hours, they have become fifteen per cent worse off. 'So the orthodox statistics tell us we are better off and indeed our productivity has risen by ten per cent (for we still only produce for forty-two hours); yet we feel worse off, and not being professors of economics, we cannot account for it. The lengthening queues probably explain why the Soviet people are reported to be more discontented and saying they are worse off, though the volume of consumption per head is stable.' The worker thus has to put in more work, in the rather unpleasant form of standing in the queues, to buy the same quantity of goods. That is suppressed inflation, a psychologically dangerous phenomenon because it opens still further the gap between what the average inhabitant is being told by his leaders and what he is personally experiencing; and because, despite his awareness that the situation is getting worse rather than better, his expectations are constantly rising.

In most East European countries there is a waiting list of many years for a telephone, which means that the office phone is used by white-collar workers to 'arrange' spare parts or otherwise fix deals and co-ordinate shopping. According to circumstances, this can account for anything between twenty and sixty minutes of a working day. The lunch break has become extraordinarily elastic in both offices and factories. In offices in Poland, the Italian jacket scheme (not unfamiliar in Fleet Street) is often deployed. The cunning office worker will keep a second jacket permanently in the office wardrobe. When he leaves to stand in queues he will drape this spare jacket over the back of his chair and scribble a note indicating that he has just popped down the corridor. Many of the bureaucratic delays in Socialist societies are not due to anti-human Kafka-malice, but to the fact that the clerks have to buy food for their families and cannot answer the telephones. In factories such tactics are rather difficult but the foreman and shift supervisors – who are dependent on the good will of the workers if norms are to be met – have devised ways of operating shifts-within-shifts, allowing workers to queue at the factory shop. To leave the factory is a more complicated task because it means passing the security guards with either a plausible excuse or a bribe.

There are of course regional differences in the theft of labour. In

Hungary, the amount of moonlighting has increased sharply in line with suppressed inflation. Workers are allowed to lease part of their factories and work in the evenings for their own profit to produce either more of the usual goods or slight variations. They organise themselves into crews and usually sell the products to the factory management. The effect of this is that workers try to conserve their energy during official working time so that they can turn out more at a more profitable rate in the evening. Sometimes too they steal materials (which technically they should pay for) and they certainly spend a great deal of official working time organising themselves for their (legal) bouts of moonlighting. Private deals have also been reported from the Balkan countries and even from East Germany. There it is a common occurrence that a plumber, having been ordered through an official agency which pays him at modest official rates, will arrive at a household. He explains to the distraught housewife that if he fixes the burst pipe according to the book it will take three days but that he can do it for a private fee – five times the official rate, or sometimes in hard currency – within the hour. More often than not the householder agrees, the plumber makes a tidy, undeclared profit and takes the next two days off, explaining to his state employer that it is a long and complicated job. In Poland, where it is illegal both to give and to receive bribes, the plumber can rely on the discretion of the householder.

When Andropov came to power, the Politburo, the Central Committee, the Party Auditing bodies and the Council of Ministers offices received a flood of letters – many hundreds of thousands according to reliable sources – complaining about shop-counter corruption. In the year that Andropov was still fit enough to make an impact on policy, he launched a comprehensive campaign against corruption, but at the same time made it clear that he would not tolerate Russians taking time off work to buy scarce goods. Labour discipline became the catchphrase and the militia was ordered to begin a nationwide crackdown, in January 1983, codenamed *Tral* (Trawl). Many of the customers cramming Moscow's stores are from the provinces, often described by the Muscovites as *meshochniki* (bagmen) or *desantniki* (assault troops), who elbow their way to the counter to fill rucksacks with food. These assault troops are playing two days truant from their factories to stock up with goods unavailable in the countryside. Initially the *Tral* was rather popular with Muscovites. Policemen and civilian vigilantes checked the documents of every shopper, to check first of all whether they were officially employed and secondly whether they had permission to leave work. At the higher levels, heads began to roll, including that unenviable post, the Minister of Domestic Trade, Alexander Struyev, who had held the job since 1965. But confronted with a stark choice between police harassment and severe restrictions on queuing, and on the other hand, rampant but tolerable levels of corruption in the retail trade, most preferred the latter. Shop-counter corruption and the latent violence of the queue may not be pleasant but at least it means that the consumer has some chance of getting what he wants. A situation where women are afraid of slipping out of the office to stand in line for an hour does not solve the problem of how to live.

The turning-point came in Moscow in the spring of 1983: the spot checks by police and the huge round-ups had cowed everybody into carrying their personal documents with them at all times and many were afraid to go into a bar during normal working hours. Perhaps the most disturbing twist in the campaign came when the police started to raid the public baths. For office workers, especially managers and their deputies, a pleasant way of breaking up the monotony of the working day is to go to the *banya*, a traditional steam bath. Here the rigid compartments of Soviet bureaucracy can be melted in the dry heat. Foreign trade managers can talk quietly to producers or department heads in the finance ministry and can come to semi-legal arrangements that lead to private commissions and sidestep the cumbersome formal arrangements. When the police started to invade the baths looking for work-dodgers, many officials were put in embarrassing situations, unable immediately to prove their identity. Back at the office, secretaries were instructed to say that their bosses were at 'meetings' or had 'just left the room'. The red faces were not just steam-induced.

For those found without official work stamps in their identity card, the penalties are harsh. The Soviet Union has had an anti-parasite law for almost fifty years, originally designed to deter those who made a living out of the black market. In recent times the law has also been applied against Jewish dissidents and Jews who have applied to emigrate. When they apply to leave the country, they are usually dismissed from their jobs as security risks. A period of anything from eighteen months to several years then ensues during which the would-be emigrant finds it extremely difficult to find a skilled job of any kind. If he refuses to take a normal job and lives off loans from his friends or from presents from overseas, he becomes liable to the 'anti-parasite' legislation. In the Soviet Union not only is the right to work guaranteed – much vaunted in propaganda at a time of high unemployment in the West – but so too is the obligation. Similar conditions apply in Romania, East Germany and Czechoslovakia, none of whom have any qualms about using labour legislation to deter emigration. For many years in Poland, the Catholic Church opposed the introduction of an anti-work-dodgers bill, fearing that it could be applied, as in the Soviet Union, against intellectuals, students expelled from university or other non-conformists. At a time when many were losing their jobs either because of official retaliation against Solidarity activists or because the authorities had asked workers to make unacceptable and debasing compromises (signing loyalty oaths to the state for example), this resistance was particularly significant. Even so, the legislation was passed in 1982 and a crackdown began on people in the queues or shopping in the market.

The resourcefulness of the Poles, however, has by and large defeated this piece of legislation. So far it has only been used against work-dodgers who have been given two months to find work under threat of being sent to do emergency relief work in flood areas or being put on special work detachments. In Praga, the tough, scabby suburb of Warsaw, it is possible to buy well-forged documents from the under-world and throughout Poland there are private companies who, for a small or not-too-small bribe, will officially state that they are employing somebody. Doctors are also prepared to sign indefinite leaves of absence for generous patients and a number of professions are so difficult to monitor – taxi drivers, for example – that the aspiring black-marketeer or even humble queuer can have a great deal of time to himself. In some cases when the authorities have tried to send dissidents on work detachments, the Church, in the form of a local bishop, has offered employment as a caretaker.

One of the changes underway in the Soviet system is a shifting attitude towards time, time lost and found in the business of living. When you arrive at Brest on the Soviet-Polish border and the train is hoisted onto a different gauge track, then your idea of time is also derailed. Time has a different meaning, is allocated in a different way. At what point does it become a hardship to queue for scarce goods? The value of a pair of running shoes is measured, but also enhanced, by the time invested in buying them. The ticket or post-office clerk closes her counter for mid-morning tea between 10.30 and 11.15 a.m. The queue remains, even relaxes a little. Later the queues will complain to their families about the sloppy work habits, but in their hearts they know that they are part of a nationwide conspiracy; the queuer abandoned her (or his) office, the phone rang unanswered between 10.30 and 11.15 a.m. There is a satisfaction too about netting a rare purchase. A Muscovite will ring proudly to announce that she managed to buy coffee today. That satisfaction extends to services; Russians talk of 'catching' taxis; that is, using stealth and trapper's guile, they lure cabs into a position where they must stop and take a passenger.

But this tolerance is changing. The formal working week has shrunk over the past dew decades (I make an exception here, as so often, for Romania which under Ceausescu operated a seven-day week in certain industries). But moonlighting to maintain standards of living, official overtime and the relentless search for scarce goods have sponged up the leisure time. Wages have gone up, there is more money in people's pockets, but there are not the goods to buy, nor the time to enjoy them. The demand is not only for better supplies, but for time. Time, naturally, cannot be sold. A rich man cannot buy a couple of hours from a poor man in order to create a twenty-six-hour day. But the wealthy can employ the poor to carry out the time-consuming tasks. The loss of time is beginning to cause serious friction, not only in queues but in all aspects of Soviet social life: one characteristic of the Gorbachev revolution is a growing impatience, as workers adapt more quickly. I took a stroll through a public garden with a Soviet psychiatrist, one of the new breed unstained by the abuses of the Serbsky Institute and other notorious psycho-detention centres for dissidents. He wears Austrian metal-framed glasses and is popular with women patients. Just as the Master, Freud, attracted the suppressed hysteric, the Viennese woman out of touch with her sexuality, so Dr Andrei has frustrated Moscow consumers on his hands. 'If somebody comes up to me and says, "I can't cope, I can't cope – the queues! the bribery! the squalor!", then I treat them, I think legitimately, as cases of serious maladjustment. They are not, of course, saying something untrue. There is nothing wrong with their perception of our world. The newspapers are saying substantially the same thing. But their immune system has collapsed – that is the problem. Until now, people have seen, and yet not seen, the crisis: that's the only way to keep sane. But now more and more people feel the friction of it all – they don't have enough corpuscles, they have lost their resistance to everyday life, they have become unhinged.' Put another way, as the system cannot be changed in a manner that would satisfy needs, the consumer has to change and find a palatable method for accepting sacrifice. Andrei charges eight roubles an hour for his advice.

The Soviet Union has all the necessary ingredients for an economic miracle. It is rich in resources and has a highly educated workforce. If, as the reforms stipulate, it were to modernise its machinery, rationalise its production, turn on the profit-motive switch and introduce sensible management techniques, then the Soviet Union could become the powerhouse of the twenty-first century instead of the confused, if not sick, giant of Europe. These are realistic goals. But the Soviet consumer does not actually believe these calculations at all, and he is already on a short fuse. Popular attitudes are changing, the Soviet workforce is the most highly educated, and the most articulate, in Russian history; there is a need for more than just better-supplied shops and reasonable wages. They want symbols of social advancement; they want more genuinely free time and a leisure industry that caters for this new-found time. So far the Gorbachev planners are not equipped for this. The economic plan which charts Soviet goals until the year 2000 envisages the production of sixty thousand videos by 1990, two hundred thousand by the year 2000. Yet Poland, largely by personal import or smuggling and the black market, already has over one and a quarter million video machines and networks of video rental clubs. Perhaps the Soviet authorities are afraid of the effect on Russians watching Western tapes instead of state television. But the main problem is that they have no conception of consumer demand. The production of consumer goods in the year 2000 is planned to be eighty to ninety per cent above that of 1985, but that still represents smaller growth than in the economy as a whole. As for consumer services, the Soviet economic miracle, following conventional market-orientated lines, should look like this: workers from the dinosaur smokestack industries will be redeployed, that is, made redundant and shifted elsewhere. The increasing prosperity of the rest of the population, the demand for time, will stimulate the growth of a proper services sector. And, hey presto! Steel workers will start taxi companies, open barbers' shops, pizzerias and computer workshops. That was the logic of the Thatcher and Reagan eras. The vision was incompletely realised in Britain and the US – and the result was an unbudgeable lump of unemployed people. The market revolution, in Thatcher terms, is unworkable in the Soviet Union. There is talk of accepting unemployment – or 'redeployment' – with sixty thousand civil service jobs to go by 1990 and, conceivably, sixteen million jobs from heavy industries by 2000. But there is no question of this redeployment happening spontaneously. Gorbachev's chief economic adviser, Abel Aganbegyan, is a late convert to unemployment.

There is an irrational fear of unemployment in the Soviet Bloc. The assumption is that it will destablise the political system, throw normal economic calculations out of the window and create, in the long term, worker opposition. There is in fact a measure of unemployment disguised as workers between jobs. But in so far as the shift from heavy, unprofitable industry to customer services involves Western-style unemployment, there can be no progress. Jobs will be chiselled away and then, administratively, workers will be allocated to state-run light industry services. If the private sector were to expand as dramatically as some Soviet economists would like, accounting for, say, ten per cent of output instead of 0.4 per cent, then labour mobility would not be so much of a problem. But a legally inhibited private sector cannot hope to absorb the overflow from the smokestack industries. There will be some juggling – early retirement schemes, women encouraged to stay at home – but the compulsory, administered shift of redundant workers into an artificially expanded service sector is bound to fail.

This possibility for enriching ordinary life remains an impossible dream; the initiative will rest with co-operatives and private entre-preneurs who stay small enough to take risks and respond to the market. All the post-Communist governments are struggling with this problem.

Hiding Inflation

There was a time, as in Weimar, when you could plaster your walls with pengos; it was cheaper to use currency than buy paper. The Hungarians are a creative people and there emerged a thousand and one uses for the notes. One could, for example, stuff cushions with them, or, deep-soaked in water until they formed a solid bundle, they could plug a hole in the roof of the garden shed. Central and Eastern Europe has a long tradition of inflation. A Hungarian born at the beginning of the 20th century has lived through the devaluation and eventual demise of three currencies: the crown, the pengo, and the so-called tax-pengo. The wild inflation of the crown took off after the First World War, that of the pengo after the Second. In the first case, the disturbing effects of a war economy, the loss of a large chunk of Hungarian territory, and the confidence-stripping effect of being on the losing side all restricted the crown. The pengo was undone by a war in which forty per cent of natural assets were destroyed and by the social changes, the move to Communism, that caused such an upheaval in economic life. The currency reform in August 1946 showed how far the crisis had developed: one new forint (equivalent to about ten US cents) was handed out in return for four hundred million million billion pengos. A second pengo, the B-pengo, was worth one hundred million billion ordinary pengos. The Hungarian National Bank had produced a new banknote, one billion B-pengos, but never issued it since it had already become worthless. Shopping was done with wheelbarrows or rucksacks to carry the notes; or rather, money was not used at all. The attempt to give money value again, the 1946 currency reform, had to be carefully prepared. Deflationary policies, or restricting the wages of workers (who in any case had been working for almost nothing over the previous eighteen months) were not enough. There had to be something to buy. But the factories were still crippled from war. The Hungarian authorities therefore hoarded goods, deliberately induced shortages, for several months before the forint came into circulation. These were gradually released after the 1946 summer and the forint appeared to gain credibility. At the same time, the government traded the country's entire home-grown tobacco supplies for Western clothes and other consumer goods. It was an immense operation, especially because of the shortage of petrol and vehicles; somehow all the shops had to be filled in all corners of the country at the same time. After a fashion, the trick worked and a Hungarian 'money miracle' was declared.

The result has been more than three decades of 'price stability', with prices of fundamental services (rent, gas, electricity) and politically sensitive foodstuffs (bread, meat) pegged at an artificially low level. As production and labour costs grew, so did the real cost of the staples. But governments were committed to keeping prices more or less at the same level, 'protecting' the consumer and using subsidies to keep the system afloat. There is, of course, nothing very Socialist about unchanging prices; rather price stability simulates a fantasy world in which the market has been abolished and in which all needs have been, and always will be, met by Mother State, a vast sow that suckles its many infants. Common sense broke through on occasion; various governments, egged on by ambitious finance ministers, have tried to roll back budget subsidies and pass on some of the costs to the workers. The political will, though, has melted. The serial upheavals in Poland (1956, 1970, 1976, 1980) and scattered strikes and unrest in Romania, East Germany and in Soviet enterprises have demonstrated how difficult it is to touch prices or fiddle with work norms. The workers, especially in the heavy industrial fortresses, believe that they have an unstated contract with the State. Shops are empty, the living is hard, so the State has an obligation to keep prices down. It is the garbled logic of the man in the bar who says, 'We're living at a basic level because of their incompetence,' (his finger jabs towards the sky, the vodka splashes) 'and now they want to make everything expensive to cover up their own incompetence! Let them work it out for themselves.'

I have argued the point in various bars in the Soviet Bloc but have made no dent on the popular consciousness. Prices have lost any connection with the rest of the economy. Tell a Polish steelworker that higher-priced meat will mean more meat in the shops and he will stare at you as if you were moonstruck. Prices are a bureaucrat's foible, part of the fiefdom. Just as a noble landowner could raise the rent of cottages on his estate, so the planning department can raise prices. But it has nothing to do with supplies. The Soviet State Committee for prices, which by rights should not exist at all, sets individual prices for just under half a million products, from tights to motor cars. Little wonder that prices are not frequently changed. When the prices of state goods are shifted, the process seems entirely random – or at least irrelevant: the price of caviar, smoked salmon, fox-fur and jewellery will double overnight, while end-of-the-line televisions will come down by twenty per cent. That was the composition of the surreal price adjustment in 1973. After martial law was declared in Poland in 1981, the government, protected by soldiers in the streets, could afford to be a bit braver. Food and alcohol prices were pushed up, smartly accompanied by one-off 'compensation' payments to the low-income earners. Since then, prices edged up without major upheaval, though the strikes of May and August 1988 showed how close to the edge the government was treading. There were no retreats, apart from the case of butter which, in a blundering manner, was made more expensive shortly before a holiday. Services, such as the traditionally subsidised summer camps for schoolchildren, became more expensive by leaps and bounds. Yet meat and bread remained taboo, and the budget subsidies were not reduced; they merely grew at a slower rate. Only the Solidarity government was able to take the risk of freeing food prices entirely.

And so it is that, in Gorbachev's words, Russian kids play football with loaves of bread. For every kilo of Soviet meat costing 1.8 roubles, there is a three-rouble subsidy. Hardly surprising that the queues begin at six o'clock for meat shops that open at eleven. Much of the economy is run on the same basis.

The effect is to push inflation underground. If it is impossible to raise prices officially (with the exception of the authorised free markets where that 1.8 rouble pork joint can be bought for seven roubles) then it must be done by subterfuge. First, many Soviet Bloc countries – all except Hungary and Poland – are operating with inaccurate shopping baskets. That is, in calculating the official level of inflation they are choosing an unrepresentative sample of goods. Food sold on the free markets is not included, for example. As the Russians spend fifty per cent of their incomes on food and, as many have to resort to the expensive private markets run by collective farmers, an important component is missing. So too are goods produced by small market-orientated enterprises – a made-to-measure jacket, or skirt, or children's shoes. Many Soviet-Bloc price commissions also leave out services. The accuracy of the officially conceded price index is therefore deliberately low. Governments also tinker with the price index, forcing down the prices of discontinued or unavailable products in order to counter-balance serious price rises elsewhere in the economy. This reinforces the impression that Soviet-Bloc price indexes have only symbolic value, crudely carved totem poles around which one can dance, whooping. One example: the Czechoslovak consumer price index for 1982–83 was officially set at seven per cent. Yet the price of beef had gone up by sixty per cent, veal by forty-two per cent, pork by thirty-five per cent, sausages by twenty per cent, fish by up to fifty-five per cent, colour televisions by forty per cent, washing machines by twenty-four, petrol by twenty-three. Prague Man, it seems, can live by bread alone.

But price rises are also hidden from the central authorities by factories who fiddle the books. A clever enterprise manager (the kind that has been amply rewarded until now) knows not only how to exaggerate the size of his production but also how to depress the price statistics. One way is to change the product mix, or to introduce pseudo-innovations. The technique is rather obvious and, for different reasons, is practised in consumer marketing in the West. Thus older-model cars are with-drawn, and a new model with only a few accessories is introduced at a seventy per cent mark-up. Tins of peas, four hundred grammes, are withdrawn to re-emerge as three-hundred gramme tins at the same price. Poor-quality jackets are substituted for top-quality jackets but the price stays the same. If quality deteriorates with unchanged prices, the real price increases. One out of every four Polish lightbulbs is defective. Soviet televisions are, on average, returned twice to the manufacturer in the first year of the guarantee. Dan Franklin of the *Economist* jokes (19 April 1988) that the most exciting thing about watching Soviet television, before glasnost arrived, was that the set was liable to blow up.

Shoes routinely wear out within months, their soles flopping on the pavement like the footwear of a circus clown. Poor quality is the factory's way of keeping up with the Plan targets, and it does not do to advertise the fact that, say, less glue is being used on shoes, or less time spent checking televisions. There is, though, a measure of collusion between the centre and industrial concerns. In Poland in 1972 planners sent directives to meat processing factories telling them to cut the meat content in sausages by an amount equivalent to a 12.8% price increase.

Some of these absurdities are supposed to be eliminated by price reform. That will entail more realistic pricing and a more accurate assessment of inflation; it should also help to bring more goods to the shops. Hungary is the pioneer of price reform and, in the context of the New Economic Mechanism introduced in 1968, set out three kinds of prices:

1.   Prices set by the State for a limited number of goods.
2.   A loose price framework for the majority of consumer goods, setting upper limits.
3.   Uncontrolled prices for raw materials, some semi-finished goods, some consumer goods.

The price system has been refined somewhat since then. In 1980, a 'competitive price mechanism' was brought in. Domestic prices of all raw materials and semi-furnished goods, including those produced at home, have to be linked to the average import price in convertible Western currencies. So the price of these goods is raised in order to force factories to economise and become more responsive to the world market.

These are interesting steps towards giving 'price' more meaning: price actually conveys information in the Hungarian economy, it is not a mere totem-pole. Poland has followed suit, at least in so far as introducing a three-tier pricing system and a more or less reliable Consumer Price Index. The result is that Hungary and Poland, in international comparisons, seem the worst afflicted by inflation.

Gorbachev's advisers are thinking on similar lines, though nobody is anxious to grasp the price nettle. By allowing a co-operative, or private enterprise, to grow so quickly, he is bringing in a form of price rise; for the better-quality food and products, the Russians are often willing to pay four or five times the state price. But first there will be a reform of producer prices (1990), then an increase in farm procurement prices

(1991) and only then, tentatively, helped in with 'compensation' payments *à la polonaise*, will there be major movement in retail prices. It is too easy for Gorbachev's opponents, their ears tuned to grumbles in the factories and the queues, to argue that the Soviet leader is reforming on the backs of the workers. Even raising – or rather, freeing – producer prices is fraught with danger. It is a logical first step. If factories are really to be 'self-governed and self-financed' then they must be free to buy from suppliers and to sell to other enterprises at a price that is negotiated, not dictated from above. The idea will be to fix (at a high level) the price of raw materials, to make some prices negotiable by contract, and others entirely free. Hungary is being closely studied by Soviet economists. But will the planners give up their price-setting rights without a fight? And what happens when the newly-liberated factories exploit their monopoly position by pushing up prices? Hungary has not completely solved these problems despite dealing with them intellectually for two decades. The Soviet Union, infinitely larger, infinitely less prepared, is trying to introduce these changes at a time of low growth.

If Gorbachev needs any further cautionary advice, he could do worse than listen to the shoppers of Shanghai. China was stuck in the same yoke of politically-induced price stability. 'Why China Has No Inflation' is the title of a pamphlet by the author Peng Guangzi in Maoist days. The usual stuff: 'The broad masses and their families under capitalism feel threatened by economic fluctuations and inflation . . . (but) many people in People's China have no idea what inflation is.' That has changed. China has established a more reliable CPI which registered inflation of 7.2 per cent in 1987 and over ten per cent in 1988. Even that was camouflage. Fresh vegetables had risen, year on year, by forty-four per cent. Like the Russians, the Chinese spend about fifty per cent of their income on food, so the rising prices of tomatoes, paprika, garlic, pork and fish were hurting. Cigarettes, alcohol, clothes, shoes, newspapers, books and electricity were also climbing quickly. The head of the Chinese price commission admitted that twenty-one per cent of all urban families had suffered a drop in real incomes. Factories and farmers using their new price freedom were pushing prices to the upper limits of permissible margins. Those who suffer most are those on fixed incomes, with no moonlighting possibilities: party and government functionaries, employees in heavy industry, teachers, students and pensioners. Each of these groups is capable of forming an anti-reform coalition and so, nervously, the Chinese leadership resorted to the old methods to soften the blows of the market: price controls, a rationalisation programme, new subsidies and 'compensation' payments for the urban Chinese. The compensation, though, was no such thing: typically eight yuan for an office employee, barely enough to buy a kilo of tomatoes on the free market.

These problems are lurking for the Gorbachev reformers. It is a classical conundrum, empty shelves or empty pockets. But more than that, it is a test of credibility. Somehow Gorbachev has to convince the Russians that the word 'price' has some semantic content, that the price rises are a kind of promise, a pledge to fill the shops, to cut the queues, to make life more expensive but easier.

Death, the great equaliser, is of course nothing of the sort. The same market disequilibrium families experienced throughout life persists into and beyond the grave. On the one side, a shortage of burial space, marble, coffins, gravediggers and embalming fluid. On the other side, an ageing population fearful of an indecent or shaming funeral which is willing to devote large chunks of their savings to a worthy burial. The money is pursued by the unscrupulous ('cemetery hyenas' in Polish) who manipulate the shortages, and the momentary lapse in concentration of a grieving family. Bureaucratic sclerosis adds to the market imbalance, aggravates the shortages and lengthens the queue. It was naive to expect the interplay of bribery and string-pulling to end at the point where one stops breathing. Sonia, in Prague, should have known better. In Czechoslovakia, if a man dies at home, the family must immediately inform the local hospital; a doctor must issue a death certificate, and an inspector has also to visit the house. This is Sonia's story:

'We rang up the hospital and they were really quite efficient, put us through immediately to the right department and the doctor was with us within a couple of hours. Meanwhile, we tried the other number that the hospital had given us, the inspector from the registry. Well, it seemed that as long as the death certificate had not been filled out, he could not authorise the body to be taken to the mortuary. The doctor came and it turned out that he knew a friend of a friend, who was at medical school with Pavel so that was okay. He gave us a chitty. Then we rang up the registry again who said something along the lines of "Well, all right, if that's the way it has to be." But by this time it was past four o'clock and the registry office was closing. You can imagine what we were thinking – Father dead in bed upstairs and us staying the night in the house for this damned inspector. So, well, of course we got hold of the inspector's home number, and we made him an offer, perhaps not quite like that, but we made it clear that there would be something in it for him. It turned out that this was pretty good investment (thirty crowns) because sometimes these inspectors start to ask whether you are officially registered in Prague and so on. He just wanted to get home and watch the football match so there was none of that sniffling around, though God knows we have little enough to hide. By this time, it was quite late and I rang up the hospital again to take the body, that is Father, to the mortuary. They said it was too late: all the ambulances were on emergency duty at this time and they could not spare one to transport dead bodies around Prague. This was ridiculous and I suppose I lost my temper a bit, it had been a hell of a day. So they slammed down the phone. Anyway, I rang up my brother-in-law, who lives near the hospital and asked him to go round and fix up what he could. Jan is good at these sort of things. He gave an ambulance driver twenty crowns to take his supper break early and ferry the body away.

'The problem with this is that according to the rules all bodies brought in by evening ambulances have to go immediately to casualty. That would have meant another examination, another death certificate. So Jan gave the driver another ten crowns to tip the receptionist, the woman who sends stretchers to the right places. Everything worked out fine that day, praise be to God. I thought at one moment that the kids would have to spend the night with their dead Grandpa in the next-door bedroom.

'But the next day, the bother got worse. First, I had to fix up with the crematorium to take Father. Can you believe it – there is a waiting list at the crematorium? They insisted I had to deal personally with them, nothing over the phone, so I had to go round, then they sent me to one office after another. I tried everything at the town office of the crematorium – breaking into tears and the usual line, "If there is any contribution I can make to some charity fund or other." Well, the woman there wasn't really interested in bribes but I think she was just waiting for me to show a willingness to give her something, to show that I was serious. The tears did not convince, but the offer of money did.

'So they fitted me into the schedule for the following day, well Father really. And still things got worse. Somehow we had to get Father's body from the mortuary to the crematorium. Jan went round again and got two mortuary assistants to make the body look presentable so that the family could see him in the open coffin. That cost him a couple of bottles of something or other and, so he says, the promise of a few litres of petrol. I was furious when I heard that. How dare people make a profit out of this sort of thing! The ambulanceman did not want to take the body to the crematorium because he would be noticed – it was a long way and if there was a queue people might note down his number and complain. But we got hold of another phone number, of somebody who drives a car for the ministry. For a bribe – I don't know how much Jan gave him – he was willing to take the coffin. That was good because the car was black and had a lot of space. I came separately with the kids. When we arrived there was a queue, maybe three funerals. But the driver said he had to go back otherwise he would be missed so we had to give him some more to stick around. First of all Jan tried to jump the queue of course, but nobody was having that . . .'

Death is not always such a complex financial transaction. In Poland, the influence of the Catholic Church is so strong that corruption has been virtually banished from the process of dispatching the dead. Undertakers are often private and though they charge sizeable sums they have to work in close co-ordination with local priests and parishes, banishing the temptation to make a quick zloty. The state burial enterprises have to be correspondingly efficient and are one of the most effective sectors of the Polish economy. In the Soviet Union, the role of bribes is different from city to city: in the Ukraine where the Catholic tradition is still evident, if not zealously trumpeted, funerals are discreet, well-managed affairs with little bribery involved. In Moscow, corruption is rife and there have been a number of reported cases of cheating and profiteering. Perhaps the most common form is the selling of the clothes, usually the best suit of the deceased, in the second-hand 'commission' shops or on the black market. As the coffin is wheeled out of sight in a crematorium, the corpse is taken out of the box and stripped. There have been a number of cases that were exposed after the crematorium workers brought in smart black shoes from corpses that proved to be made of cardboard. It emerged that professional under-takers, especially in some Western countries, have special cardboard artificial shoes to dress the dead as they lie in open coffins and thus keep down the cost to the relatives. Somehow consignments of these shoes had been imported by Soviet funeral enterprises. Crematorium workers, either not fully realising this or hoping to get away with it, sold the shoes to the second-hand shops who then sold them to ordinary customers at high mark-up prices. The first rainfall soon exposed the racket.

Legitimate private enterprise can eliminate some of the more sordid transactions faced by Sonia. A funeral co-operative in Moscow has set up a special embalming and cosmetic service for corpses. It supplies the coffin suit, books a place in the crematorium queue and can help organise the funeral service. All for a hefty sum, of course. But private entrepreneurs, seen by the dogmatic opponents to Gorbachev as a breeding-ground for crime, can actually fulfil useful tasks. First, a private undertaker is taking over a job that used to be performed by State mortuaries and which was abandoned because of a shortage of manpower. Second, it can wipe out some phases of grave-robbing; the private individual bribery (instead the co-operative itself arranges the payoffs). How can consumers, in this case mourning families, be shielded from crooks who exploit chronic shortage? There are legal sanctions but, as an interesting case reported in the Romanian lawyer's journal, *Revista Romana de Drept* (issue number 3, 1983) revealed, the result can be more bewildering than rewarding.

A coroner, while performing an autopsy, removed false teeth containing eight golden crowns from the corpse with a view to selling the gold on the black market. This immediately sparked off a debate among Bucharest legal circles. The Timisoara court found the coroner guilty of profaning a corpse because the denture was not a removable one and was therefore considered as much part of the body as his natural teeth, or his ear or leg for that matter. The legal scholars interviewed by the magazine agreed with the court verdict: the coroner had violated a corpse. But there was considerable disagreement about the ownership of the recovered denture, a crucial point not only from the point of legal precedent but also because such looting of corpses is common practice in the country. Some of the lawyers argued that so long as a man is alive, the denture – or wig, or wooden leg – is part of his body and cannot be considered an object of theft. But as soon as he is dead and the denture isolated from the corpse, then it can be considered an asset in its own right. As such, it is included in the estate of the deceased and if the heirs initiated the appropriate processes and legal proceedings, they could claim the denture. The Court of Appeals, however, decided that the family members were not entitled to the denture since they, like the coroner, had no right to detach it from the body. This verdict is a flawed one, as Romanian lawyers have pointed out, since it is a third party – the coroner – who removes the denture and an illegal act cannot be imputed to the relatives simply because they stand to benefit.

Private companies can provide a form of control on state corruption; certainly a good mortician would have caught out the crooked Romanian coroner. Co-operative, that is private, undertakers have now opened up in several Soviet cities, established by well-educated young people kitted out in sober suits; a Western reporter even found one, a twenty-seven year old former metallurgical engineer, in the dismal steel town of Magnitogorsk (N. Y. *Times*, 16 August 1988). The new breed of undertakers can bring order into the funeral market and perhaps, with order, dignity. But few people can afford the fees: it is still cheaper to bribe. Plainly some intermediary is needed if bureaucracy and shortage are to be defeated. Alternative methods of beating the system – the use of connections or barter – are inapplicable; it would be unduly morbid to cultivate contacts in the funeral parlour in the same way that one nurtures garage mechanics. The problem is, at what point is it unacceptable to make a profit out of misery. In the Soviet Bloc, the limits of public tolerance are even narrower than in the West; hardline Marxists on the one hand, the Catholics of Poland, Hungary, Slovakia and the Soviet Baltic on the other, share a common revulsion for the private undertaker. The result is that most of the new private undertakers are geared up to making quick profits rather than establishing life-long (so to speak) businesses; a natural reaction in times of political uncertainty and tepid popular acceptance. Of all the modern Capitalists-in-Communism, they are the most vulnerable. A confidential opinion poll in Hungary in the late 1980s showed that there was widespread acceptance of the idea of private enterprise and that such companies gave better-quality service. But at the same time, they were judged not fully reliable in the sense that their continued existence could not be counted on. Private businessmen were also as likely as state employees to cheat customers.

Private innovation may thus not be a complete solution to the Soviet Bloc's funeral gap. There should be some caution about the number of co-operatives – in the thousands by 1990 – in the Gorbachev era. Many were opening, but many were closing too, either because of pressure from the authorities or because of misjudged demand, or more frequently, because they were satisfied with a reasonable, swiftly realised profit and wanted to move into something new. Andrzej, a tall, rusty-bearded Solidarity member, came to my office one day with a request. In partnership with his wife, a beautician, he had planned to set up a funeral parlour, but in the previous week he had been stopped after drinking at a party and was sure to lose his driving licence. That ruled out a hearse service. His request: to get hold of fifty plaster dogs, about the size of garden gnomes, from a department store in London. His plan, in the spirit of Gorbachev, was to set up the first pet cemetery in the post-Communist world.

5

A Roof For Ewa

Ewa was a simple girl who hated her mother. The family lived together – the parents, a grandmother, a widowed aunt, Ewa and three other children – in a large farmstead, east of Bialystok near the Soviet border. Ewa developed more quickly than her contemporaries and started to put demands on her mother – a brassière, lipstick, time off from household duties – and the arguments, harmless enough when the girl was thirteen, flew out of control, lingering in the house for days. At eighteen, a few weeks after her birthday, Ewa left home, hitch-hiked to Bialystok and took the train to Warsaw.

There was enough money for a fortnight and a promise of a job in a bakery. The advertisement pages of the newspapers, written in the crisp, telescoped language of the genre, did not offer much hope of accommodation. Everybody seemed to want to buy or rent or exchange; there were only ten or twenty offers, coded and opaque. One apartment could be bought by a 'person coming back from abroad'. Simply put, somebody wanted to sell their flat for dollars. But there was some hope too: three people wanted single women to share an apartment. She rang a number and was told that the price was 'negotiable'. An old man in Praga, two rooms and a kitchen, communal lavatory. He said he wanted a housekeeper and put his hand up her skirt. The second was a middle-aged divorcee living in the Ursynow housing estate. He said that Ewa wasn't his type. Coming down the stairs – the lift was out of order – she passed a girl on the way up, long black hair piled up, perfume clinging. Ewa had never seen anybody so sophisticated in her life. The final advertisement was another old man, but cleanly shaven and not smelling, like the Praga landlord, of cat's urine. It was a comfortable one-bedroomed apartment. There was a convertible sofa but Ewa knew what to expect. She was tired and had not bathed since Bialystok.

Ewa lived with the man for a year, unable to leave: she could not keep her job without an official residence permit, she could not have a permit without a job. Her priest, who told me the story, describes the phenomenon as 'housing prostitution'. By trying to restrict the number of people migrating to the capital from the provinces, the authorities are pushing young women onto the streets; it is often pimps who have accommodation to spare. Ewa too ended badly. Her gratitude to the landlord soon turned to resentment; she was sexually abused but at the same time she was able to bully the man. She drank hard, was reprimanded and for no very clear reason, killed herself, gassing the whole apartment. The priest, her confessor, agreed to conceal the cause of death so that the family could bury her decently.

Although the literature of the nineteenth century is full of Ewas, she was a victim of the great post-war housing crisis of Eastern Europe. In Poland where there are 2.1 million families (about six million people) on the waiting list, where the wait for an apartment is now 16 years in Warsaw and where the authorities place a high premium on residence permits, desperate measures are often called for. Moscow, Warsaw, Leningrad – all cities battered by the Germans during the war – are like honeypots to young people in the countryside. To change one's life, to scale the social ladder even in a small way, to earn a reasonable wage, to find a husband or a wife, to escape the deadening tedium of the village and the scrutiny of the family, to learn a trade – all this requires a move to the city for the ambitious young. But the authorities are afraid of depopulating the countryside too rapidly and are worried too that aspiring city-dwellers would overwhelm the state's building potential.

Trekking into the urban hinterland of these new city sprawls, it is difficult for a Westerner to see the attraction for provincial youth. I know Ewa's home terrain quite well: there is no cinema within a hundred kilometres apart from the fleapit in Bialystok, no night life, haphazard bus services, a dearth of intelligent young people. But the alternative, in the housing estates, offers little warmth. Ursynow on the fringe of Warsaw is so vast and so new, so prematurely aged, that residents do not know the names of the streets after ten years, nor indeed do they appear on the Warsaw street map. The place is full of young families, but the local school is spilling over – 40 to a class – and most children have to commute across the city. The health centre is poor. Most apartments do not have telephones and cracks are zig-zagging their way through the concrete. I found a similar picture in Leningrad and in East Berlin.

Tagging along with Mikhail Gorbachev's party in East Berlin in April 1986, I discovered Marzahn Estate, tastefully laid out but drained of colour as if after a long illness. The place had been given some flower tubs ahead of the visit and a splash of paint but one had no sense of being in or near a grand, historical city. Social life was centred on the supermarket which was both well-stocked and expensive; it had a monopoly, the small corner shops, the so-called 'Tante Emma Laden' having been wiped out by the planners. To simulate some form of communal living for Gorbachev's visit, the official choreographer had laid on a group of local teenagers to play handball. They were positioned near one of the most colourful edges of the estate and looked well-trained. Everybody else on the estate had been confined to their one- and two-bedroomed apartments by the security police who told them to stay away from their windows. They could watch the whole performance later that night on West German television. Suddenly, though not at all surprisingly, a strapping youth threw a ball at Gorbachev. He caught it and returned it with a slight wheeze. The party clapped and two people laughed. This was later described in the East German press as a 'spontane Ballwechsel' – a spontaneous exchange of balls. Two important points had been established. First, Gorbachev was fitter than Chernenko, Andropov and Brezhnev. Second, Marzahn was a pretty lively sort of place in which anything could happen.

The shift from country to town, and the barrack-like existence of the housing estates, is of course not specific to the communist system. What is different is the scale of the rehousing and the reluctance of the architects and builders to adjust, over the years, to the more sophisticated needs of the residents. It can be argued, though, that the post-war building programme is at once one of the greatest successes of communism and one of its greatest failures. Success because the mobilisation of building reserves after the war was an astonishing achievement. The pace has not slackened: between 1956 and the mid-1970s about 44 million housing units had been built by the state and co-operatives in the Soviet Union, more than anywhere else in the world. Nowadays the Soviet authorities say that 110 million square metres of housing are built in a year and 11 million people move into new apartments. About 30 million square metres of co-operatives, in town and country, are completed annually. Even if most of these apartments are boxes (Lenin in 1920 defined the minimum living norm as nine square metres per person and the proportions have not changed much since then) this is a staggering turnover. It also underscores the size of the problem: all those old Second World War battlegrounds, Kursk, Smolensk, Kiev, have to cope with the legacy of the German bombardment, with a manpower shortage and with population growth. Although demographic trends have slackened (the Russian rate of reproduction is stagnant or dropping while the Muslim areas of central Asia are the big population-growth centres) there are more and more people to be housed.

The raw figures say something about the expenditure of human sweat, but they also conceal a great deal. Something has gone badly amiss with Soviet-Bloc building programmes. Dissatisfaction with housing has been identified as one of the three root factors in industrial unrest, along with sudden drops in real wages, and consumer goods shortages (see M. Holubenko, *Critique*, spring 1975). Central planners plainly want to avoid trouble and draw up ambitious construction plans. The Housing Lobby, or mafia, can be identified in the Central Committee of every Communist state. It fights for materials and manpower, in the sure knowledge that this will translate into political influence. Pressure is exerted all the way down the ladder of command to maximise the number of apartments that can be built. Everything depends on these promises being honoured on paper. Construction teams receive their bonuses according to Plan fulfilment, city bosses and party chiefs build up their base on the strength of the figures. A report by the Polish Supreme Chamber of Control demonstrated what these promises look like on the ground. The report, released in 1980, was an attempt to lobby for position in the period after the fall of Edward Gierek. But its findings are sound and are a frank indictment of the planning process in all the Bloc countries.

Examining the performance of the building industry in 1979, the NIK team found that by October only 78 per cent of the housing construction plan had been completed. Houses were being passed over to housing co-operatives unfinished, habitable only on paper, without heating, lifts and other basic facilities. But on paper, the Plan had been successfully fulfilled. The first few months of 1980 were then spent on finishing the houses that were technically completed the year before. This hangover effect causes crushing delays and wastage. Cement mixers and grinders would be delivered in January or early February to a construction site marked on the programme. But the place would be deserted – the work team, weather permitting, would be busily completing houses elsewhere that on paper were already occupied by happy couples. The machines, once delivered could not be taken back. They were covered with a shroud and left to survive the winter. According to the NIK report the practice of counting bare walls as completed houses started in 1975. The Controllers informed the government immediately, but the information was supressed, and in

1978 the Gierek leadership claimed that it had built the largest number of apartments in the post-war history of Poland. A year later, in fact, a large proportion of those same record-breaking apartments were still unoccupied.

NIK took another look at the housing industry in 1986. Nothing much had changed despite a change in leadership and a much-trumpeted economic reform. Plans were still being faked. The Wroclaw Building Enterprise, for example, found in November that it had to complete 304 flats by the end of the year. December is known as the month of miracles in the mythology of the communist construction industry. So nobody was very astonished when the state company managed to complete its tasks by year-end. The last building, containing 116 flats, was handed to the local co-operative on the last day of December. There was no exterior plastering, the walls were unpointed and in some cases the apartments had no floors. People moved in, undeterred by the abandoned pails or the walls that slanted like the vision of a drunk. By the following spring the builders had put some of the things right, but only a few, and at great expense.

The housing shortage illustrates the simple recurring formula of centrally planned economies. First the planning apparatus is unable to cope or even adequately to define the problem. The pressure to produce results leads to cooked books, poor quality, and wholesale corruption. The faking of results conceals but does not eliminate shortage. The shortage, when it is tackled in the classical form of central distribution – the queue – encourages bribery, and guarantees misery. When market forces are invoked either legally (in the form of co-operatives) or illegally through crooked estate agents, corruption spreads through the whole system; it becomes impossible to live without cheating. In the Soviet Union, the principal way to acquire a roof over one's head has been unchanged since the Bolshevik revolution, and so far it seems that Gorbachev is unwilling or unable to introduce more market elements into the equation. Gorbachev himself lives in a rented apartment and his advisers, otherwise open to questioning the principles of ownership, are not convinced of the desirability of creating a class of private property owners. That gives city housing departments immense power, a power unparalleled in the Soviet Civil Service. It also makes them a honeycomb of corruption.

There have been cases of personnel directors of housing departments selling jobs in the section, in the knowledge that even a secretary can supplement her salary with bribes. The old worker-peasant system, in which worker families were given priority, has been replaced by a more haphazard pattern of allocation in which subjective calculation of need becomes the main criterion. The trick is to know exactly what level your application has reached and to ensure that your bribe goes to the appropriate official. This information in itself requires a bribe. A bribe for information, for consideration, for a recommendation and ultimately for a decision in your favour. Some elements in the equation are still beyond bribery: a letter of recommendation from one's Party cell, for example, cannot be bought with money, only with an exaggerated mime of allegiance, or by taking on unpleasant duties.

Factories have some power over the allocation of apartments, can establish their own housing co-operatives, build their own property, and buy their own materials. This is a precious independence in the Soviet Union, for it means that the factory can compete with others for scarce manpower. Wage payments fluctuate only within a narrow band in Soviet industry, making the offer of an apartment a valuable carrot. A famous cartoon in the satirical weekly *Krokodil* shows a scene outside the door of a personnel department of a factory. A crowd of flat-capped workers has gathered clutching requests to be relieved of their duties – the official first step to resigning – and apparently gossiping with revolutionary fervour. 'What's going?' says a worker in the phrase used to ask after scarce goods. 'Housing,' says a woman. 'But where?' 'At the factory down the road,' comes the reply. In industries where the competition is sharpest for manpower, the factories will engage in a spiral of corruption to obtain as much building material and building land as possible to attract workers. Local Party chiefs are given a 'tribute' – no Party dignitary in a region which contains a car factory need fear that he will have to use the bus – and a network of bribes and sweeteners encompasses the whole local government machinery. In these cases the housing departments lose out but they can catch up well enough in other ways. To bribe the local Party *apparat* is of course also to bribe the local branch of the KGB and militia, for these alone have the power to interrupt the relationship.

Some people can jump the queue: members of the writer's union receive more space, as do academicians and party bigwigs; others such as senior officers have their own network, independent of the Housing Department. But the queue is still the central fact of life; standing in it, or hopping to the front, few Russians escape it. It can take sixteen years to reach the head of the line, and in the meantime one has to live somewhere. Many young people enter middle age still cooped up in the same apartments as their parents. This has all the advantages of the extended family – grandmother takes care of baby, the infirm have someone to buy their meat and collect their medicines. But such living also stunts young families – many spend their lives dependent on financial support from their parents – and stirs up tension. A prominent Warsaw defence lawyer opened up his casebook for me and demonstrated that out of six murder cases he had defended in the past three years, five were the direct or indirect result of cramped existence. The saddest cases are perhaps couples who have divorced but who cannot find a second apartment. Searching for an apartment in the winter of 1981, I came across one such couple. The living-room had been divided by a plush but dusty curtain, the front door was heavy with locks. For the past two years the couple had had to stay together, conducting their love affairs and their dinner parties and their private conversations within yards of each other. This couple at least owned their own apartment. Far worse off, it seemed to me, were the majority of Russians, Poles, Bulgarians or Romanians who pace out the years on a waiting list by living in a communal house. Through connections Igor had found a room in an old merchant's house near Izmailski Park. There was a long underlit corridor where most of the residents left their outdoor shoes. The corridor fed into five rooms. In each room there was a family. Igor, an engineer and technical translator, lived with his wife, on maternity leave from Aeroflot, and a baby. The room was more or less in line with Lenin's norm – about 20 square metres, with a good high ceiling. This was particularly prized because the buildings slapped up in Krushchev's housing drive, the usual thin-walled new-old constructs, had ceilings that would have crushed Alice in Wonderland. The room had been done up nicely, though their clothes were hung on free-standing clothes-racks pilfered from a shop. The problem came in the sheer mass of people wanting to use the lavatory, bathroom and kitchen on the other side of the corridor. The refrigerator had locked compartments to prevent theft. Cooking times were laid out in a roster, the lavatory was a free-for-all, with a queue beginning before six o'clock in the morning. Nobody seemed to regard the situation as unusual.

Even for such accomodation (the English term 'flat share', with its vision of three temp secretaries making do in Kensington, does not seem adequate) there is fierce competition. At the Rzhevsky Baths, just off Prospekt Mira in Moscow, there is a stretch of ground about the size of a cricket pitch where, every Sunday, aspiring tenants and landlords patrol up and down with placards pinned to their overcoats. The look is of the man wearing sandwich boards on Oxford Street proclaiming the evils of meat and the imminent collapse of the world: multiply this eccentric by thirty and add in a bit of noisy haggling and you get an idea of the scene. These placards, though, are not testimonials to vegetarianism but straightforward advertisements: a two-room apartment in the suburbs is being offered in exchange for a one-roomed apartment in the centre, rooms are being let but to students only, or to childless couples. Surrounding the walking advertisements there are perhaps forty or fifty Russians. Their stories, complex, deduced from their quickfire conversation, express a fragment of Russian reality. Ewa, one senses, would have understood the scene had it been played out in Poland.

Some of the takers were straightforward enough – a pregnant woman looking for extra space – but others were desperately trying to break out of catch-22; no Moscow job without residence, no residence without a job. These open-air accommodation bazaars are rarities elsewhere in Eastern Europe. Word of mouth, messages stapled to trees, plastered on lampposts and walls, and of course newspaper classified columns are more obvious pitches for this kind of market. One of the most sordid expressions of the housing crisis is the growth in marriage bureaux, some legal, many not, which specialise in arranging marriages between provincial girls and Warsaw or Moscow residents solely to obtain official registration. In Warsaw the going rate is the equivalent of three months' wages, paid by the girl to the happy spouse. It is a formalised version of the relationship that plunged Ewa into the depths. But it is dangerous to make generalisations about the Eastern Bloc, especially in social issues where different historical and demographical factors are at work. The poor housing conditions apply to every major city in the Soviet Union, to the industrial centres of Poland, to Bucharest and East Berlin. There are difficulties in Budapest housing, but nothing to compare with Leningrad. In Prague the housing list also moves slowly, but most interim accomodation is of high standard. There are few slums on the lines of the Soviet *trushchobi*. And even in the same country there are substantial differences; the chubby young mayor of Erfurt, near Weimar, told me that the housing list of his medium-sized city was 300 and that most of these were divorcees or expanding families. There was no one living rough and no slums. It was difficult to fault him. (He had just rattled off a statistical profile of his city, including refrigerators and cars per household and the remarkably precise calculation that there were 12 punks in his domain. 'That is one punk per hundred thousand of the population?' Yes, he replied without humour, 'But it's a

downward trend – one got his hair cut last year to join the army.')
Contacts in Erfurt appeared to bear him out; a young teacher with wife
and two children, a non-party member, lived comfortably in a two-
bedroomed apartment that compared well enough with his West
German equivalent.

The common factor, though, is a steady embourgeoisement, the
wish, in the face of desperate shortages, to establish roots, and build for
one's own family. One of the most successful magazines to be set up
after martial law was imposed in 1981–82 was *Murator*, instructing
Poles how to build their own houses and country cottages. As the years
have marched on, as the economy deteriorates still further, so articles in
Murator have become steadily grander, containing architectural
projections of mountain chalets and Dallas-style ranches. 'There is a
hunger to build,' explains one of the editors, Lech Stefanski, 'as things
get worse, so people want to develop something themselves. It is a
change of mentality. Instead of waiting for the government to dispose
and decide in a year or ten years to allot you a low-rent flat that you don't
much like, you build for your family, either privately or in a co-
operative. Of course there are chronic shortages of materials, but you get
hold of them, by hook or by crook.' More likely crook, of course. Janos
Kennedi, the Hungarian dissident, has set out in a comic samizdat text
the problems of building on one's own account. The text is called 'Do it
Yourself.' This is how Kennedi describes the mating ritual involved
before a buyer and seller get together to clinch an illegal deal: 'He
insisted on telephone conversations under false names (we were never
allowed to call him), on semi-secret meetings in coffee houses where he
was suspicious even of the regulars, mainly elderly ladies. Together we
went on Sunday excursions in the hills; we sat in secluded forest
clearings, scratching in the dust with a twig the complex moves from flat
to flat and house to house. He dropped envelopes in our letterbox
(addressed in letters elaborately cut out from newspapers) containing
railway tickets for a return trip to Debrecen, so that we could negotiate in
secret on the train. I had to watch the most boring football match of the
season to discuss with him the methodology of transferring funds . . . on
one occasion, we had agreed to meet secretly at a street corner
somewhere in the suburbs, but he just passed us by, indicating with a
wink that he was being followed.' In the end, the deal did not go
through.

Building your own house in a centrally planned society means either
thieving or bribery. Bricklayers are lured away from official construction

projects because there is no such thing as a private bricklayer. Cement, mortar, window frames, glass are diverted from factories (the Soviet Union enjoyed a boom in dacha construction between 1978 and 1980 thanks to materials spirited away from Olympic Games construction sites). It means 'borrowing' trucks. It means taking months off work while one labours on the site, making sure that the workers do not drink themselves into stupor, driving around the country to find wood panelling or bathroom tiles. It all costs a great deal of money.

As Zita Maria Petsching of the Hungarian National Bank puts it, the explosion of costs makes private house construction both expensive and a sound investment. 'The price of homes built by the National Savings Bank increased by 100–200% during 1985. The price-conditions of private builders became more and more difficult too. According to our estimates the price of land increased by 500–600% and material costs tripled – not including bribes. The costs of transport have increased even more, and the fees private builders charge have also tripled. Several features and processes underpin the above figures but let me give you two more data: between 1970 and 1984 consumer prices doubled and the nominal wages of workers and employees increased by 130%.'

To get hold of a private or co-operative home, the Hungarians have to moonlight, sometimes illegally. Married couples, both holding down two jobs, are now a common phenomenon in Budapest. Mrs Petsching thinks that the drive to own property, though desirable, could be creating a new form of exploitation: 'After buying their homes, many of them do not stop these additional activities as they have to pay back their debts. This process leads to the quick over-exploitation of labour. In this new paradoxical situation people's lives are lived for their homes; the homes dictate their lives.'

Perhaps the most inflation-conscious citizens of a planned economy are its leaders. Certainly one can see a shift in their living habits since the war. In the 1950s and 1960s it was enough for those in power to rent (for nominal sums) large luxurious apartments and enjoy the use of state-owned country rest homes and dachas. A touch of class was often provided by the permanent loan of antique furniture from national museums. But in the 1970s and 1980s, leaders wanted something to pass on to the children. Prisoners and military conscripts have been used to build private dachas and apartments in every corner of the Bloc. One of the most concrete results of détente in the 1970s was – Western concrete. Not to mention West German bidets, Italian furniture and Dutch tiles. In the Gorbachev era, the political builders are a little more discreet, for there is no knowing when evidence may be turned against them. At the moment, it is safest to be both a builder and a reformer.

The legal way for the relatively well-off to buy accomodation is through a co-operative. This functions on the same lines as in America and other Western countries. A deposit, usually about 40 per cent, is paid to a trust representing a community of owners. The rest is paid off over some 15 years.

The private market in Poland has grown up because of the financial problems of housing co-operatives. Put rather crudely, the situation is this: the slipshod construction techniques of state builders and the faking of results have exerted more pressure on housing co-operatives which are taking over half-finished buildings. There is a desperate need for cash, especially dollars to buy spare parts and to pay off freelance work teams. So the co-operatives sell some of their apartments to Locum, which is the only official agency empowered to sell housing to private citizens. Locum sells apartments to foreigners at 400 dollars a square metre and to Poles in a combination of dollars and zloties. The semblance of a private market has sprung up as the direct result of the failures of the central plan. Here comes the rub: even Locum now has a waiting list. You could go into the Locum offices and spread forty thousand pounds onto the desk of the chief director and he still would not be able to find a place through his official network. In 1978 Locum sold 7,500 flats for dollars, in 1987 it sold only 700 and the waiting list was in the hundreds.

Anything, it seems, touched by the dead hand of the state, will produce shortages and queues. The result is a free and almost entirely illegal market. Lawyers function quasi-legally as estate agents and play some of the tricks practised in the West, keeping both buyer and seller apart for as long as possible, taking a cut from both, pushing up the price and splitting the difference with the seller, buying up underpriced property on his own account. There is no recourse for the apartment buyer. First there is no such thing as an estate agent so it is impossible to be cheated by one. Second, the agent is also cheating on behalf of the buyer in order to sidestep taxation or repressive legislation. In 1985, Poland passed a housing law which is regarded as something of a model for other communist countries worried by Western-style house profiteering. The law says that there can be only one apartment per family. It also imposes a huge tax (in theory up to 80 per cent of the notional profit) on any housing that is sold within ten years of purchase.

The first proviso is sidestepped by means of the fake divorce. Happily married couples arrange divorces through specialist lawyers in order to own two apartments. The second apartment is then usually rented on the free market. (If the landlord can find a foreigner willing to pay dollars he is certain to become a zloty millionaire.) The hearings in communist divorce courts are nowadays about the property relationships: care of the children, and prospects for reconciliation, occupy only a small part of the judge's questions.

The ten-year rule has made rich men of many housing department clerks. It is cheaper to give a clerk a bribe of several hundred pounds than pay the crushing tax for breaking the ten-year restriction. Everyone appears to be united in wanting to cheat the tax office. When a Pole buys a new apartment, either through a lawyer-cum-estate agent, through Locum or through a direct transaction, he is supposed to pay a purchase tax equivalent to five per cent of the value of the property. The lawyers therefore draw up two sales contracts – a real one that is promptly hidden, and a fake one, undervaluing the property, for the tax office. But the tax office is naturally wise to this and produces its own regular updated version of free-market prices, and calculates its tax estimate from that. The lawyers then argue that the property is in a dramatically bad state of repair and try to pull the tax estimate down. So many bribes are exchanged and quiet deals struck that it is impossible to keep track of the complete transaction. A further oddity: nobody bothers to inspect the property; the bargaining is conducted in a vacuum, for the joy and profit of it all.

How could widespread privatisation improve the housing crisis in the Soviet Bloc? The proposal was made, rather vaguely, in a Solidarity research programme entitled 'Five Years After' (that is, five years after the 1980 Gdansk agreements which not only created a free trade union but also set out demands in areas such as housing and health). The ideas, however, add up to little more than the gut feeling that anything must be better than a centrally-planned building industry and its endemic corruption. Gorbachev, in 1988, commissioned a team of economists to look into the possibilities of private house construction. But their brief was a narrow one, and the experience of the most advanced privatisers, Hungary and Poland, does not offer much encouragement. As long as privatisation remains partial, no great impact will be made on the housing picture; key components of the contruction industry will always stay in the hands of state concerns, however liberal the regime. There is scope for private enterprise in three phases of the building process: the acquisition and use of land, the production of materials, and the organisation of house building. But these elements interlock; to allow, say, private cement factories might improve cement supplies, but would foster corruption in other parts of the industry.

Property developers are forbidden by law in Soviet-Bloc countries, though there are some plans to make it legal to build one's own home and sell it at a profit. Even if developers could operate legally, they would have to solve the problem of land ownership. State-owned land typically has no sewage or irrigation, no telephone connections or electricity. Privately-owned land is usually earmarked for farming and cannot be converted without special permission. Most Western countries face similar hurdles – in Britain too there is an obligation to seek planning permission from the local council. The difference is in the time-span. It took almost ten years to free the fields of Ursynow from their protected arable status and make them available for a housing estate, Warsaw's largest. Permission had to be squeezed out of the Ministry of Agriculture, and even the Council of Ministers. That was for a large and, as everybody agreed, urgently needed state-sponsored housing project. Private builders face a more daunting task. In the whole of Poland only 30 per cent of open land has building permission. Even when the builder has managed to acquire a patch of land, he faces the problem of how to package it: the municipal authorities frequently forbid certain kinds of building and insist that part of the territory stays undeveloped.

The Byzantine complexity of land acquisition, the first stage of house construction, naturally breeds corruption. Dogmatic Marxists who claim that corruption is spawned by the private sector can pick up some ammunition from the housing industry. Private builders cannot wait for three years or more while various courts decide the fate of their land. They start to build before permission is granted and, as one cannot disguise a house, they bribe the local authorities and the police. Criminal charges are usually not dropped but the hearings are delayed and the private builder ends up paying a fine on top of the bribes. The bribes would of course have been unnecessary if it were not for the bureaucratic barbed-wire fence erected around the laws on transferring land.

No communist or post-communist country has a unified organisation that can buy, divide, build on and sell land – no property developers, in other words. Hungary comes closest because it is generally more intelligent about how to treat the laws of 'speculation'. If a housing co-operative wants to buy land then it bribes officials by offering them apartments in the future housing development. Later, if the co-operative wants to resell the building for a profit, a new chain of bribes is set in motion.

The other aim of privateers in communist society is to break the monopoly on the production of building materials. There is a chronic shortage of the most basic materials, from cement to piping, glass to nails. Most can be produced simply; the shortages are solely the result of a state monopoly and the inflexibility of central planning. One of the constant blunders of state builders under communism is that they use too much cement. This is not a question of protecting citizens from nasty winters: the per capita tonnage of Soviet cement easily exceeds that of Sweden and Finland, countries not famous for their winter sunshine.

The fact is that the state cement producers expand their power by turning out more and more of the stuff. Because they employ thousands of workers they have a foothold in the official trades unions and, frequently, the ear of sympathetic politicians, and they resist any move towards lighter construction. 'Heavy builders' – architects who favour tomb-like slabs or Pharaonic temples – are encouraged. When Polish private businessmen and co-operatives wanted to move into the pre-fab business, they found themselves squeezed by the state companies who dropped their production of light bricks. The move was deliberate, to preserve a monopoly, and pre-fabricated homes – a partial solution to the housing crisis – were doomed as a result.

Private companies in Poland and Bulgaria have started to make glass and ceramic tiles. But in Poland, the state still has a monopoly on the production of window panes. Private companies can turn out frames, can produce glass, but window panes for apartments stay firmly in the hands of the state. Most factories make only one-sized window panes to fit a standardised apartment block. Result: plenty of frames but no windows. The shortages vary from one country to another; the quality of production is usually higher in Hungary, and in Czechoslovakia housing materials are made in factories that operate on virtually Western management methods. If a Czech can buy his land – as complex a process as in Poland – then he will be allotted certain materials. That cuts out some of the plundering of building sites common elsewhere in Eastern Europe. Most communist countries, though, complain of shortages – openly recorded in the local press even before glasnost – of connecting walls, or of doors that are directly caused by clumsy state planning. In the housing sector, the Plan has been designed to protect inefficient and frequently corrupt state enterprises.

Faced with these problems it is difficult to see how the privatisation of one segment of the industry will help significantly. Lech Stefanski estimates that even if private builders were given completely free rein (a near-impossibility, he admits) the number of completed apartments could double but still be well below 200,000 a year. But he stressed: 'This is not just a question of private enterprise or state. There is a role for small businesses of all complexions providing they are efficient and modern enough to respond to demand.'

That is one lesson for the nervous reformers in Moscow: responding to demand is a question of scale and flexibility, not just ownership. If the market is to play a serious role in solving communism's problems, then the old Brobdingnagian philosophy of 'Big is Beautiful' has to be discarded.

6

Corruption On Wheels

One of the most effective pieces of political propaganda to be deployed in a US election was the poster portraying Richard Nixon and asking, 'Would you buy a used car from this man?' The second-hand car business in the West has long been synonymous with fraud. Too much depends on trust, the guarantees are thin, the expertise of the customer limited. Has the mileometer been manipulated? Is the engine number correct? Why does the engine sound, well, funny? The salesman has to simulate the authority of an independent expert while at the same time pressing home the deal. Even for aspiring Presidents, this is a difficult act. In Eastern Europe and the Soviet Union, the used-car market is one of the commanding heights of the corrupt economy. Not only is it open to the kind of abuse common in the West, it is also an important stepping-stone for a black marketeer who wants to treble or quadruple his fortune: it is the quickest way to become a millionaire.

Cars, of course, are a measure of national well-being and prosperity. In the 1950s the domestic car industries of Eastern Europe produced only a few thousand vehicles a year. The Soviet Union turned out only 64,000 cars in 1950 and 300,000 trucks: in the same year the US produced about two million cars.

In East Germany, the Soviet Union and Poland, the war had wrought so much destruction that the main concern was building – houses to live in, roads to drive on, hospitals and factories. Other countries like Bulgaria had such a poorly developed industrial base that the production of cars was seen as an unnecessary luxury, at least in the early post-war years. Instead the leaders and medium-ranking officials made do with a handful of imported vehicles from the Soviet Union, the pre-war models and some cars and trucks left behind by the Germans. Even as late as the 1960s it was possible to cross through the Wall from West to East Berlin and enter a virtually car-less world. On one side of the Wall, young men would cruise the Kurfuerstendamm in open-topped Mercedes and Porsches; on the other, barely a kilometre away, it was possible to walk down the centre of the main streets without any risk of an accident. But as the economies picked up so too did a phenomenon known as 'automobilism'.

East Germany, ahead of its communist allies, now has 200 cars for every 1,000 inhabitants (compared to West Germany's 430), while Poland has 100 cars, and the Soviet Union 50 for every 1,000. The cities are ill-equipped for the motor age and central Budapest in rush-hour – an hour that seems to come earlier every year – risks comparison with Milan. Driving habits have also adjusted to the standards set by the Italians. Every motorist sees himself as a cowboy breaking a mustang in a crowded rodeo.

The problem is this: production has not kept pace with demand, nor with the rise in incomes. Not only do most adults want a car, they have come to see it, in the Western manner, as indispensable to their lives. Cities have grown and so have distances from home to work. The shortages of food and other consumer goods have put a high value on the car as a means of driving out to the countryside to buy a pig from a farmer, to collect ceramic tiles from a building site, to scout around the five furniture shops in the capital to see if there are any mattresses available. The planners were taken by surprise. They anticipated a steady growth in output, say ten per cent a year, and trusted the central administrators to lower expectations.

But even with foreign assistance (Fiat counsels Moscow and Warsaw, Renault is active in the Soviet Moskvich factory, and Volkswagen advises East Germany), output targets are unrealistic. I flew to the boggy banks of the Volga, south of Moscow, to see whether the Soviet car industry would ever be able to meet the domestic demand. Amid the cranking and the clamour of the Togliatti plant, a huge Pharaonic construction built with Italian help, it was difficult to hear the explanation; indeed, there was none. Even when the antiquated production lines are eventually renewed (the plant was completed in 1970 but still has the air of the 1950s, posters of exhortation and encouragement covering cracked concrete) there is not much hope for the aspiring Soviet driver; it is the export quotas that are due to increase. An ambitious muddy parking lot stood empty, deserted as a parade-ground in wartime. Few of the workers could afford their own cars. ('A classic case of alienation,' I told the guide. Such tours always have a combative element: over-sceptical Western correspondent is pitted against over-cautious – to the point of mendacity – minder. 'Don't understand – how you mean alien?' 'You know, Marxism. Workers slaving away on making things they can never afford.' Cupping his ear to protect it against the factory noise which had indeed become mysteriously louder in that moment, he shouted, '*Alien*, yes, good film, very good. You like the cinema?') The Soviet car industry, mainly Togliatti, produces about 1.3 million cars a year, 600,000 of them Zhigulis. But about a third of the total are destined for export (the Zhigulis are renamed Lada) while the domestic demand is bottomless.

It is the same story throughout the Communist world: car stocks account for only about seven per cent of world stocks, somewhat under developing countries. But the people of Eastern Europe are measuring themselves against car ownership in the West. Thus in Poland, about 292,000 cars were produced in 1986 and a large chunk exported to other Comecon states (especially Hungary, which has no car industry of its own) the West and China. Yet annual domestic demand is reckoned to be 400,000.

Export quotas are not the only problem. The models are old and there are constant design modifications. And there are shortages of materials, of steel, glass and engine parts. The factories operate outdated machines and use, even in the Gorbachev era, outdated management principles. When Japanese consultants explained to the Poles exactly what shop-floor changes would be needed if they took up a modernisation contract, the personnel director exclaimed, 'We will have a revolution on our hands.' The Japanese work-team system, with its short tea breaks, intensive robot-assisted labour and voluntary breaks for volleyball, is difficult enough to graft onto the workforce in northern England. In Eastern Europe (where since the Solidarity era, workers sometimes bully their managers) the system is unthinkable. The Soviet Bloc will be saddled with inadequate production for decades to come.

The result is a queue. To buy a car in Eastern Europe you must either have the loving patience of a Franciscan, a fistful of dollars, or the bargaining instincts of a horse trader. Sometimes you must have all three. The queue for cars is, of course, notional, for it lasts for years. Money is deposited in the state savings bank in return for a lottery ticket. This decides whether you will receive your car in 1990 or 1995. The waiting time varies according to country and make of car: in East Germany you might have to wait ten years, in Poland six. If you are lucky your number will come up quickly. Then you have to pay the rest of the money and the car is yours. The price of the car is fixed at the moment of sale and so is more or less inflation-proof. Despite the burden of waiting for so long, it is by far the cheapest way to car ownership. The lottery system is shrewd in the sense that it deflects discontent, introduces the element of chance (a Polish priest once told me, 'The car lottery has brought many people Back to God. The Blessed Virgin Mary receives many requests and offerings from young couples before they set out to buy their ticket') and gives workers a stake in the country. That is the theory, anyway; it is how socialists explain this very non-socialist form of distribution. In reality it spawns corruption and a variety of markets. There is for example an effective futures market in which an aspiring motorist can trade in the promise of a Lada in 1990 for a Wartburg promised for 1992. Those who draw tickets for a car delivery within six months find ready buyers on the black market. Big speculators buy up dozens of such promises, collect the cars and put them on sale on the free market with a five hundred per cent mark-up. The tortuous ways of car purchasing have also thrown up loan sharks. If you draw a ticket for a car delivery within the year, it has to be redeemed quickly, sometimes within a week. The buyer, who had been reckoning on another two years or more to scrape up the rest of the money, has to borrow, if not from friends then from local loan sharks who operate in effect like private bankers. In Moscow and Kiev, illegal bankers will provide cash on the nail at 14 per cent interest. The have musclemen to call in bad debts.

There is another way to jump the queue and still pay the relatively low official price. Every waiting list in East and West has a priority code. Certain classes of customers are entitled to a quick sale – doctors, farmers, miners, workers with 'special achievements', invalids. Priority on the car waiting list is a perk for government officers, a sensible concession to those who have to travel widely in their jobs, an incentive for good workers.

In Poland the system used to work like this: the Minister of Machine Industry, who was in charge of car production, printed several thousand 'Talons', special coupons, which were then given to other government departments to be allocated to the people entitled to jump the queue for cars. The coupon, a piece of pink paper no bigger than a page in an exercise book, is supposed to contain the name of the recipient of the car and the make of the car. The lucky man can then travel to the factory, show it to the sales officer and collect his vehicle. But the coupons were supplied to the ministries completely blank – and they thus became part of the armoury of unofficial privileges to be bestowed by government dignitaries. A case in point was the head of the Polish government's

Planning Commission during the 1970s, Mr Tadeusz Wrzaszczyk who apart from his Talon allocation managed to get extra supplies from his friend, the Minister of Machine Industry. Mr Wrzaszczyk's deputy in the Planning Commission was Mr Jerzy Kozarzewski. His official salary in 1979 was 13,000 zloties a month, but through running a racket for his boss he managed to net 400,000 zloties a month, making him one of the richest men in Poland. The business began in 1978. Kozarzewski gave his assistant a Talon and said that he had no need for another car – the assistant should dispose of the Talon for an East German Wartburg as best he could. The assistant offered the Talon to an assistant in a butcher's shop who had always managed to secure a supply of the best cuts and joints to the chiefs of the Planning Commission. Had the assistant waited for several years she would have been able to buy a Wartburg at the official price of 155,000 zloties, had she gone to the private used car market she would have been able to buy a car instantly, but for 240,000 zloties. The Talon allowing one to jump the official car queue was therefore worth at least the difference between the official and the private price of a Wartburg. The man from the Planning Commission wrote out the shop assistant's name and she paid him 85,000 zloties. With various deductions along the way, the sum reached the pocket of Kozarzewski.

The business began to take off after that. Kozarzewski, with the help of his boss, began to release a flow of these Talons on to the black market. His assistant was spending most of his day on the Warsaw car market spinning off the coupons to farmers, private producers, managers, moonlighters, and even a professor. They would pay 100,000 zloties for a Wartburg coupon, 150,000 for a Soviet Lada and 250,000 zloties for a Polski Fiat – and would do so happily, for it meant that they could pick up the car within a few days. Eventually the Planning Commission racket had to include ever-larger circles of underworld contacts. There was no point in hanging on to such large wads of Polish currency so it was converted through third parties into dollars and into gold coins. Kozarzewski was eventually arrested, as were a number of his underworld contacts, to face charges of car fraud and abuse of privilege. Wrzaszczyk, though not facing detailed charges, was also put in jail.

Pressure from Solidarity brought a suspension of the Talon system. Too many people were playing variants on the Kozarzewski game and there was a trickle-down effect in the whole society. Doctors would be bribed to provide certificates attesting physical handicap; the recipient would jump the queue, buy his car at a bargain price and resell within days on the used car market, netting a huge profit. By 1984, with Solidarity outlawed, car coupons were back again, under a different name and distributed by 13 different ministries. Only the Solidarity Government, in 1989, managed to squash the system.

How else to buy a car? As usual, dollars are an advantage. Every Comecon country now permits its citizens to buy cars that would normally have been earmarked for export. They are usually of better quality, and can be delivered within days. The snag is that the customer has to pay not in his native currency but in dollars, pounds and Deutschmarks. In countries where possession of hard currency is forbidden or strictly limited, this simply amounts to yet another privilege for the privileged classes. In the Soviet Union those who are allowed to work abroad – advisers, say, to the Vietnamese government or ballet dancers, or writers published legally in the West, foreign traders or diplomats – receive part of their pay in Certificate Roubles, a kind of hard-currency substitute that can be used to buy goods in short supply, including cars. The truly privileged can go a step further and import Western cars. The Bolshoi Ballet prima ballerina has a Citroën and Range Rover. The chess player Anatoly Karpov has a BMW, the KGB colonel and erstwhile British correspondent Viktor Louis has six collector's models, including a 1938 Bentley convertible. The tone was set by Leonid Brezhnev, who had a fleet of luxurious Western cars given as presents during his tours; they included a Rolls Royce and a Lincoln. He would drive them fast and erratically while on holiday by the Black Sea and thought nothing of asking manufacturers to respray their presents if he was unhappy with the colour. These times, of course, have passed.

In East Germany, the right to work and travel abroad was even more difficult to achieve than in the Soviet Union. But hard currency could be transferred from relatives in the West and this in turn led to the swift purchase of an export car. For Poles, access to hard currency was not a privilege but almost a daily necessity. The black market was so pervasive and elastic that dollars were virtually the second national currency. If a Pole has large quantities of zloties, then he can change these into dollars easily and swiftly and buy an export car. There is no need to wait until an opportunity arises to work abroad. But the cars are expensive. The Solidarity Government of 1989–1990 was pledged to introduce a free market – but it was also protectionist, slapping high import taxes on Japanese and Western cars to ensure the competitiveness of domestic cars.

The preferred route to car ownership is thus more often than not the free market. It is cheaper than buying for dollars, quicker than buying in the state lottery. One of the many paradoxes of the East is that cars actually gain in value. In the West, unless they are hand-finished Morgans, they depreciate with every mile travelled and every winter survived. In Poland, every car is a Morgan.

The trip to the Aleja Krakowska in Warsaw, the road jammed bumper-to-bumper with second-hand cars waiting to be sold privately, shows the simple truth that when money loses its value any durable good in short supply becomes an investment. Few bank managers in Britain would recomend the purchase of ten refrigerators as an investment for the future; in Poland and the Soviet Union over five years those refrigerators can quadruple in value, irrespective of the fact that the icebox may have broken. Along the Aleja on a Sunday morning, there will be a five-year-old Mercedes for the equivalent of 35 years average salary, a small Polish Fiat, ten years old, goes for the same price as a new model; an eight-year-old tractor goes for the equivalent of the yield of twelve harvests from a healthy smallholding. More millions change hands than on any gambling casino. Rarely is the sum paid the result of hard toil; rather it is the final stage in a complex chain of black-market transactions by both seller and buyer. Two dealers of my acquaintaince pursued the road to fortune if not fame, on the Aleja Krakowska. One, in partnership with his brother, left Poland as a tourist in the summer of 1979. They both worked illegally as waiters in West Berlin for a month and with the help of a number of side deals managed to save four thousand marks for which they bought a very battered, scarcely functioning Mercedes. It lasted somehow or other until Warsaw where the boys re-equipped it as best they could, resprayed the bodywork (mainly to cover up the rust), and took it down to the Aleja. There they sold it for the relatively modest sum (prices were depressed at the end of the 1970s) of a million zloties. Half that sum then went towards buying two new Polski Fiats from people whose lottery tickets were about to become valid. By putting an extra 50,000 zloties on top of normal purchase, they found people willing to start standing in the queue again. Dealers, though not these brothers, often study accounts of drunk driving cases and approach anybody who has been banned from driving for a year or more in the reasonable assumption that the car is not needed and that the erstwhile driver will need money to live and to pay off court fines. The two spanking new Polski Fiats were then resold, one on the market at a 100 per cent mark-up, the other a year later when the shortage of cars had become so acute that the black-market price had soared. With further subsidiary deals, the brothers converted the four thousand marks to a fortune of hundreds of millions of zloties, enough for a substantial villa outside Warsaw and a bit left over to lay the foundations of a corduroy-jeans factory.

The second case, Andrzej, is a more conventional case study of black-market success. He started at the age of 16 as a small-time money-changer in front of hotels. With a small float of 20,000 zloties he bought dollars from tourists at a rate better than the official but still well below the true black-market level, then sold the dollars at a higher price and constantly increased his pool. This went on until one of the main currency-dealing kings of Warsaw asked him (persuaded him, say Andrzej's friends) to join his group. This was a closed shop of hotel porters, waiters, taxi drivers and free floaters who are given their float daily by one of the administrative heads of the currency racket and return it at the end of the day with a hefty profit, part of which can be retained by the dealer himself. This minimises risk – the leader of the group is responsible for paying off the police and paying fines – but is not very encouraging for a young man who wants to make his way in the world. Andrzej used cars to get out of the gang and is now a quasi-respectable dealer. He had a priveleged beginning in the business in that he dealt solely in dollars – no question of shovelling millions of zloties from one side of a table to another – and though the profits sound less spectacular (he can make about 800 dollars on a transaction) he has amassed a significant fortune of about 400,000 dollars (his wife's estimate). This in Poland was enough to buy two dachas, rent a ski chalet, run a nice car and ensure that neither he nor his family need ever work again. But he prefers to keep his wealth in dollars ('mobile wealth' he calls it) so as not to excite the interest of the tax authorities, or for that matter of rival underworld figures.

There are other odd characters in the market. Sitting in the back of a truck, supplied with a constant flow of coffee from the top of a vacuum flask, there is the Gypsy King of Warsaw. He lives in rather a grand house in the run-down suburb of Marki while his relatives live in motorised caravans anchored in nearby streets. His main source of income is Transit vans and pick-up trucks. In the Warsaw market, farmers flush with cash from the harvest go to him first. He sits picking his teeth and waiting for his aides, who prance like chamberlains in an Imperial ante-room, and sift through likely customers. Young gypsies spread throughout the market supply him with the latest prices. Vodka is essential both to dull the critical senses of the customer and to make a festival out of a hard-nosed transaction. The mood up and down the street and in the hinterland of the market is that of a nineteenth-century horse auction. Buyers demand that bonnets be lifted in the same way that their fathers once wrenched open a mare's jaws. The zloty equivalent of hundreds of thousands of pounds changes hands and the state – in the form of the official sales contract which hopelessly understates the real value of the deal – is mentioned only in laughing asides. It is the perfect place to launder money. Buy a car with dirty money and sell it the same afternoon for a small profit: that is a kind of bliss for the boys from Praga, who have crossed from their battered neighbourhood to size up business. But most Praga men, more at home running prostitutes, selling stolen furs or caseloads of whisky, are out of their depth in the car market; it is a place for professionals and for those adept at off-loading large sums of money.

The car market demanded sophisticated players because the best deals were often made by arrangement, out of hours, with go-betweens from Western Embasssies. One of the perks of being a British (or American, Canadian, Australian) diplomat in Eastern Europe was that one could import, duty-free, a sturdy Volvo, Mercedes or Rover. After three years when the diplomat's tour was over he placed a bland advertisement in a local handout along the lines of: 'Ford Granada, 1980, good condition, recently serviced in West Berlin, highest zloty offer.' Then the bidding began. Dealers made their zloty offer in anticipation of a sale on the grey-black car market. A good American car might in this way fetch seven million zloties, which at the 1988 rate of black-market exchange was seven thousand dollars. Not bad for a fairly bruised vehicle. But better still: the diplomats could then pay the zloties into the embassy account and receive the equivalent at the official rate of exchange. Seven million zloties, at that rate was closer to 35,000 dollars – a neat profit and an illustration of how even Western taxpayers are stung by the black markets of the East. The customers with the most zloties to dispose of are so-called Polonia businessmen who are licensed to trade with the West. A clever car-market dealer will therefore try to put car-trading embassies in touch with their richest customers.

There is some zest in the Warsaw, Moscow and Hungarian car markets (the Hungarian market is so devious that it has become the subject of econometric analysis – see *Soviet Studies*, 36, 1984); the same unfortunately cannot be said of the East German market. As in the neighbouring Communist countries, there is a great deal of uncertainty over what is legal or illegal. Car markets are obviously a focus of great underworld wealth. The Poles, the Russians and the Hungarians know when to turn a blind eye to a necessary market mechanism. But the Prussian civil-service traditions run deep in East Germany and it is my impression that ordinary East Germans were far more nervous about secret police (Stasi) informers than the Russians were of the KGB. A visit to the large parking lot near East Berlin's Schoenefeld airport is a rather depressing affair. As you enter the market, both buyers and sellers are charged five Ostmarks by an official attendant, his peaked cap perched at a spry angle. From that point on, in theory, the state leaves you alone until the sale is completed. But every buyer – some of them are after spare parts rather than a whole vehicle – sees an *agent provocateur* in every seller. Only the Palestinian and African students have no inhibitions, kicking wheels and getting the sellers to shine torches underneath the chassis for no very obvious reason. There is the same topsy-turvy logic of a thriving market in a country that discourages markets. A Trabant costing 8,500 East Marks on the official net goes for sixty per cent more on the Schoenefeld parking lot. The more solid Wartburg (the Trabant has in its time been compared to a faulty electric razor, a mechanised lobster and a foul-smelling hair-dryer on wheels – but still managed to convoy thousands of East Germans to the West in 1989), earns a bigger mark-up. But it is modest stuff compared to the wheeling and dealing in Warsaw. The key lies in the final phase of negotiation (which is dry – strictly no schnapps). The buyer and the seller agree to go on a test drive. In fact they want to avoid eavesdroppers. But the fear of 'provocation' is so strong that few sellers or buyers try to push a hard bargain. There was talk a while back of one seller who was wired up, recording the whole transaction for use by the East Berlin fraud squad. That anxiety serves to yield, almost by accident, a fair price.

The free markets in cars are scattered throughout Eastern Europe and are not necessarily concentrated on the capitals. Provincial markets especially are the logical destination of 'hot' vehicles. The Georgians and the Armenians who trade between their own regional markets and Moscow are adept at respraying and deleting the engine numbers of stolen cars. Now that the Moscow Fraud Division has computers, the process has become more complicated. Cars have to be bought and sold very quickly if the police are going to be fooled for long. Still, the technique is to keep moving over provincial Soviet borders since each individual car theft is the responsibility of the local police command.

The safest place to trade is probably Siberia; the police do not ask too many questions and there are large sums of cash in circulation (workers from the gas pipeline, the oil rigs or prospecting engineers are given heavy bonuses).

East European car markets are proving to be a link between organised crime in the West and the black marketeers of the East. As other chapters show, there are already different connections – in drugs, prostitution and techno-banditry – but the East–West car market is not of the same calibre, usually improvised by gangs of émigrés and dictated by the need for a quick one-off profit.

Stolen cars have to be disposed of swiftly, before they are registered on a computer, so the short sprint from Austria and Northern Italy into Hungary has become a favoured route. Yugoslav car thieves based in West Germany have also been offloading hot cars in the Balkans. This is strictly smash-and-grab crime. However, a degree of sophistication is creeping in. Some Swedish citizens, including Polish émigrés, decided in 1986 that there was a huge demand in Eastern Europe for Western luxury limousines, and enough hard cash available to make the operation very profitable. The gang used forged driving licenses to rent cars in Copenhagen and either drove straight to the Gedser–Warnemuende ferry (which takes vehicles to East Germany) or to Sweden to board the ferry to Poland. Control on the ferries is minimal and the Polish and East German customs guards check mainly the engine volume and the year of production rather than demanding the purchase certificate. One variant of the racket was to rent a car in the West (West Berlin is a favoured target) and let a friend steal it. The client then waits for some time before reporting the theft – in seven hours, the friend should have cleared the East German and Polish borders. Once in Poland the BMWs and Mercedes changed hands so quickly that the original, forged purchase certificate became irrelevant. Most of the current owners bought their cars – about 200 were dumped before the gang was unravelled – quite legally from another legal owner.

East–West theft is embarassing. It highlights the fact that the government is tolerating a semi-legal market because of the deficiencies of central planning. 'Such a market cannot and will not continue forever,' explained Dr Ludwik Kracucki, a wily ideological adviser to the Polish Communist leadership. 'That we make use of some market mechanisms to meet demand does not mean we accept them as a permanent feature of our system. We do not like crime and corruption any more than you do – and by the way not all markets produce crime – but until our system of production becomes more efficient then we must live in this state of compromise.' But what is the chance of the East European car industry ever gearing up to demand? Minimal. There are ways of choking back demand – raising the price of petrol, making more spare parts available, improving public transport – without resorting to drastic police-state behaviour (for example by rationing cars to one per household). But the fact is that most Communist authorities do not radically object to the existence of car markets, since they sponge up such huge sums of black-market money.

The various financial ministries in both Poland and the Soviet Union are worried though that much potential revenue is eluding them and the police too seem uncertain whether to treat the car market as a centre of corruption and criminal activity (and therefore a high-priority target) or a slight embarrassment. Certainly, in a more mercenary vein, officials seem to regret that a great source of bribes is passing them by. Some of this frustration is evident in a report drawn up by Warsaw's Central Anti-Speculation Commission. The car market, it says, 'evokes justified protests from those who would like to see our car markets working normally according to the sound principles of supply and demand, as well as the anger of those who are indignant at the easy and enormous earnings of people dealing with the sales of new cars.' The report, not published in the official press, then went on to propose either: (*a*) the setting up of a state monopoly to control the selling of all second-hand cars (though this would actually run counter to the property rights guaranteed by the Constitution) or (*b*) treating all second-hand car sales as speculation (an obvious nonsense as black marketeers must form only a fraction of the two million private-car owners in Poland and the right to sell at the price you think fair is a fundamental civil and economic right). The report was just groping in the dark in the absence of any clear political guidance. In East Germany and Czechoslovakia (where the main black market is in spare parts) the waiting period for private cars was a major source of discontent. The Polish government, smarting from years of upheaval following the overthrow of Gierek, the rise and fall of Solidarity, and the bitterness of martial law, was reluctant to open up new consumer wounds. The Minister of Domestic Trade suggested in a confidential report that special companies should be set up to deal in second-hand cars and that any car less than three years old should be sold through these state agencies. Cars older than three years could be sold privately but only under state supervision. The Ministry of

Finance, which could see an El Dorado of bribery opening up if these suggestions were followed, made a counter-proposal: before entering a car market, state experts and agents would closely examine each vehicle and fix a price framework according to its technical condition. Under no circumstances could a private market price be more than the official price of a brand-new car. Mutual jealousy and tensions between the two ministries have not helped and the result has been complete paralysis on the issue of controlling one of the world's most lucrative black markets. The Solidarity government has not come up with any miraculous solutions either.

The state has set itself the responsibility of planning the economic life of its citizens. But it cannot produce enough and has, in planning future production, constantly underestimated demand. Faced with such a huge need for passenger cars it has been forced to accept a form of market economy. But the confusion of ideology with economic reality, and the legal turmoil, means that the market is imperfect and inefficient. This in turn has helped to create a criminal automobile class. One of the pitfalls of reform under Gorbachev is that in the first years of market experiment it will spawn a new generation of criminal entrepreneurs. If one frees the market at one level – handing over car distribution to independent operators – but is unable to increase production in the state-run factories, then the result is simply astronomical pricing. The most the state can hope for is to skim off the profits of the car dealers. The police, responsible for enforcing unenforceable laws, are pushed offstage, to gape helplessly at the growth of a new breed of crook.

PART III

Subterranean Markets

7

The Soviet Underworld

Against all expectations, Ola Cherkasov died in bed. It was, admittedly, a prison bed with hard springs and rough blankets but he at least went quietly, in his sleep; the passing of a Soviet Godfather. In his day Cherkasov was the acknowledged head of the Moscow underworld, one of the early founders of Western-style organised crime. Like the *padroni* of Corleone, he lived modestly (though he affected black shiny leather shoes, conspicuous footwear in the Soviet Union). He received tribute from scores of footsoldiers, employed a private banker and a crooked lawyer, and paid retainer fees to several Moscow detectives. His 'family' was connected not by blood but by shared labour-camp experiences. The Gulag archipelago with its network of camps and prisons has created a real criminal class in the Soviet Union. Cherkasov when I saw him was already a trembling old man; but he became young with storytelling. How they settled accounts in the camps! Imagine slicing a man's finger off, as punishment for some infringement of the mafia code, in a place where no knives were allowed. The problems, the problems! He had fond memories of the political prisoners, many of whom became victims three or four times over by being exploited by the crude rituals of the criminal inmates. Cherkasov protected some, threw others to the dogs. It is difficult to see cruelty in an old man, but it comes out in the language; in the foulmouthed verbal combinations of a virtually impenetrable camp slang. Cherkasov loved his stories because his 'family' was connected by gulag myth and memory: it was an instrument of power. Cherkasov was the king of his camp and so became king of the underworld after his release; outside was not so very different from inside. Later, organised crime became a more sophisticated creature, part of the market society, serving customers rather than delivering victims. The simple ability to survive and face down opponents was not enough in Gorbachev's Soviet Union, where life was accelerating. Police and Procuracy officers were rotated more quickly, were better educated, less liable to accept bribes. New opportunities were opening up for channelling dirty money into the legal economy, for making more cash in a year that Cherkasov had minted in a decade.

His power seeped away; he had hoped for an orderly succession but instead there were fights that tumbled onto the streets, Palermo moved East. Cherkasov the king was arrested for selling pornographic magazines: it was the final blow to his crumbling status. Shortly before he died, an imprisoned member of his 'family' carried out his last wishes and slipped onto his feet a pair of black laminated leather shoes.

Everyday life in the Communist world, crippled by an antiquated and patently inefficient central planning system, is suffering from arterial blockages, a kind of consumer sclerosis. The distribution of cars, food supply, all the fundamental services from birth to death, function at their lowest level of competence; illegal or semi-legal markets have sprung up to keep society alive. In the West such markets are of course considered normal and desirable. But there is another category of market for goods and services that even in the West would be considered criminal: for gambling, moonshine alcohol, drugs or prostitutes. How do these illegal markets operate in the Soviet Bloc? How deep are the criminal roots of the capitalist revival in Eastern Europe? How will Gorbachev deal with them? And how, with market forces unbottled in other sectors, will the criminal underworld adapt?

Walter Lippman, writing in 1931 in an America still influenced by Prohibition, took the view that organised crime has a social function. Whereas an ordinary criminal – a burglar, say – is wholly predatory, the underworld offers something in return to the respectable members of society:

'The underworld has a different status. Its activities are in some degree countenanced by the respectable; from among them it draws its revenues; among them it finds many of its patrons; by them it is, in various ways, protected.'

Organised crime in other words performs services for which there is some kind of public demand. In the first place, says Lippman, there are the 'persistent and outlawed human appetites'. 'There may be those who have never craved liquor or lusted for women or wanted to bet, but such men are too rare to be counted in considering social policy.' But organised crime, under capitalism, serves another function.

'Given an oversupply of labour and an industry in which no considerable amount of capital or skill is required to enter it, the conditions exist under which racketeering can flourish. The effort to unionise in the face of a surplus of labour incites to the use of violence and thus to preserve and enhance the worker's standard of living. Labor unionism in such trades tends to fall into the control of dictators who are often corrupt and not often finical about enlisting gangsters to enforce the closed shop. The employers, on the other hand, faced with the constant threat of cut-throat competition, are subject to easy temptation to pay gangsters for protection against competitors. The protection consists in driving the competitors from the field.

'The fact that racketeering seems to infest the small, unstable, disorganised industries suggests rather strongly that we have here a perverse effort to overcome the insecurity of highly competitive capitalism, that the underworld through its very crude devices serves that need for social organisation which reputable society has not yet learned how to satisfy. Indeed, one might go further and at least inquire whether certain forms of racketeering are not the result under adverse conditions of the devotion of legislatures, courts and public opinion to the philosophy of *laissez-faire*.

'It would appear at least that rackets are in large degree perversions of the search for economic security, a diseased compensation in the lower reaches of capitalism for the instability of proletarian life, and the terrific struggle for existence which prevails in a population uprooted from the land, unprotected and undisciplined by its own guilds, and subjected to the daily hazards of the open market.'

It is instructive to compare the rise of organised crime in early-capitalist America with the astonishingly fast development of the criminal underworld in the present-day Soviet Union. There are, of course, stark differences. The same people satisfying the 'outlawed appetites' for prostitutes or moonshine are also running, or exploiting the car market and are active in several other more or less legitimate activities. Gorbachev has drawn an invisible frontier between those markets operating in everyday life and those catering for 'outlawed appetites'; he has in this sense helped to create the idea of organised crime in the Soviet Union. Previously, the frontiers were blurred, there was one broad spectrum of illicit black-market activity: no distinction was made between selling smuggled food or privately produced meat, and selling moonshine. Nowadays, officially licensed private shops legally sell coffee and chocolate that has almost certainly been smuggled across the border, while some 40 per cent of police activity in all the major Soviet-Bloc countries is taken up with raiding alcohol stills. There are other differences too: obviously, organised crime has not moved into the labour unions. But with the rise of the co-operative –that is, the legal, private–sector, organised crime is enjoying boom years. Lippman's diagnosis, that organised crime satisfies a primitive need for economic security, applies to the flourishing protection rackets in several Soviet cities. More, the new Soviet criminal gangs provide a negotiating partner. Isolated prostitutes (often without pimps in the Soviet Bloc) benefit from organisation, since their influence on police control is minimal. A mafia godfather has infinitely more clout with police and politicians, and can let her work undisturbed; to forward 20 per cent of her earnings to the mafia may be irksome but it makes some sort of economic sense as long as there is the prospect of police harassment. Petty criminals – small-time drug dealers, whores, loan-sharks – are both the victims and beneficiaries of organised crime. The ordinary citizen is by and large untouched; he is a customer for the services provided by the mafia.

Gorbachev's encouragement of the co-operative movement has altered the terrain for organised crime in the Soviet Union, brought it closer to Lippman's America. Like prostitutes or taxi drivers or illegal distillers, proprietors of private businesses in the Soviet Bloc are lonely and vulnerable; they are forced to break the law in a number of small ways, but, most difficult of all, they are having to compete in a system that has drained the competitive instinct. For Jusefa, the Jewish restaurant next to Moscow's Paveletski Station, the problems began soon after the gala opening. The mini-bus, used by the 12-man co-operative to deliver food, was stolen and, when it was found a few days later, was no more than a burnt-out shell. A replacement car was immobilised by sugar in the petrol tank, the wiring in the restaurant was sliced, the windows smashed. The demands for protection money began to trickle in. Yuri Peresovski, the president of the co-operative, was asked by telephone for 500 roubles a month protection fee. The restaurant (at least in 1989) was making good money – the takings were over 1,000 roubles on opening night – but Peresovski refused. Then the protection mafia used the most poisonous of Soviet-Bloc weapons – rumour. Soon it was said, credibly but untruthfully, that the nationalist, anti-Semitic group Pamyat was beating up clients coming out of Jusefa. Takings dropped to under 400 roubles a night. Similar tactics were tried against the Lasagna, Moscow's new Italian restaurant, and the '36'. Moscow rumours said that the Lasagna had been destroyed by a bomb, that the boss of the '36' was about to be killed in an underworld contract. Suddenly, eating out seemed rather dangerous to the Muscovite. In this strange world of contained competition, where restaurants and clothes boutiques fight for trade but the rest of the economy muddles on as usual it is difficult to find out how the co-operatives are coming to terms with the threat from organised crime. In 1988 Colonel Dr Alexander Gurov, head of a Soviet task force on organised crime, asked 109 colleagues throughout the Soviet Union for their assessment of the co-operative movement and its relationship to crime. Over 80 per cent said that co-operatives were being blackmailed, 52 per cent said co-operatives were regularly paying protection money. The protection racket was spreading: doctors with legal private practices were receiving menacing visits and private taxi drivers, operating from profitable places like airports, were being pressed to hand over the equivalent of 150 pounds a month.

But co-operatives offer other opportunities for organised crime. Above all, Soviet gangsters can launder illicit cash through the accounts of co-operatives. Some 25 per cent of Soviet co-operatives are said to have Soviet mafiosi as sleeping partners. In Poland, a similar pattern applies to so-called Polonia companies, set up by Western citizens of Polish origin to stimulate small-business exports. Since such companies are having to import raw materials in dollars and make much of their profit in the local currency, zloties, they are an active participant in the black market. The most notable difference between Italian and American mafia profits is dictated by the institutional and informal barriers dividing the legal and illegal or outright criminal economies. In Italy, even after some strict anti-Mafia legislation in 1982, capital moved with ease from the narcotics trade into the building sector, the haulage business or the stock market. In the US there are tough, and enforced, laws on capital from suspect sources. The result is that illegally earned money often stays in the illegal market, moving from heroin sales into gambling or prostitution. Indeed Las Vegas, as a gambling centre, was virtually the creation of gangsters looking for a profitable outlet for their cash. The legal restrictions are such that it is actually safer for the US mafia to keep their money circulating in the illegal market than to try and break into respectability.

Soviet organised crime is trying to use the co-operatives and the private sector in general to build, like its Italian counterpart, a bridge to the respectable world. One reason for this is that there are only a limited number of ways one can spend a rouble fortune. Building an extravagant villa with a swimming pool in a socialist society attracts suspicion rather than admiration. Ostentatious wealth is still grounds enough for the Soviet police to open an investigation. Partnership in a legal, profitable private company is the perfect alibi, the easiest road to the laundry.

The recent history of Soviet mafias shows that even before the consolidation of Gorbachev, this was the natural trend for the underworld. The entrepreneurial instinct flashes and sparks.

Three criminal generations have come and gone since Cherkasov was at his peak. The first to slip his control was 'Mongol', so called because of his high cheekbones and slit eyes. He was born during the war, but by the 1960s had broken away from Cherkasov and was already in command of his own mafia – 31 soldiers and officers, including seven women. Mongol had been in prison but not in the Siberian camps; his was a different nobility, less sentimental, enforcing discipline with brutality. He seized control of the Moscow drug business by having his men pose as customers. They forced themselves into the flats of the dealers, bundled them into cars and tortured them with burning cigarettes. The dealers were persuaded to reveal the full lists of their customers and were then murdered. Mongol was captured in the early 1970s and his gang was shattered. His successor, a former officer in the Mongol mafia, was nicknamed 'The Japanese'. He rebuilt the group, armed them with guns, and moved into assault and blackmail. Eventually he too was trapped: the arrest, in 1981, was one of the most spectacular ever witnessed in Moscow. 'The Japanese' had summoned his officers for a strategy meeting, but one of them had tipped off the police. Hundreds of militiamen crowded into the backyard of an apartment block and the area was circled by 32 patrol cars.

By the early 1980s, according to Colonel Gurov, there were mafia groups everywhere, each controlling a rigidly defined territory. In Moscow, organised crime had hold of the Balschicha, Luberzy, Puschkino and Orechovo-Sujevo districts. There were powerful 'families' in the Ukraine in Kiev, Lvov, Odessa, Donetsk and Brezhnev's old power base in Dnepropetrovsk. There were mafias in Moldavia, and in the towns of Tambov, Pensa, Yaroslav and Perm. Gurov believes that none of these mafias has been completely broken. Not all, however, operate at the same level of sophistication. At the lowest level, there are simply organised groups of professional criminals who plan crimes together, form coalitions but have no power. Then there are similar groups who are protected by corrupt officials. And finally, the most influential clans, under single unified command and with political clout. At the top level, the mafia operates on the Cosa Nostra or Sicilian model, with a military hierarchy: liaison officers, footsoldiers, hit-men, intelligence and counter-intelligence, a banker, and adjutant.

The second generation emerged in the 1980s in the ugly shape of

Sergei 'Boxer' Vasiliev. He began by taking over the thimbles racket in Leningrad. As described in the chapter on gambling, this game is a variant of Find-the-Lady; a good team makes 20,000 roubles a month. In Leningrad, there were several such teams, mainly Georgians. Vasiliev's men bullied the Georgians out of business. This improved Vasiliev's cash flow. His mafia now set itself up in competition with the officially run second-hand car market. As the state persistently under-valued traded-in cars, Vasiliev's men had no problems finding people willing to sell him cars at a generous mark-up. Fleets of cars were driven every week to the more remote republics of the Soviet Union and sold at great profit. A combination of brawn and bribery had brought Vasiliev from a clearly criminal position into a quite legitimate business (in the Western understanding – 'speculation' is still a grave crime in the Soviet Union). Boxer was by now in a very powerful position: the car market is the pulse of a city. Two things happened. First, Vasiliev started to live according to his wealth – something that Mongol or Japanese, schooled by prison, would never have attempted. He drove Western cars, modest enough in the West – Toyotas, Ford Granadas – but a sensation in Leningrad. More, he changed them every three weeks. Vasiliev had plenty of enemies inside the underworld; now he began to make them outside. Second, Boxer felt the drive to respectability. With his car profits, he moved into the fashion business. It was easy enough to put a vice on the legion of amateur or private tailors in Leningrad. Soon he had a monopoly on the production of fashionable clothes and forced boutiques to accept them. To the tailors he paid 'wholesale' rates, and sold, of course, at 'retail'. At his peak, Boxer had 150 employees arranging deals throughout the city. In Britain he would have been awarded the OBE; in Leningrad, in April 1987, he was arrested. Eventually he was tried and sentenced to several years in jail but for the police it was a difficult case. Boxer's men intimidated witnesses so crudely that they had to be permanently guarded. Even now, with Boxer behind bars, at least three witnesses have suffered serious accidents crossing the street.

The third, emergent generation does not have the same dominant personalities. They try to stay clean, leaving day-to-day negotiation to subordinates. Cash is invested in the co-operatives by front-men; at parties, they are sober, with carefully cut hair. They have no political opinions and are therefore welcome in politicians' homes. If bullets ring out at night, they deplore the rising crime rate over breakfast. There are, of course, exceptions. The southern republics are still the wild frontier:

at about the same time that Mikhail Gorbachev was addressing the Party about dragging the Soviet Union into the 21st century, Narik Karganjan, one of the main Tashkent godfathers, was peppered by a machine-gun fired from a passing car. He was about to have dinner, and, as was customary, had surrounded the restaurant with eight gunmen.

The saga of the New York gangs charts the rise and the gradual absorption of different immigrant groups: there were Jewish gangsters, Irish, Italian and, nowadays, Russian émigrés. Organised crime has become an evolutionary stage in metropolitan life: what has happened to the grandchildren of Al Capone? Perhaps they are college lecturers or (their grandfather would have approved) on Wall Street. Organised crime contains both brutal villains and entrepreneurs; the businessman, in Italy and the USA, is now in the ascendancy. It should be no surprise that a similar process is under way in the Soviet Union. Men like Boxer in Leningrad are 'venture capitalists', speculators. But they go beyond that: their gangs and mafias which control billion-dollar criminal industries (notably illegal distilleries) and which influence the black markets that support everyday life, have all the hallmarks of fully-fledged capitalist enterprises. Soviet mafias tend naturally towards monopoly, and this limits their scope. Whereas the Sicilian mafia, via the narcotics trade, has developed global ambitions and strategies, Soviet mafias confine themselves to controlling the business of a single Soviet Republic, whether it be Uzbekistan, Tadzhikistan, Azerbaidjan, Georgia or Kirghizia. Sometimes this requires corrupting officials and politicians in Moscow too, but at no time has there been a mafia that stretches throughout the Soviet Union; geography inhibits the monopoly. But, on a regional level, gangs and mafias function like firms fighting for a bigger share of the market. At the sharp end, these market disputes can end with gunfire and knifings. But more commonly, weaker gangs are absorbed, gang leaders co-opted until the mafia controls the business. In a centrally planned economy, it makes more sense for a single mafia to offer weighty bribes to the local political chieftain than for rival gang leaders to buy off relatively low-level police officers.

Mafia-supported enterprises, in West and East, have the competitive advantage of being able to raise large amounts of capital quickly. A normal capitalist concern builds up capital by accumulating profit over years and has access to loans and other capital-raising techniques. A 'capitalist' (that is, private or co-operative) company in the Soviet Bloc is much more restricted. Borrowing is difficult, stock markets (so far only in Budapest) primitive, and profits subject to steep and fluctuating taxation. To set up a private car-repair shop in Poland would require start-up capital of anything between 200 and 300 million zloties. Yet the average monthly salary in early 1990 was around 400,000 zloties. But consider this: 400,000 zloties at the black-market rate was less than $40. Any criminal operation with access to dollars could provide the capital without much ado. This is happening throughout the Soviet Bloc as doors open to private enterprise. Either criminal profits are being ploughed into private industry, or criminal cash is being loaned, at competitive rates, to aspiring entrepreneurs. Schumpeter, in his *Theory of Economic Development* (1959) identifies the entrepreneur as someone who invests resources that come from outside his personal estate. But whereas Schumpeter was referring to the banking system, in the Soviet Bloc the function is increasingly taken over by mafia money. 'Boxer' raised his start-up capital from the thimble business: the 20,000 roubles earned by one of his teams in a month was the equivalent of over eight months of honest work. In an immobile system, the man with mobile capital is king.

The emerging entrepreneurial revolution in the Soviet Bloc has also dictated a shift in the relationship between organised crime and the authorities. In the Brezhnev era, the growth of the black market was a substitute for economic reform, that is, in the absence of political will to improve and overhaul economic production, it became policy to tolerate black-market forces which were at least satisfying the needs of some consumers. Accepting the black market was tantamount to encouraging it and led, inevitably, to political and legal immunity for the main marketeers. The mafias took this one step further, not only making the black market a substitute for reform, but also presenting organised crime as an alternative for government. The Uzbekistan mafia was a direct reflection of weak and inefficient government, was accepted because of a general contempt for the authorities, and operated according to strange cabalistic rites.

Uzbekistan is the cotton-producing centre of the Soviet Union. The textile dominates the life of the Southern Republic; schoolchildren have their classes cancelled to help in the harvest, and women work on the farms or in the spinning mills. The American Civil War put an end to cotton imports and since then Czars and Party chiefs have encouraged, demanded, that Uzbekistan supply the cotton for the country. No other major industry was developed.

The Uzbekistan mafia arose from this 'monoculture'. Sharaf Rashidov understood cotton, and more valuable still, understood Moscow's dependence on Uzbekistan's prime product. Brezhnev complained about shoe production, but never complained about shirts; one Republic and, effectively one man, Rashidov, could determine the Soviet Union's ability to supply clothes to its people. Rashidov was head of the Uzbek communist party for 24 years, during which he was awarded 10 Orders of Lenin for his loyalty and his remarkable cotton figures. The revisionist accounts of Rashidov portray him as a typically corrupt Brezhnev crony who manipulated his friendship with the Soviet leader to enrich himself and his confederates. It was not quite like that. Rashidov was a quiet, introspective man who preferred writing his memoirs, and forgettable poetry, to making deals. He had been a soldier in the war, and a Party man all his adult life. As he climbed the ladder he brought his friends and family with him; that was the Central Asian way. A non-voting member of the Politburo, he travelled to Moscow frequently and fortified his position. Brezhnev was his patron, and Brezhnev could demand tribute: when the Kremlin leader asked for an increase in cotton production, Rashidov really wanted to oblige.

It says something for Rashidov's intelligence that he soon realised it was impossible to step up cotton output at the pace required by Moscow. Cotton is a vulnerable crop and, barring a revolution in agricultural science, there is only one way to grow it. The margin of improvement comes only from cutting out wastage, modernising the storage. This Rashidov did, but there were no miracles. And so, as he was a man who preferred consensus, as he did not want to lose face in the Politburo, as he owed his patron good results, he introduced one of the Biggest Lies in Soviet history. He added several hundreds of thousands of tonnes to the cotton harvest every year. Each collective and state farm inflated its harvest. Each regional director added some further percentage points, and by the time the report reached the Ministry for a final rounding-off, it was an entirely fictional sum. Those who could have blown the whistle in Moscow were handed suitcases full of roubles. The whole Republic was in thrall to a lie. Naturally, the Uzbeks were paid according to the fictional production figure, and the money trickled down. There, said the Moscow press, was a man who could make Soviet agriculture work! A personality cult was encouraged by Rashidov's colleagues since it could block more intensive questioning, could scotch rumour. Gold busts of Rashidov and Brezhnev were sculpted in the Uzbek academy of arts, tapestries depicted the two leaders in gold thread, a documentary film-maker was engaged for a biographical sketch.

To keep such a large secret for such a long time, many people have to be rewarded for their silence, made active members of the conspiracy. Most of these new-found conspirators were content with promotion, since, in Soviet Central Asia, high position brings wealth. Akhmadzan Adylov wanted a little more. He was a Hero of Socialist Labour and the prototype of three commissioned novels that depicted a brave, outspoken communist fighting for literacy and progress. Adylov ran the Fergana Valley region like a feudal chieftain. On the grounds of his estate, surrounded by armed men on the farm payroll as gardeners, he kept peacocks, 50 pure-bred horses, and several mistresses (though not, presumably, on the same stretch of lawn). Rashidov had appointed him to run three state farms whose productivity was essential to the cotton figure. There were 30,000 workers under his control and twice a week, he would drive around the estates, bullying the workers. If he saw any slacking, they were brought in for punishment at the end of the day. Typically, Adylov would address his workers from a granite pedestal in front of a silver bust of Lenin. Offending workers could be stripped and beaten in public; others had ice-cold water poured under their shirts. In private, he would supervise the branding of workers and personally whip delinquents, including pregnant women. Those identified as persistent slackers were set to work, for 15 hours a day, digging underground tunnels to join the office buildings. This was effectively a prison: one man testified during the Adylov investigation that he was beaten unconscious after refusing to accept a foreman's job. He had refused, he said, because those who took on responsible positions invariably 'die in three or four years, from a stomach disorder or a car accident, or simply disappear.'

Adylov's case, although a perverse extreme, demonstrated that there was quite simply no government in Uzbekistan. Loyalty to Rashidov and his secret had replaced any other criterion for preferment; there were no controls. The only requirement, apart from a successful harvest, was a perfumed relationship with Moscow. The climate of lawlessness created a profusion of rackets. The various warlords allowed dozens of 'families' to run the black market in housing, in cars, in drugs. Educational diplomas were bought and sold; so were jobs in the Party, at university, in the police, in hospitals. The system of tribute – cash presents offered to one's superior on his birthday, his wedding anniversary, on national holidays – doubled and trebled income. Rich fathers would buy jobs for their sons in the sure knowledge that it would be a good financial investment. The mafia involvement in this immense network is almost impossible to define, since the whole Republic, 20 million people, appeared to be active in some form of patron–client relationship. The boss of the drug mafia paid his tribute to 'his' regional Party chief – but did that make the politician into a godfather, or just another bribed policeman? The Knapp Commission which investigated police corruption in New York (in 1971) divided bent policemen into either 'meat-eaters' (who aggressively misuse their power for personal gain) or 'grass-eaters' (who passively accept the pay-offs). But the Uzbek government and mafia chieftains – interdependent and often inter-changeable – were omnivores. Perhaps the only grass-eater in the Uzbek elite was Rashidov himself; it was enough for him to survive to become rich. Mafiosi, by any definition – drug dealers, say – were elected to the Supreme Soviet and arranged, or bought, the highest Soviet awards.

This blurring of the criminal and the respectable (that would be the envy of the old men in Palermo and Corleone – how dearly they would like to be declared Commendatore della Repubblica!) paralysed the Soviet authorities even after the death of Brezhnev, Rashidov's protector. How was one to clean up the stables in Tashkent when the Uzbek militia were moonlighting as personal bodyguards to mafia chieftains? It was as if the mafia had ousted the Communist Party; only another *coup d'état*, an armed invasion, could bring the Republic to rights.

A few months after the death of Brezhnev, the head of the anti-corruption squad (OBKhSS) in Bukhara was caught accepting bribes; the local police chief and two department heads were arrested. In the old days, this could have been quietly forgotten. Under Chernenko, with Gorbachev coming up fast on the inside track, it was decided to take the matter seriously. At least for a month or two. A team was sent from Moscow to investigate.

The Moscow detectives discovered soon enough that the whole Bukhara elite was involved. The Party chief of the city, Karimov, was arrested. The police bluffed their way past Karimov's bodyguards, saying they had brought presents for the chief, and found him hungover after an all-night party. The handcuffs were slapped on him and he was hustled out to the car. The number plates were changed – to dodge the Bukhara police road blocks – and Karimov was delivered to the Moscow plane.

Karimov's villa was searched, and his garden dug up, producing a

coffer of Czarist gold, jewellery, watches, three suitcases of rouble
notes. The Uzbek mafia felt twinges of anxiety. One investigator was
offered a million roubles (tempting for an officer earning 365 roubles a
month) if the Bukhara case was treated as a local affair and the
defendents tried by an Uzbek court. But Karimov was already giving the
investigators new leads: he admitted paying Yuri Churbanov, deputy
Interior Minister and Brezhnev's son-in-law, 10,000 roubles. The
reason for the bribe? Karimov wanted to ensure that a report on
shortages in Bukhara did not go further up the ladder in Moscow.
Specifically, Karimov was worried about the cigarette shortage, created
partly because he had clinched a deal with a black marketeer to drive up
the price of illegally sold cigarettes. Karimov's fortune in tributes had
been spent in setting up scores of dummy trading companies with a
turnover of hundreds of thousands of roubles. Those profits were in turn
converted into gold coins and ingots, and into a hectic social life.

The Bukhara trail led to the heart of the cotton scandal. The chief
investigator, Telman Glydan, was threatened with assassination every
step of the way. When he was delivering a suspect by plane to Moscow,
the pilot noticed only just in time that a steel cord had been tied across
the runway. Glydan's men bought air tickets in false names, used army
helicopters, regularly changed their numberplates, wore bullet-proof
vests. When Adylov was interrogated he told the prosecutor: 'You'll put
us behind bars now. So what? Fifteen years from now, we'll put you all
away and destroy your children. I'll find millions of roubles to do it.'
This was not an idle boast. Colonel Gurov estimates that a current
murder contract in the Soviet mafia costs between 30,000 and 100,000
roubles. In Rashidov's heyday, professional killing – for instance, of
farm directors who refused to inflate the cotton quota – was far cheaper.
By 1988, the investigation, which had strayed into a labyrinth of
specialised mafias, had succeeded in arresting the Republic's premier,
four central committee secretaries, two ministers, six provincial party
chiefs, and hundreds of lesser officials. Churbanov and eight members
of the Uzbek mafia were handed long prison sentences. And Rashidov
committed suicide.

Rashidov was buried in a fine mausoleum in the centre of Tashkent,
near the Lenin museum. The tomb was a source of pilgrimage for
Uzbeks who failed to believe that he was connected with the mafia; roses
and carnations piled up day by day. In 1988, at dead of night, his body
was removed and buried in an anonymous grave in a remote village,
Rashidov's birthplace.

Other Soviet republics face similar, though perhaps not quite such penetrating purges. What Rashidov achieved for cotton, others might be accomplishing for rice, or maize, or livestock. The purge thus signalled that Gorbachev would not tolerate any coalition (or, as in Uzbekistan, a full-scale merger) between local governments and organised crime. But it went further than that. There was a loose politico-mathematical formula, along the lines of: Brezhnev ally=corrupt governor=mafia overlord=poisoned obstructive bureaucracy=opposition to reform. If there were traces of any element of this formula, Gorbachev pounced. When, in 1988, there was a fierce controversy between Armenia and Azerbaidjan, Gorbachev's spokesmen privately blamed the entrenched mafias in these republics. The Soviet authorities were about to crack down on these gangs and the mafiosi responded by fanning nationalist discontent to deflect attention from their activities, ran the logic. When earthquake assistance went astray after the deadly tremors in Armenia in the winter of 1988, Gorbachev himself blamed the Armenian mafia. It is of course true that Armenia and Azerbaidjan can boast elaborately organised criminal networks. But there was no real proven connection, no evidence offered of political calculation by the mafias. Gorbachev, it seems, is convinced that nationalist unrest – and the threat to unravel the Soviet empire – is the most potent challenge to his reform policies. It is difficult to say so aloud since that would acknowledge a fundamental flaw in perestroika (namely, that economic restructuring cannot be carried out at a uniform pace). And so gangsters, an easy enough target, were invoked.

This was more than sleight-of-hand; it is fundamental to the Gorbachev line that the fight against corruption equals the fight for reform. But this is not a necessary equation. First, there are many opposed to Gorbachev's reforms who have no active interest in corruption: steelworkers, say, or pensioners. Second, political corruption, though it might ebb and flow, is not endemic to any particular economic or political system. There is no reason to believe that links between party or police officials and organised crime will disappear in a reformed socialist system. Finally, Brezhnev protégés, and those they protect, are not necessarily opposed to reform. Gorbachev, after all, rose and rose under Brezhnev.

But can one go further? Are not the Soviet entrepreneurial gangsters natural suporters of a reform that is supposed to encourage private initiative? Is it a bad thing that the Soviet mafia is laundering its money through co-operatives? After all, how clean was the money that funded the capitalism of the Victorian era? Surely, one might argue, as long as the relationship between organised crime and government does not approach the Uzbek nadir, as long as violence and blatant intimidation is kept in check, surely there is something positive to be harnessed? Walter Lippman wrote on similar lines about American organised crime in the 1930s; Prohibition was an unreasonable policy, the bootleggers were providing a valuable service, why not channel this energy?

There is a fatal seductiveness about this argument. The encouragement of organised crime can never, of course, become official policy, least of all in a communist state where social envy is such a potent mobilising force. But even quiet tolerance of the mafias would be a misjudgement. True, they accumulate capital in a system that now acknowledges this as a virtue. But the mafia, in West and East, is deeply uncompetitive. It has, as Thomas Schelling writes (*Journal of Public Law*, vol. 20, no. 1, 1971) a hankering for monopoly; shootings and murders are in the name of repressing competition, because, despite the flashes of entrepreneurialism, organised crime is not efficient. The Mafia has traces of capitalism, but it also embodies some collectivist attitudes. Organised crime functions not only as a firm, but also as a trade union, organising individuals who might not be able to organise themselves or survive without an organisation. As Colonel Gurov reports, many of the current Soviet mafias, such as the so-called 'Administration' clan in Khabarovsk, operate social support funds. These finance the legal defence of arrested mafiosi, arrange regular food parcels and support relatives. That was once common practice among Sicilian Mafia families but is now rarely observed. Jailed mafiosi are assumed to be rich enough to bribe prison warders and arrange their lives themselves. The Soviet mafia practice apes the state itself; the mafioso does his day's work and expects to be looked after unto the grave.

The debate about the true nature of oranised crime matters because it frames the correct social response. If the legal marketplace is to be expanded in the Soviet Bloc, should not the market for gambling, alcohol and other 'appetites' be loosened too? Much depends on how organised crime would exploit the opening. Schelling argues that the legalisation of gambling would prove a boon, because it would expose the fundamental inefficiency of the mafia. 'The Organisation is skilled and experienced in the *suppression* of rival gambling services, especially in suppressing rival *illegal* gambling by collusion with the police. Its success, with or without the police, is appreciably due to the inability of the bookmaker to seek the protection of the law.' The history of Prohibition and its aftermath suggests strongly that organised crime does not thrive in the face of legal competition. Gorbachev then should be consistent and legalise some of the presently criminal markets. At the same time he should re-tool the economy, create an adequate infrastructure of services that would rob the mafias of some of their functions. If the Soviet banking system were more responsive to the needs of private enterprise, then the whole loan-sharking division of the Moscow mafia would collapse.

A great deal more should be done if Gorbachev is to establish a *moral* basis to his reforms, if he is to carry out his promise to shape and purify the New Socialist Man. As in Italy, there are two conflicting attitudes to organised crime. The first says: the mafia does not exist, it is simply a collection of patron–client attitudes active in the legal and criminal worlds. There is no conspiracy. The second says: the mafia is everywhere, it has penetrated every institution and, though not every mafia relationship leads to murder or a payoff, it is as tenacious as a spreading tumour. Both attitudes foster a kind of paralysis. Gorbachev's Soviet Union is only just admitting to the existence of a prostitution problem (previously officials would swear that there were no prostitutes under socialism; they were ideologically impossible and so did not exist), to a criminal underworld with distinct codes and political connections. But if the Soviet Union is to admit to Western-style social ills, it must at least consider Western-style solutions. There are no completely satisfactory models – though Soviet officials say privately that Sweden has an acceptable level of crime.

The lesson of the regional mafias, such as Uzbekistan and Armenia, is that there should be tighter control over republican governments. The Soviet ruling class has to be schooled in a manner that provides for uniformly high ethical standards. But how does this square with Gorbachev's desire to de-centralise the economy (and, therefore, the social system)? It does not. The Gorbachev paradox is that to free the economy he must strengthen political control at the centre.

Gorbachev's attitude to organised crime (publicising its practices, dispatching honest cops to dishonest republics) appears to be improvised; there is no real blueprint. His book *Perestroika* concentrates on the question of increasing supplies, of modelling a more responsive economy and skates over the intriguing relationship between the Plan, the Market and Crime. Somehow, though, he will have to find a way of satisfying the 'outlawed competitor'. To fail in this would provide the necessary ammunition for the critics of Gorbachev who argue that reform brings anarchy.

8

Katyas and the Fall From Grace

Late one night, when good girls were in bed, Olga was being beaten up. It was in front of the National Hotel and everybody in the lobby knew what was going on. 'Look at this,' said the desk clerk to no one in particular, 'they're beating up a katya.' A katya, the diminutive from Katerina (more specifically Catherine the Great, whose image appeared on old 100-rouble notes and who had fabled sexual energy) is slang for prostitute. 'They' were two men, barely discernible, so quickly were their legs and arms pistoning into Olga, who was slipping to the floor like a discarded garment. The National Hotel faces Red Square. A few yards away over a thousand troops and a battalion of militia are in barracks and within the hotel itself there were enough KGB agents and informers to fill a discotheque.

Nobody intervened. I was not keen to go out. It was a bit cold, the nippy October of 1976, the first snow not far away. 'It's a domestic matter,' said the clerk turning away from the window. Olga was not moving. 'They are her friends, and they must punish her.' Later, twelve years later, the Soviet press would write about the Olgas and the katyas, lament the fact that they were being scarred by pimps and gently raise the question of what to do about something quite as old, as nineteenth-century, as prostitution in the modernised, go-ahead Russia of Mikhail Gorbachev.

There are 3,500 registered prostitutes in Moscow but the real number is probably twice that. The man who keeps track of them is Major Sergei Adzhiyev in Militia District 69 who – informally since prostitution is not really a crime – is head of the vice squad. He is very proud of an alphabetical card index, the kind you can flip through, which refer to meatier files in a big olive-green metal cabinet. Personal computers have not reached the 69th Precinct.

'Give me a name,' he says.

'Irina.'

'And you last saw her at?'

'The Bolshoi, cruising in the interval.'

'Difficult, the Bolshoi. Try a hotel.'

'The Ukrainia.'

'Good, so here you have it. One metre 67, big girl, brown hair – you can never be sure of that though – and, let me see, lives in the Sokolniky Park district. That'll be her. Medically, quite clean, so it says.'

The Major built up the archive from scratch because until recently prostitution has not been against the law in the Soviet Bloc. Prostitution did not exist – that is, could not exist: it was a remnant of capitalism, developed socialism had long ago taken away the pre-conditions for the business and so, Q.E.D., there were no whores and no call to punish them. Those who think that Soviet police are pitted against glasnost should talk to the Major; policemen were fed up with double-speak about non-crimes like prostitution. Many policemen on the beat trying to glean information about a burglary or a moonshine distillery would go first to the local prostitutes, yet they could not be named in the report, could not exist. Now they do exist, and they can be punished – 100 roubles for the first soliciting offence, 200 roubles for the second offence within a year. That is a kind of progress. On the wooden seats of the waiting-room in the 69th, there are two or three girls a night waiting to be booked.

The Major has three broad categories on his files, ranging in age from 14 to 70 years. There are the Centrals, well-brought-up youngish women who have fallen on hard times; crumpled looks, a drink problem. Then there are the Primitives, who can be purchased for a glass or two of moonshine vodka. And then the vast majority, the Social Drifters who edge their way into prostitution after a broken marriage or as part of a move from the country, who develop and work a regular patch in the railway stations or cafés, professionals with a fixed rate and fixed hours. But these file categories tell only half the stories. There are the fragrant women who patrol the foreigners' hotels, charging dollars, seemingly undisturbed by the KGB. They do not figure on the Major's list and are plainly the responsibility of another department. There are the women who work only in the summer, living in Moscow but taking long professional holidays in the Black Sea and reaping the harvest of Westerners or, at a pinch, the well-heeled Russians. There are trade-delegation girls, Sokolniky Park girls, women who come out only for the big exhibitions – the Moscow Book Fair, say. There are students (as was admitted in the *Moscow Komsomol* paper) supplementing their grants. There are housewives saving for a co-operative apartment. And out of

Moscow, the situation is reproduced on a smaller scale, in Leningrad, Baku, Kiev. But there are also oilfield girls and gas-line girls and women who prospect for prospectors in the Far East. Siberian incomes are very high, there is little to spend the money on, and many men have left their wives and families behind in the more comfortable western and southern republics. The demand for prostitutes in Siberia is so large that the nubile womenfolk of whole ethnic groupings such as the Nenets are in the business. Traditional hunters and trappers take to drink and young daughters, for whom the Russian-language classes at school were a penance, now amuse the roughened engineers, earning more in a week than a months' fur-trading by their fathers.

Major Adzhiyev knows his list is, at best, incomplete. The record will expand rapidly with the overt criminalisation of prostitutes in the Russian Federation and in other republics. Previously the police had to charge women with 'parasitism,' earning money without having a legally recognised job. This was not an easy article to enforce since women are under no obligation to work and the burden is on the police to show that the prostitute is living on illicit money. That is not an impossible task, but for most active police precincts it was too much bother. A combination of glasnost and AIDS has forced a change in the legal formula. The Gorbachev approach to prostitution was shrewder than his policy on that other prime underworld activity, alcohol abuse. The frontal assault on the sale of legal and illegal alcohol has produced few positive results; rather it has pressed one of the most versatile Soviet industries, moonshine distillation, rapidly to change its means of distribution and, of course, to raise prices. Now workers are bringing even less of their pay packets home. The line on prostitution, though, is simply this: we have a problem, let us find out as much as possible about it and, as a mild deterrent to the girls and their customers, publicise our findings. Making soliciting a magistrate's offence means that more women will end up on the Major's files and help provide a form of control in the age of AIDS, since all registered prostitutes have to be medically examined. They call their clean bill of health 'a driver's licence'.

Punishment – a hundred-rouble fine is a slap on the wrist for a good whore, who can earn that in one night or two – is one of the few effective AIDS controls available. The Health Ministry ordered 600 million condoms from the Oil and Chemical Industry Ministry under the 1988 plan but had this reduced to 220 million because industry did not have the capacity to make more, or the hard currency to import. Even to meet the 220 million target, the rubber industry had to stretch the quality thin. The supply worked out at less than two condoms a year for the adult population of the Soviet Union. The result: a black market in condoms, with most sexually active Russians not bothering, and a concentration of condoms in Moscow and Kiev and Leningrad but a complete dearth elsewhere. Dr Igor Kon, a Soviet sociologist who has been trying to drum up AIDS awareness, says, 'Promotion of condoms in this country is regarded as corruption of the youth. If you complain about the poor quality of ours to anybody, he just shies away as if you were asking to look at a collection of pornographic postcards.' Most other East European countries have similar problems. Prostitutes are thus particularly dangerous, even though the number of AIDS cases is still relatively small: in 1988 there were less than a hundred carriers in the whole of the Soviet Union.

The supposition is that AIDS is still essentially a foreign infection, that women who ply the Russian-only trade are not at great risk. Major Adzhiyev can find in his files complete prostitute dynasties, a grandmother, mother and daughter all on the street at the same time, who have never suffered serious venereal infection.

The Moscow police carry out irregular sweeps of the hotels, load the women into buses, take down their particulars and then let them go. The order from the top appears to be to obtain maxium information about prostitution since this is the first step in the fight against AIDS. The prostitutes' milieu in Moscow believe that something is being planned: perhaps legal or semi-legal and medically controlled brothels, perhaps really tough jail sentences and re-education courses. One penalty that bites is the removal of the Moscow residence permit. Before the 1980 Moscow Olympics, the Moscow militia rounded up 70 prostitutes and dumped them at kilometre 101, just outside the city limits. But to enforce this at the moment the police have to catch a prostitute three times in a year, which is more difficult than it sounds. Moreover there are a dozen ways around the rules. Withdrawal of the residence permit can actually work in favour of hotel prostitutes. Under the regulations in the Soviet Union, Poland and Czechoslovakia no girl can be in a man's room after ten o'clock at night. And no Moscow, Warsaw or Prague resident can stay in a hotel in their city of residence without special permission. But there is nothing to stop a prostitute, officially resident in say Kaliningrad, taking a hotel room in Moscow and during her stay, visiting other people's rooms.

The history of prostitution in eastern and central Europe is an intricate and intriguing patchwork of corruption, hypocrisy and greed; in short, very similar to the history of prostitution in the West. The accounts of the prostitute's trade in the nineteenth-century London underworld can be almost precisely matched in nineteenth-century Russian or Polish literature, and the fundamentals are little changed today. It has always been something of a mystery to me why prostitution should be the oldest profession (why not butcher, or interior decorator, or gardener?) but it is plain that as a business it is one of the least susceptible to change.

The free-loving strand of Bolshevism, as represented by Alexandra Kollontai, was stifled soon enough and any chance of the Russian Revolution leading to a sexual revolution was lost by the late 1920s. The Party had to enjoy moral superiority and that meant for the most part dour (sometimes serial) monogamy, the use of extra-marital affairs as ammunition in party infighting, and a kind of provincial horror at any flouting of traditional sexual codes. As recently as 1983, General Jaruzelski's allies in the Polish leadership used a rather public affair to discredit and oust the hardline Foreign Minister, Stefan Olszowski. Amost all of the Soviet-Bloc leaderships now have regularised relationships, stable if somewhat sterile marriages, because of the Party's collective prejudice against ostentatiously disorderly sex lives in their leaders. The historical trend of prostitution is best illustrated by Poland, which during its brief period of independence between the Wars enjoyed a boom time for courtesans. Brothels were abolished in 1922 but there were no strict penalties against prostitutes providing that they underwent regular medical check-ups and carried valid health certificates. Before the Second World War there were some 50,000 unregistered prostitutes in Poland, and they became the subject of considerable scientific interest. One survey of 600 Warsaw prostitutes in 1939 found that 43.5% were illiterate, 64.5% came from large working-class families, 49.5% said they had no choice because of unemployment. During the war the Germans introduced brothels in all the major towns of occupied Poland, but they were scrapped again in 1945. The massive displacement of people – Poland was shifted westwards, its eastern territories handed over to Stalin and western land granted fron dismembered Germany – encouraged prostitution; young women who lost their homes found themselves in an urban sprawl like Gdansk or Warsaw without a foothold on the black market. Gdansk and the other Baltic ports were particularly attractive as sailors were relatively affluent and brought in scarce goods or dollars. Private bars sprang up –

by 1947 there were 60 privately-owned restaurants and clip joints in the Nowy Port district of Gdansk – and a red-light area was born.

Prostitutes were registered from the beginning, from 1945, by special sanitary commissions. But the political changes in Poland had their impact on prostitution. On the initiative of the Polish Women's league, a national committee for fighting prostitution was established. Many of the women were forced to take on office jobs. By 1949 the national committee was also abandoned and responsibility for prostitution control was handed to special police vice squads. The Stalinist model imposed on Poland took its toll: the nightclubs were closed down or driven out of business, tourism virtually dispppeared and foreign seamen were often barred from setting foot on shore. By 1952 the militia had only 1,551 prostitutes on their books. The familiar line was adopted: prostitution had died out because it was a perversion of capitalism. The vice squads were dissolved and a great victory was declared.

The Stalinist years pushed prostitutes more deeply into the criminal milieu; only the protection of the underworld and black marketeers saved the women from starvation. The women who still remained active tended to concentrate on the railway stations. For many whores in the Soviet Union, that remains their stamping-ground: the large, well-heated waiting-rooms in the Kazan, Leningrad and Yaroslavl stations in Moscow, with their extraordinary jumble of luggage, paper bags, peasants and travellers, are also a pick-up terminus. The women, well-wrapped in winter, coquettishly dressed in the summer, have their prices chalked on the soles of their shoes.

The death of Stalin, the rise of Krushchev and of Wladyslaw Gomulka in Poland, created a new atmosphere. By the end of 1956 there were nightclubs again, foreigners began to cross the Iron Curtain more frequently and, for the professional girls, it was like the Klondike Gold Rush. Every opening to the West – the expansion of the Poznan Trade Fair, a new ferry route between Sweden and Poland – brought business. The number of registered prostitutes in Poland measures out the political 'thaw': 1,551 in 1952, 3,137 in 1959, 7,267 in 1962, 9,847 in 1969; growth figures to please the hearts of number-crunching bureaucrats. The Western investment boom of the 1970s, the financial face of Ostpolitik, brought British, West German and Japanese workers to the Soviet Bloc. Settled for several years as they worked on major construction projects, they changed the structure of prostitution in small, shyly-industrialising provincial towns. I owe some thanks to Michal Antoniszyn and Andrzej Marek, two Polish sociologists, who in their restricted-circulation book *Prostitution in the Light of Criminological Studies* have produced a unique record of how a group of British construction workers managed, in the 1970s and 1980s, to transform Wloclawek in central Poland. Their sample, 40 prostitutes in Wloclawek, 100 in Gdansk, is good enough to draw some general conclusions. Wloclawek is a sleepy, grimy sort of place with the usual problems of an East European township: too many farmers' children moving to the town for work, cramped housing conditions, food shortages. Two big new investments projects were earmarked for the town in the Gierek era: a fertiliser plant and a furniture factory. In came Western money, followed by French, British, West German and Japanese workers; by 1972 there were 2,200 of them, enough to boost the hard-currency black market and stir up a drunken trade in the local night bars and discotheques. The number of prostitutes doubled between 1975 and 1981 and though most foreigners have now left (martial law chased away all but a hundred), Wloclawek still has an active red-light district. The British clients, mainly 'on the lump' in Glasgow and Liverpool, taught their Polish colleagues how to strike and made impossible demands – a regular supply of lavatory paper – from the Polish management. The friction on site spilled into the streets where the Friday-night brawl became a social fixture.

The girls did not mind; as the Polish economy slid out of control, the prospect of a British husband, or at least his wage packet, beckoned. The sociologists who looked at Wloclawek point out that their sample understates by far the numbers involved, excluding, for example, girls under 18 who in the late 1970s became an important part of the prostitution scene in Wloclawek. The identikit that emerges from Wloclawek and Gdansk is surely true for much of the Soviet Bloc: 72 per cent were aged between 20 and 30; about 70 per cent were single, almost half the sample had children housed with mothers; 18 per cent came from peasant families, 65 per cent came from professional backgrounds (those who worked in restaurants rather than on the streets); most had only primary education. On average, the sampled women had 300 clients a year; 62 per cent of prostitutes spent whole nights with their clients, though younger women preferred shorter and more frequent contacts. 'It has become customary,' says the survey, 'for prostitutes to take Saturdays off. On Saturdays they do not visit their regular nightclubs but watch television or meet their families or permanent boyfriends. The choice of the free day is down to many reasons: a wish to imitate people with ordinary jobs, for example, but also the need to avoid being seen by Polish relatives or neighbours who frequent nightclubs on a Saturday.'

The registration of prostitutes by police is based on shaky legal foundations, since the Soviet-Bloc countries have signed the UN Abolition Act of 1952 which bans the penalisation or compulsory control of prostitution. The new Soviet approach of fining prostitutes also violates the UN Act. In Bulgaria, whores are usually prosecuted for vagrancy and similar devices – 'parasitism' – are applied elsewhere. In Poland the legal structure is aimed at the milieu of the prostitute: 1 to 10 years jail for procurement, jail and fines for living on undeclared earnings, or renting accommodation for immoral purposes. The spreading of venereal disease is also illegal (up to 3 years in jail) and this may become the basis for future anti-AIDS legislation. The laws against those helping prostitutes have changed the traditional relationship between pimp and prostitute. Hotels, aware that they could be prosecuted if they allowed prostitutes to work in their rooms, imposed rigid rules: porters helping girls to enter rooms have been prosecuted in both Poland and the Soviet Union. At first, prostitutes were banned outright from hotel foyers, but in Poland this was successfully challenged in the courts: she can stay in place, shimmering between the palms, providing that she does not violate the 'norms of decent behaviour' by, say, getting drunk. The front line then shifted to the hotel room. Hotel guests with women in their room after 10 o'clock can expect a rude intrusion. There are a dozen ways of avoiding this restriction and most hotels have given up the struggle. But the role of the pimp, so much in evidence in pre-war Europe and still thriving in the West, has faded in the East. There is a complex criminal infrastructure helping the women to ply their legal trde: hotel porters, doctors who treat sexual illness and issue fake health certificates, fictitious husbands, landlords, taxi-drivers and the travel agents who ensure that the more mobile prostitutes are booked into the right corridors of the right hotels in the most lucrative holiday or business centres. Waiters, cloakroom attendants, sometimes musicians, keep chosen restaurant tables reserved for prostitutes. 'In Gdansk, but also obviously elsewhere,' write Antoniszyn and Marek , 'there are many taxi-drivers who work only at night and exclusively for prostitutes. In daytime they drive them to the hairdresser or the doctor, then on to the nightclubs, and patiently wait to take them and their clients home. Taxis rarely become the actual "workplace" but the drivers certainly draw a profit from the business.'

The taxi-driver does not qualify as a pimp, though sometimes he functions as a bodyguard. Younger prostitutes sometimes use their boyfriends to keep accounts and even to drum up trade, and the survey cites two husbands acting as a classical exploiters:

"Roma", 28, mother of two, says her husband was obsessed about getting a new proper car. Together with a friend he had the idea of persuading their women to make money in the "easiest" way. At first, "Roma" thought it was only a bad joke but her husband soon took her and the other girl to a café, left them alone at the table, and later confiscated the first 30 dollars she earned. If she refused to go out, her husband simply beat her up. On one such occasion he hurt her so badly that subsequently he had to serve a jail term. But "Roma" didn't give up the chance to make easy money. In the mornings she works as a clerk in a school; the evenings transform her into a habituée of restaurants. She says that if forced to choose, she would rather keep her second job since it makes better money and that makes her a bit more satisfied with life.

'Another similar case is "Gienia". She had 3 children and a sailor husband who was sacked for drug and alcohol abuse. Once back in Gdynia, he needed more and more money and decided to use his pretty wife. For the last two years "Gienia" has provided for the household, children and husband's habits.'

Usually, though, force is not used. There are two fundamental differences in the nature of prostitution in East and West. The first legal: if pimping and procurement can be punished, and prostitution not, then the balance of advantage shifts to the women. In Western countries there is a criminal dependency between the pimp and his women, a shared risk. Second, in Britain, the USA and West Germany, the pimp is often the main supplier of drugs. So far, drug abuse among Soviet-Bloc prostitutes is not a major problem. (Though I recall meeting one reformed prostitute at a drug rehabilitation farm run by the Monar charity outside Warsaw. She used to make $100 a night, most of which went on heroin for her addicted boyfriend. Now, at the farm, her hair shorn and boots clogged with mud, she looks like Wurzel Gummidge.)

A typical pimp is Artur, whose story was told in *Kultura* (Warsaw April 1986). For some years now wealthy Arab businessmen have been travelling to the Gdansk area for sexual tourism. A chartered Boeing 727 takes 60 businessmen to West Berlin and several Mercedes limousines are then hired for the short drive through East Germany to Poland. Artur handles four women who cater for the trippers and other Western clients. He told *Kultura* that his profits amounted to about half a million zloties in a good month – a huge amount compared, say, to the salary of a teacher but not that impressive when converted into hard currency (about $400 at the then rates). The petro-dollars are handed directly to him by the businessmen, who prefer to deal with a male; Artur converts some into zloties, launders the larger notes through private Polish companies, and deposits the rest in bank accounts. He is 28, a graduate at Gdansk Polytechnic, speaks English and a bit of Arabic. 'He has had several offers to go to Kuwait and set up a branch of his business there. He declined – he regards himself as a professional and wants to be independent. Abroad, he would have to buy his way into everything and in the end his profits would be smaller than at home.'

Artur visits two cafés to make sure his girls have turned up for work. He organises his schedule for the following day. Afterwards he is free to go home and watch a film from the largest private video collection on the Baltic Coast. 'If I were ordered to make my business official and pay taxes, a first-rate brothel, comparable to Hamburg or Paris, could be set up. We would settle our accounts with the tax office every month.' A lucky man Artur: that is what they say around the Nowy Port district; too lucky, perhaps, to survive.

Dollars are, of course, the engine of the business. There are three categories of clients; rich foreigners, poorer foreigners and locals. A kind of guild exists and nobody admits to lowering prices or stepping out of their categories. Rich means American, British, West Germans, Scandinavians, the valued (clean, quick) Japanese. Poor means African students , sailors. The true professionals are adaptable, dressing down, for example, if a ship is in port lest they intimidate sailors with flashy clothes. The rates vary, according to season and place: $20 for a sailor in Odessa, $100 for a businessman in Prague. The differences become plain in central Warsaw. On Friday night at the Black Cat club, in the subterranean part of the Hotel Victoria, the girls sit along the bar or at reserved tables. They dress fashionably, mainly in white so that the strobe lights will pick them out, and stride regularly to the lavatory to catch the eye of Western revellers. Professional girls outnumber guests by about 3:1, an acceptable ratio for attack. Waiter service is deliberately slow to force the customers to approach the bar where they are, in turn, accosted. Nobody is shocked, since it is clear from the beginning what the club is designed for; obviously not the floor show of chorus girls, some of whom appear to be mothers or aunts of the women at the bar. To make doubly sure, a hotel porter discourages any unsuspecting mixed party of guests from entering. At the end of a long night, assignations are made and the girls, entering a lift near the underground garage, make their separate way to the rooms to cement East-West relations.

A few hundred yards away, on the same evening, there is a different scene. The area intersected by Marszalkowska, Chatubinskiego, Wspolna and Poznanska Streets is nicknamed Place Pigalle: this is zloty prosititution. The area is poorly lit, has useful patches of waste ground. On a Friday between 50 to 70 women patrol the area and the bargaining starts from about 50,000 zloties. There is a hunchback, a young, obviously mentally retarded woman, somebody on crutches, but also passably attractive women excluded from the dollar-earning elite. It is not a competitive beat. Most clients are drunk, many of them up from the country. Their choice, in the half-light, appears to be completely random. Later some will be found unconscious, picked clean of their harvest earnings. There are brawls all weekend but the police rarely intervene, treating Place Pigalle as a kind of large disreputable family prone to quarrels. When they move in to do a spot check on prostitution (as in Operation Corinth, 1986) they trawl a fair number of amateurs: a 48-year-old Social Studies teacher supplementing her income, many women on maternity leave, a few nurses.

In summer, the picture changes. In Place Pigalle there are more students, shop assistants trying their luck and, by early September, more farmers as customers. In the Black Cat, the shrewdest girls are making plans for the Black Sea. Seaside prostitution is a big money-earner since West German travel opened up the relatively cheap resorts in Bulgaria, Romania and, increasingly, the Soviet Union. There is sharp competition. In Bulgaria, the local prostitutes are known as 'black seagulls' and tend to be gifted and frequently under-age amateurs. Various clubs have been denounced in the Bulgarian press: the Roman Colosseum Discotheque in Plovdiv, renowned for its 14- to 18-year-old boy and girl prostitutes, and the Aquarium, also in Plovdiv, which was a haven for slightly older girls. But in Varna, the market is almost entirely professional. It is a strange place, Varna, in the summer. As East Germans could not travel to the West they used to arrange trips to Bulgaria. Their relatives from West Germany meanwhile came on package tours and between the concrete hotels, in discreet corners there were moving scenes of family reunions. The East Germans, evading their tour leader, came to the West Germans in their plush hotels. By the same token, East German girls came to Varna to find West Germans husbands. Bulgaria itself is amost an irrelevance; the only important venues are the hotel room, the beach, private places. The elites of

Eastern Europe still come to Bulgaria taking advantage of a network of VIP rest-homes where the accommodation is substantially cheaper than Ibiza. There are the package tourists, the 'singles' tours, the Western trade-union leaders. And, swimming in the crowded waters, the metropolitan prostitutes, both male and female, from Poland, Hungary and Czechoslovakia, seeking out lonely West Germans and their loose, attractive Marks. Together, in a good Varna discotheque, it is possible to see the whole zoological display: the young, spoiled children of Polish party leaders, husky Bulgarian girls, the travelling professionals, the West German mechanic on his first foreign holiday, a slightly bulging lady from Bochum with a charming Bulgarian boyfriend. They dance to the usual throbbing beat and barely talk at all.

It is difficult to write about prostitution without making it sound like a mass phenomenon; plainly, it is not. The forces that govern demand and supply are interesting and, in the age of AIDS, important to understand. But though AIDS obviously endows prostitution with a new seriousness – above all it has re-activated the legislation and the brothel debate in Eastern Europe – prostitutes themselves are not taking their 'profession' as seriously as in the past. The Polish survey of prostitutes in Gdansk and Wloclawek showed that most women stayed in the job for three to four years. For over a century prostitutes have talked about giving up their job as soon as they come into a nest-egg. But now, at least in the East, this has gone beyond self-delusion. The relative earnings are high in the Soviet Bloc and the money is easily laundered. But the social composition is also changing; there are more women with secondary or higher education entering, and leaving, the field. Three years of prostitution, legally permitted, can bring in earnings equivalent to a lifetime of university teaching. In the East, as in the West, the notion of the job-for-life is changing; the idea of being prostitutes for a while and then doing something else fits into this conception. Young prostitutes in the Soviet Bloc, when they talk articulately of their lives, treat the interlude as part of the adventure of creating hard currency out of soft, wealth out of easy, high-risk work. Partly because of lack of legal sanctions, there is no moral dimension.

The idea of prostitution as a wealth-creating adventure was best represented by the 'Dziwex' affair in Poland. This was a monstrous racket. Italian nightclub owners conspired with the official state entertainment agency (ZPR) to export Polish girls as dancers or, in many cases, prostitutes. Between 500 and 1,000 women were involved over several years in the late 1970s and early 1980s.

According to the Polish indictment, the main Italian partner, Carmelo Carsalia, head of the Olivero Artistic Agency, was supplying girls to about 50 nightclubs throughout Italy. The standard pay-off to the Poles was $500, spread among various beneficiaries, plus three dollars a day for the duration of the girls' stay. The recruiting grounds were 'dance centres' which sprang up in the 1970s. The word soon spread that talent scouts were visiting training sessions even in such out-of-the-way places as Rzeszow near the Soviet border, Western impresarios in well-cut suits, with manicured hands. And so, throughout Poland, girls who had never dreamed of going on stage, who thought *Swan Lake* was a nice place for a summer holiday, enrolled in the schools. The balloon eventually burst: Polish security police broke open the door of a suite in the faded Europejsky Hotel in Warsaw and arrested, on a chill February morning, both Carsalia and his deputy. The business was slowly unravelled. But as the trial developed, so the motivations became more opaque. To defend themselves against charges of procurement and white slavery, the main conspirators – dance teachers, who picked out the most promising candidates, and the ZPR staff – argued that they had no idea what the women would have to do when they arrived in Italy. Witold M., later jailed for a year, said of the prostitution connection, 'I couldn't even invent such an idea.' But before the trial began he gave a rather different impression: 'As soon as we arrived in Italy, I found that they only needed me to bring the girls over. I was isolated immediately. The girls were disappearing. Judging by their looks and manners I knew they were whores. One day I tried to enter the girls' room but I was blocked by a heavy, Franco Frani, who threatened me and told me not to get inquisitive.' Janusz K., also jailed, was a choreographer who 'trained' the girls and delivered them in batches of 30. He received about $11,000, a small fortune in Poland and enough to make one suspicious when he testifies: 'I was told my responsibility extended only to several minutes' artistic performance a night. What happened before or after the show was none of my business.' The Poles thus used the spectre of organised crime to get off the hook; the Italians were simply too menacing to probe deeply into the mechanics of the deal. And indeed the Dziwex affair is full of mysterious deaths; the car crash, for example, of the Polish consul in Milan who regularly extended the passports of the girls.

What actually happened in the clubs is also somewhat unclear. The girls performed a token, heel-kicking dance and drank with customers, for which they were paid the paltry sum of 1,000 lire (less than a dollar) per drink. Their earnings rose only when they persuaded the customers to enter curtained-off rooms, *séparées*, and buy bottles of over-priced champagne. Other business was transacted, but that seems difficult to prove. It was one of the rare trials in Eastern Europe when it was necessary to prove the practice of prostitution, and, in the end, it was impossible. The Italians, arrested and then released on large bail (and thus allowed to flee the country) were the only ones who could have pronounced it a procurement racket. The managers received mainly suspended sentences, the women who had orginally complained withdrew their testimony (though because of Polish, not mafia, pressure) and the honour of Polish maidenhood was saved. A key witness, Iwona S., talking to *Polityka*, demonstrated that discretion is sometimes the safer option: 'I'd like to have this whole nightmare behind me already. I knew a lot about what was going on in Italy, but I'll keep it to myself. I'm afraid. Aren't you afraid to write about it? Now I regret I said too much last year [1981, when the indictment was being drawn up]. Some of the girls were forced into prostitution not so much physically as psychologically. They didn't have their passports, had debts with the Italians, had to pay for board and lodging. And there were girls who knew what they were letting themselves in for. The people who are being tried right now also knew about it. Will I tell all this to the judges? No, I've had enough and don't want to live in fear any more.'

The current version of Dziwex, which also exploits the easier travel regulations in the Soviet Bloc, is an international marriage-agency fraud. The West German newspapers are full of lonely-hearts advertisements, many of them placed by agencies who specialise in Thais, Filipinas or Poles. One agency issues a catalogue with photographs of Polish girls, each marked with a number. For a fee, every West German customer has the right to receive five sample candidates. The girls have already been talent-scouted in Poland (and, to a lesser extent Hungary and Yugoslavia), issued with fake Red Cross invitations, met at Bielefeld Station (the main terminus for this kind of business) and taken to boarding-houses. The girls 'rejected' by the clients are submitted to others until a marriage is eventually settled. But in the meantime they have to pay their keep. As the Detmold prosecutors established, many of the girls are sold to brothels at DM 10,000 each. The key to this East-West traffic, which has been going on throughout the 1980s, is the link between disreputable marriage agencies, since it is East European agencies, now quite legal but unregulated, which are the principal 'talent-scouts'.

The connection between criminal enterprise in East and West has never been more evident than in the field of prostitution. Since prostitution ranks so low in the criminal scale in the East, since procurement is almost impossible to prove, and since there is a regular supply of young women frustrated with their social lot, the potential for organised crime is huge.

9

A Bet On The Side

Karlshorst is an S-Bahn ride away from the ruins of Berlin Wall. It is the most obviously Russian spot in East Berlin. The old Wehrmacht barracks, red and grey, now house a Soviet guard regiment. On a Sunday afternoon, in a lazy Berlin summer, the air thick as gravy, the windows of the barracks are open and the sentimental blare of Volga Radio, the Soviet Forces Network, drifts out onto the street. Two soldiers on an afternoon pass pause in front of the Russian-language notice board, then stride past an East German cinema (showing a soft-sex film thinly disguised as an educational movie), a café where they are forbidden to drink, past girls who watch West German television every night and who worry about J.R. and Sue Ellen, and past a crowd of uncharacteristically jolly lumpy shortsleeved Germans. The soldiers, peasant boys who might as well be on the moon, pause.

'*Eto ippodrom.*'

'*Eto chto?*'

'*Ippodrom.*'

He makes a fast walking movement with his fingers. They laugh, for no reason. They have discovered Karlshorst race track. It is, like the cakes, the beer, the films, and the girls, forbidden territory, but it makes them feel at home, even a little excited. Inside, money is being made and lost.

A Sunday afternoon at the races in East Berlin is time-travel, an expedition into the 1920s or beyond. Fat ladies, arms like Prague hams, stroll with their skinny consorts who blink and wheeze like off-duty miners. A brass band, as un-Prussian as it is possible to be in Prussian Karlshorst, burps and bleats. Glasses of beer rest on the floor for the interval. Queues form for sausages and beer and ice-cream but most people promenade alongside the white fence that divides the grandstand from the track. The grass is scattered with broken glass and losing betting-slips; inside the main betting hall, which advertises the races like a train departures board, the floor is confettied with paper. Each discarded slip represents a loss of a few Ost-Mark; the profits for the state bookmakers are plain to see. Polite matrons hand out the winnings, but nobody whoops for joy. The latest trot is announced, bets are hastily placed, beers are gulped and there is a flight to the stands. The trotters – two-wheeled light carts pulled by fit steeds that are forbidden to gallop – sprint around the circuit. There is a fine bawling and shouting; un-German, you think, but actually *Berlinisch*, working-class *Berlinisch*, a relief from the daily self-possession of the embourgeoised DDR. The earnings and losses seem peripheral; the race, too. Then you spot them, conspicuous in their camouflage: a sharp man in a red shirt with an Interflug shoulder-bag conferring with a plaid-shirted operator in sunglasses. These are the crooked bookies. Plaid-shirt has Carl Zeiss binoculars but does not watch the course; his eyes roam the stands and settle briefly on likely punters. Business is contracted near the lavatory, odds scribbled onto a programme and handed wordlessly to enquirers. After the race it is difficult to find them – a feature of bookies everywhere.

It is said that they manage a few thousand poundsworth of business in an afternoon; enough, in a month or two, to finance their secondary business in the second-hand car trade. A day at the races, betting legally or illegally, quenches some of the thirst for gambling. Placing and losing or winning money on a day off: that is an excape from the grinding railway schedule of a centrally-planned existence. There are many, perhaps too many, certainties in the working existence of the Communist Bloc. The trains may not run on time, but most certainly they will arrive: the apartment, the country allotment, promotion, a job for life, the type of education and health care, the exact level of pension, everything can be charted in advance. Yet most central and East European countries have had to suppress long traditions of gambling, of games of chance. In Russia, there were the upper-class card and casino gambling depicted in Dostoyevsky's *The Gambler*, but also the peasant and urban working-class distractions, the card-sharpers and the dog-fighters. Industrialisation in Eastern Europe created distinct patterns of working-class leisure and gambling habits that persist until today. Mayhew's investigation of the nineteenth century underworld in London revealed an existence not so very different from Berlin or Budapest. But under Communism, gambling was declared illegal. Strictly speaking, like prostitution and crime itself, it did not exist; it was a remnant of capitalism. But provisions were made to trap the practitioners of this non-existent crime: Article 210 of the Russian

Federation penal code provides for one-to-five-year jail sentences for introducing a minor to gambling. Ideologically, the gambler seemed to resemble the private capitalist too closely. He put up money, he risked it, he won it, usually at somebody else's expense. The analogy is not precise, but close enough to stifle legally the gambling spirit. In the Soviet Bloc, only the lottery and horse-racing offer legal outlets. There are officially sponsored hard-currency casinos in Hungary and Bulgaria (in the Hotel Vitosha where, over the green baize of the roulette table, Mehmet Ali Agca met the men who would set him up to kill Pope John Paul II) but locals are excluded. Passports have to be shown at the door. It is in the nature of legal, yet ideologically unsound, institutions that they attract the semi-legal and outright criminal. Nowadays, illegal gambling profits are an important element in the criminal underworld of the Soviet Bloc. The cash comes not only from the horses, the lottery (where sale of winning tickets contributes a flow of new cars to the black and grey markets), but also from rigged football and volleyball matches and elaborate networks of bribes and betting in all the major team sports.

The Sluzewiec course in Warsaw has none of the *déclassé* charm of Karlshorst, nor the fake grandeur of the Moscow Hippodrome. It is a bit like a poorly designed factory, abandoned in mid-construction. And, in fact, the industrial analogy holds: it has a turnover of about 16 million US dollars, packing three million spectators a year into the stands. From the beginning the Polish authorities had been determined that if there was to be legally sanctioned gambling it would be *socialist* gambling. There are no private competitors. Instead eighteen state-owned stables are in competition. Trainers, grooms and jockeys live around the track and are paid by the state (coming under the competence of the Ministry of Agriculture). Their salaries are about the same as workers in the meat-processing industry, and there is no effective incentive scheme. If a jockey comes first he receives about £4. It thus pays him to lose a race in return for a decent bribe There are a dozen ways to nobble a horse or throw a race. Zig-zag riding helps you to lose ground, and, if the conspiracy involves several riders, the faster horses can be boxed in along the inside track. In Polish jockey-jargon this is known as 'caging'. For important races, horses are doped; testing is not compulsory and security is weak.

The racket in Sluzewiec is run by a group of track bosses with links to outside syndicates that often represent several hundred punters. In Warsaw, it is reckoned that between seventy and eighty per cent of the 600 races (official 1987 estimate) are rigged. The managers pass on their decisions to the syndicates and word-of-mouth takes over. Bets are placed at the official bookmaker or through the illegal bookies who play with odds to hoodwink punters outside the syndicate. Almost all of the 450 workers at Sluzewiec are in on the deal and though it is illegal for them to bet or to leave the course on a race day, they slip over the fence and place money through relatives. The business is so profitable that it has taken on the elements of organised crime. Track judges are bought off, unco-operative jockeys are beaten up. The track club-house, over-looking the course, houses a seven-man technical commission which is supposed to invalidate suspicious races, but such is the power of the Sluzewiec mob that judges are fired the day after they make unpopular decisions.

A new track director, Jerzy Michalowicz, tried to clean up the business in 1987 and suspended trainers and jockeys. Using their rights under economic reform, the employees exploited their democratic forum, the Worker's Council, to vote Michalowicz out of his job. The official resolution said he was 'incompetent, arbitrary, and a liar'. The Ministry of Agriculture demanded his reinstatement, but the Sluzewiec mobsters stood on their democratic rights and refused.

The Moscow Hippodrome operates similar fiddles, though not on such a grand scale. Jockeys throw races and the side-bets are huge, perhaps ten times larger than the average wager in Warsaw. A winning bet at long odds at the illegal bookmaker can net some £15,000; fewer races are fixed than in Warsaw, but the pickings are juicy.

There is a metaphor groping to get out of these racing stories. An economic enterprise, poorly managed, underpaying its staff, without serious incentives, bends the rules and plays the black market rather than undertake reform. The authorities tolerate the situation as long as revenue keeps flowing and, when it finally decides to make changes, finds it is too weak to act against entrenched and corrupt interests. Mikhail Gorbachev would do well to visit the Hippodrome.

Gambling in the Soviet Union took off in the 1960s. It was partly the new prosperity, of course, the formal ending of the years of reconstruction and sacrifice. Perhaps too there was a connection with the Khrushchev 'thaw,' an emerging sense of individual enterprise and profit. But if you talk to reformed criminals from that period a more prosaic explanation emerges. Preferential salaries were being handed out to anybody in dirty, but hard-currency earning jobs. Coal miners from the Donbass, diamond diggers in Yakuta, fisherman in the Far East, sturgeon farmers, gold prospectors: all worked the skin off their fingers and all received large wages. Their money was virtually unspendable in the provinces; some was sent back to wife and family in Russia, some went into savings accounts, but most formed a stony reassuring lump under a mattress or in thief-proof purses hung around the neck. The professional gamblers found a ready market in these men who had by dint of some psycho-economic quirk lost their sense of money; money-rich in a society with nothing to buy. Card-sharping teams set up operation on the long-distance trains from Siberia. Even now, with money harder to get in Siberia, the sleeping cars from Irkustk to Moscow are elaborate gambling dens. There were, and are, any number of games to part the prospector from his money. One is *zhelezhka*, in which you guess the serial numbers of rouble notes. Another, even more childish in its conception, has the dealer laying down cards one by one on a suitcase in the middle of the compartment. If a card in the left-hand pile matches one in the player's hand, then the dealer (the bank) takes the player's money. If the card in the right-hand pile accords with the player's hand, then the player cleans up. It is not so very different from Snap!, but fortunes were, and are, being lost on the game.

The rise in professional gambling was also linked to the freeing of prisoners after the death of Stalin. The Gulag camps have educated several generations, and forged a criminal class with its own traditions, codes and trades. The first illicit casinos in Moscow appeared in the mid-1960s, apparently to answer the need of racketeers for high-stakes gambling. They were also places where black marketeers, from different branches but often with similar camp experiences, could form coalitions. The black market in Moscow has always been better co-ordinated than in Warsaw or even Odessa. In the Brezhnev time, the police picked up big pay-offs from the marketeers and it became financially sensible for the dealers to group together and buy protection from the same officers. The accession of Yuri Andropov and the weakening of Moscow party chief Viktor Grishin threatened the established protection chains; 1982, as a result, was a time of mysterious murders in Moscow. Some recent emigrants to the West speculate that the bent policemen were either encouraging blood feuds in the black-market milieu, or actually commissioning murders of possible informers. At the time the Moscow Criminal Ivestigation Bureau, responsible for homicide detection, became an acutely politically sensitive place. By the late 1980s, the atmosphere had calmed down somewhat but the fear and loathing of the Andropov years had frightened the fat cats of the black market away from the casinos. In their heyday, they were a marvel: an almost perfect reproduction of fake 'gentlemens' club' atmosphere of Western gaming houses. In the Lomonosov district I was taken to a drab high-rise block, one floor of which was reserved for Palestinian 'diplomats'. Higher, on the seventh floor, I was met by a heavy-set man wearing, unusually for Moscow evenings, a tie and dinner-jacket. With the polite menace of his Western counterparts he barred entry until my companion vouched for me convincingly. No bribe was offered.

The corridor opened up into six apartments, like a conventional Moscow block. But three apartments on one side had been knocked into a single room, the gaming room, the three apartments on the other side were clearly rented by the casino organisers. One had been cleared of furniture and my companion explained that this was a dance floor, though on my night there was no dancing and no music. The casino was a 'cave', electric candles had been fixed to the wall, and red flock wallpaper added to the murkiness. The one strong light was a tinkling chandelier ('Bulgarian,' said my companion proudly) hanging over the roulette table. Beyond the roulette wheel, there was a card table and beyond that a black Formica bar with drinks. Three girls, dark Georgian beauties, sat on corduroy chairs waiting for their companions to win. There were perhaps thirty gamblers, too many even for the extravagantly constructed room. The windows remained locked, in the grand Russian tradition, and everybody sweated. In the lavatory there was a bottle of aftershave for the use of guests; nobody stole it, and indeed nobody used it. Wooden chips, nicely polished, were issued from one of the rented apartments which served as the bank. The gamblers would place their banknotes in discreet brown envelopes, and hand them to the messengers who walked the ten yards to the 'bank' and brought back chips. In a Russian gaming room, roulette is not for spectators; each player clenched his face with concentration and crushed a good-luck charm (one had a Jaguar key-ring) in a balled fist. The chips were slapped down with angry energy, as if it were a grudge match in the World Chess Championship. There were no drunks, little noise; serious talking seemed to take place in one of the other apartments. It was the most un-Russian night of my Russian days.

Now you can play roulette on the streets. Outside the most strategic of Moscow metro stations, or on a corner of the Arbat, or in front of a supermarket (one should perhaps use quotation marks for 'super-market'), there are sharp young men, what used to be called spivs, with plastic roulette wheels small enough to slip into a shoulder bag or briefcase (the kind that Russians use to carry their lunchtime sandwiches). There are nine paper cards, each with four numbers. Punt your five roubles on one card: if the rulyetka ball falls your way, you win 40 roubles. The game does not start until all nine cards are covered with banknotes. The crowds throng and it is easy money. If the ball falls on zero, the bank picks up everything. If it does not, the bank still makes five roubles a game. Ten games an hour, and the banker has netted a week's average salary. Look-outs are posted and if there suspicious mumblings from the crowd – say, if zero comes up twice in an hour – then somebody whispers '*Militsiya*,' the wheel is slipped into the briefcase, the cardboard box is kicked aside, and the punters go about their normal business.

The only investment capital is the bribe to buy a stamp in one's labour card; without this work permit, the street croupier could be jailed for parasitism. Increasingly, though, street gambling is falling into the hands of young veterans from the Afghan wars; they sometimes have disability pensions and even if they do not, neither police nor magistrates are keen to prosecute. There have been Soviet press reports of organised gambling groups who specifically recruit Afghan veterans. It makes sense: a significant number returned from the war (1979–1988) with a taste for drugs and most are having adjustment problems. Certainly ex-soldiers are the most active in the 'Find the Lady' racket in Moscow, Leningrad and Kiev. The game is familiar to Londoners and New Yorkers. Three beakers are laid out, a ball is concealed under one (or, as a variant three cards are used, one of them a queen, a 'lady') and passers-by put 10 roubles on their bet. Usually they lose. The game has a faster turnover than *rulyetka*, is easier to conceal. The Soviet press, though it has perhaps become too free with the word 'mafia', says that these operators (each of whom can make 20,000 roubles – £20,000 – a month) are under the control of organised gang leaders. Some of the street dealers are paid off in drugs. There has been at least one murder and in one case a dealer had his fingers smashed with a hammer. In one territorial dispute, a hundred young mobsters pursued a rival dealer off their terrain, chased him into a bar and when he drove to a militia station to take refuge, dismantled the vehicle on the street, shattering the windscreen, emptying the petrol tank and slicing the seats. The police did not intervene but took photographs from the safety of the station.

Gorbachev's Russia is an odd place. The political uncertainties, coupled with the unbottled genie of individual enterprise, have encouraged hit-and-run criminal operators. A group of ex-soldiers, or ex-camp inmates, spot an opening and rely on the natural demand, the enthusiasm for chance. They can start up and wind down their operations within a few months and then move their profits elsewhere, into cars and vodka, the black-market staples, or into 'futures' (computer software, videos). But they run their business outside the usual criminal hierarchies and the old-established criminal trades. The police, to be effective, have to be 'market-oriented', able to pick up trends, adapt detection methods, work out how to apply existing laws to new variants of old crimes.

But police officers I have spoken to in the Soviet Bloc suggest that most gambling money has been ploughed into football. The syndicates that run football gambling are the most powerful in the business; frequently they have political backing. They are neither fly-by-night operators like the Find-the-Lady gangs, nor as closely knit as the Sluzewiec racing mobsters. They are respectable *salonfaehig* profiteers. To understand how the football gangsters have reached their ascendancy, it is necessary to explain a few aspects of sport in the Soviet Bloc. Professional sport in the West is a branch of the entertainment industry; it is Sport Inc. In the East sport, in its ideal construction, is part of the educational process. By their example athletes are supposed to demonstrate the correct deportment of New Soviet Man. A typical example comes from the Rumanian sports writer Adrian Paunescu: 'In Caraiova and in Dolj County there is an exceptional atmosphere that encourages emulation of the team's achievements. The revival of Universitatea Crauova is thanks to the way the team works and to its unselfishness, its patriotic fervour, and the promotion of the sort of excellence desired by the authorities in industry and agriculture.'

That is rather like telling the Liverpool Port Authority to buck up and follow the example of the city's football team. High expectations are pinned on the Soviet-Bloc sportsman. This adds to the usual professional pressures. They have a limited life: from the age of 40 few athletes can expect anything more than a coaching or managerial job; some drift into sports journalism, others pursue careers in the army or the police, which sponsored them in their youth. Their middle age is safer than in the West, but the profits are meagre by comparison. A good, protected Soviet athlete has his own car, a club apartment, a basic salary of 180 roubles a month from his sports association (Dynamo, Torpedo, etc), another 40 roubles if he has represented his country, then there will be bonuses from his team's patrons, or friendly town council, and extra payments for playing matches outside the normal programme. But while this adds up to a generous wage, their monthly income falls short of a single goal bonus handed out to a Western footballer, or the appearance fee for a runner. The use of sport as a role-model means that personal profit is played down and concealed entirely from the broad masses. Yet the reality is that quasi-professional sport in the Soviet Bloc has become a form of social mobility, a way for rough provincial boys to make their fortunes. From the beginning they live the Big Lie: professionals who must pretend to be amateurs and who, as part of the pretence, must be paid substantially under the odds offered to their Western counterparts. There is an extraordinary pressure to succeed and thus prolong their newly-acquired lifestyles; few refuse the possibility of 'drug-enhancement' when it is offered. There is also constant pressure from below as increasing numbers of young people are talent-scouted and encouraged to test their mettle against older athletes. Viktor Korchnoi, the Soviet Grandmaster who defected to the West, tells of an early chess tournament in which he was under pressure from the Soviet team managers to lose a game with a younger player and thus allow him to reach Master status.

That is relatively harmless: only the sport loses. Soviet boxing has seen many examples of fighters who were either paid to lose a match – and thus allow a favourite to come through – or who were promised the opportunity of foreign travel. The system is geared to 'success', and discriminates against the ageing or the merely good. A sportsman who has peaked is asking himself constantly: what next, what next, what about the rest of my life? He needs, in a society that cannot offer him a lucrative commerical follow-on career, as much money as he can grab.

The dilemma is particularly acute for the footballer. The sport attracts fierce regional and city loyalties, as in the West, often the city council is helping to finance the club and feels proprietorial about it. A great deal of money chases the ball.

Hungary is football-crazy, but unfortunately not football-talented. The country has ten million people of whom three million consider themselves to be experts on the game. The other seven million are either audiences, willing or unwilling (in the case of many women), or are too young to understand why their father is shouting at the television screen, then later on the phone, and later still in the cafés. To exploit this obsession, the Hungarian authorities established a 'Toto' pools scheme which operates much as in the West. Every week the punter fills out a coupon predicting the results of ten or more of the matches to be played at the weekend. Those with correct guesses win a large proportion of the money that is paid out for each coupon. In the long sultry summer by the Danube as many as a million Hungarians a week fill in the pools coupon. But because First Division teams are on holiday during this period, the draw is made on the results of second-division and factory teams. These are often very poor players and their matches are famed for their stupefying boredom. But a gamble is a gamble and a game is a game. In 1981 and 1982, a group of enterprising Hungarians realised that there was a killing to be made out of this weekly performance. Two crime syndicates were formed – at first neither realising that the other existed, but then as the season wore on, merging their interests – and dozens of part-time assistants engaged. The main syndicate would meet every Sunday in a back room of a Budapest restaurant and discuss which matches should be rigged for the following Saturday. A source in the pools association had already tipped them off about which team would play where, so the syndicate often knew before the team itself. It was sufficient to fix six matches, though on one memorable day, June 27 1982, the syndicate managed to rig nine out of the 14 games played. Scouts were then sent to the town or factory involved to spy out the land, and assess which was the stronger team in a draw. Usually it was enough to bribe the goalkeeper, the striker and the coach. But the pattern of bribes had many permutations: if the team was weak in defence then it was sufficient to bribe the forwards and wingers not to score and wait for the opposing team to do the rest. If the team showed particular talent and was none the less pencilled in for defeat, it was more or less obligatory to bribe the referee (who would in turn pass some of his payment to the linesmen). In general though, the goalkeeper was the crucial man. Many of them bought nice cars that season.

There were typically Hungarian twists to the saga. Until both syndicates realised the existence of the other, the teams sometimes managed to collect two sets of bribes. One syndicate would arrive on Tuesday and ask for a 2-0 result, and the following day another syndicate's representative would arrive and ask for another score. On a number of occasions (in all 66 games were fixed) the two syndicates would bribe *both* sides to lose, leading to scenes of high comedy, goalkeepers throwing themselves headlong in the opposite direction to the ball, the forwards of both sides striving to lose possession as swiftly as possible. When the two syndicates merged, a more rational way of operating was introduced, as befits the cradle of economic reform in Eastern Europe. Players bribed to lose matches had to put down a cash deposit before each rigged match, and got their money back, together with the payoff, only if the result was as planned. This incentive scheme worked well enough, though it sparked off many on-field arguments with key (and thus bribed) players yelling abuse at unbribed team-mates for playing too well.

The authorities began to realise that all was not well when they studied the winning numbers of the pools coupons week after week. The numbers were often consecutive, suggesting that the winners were all part of the same group or at least lived in the same small area. An investigation was launched on the assumption that there was a major abuse within the pools association itself: perhaps an employee of the association was somehow contriving to send in coupons? But this was not the case, and anyway such an investigation could not explain why the winners were so consistently correct. Then one rigged match came to light – and another, and another. There was a minor revolt among the great mass of unbribed players who were worried that the deliberately bad playing of their team mates was going to lose them their end-of-season bonus. Eventually, the police found that the syndicates had cheated their way to at least 29 million forints (645,000 dollars) and probably double that amount. The football association suspended 260 players and 14 referees and sought suspended jail terms up to 2.5 years to 19 players. The ringleader of the main syndicate was a 46-year-old plumber, Jozef Farago, who was given six years in jail and ordered to pay 10 million forints to the pools association. Four accomplices received similar sentences. During the interrogations and trials the gang revealed itself to be astonishingly resourceful, seeking out the advice of mathematics lecturers on correct permutation technique and to assess risk factors, as well as preparing the most careful analysis ever conducted into the strengths and weaknesses of Hungarian football.

The Hungarian authorities immediately cancelled the 2.5 million forint end-of-season bonuses for players and coaches and introduced new regulations to make clubs self-financing, operating solely from gate takings and other more conventional earnings.

But the damage had been done, not only to Hungarian sporting credibility but also to football establishments throughout Eastern Europe. In the Soviet Union, match-rigging and associated corruption had already been uncovered in 1977. Then it was disclosed in the official press that the results had been fixed between Dynamo Kiev and Zenit Leningrad and between Lokomotiv Moscow and Zraya Voroshilovgrad. The motivation for these and other similar match 'arrangements' is usually to do with a private wager rather than the large-scale pools rigging witnessed in Hungary. In Soviet Georgia and Azerbaidjan it is common for football teams to enjoy the patronage of a local underground millionaire who views the team as something of a personal plaything. When Tbilisi play in Moscow, it is instructive to see what happens after the match. Depending on the mood – that is, depending on the result – the team will go out to one of the top restaurants, where, with the underworld financier paying for the champagne and cognac, they will drink themselves under the table. Clashes have been known on home ground when rival teams were taken to the same restaurant by rival financiers; abuse flies across the restaurant floor and limp bodies, exhausted by the match, the alcohol and the shouting, are dragged discreetly out of a side door. There is of course nothing particularly corrupt about drinking with a corrupt millionaire. But usually it is these patrons who are actually rewarding the goal-scorers, making the match financially worthwhile by handing out handsome bonuses to the players. Not only does the patron buy valuable kudos with the local authorities with the apparent altruism, but he also makes a number of side-bets with the patron of rival team supporters. These bets are made in roubles in multiples of thousands, or in gold. Other corruption scandals in Soviet football have involved the Black Sea team Odessa Chernomorets, which recieved a million-rouble training camp paid for by the Odessa Steamship Line, as well as bonuses between 2000 and 3000 roubles to each of five players. Odessa was obviously eager to establish the club's position in the First Division. The Odessa Port Authority provided 50,000 roubles in financial incentives to the team, factories in the area provided other luxuries, and the club, in league with the housing committee, laid on luxuriously furnished flats as well as cars and pocket-money.

This abuse of state funds is not viewed very seriously by the local police or KGB, who are frequently entertained by club managers. Town dignitaries including the deputy mayor are on the board of governors and the team is regarded rather in the way that grandparents indulge their offspring. The Chernomorets scandal only came to light because the team was not producing very good results and because of the rowdy behaviour of some of the team; in general such business is regarded complacently as a colourful part of local life.

The Hungarian scandals changed that. Coupled with poor 1982 World Cup performances (by all Communist states bar Poland and the Soviet Union) the scandal on the Danube allowed the critics of the closed football mafias to flash their knives. This was more than a pools fraud, declared the Young Turks in Eastern Europe, it showed the fundamental rottenness of the sports establishments in all their countries.

In Bulgaria they have cracked down. The 1980s, a decade of football trials, saw the football establishment purged from top to bottom. It was not difficult to gain access to the dingy courtroom where Dymitri Nikolov, president of the Bulgarian football federation, was in the dock. He, and the head of the International Contracts Section, Dazo Nanov, were accused of raking in commission, putting a price tag on arranging fixtures, stealing the pocket-money of the national side. The state prosecutor, a middle-aged man with a taste for Roman poses, droned and shouted as if Nikolov was on trial for his life. In fact he seems to have been no more than a cheat, in the live-and-let-live mode. Something of a star too, thanks to his regular television appearances as a football commentator (and a fierce public scourge of corruption on the field). Both Nikolov and Nanov received $500 for their team's matches in Argentina, Nikolov picked up DM 3000 when Bulgaria played in Athens and he accepted Bulgarian currency from Norway and Brazil. 'I believed,' said Nikolov from the dock (handcuffed, tie-less lest he hang himself), 'I believed it was a common practice for managers to give money.' A profitable match was held against the junior team in Wales during the European championships. Nanov and the national coach were called into the President's office and in Nikolov's version, the following conversation took place:

'Wales is an expensive place.'

'Yes, Comrade Nikolov.'

'I want there to be maximum savings. No waste. No unnecessary spending.'

'Understood.'

Nanov duly forged the Cardiff hotel bills and obtained some fake restaurant receipts. 'They returned,' recalled Nikolov, 'and informed me that they had saved £3,100. I was amazed by their economising but we eventually distributed it evenly among the three of us.' Another typical fraud: the Bulgarian Sports Federation paid the air fares to Zurich for the national team, but the Swiss had agreed to cover the costs and sent Nikolov a cheque which he split with Nanov.

When Nikolov's pretty daughter was about to be married, the President's secretary communicated the fact to the various heads of provincial sports clubs. One supplied 120 bottles of wine for the reception and 50 kilos of fresh trout. Another bought some old damaged furniture from Nikolov and supplied a completely new suite which Nikolov duly passed on to his daughter. Seaside holidays were free because Nikolov allowed players from the resort to take part in an international with Greece. Nikolov's problem was his seniority – that was how he explained it in court. Everybody working a fiddle felt they had to pay tribute to the President even though he was not personally involved. A DM 30,000 bribe came in from a West German advertising company for transmission rights: the sum was split with Nikolov. When Chardar Svelkov was bought by an Austrian team a $1,000 commission was paid to Nanov, who then shared it with his boss.

Down the ladder, everybody else was making money too. Referees formed their own club of corruptible umpires which they called the 'Fast Reaction Society'. As a result the Bulgarian national final, between Levski and CSKA, had to be refereed by a West German: no Bulgarian could be trusted, since each club had bought a pool of referees. Sports journalists were put on the club payroll, and coaches, trainers and players were throwing matches at the rate of two out of every three. The money, as in Hungary, was collected from bets and side-bets made by gambling syndicates. Eventually the Bulgarian Politburo held a special session devoted to the state of football, since it was patently clear that the soccer field was now little more than a theatre stage where people came on, played their parts, simulated effort and finally walked of to their waiting, brand-new cars. While Bulgarian wrestlers and track athletes were picking up gold medals, national football had collapsed. In the resulting purge, scores of footballers were fired from their mythical jobs in factories, trainers were fired and fined and jail sentences were sprinkled around the establishment. At least two dozen players were banned from sport – any sport – for 35 years. And Nikolov and Nanov received 18 years in jail.

The rigging of matches can be monitored with relative ease – a team that loses consistently is either incompetent or has been sweetened. But the question of 'black funds' is eluding most of those central authorities who want to reform the soccer establishments. These funds are accumulated by clubs largely through the sale of unregistered tickets – in effect many East European clubs have become their own ticket touts, limiting the officially paid and officially taxed gate while printing hundreds of extra tickets to sell privately. These funds have become the dynamic force of the whole game; they finance, for example, the transfer of players between clubs.

Black funds in Czechoslovakia are used to lure players away from rival teams. A car, a cash bonus of 150,000 crowns and a three-room apartment comprise a typical package for a transfer. The ultimate aim of these transfers is to increase the gate – as in the West, falling gates are a problem – but is also an attempt to mount the hard-currency bandwagon. By exporting players to Western clubs, sports associations in the East can earn themselves a fortune, at least part of which is salted away into the hands of private sports entrepreneurs. According to the Central Sports Office in Warsaw, a body that seems to do everything and nothing, some 200 Polish sportsmen were officially 'exported' to the West between 1978 and 1988, most of them soccer players but also over 30 ice-hockey stars and 40 handball players. Big Western clubs in Italy, Spain and Austria now regularly come on trawling visits to Eastern Europe. If discovered by the local team management they are virtually forced-fed caviar. In such transactions the money paid by the Western club goes to the Polish Football Federation, not to the club itself, a handling charge is paid to the Central Sports Office, and the parent club receives a payment not in dollars but in zloties, exchanged by the national bank at the official rate. But this is only half the story. If a Western club is very eager to net a player then it can do a separate secret deal with directors of the parent club so that they can actually feel dollars between their fingers. Players get no money for the transfers as such but are paid separately by the buyer: for example, Juventus of Turin paid Widzew Lodz $1.8 million (not all of which went to the soccer federation) for Zbigniew Boniek. Boniek himself was rumoured to have been paid $1.2 million for his signature. Clubs can reach private deals which allow them to use Italian or French training facilities for three months in a year, and many sports writers in Eastern Europe suspect that football directors have private bank accounts in the West. When the Czechoslovak authorities decided after the 1982 World Cup to ban all soccer players and coaches from seeking contracts with foreign clubs for at least a year, it was not just a way of trying to conserve the thin strands of Czech footballing talent but also a punishment to clubs for not fostering enough skilled talent.

It is a little heavy-handed to suggest that the Gorbachev revolution can transform the Soviet-Bloc football scene. But glasnost – controlled candour – and perestroika ('restructuring') could probably work more effectively on the football field than on the factory floor. Although there will always be large quantities of cash devoted to gambling (certainly for as long as there are consumer shortages), the control of gambling money could be taken out of the hands of organised crime syndicates. Glasnost on the subject of transfer fees would be a start. Poland now publicly announces transfer deals. Widzew Lodz was offered 21 million zloties by Gwardia of Warsaw for the player Dariusz Dziekanowski, Gomik of Zabrze paid 10 million zloties for another player. Fees of about 2 million zloties (advancing in line with the black-market rate of the dollar) are the most common. As in the West, the players receive a percentage of the transfer fee. There is no secret about any of this, and the assumption is that the announcement of the fees puts public pressure on the players to show that he is worth his salt. The quality of Polish soccer has improved accordingly. Making clubs more financially accountable, indeed profit-orientated, also contributes to the standard of play. These are the long-accepted principles of the Western market economies and, in general, they work: that is, the clubs with the most attractive (or most successful) football draw the biggest gates. Glasnost and perestroika, without imitating strict market conditions, can achieve similar results. If a crime syndicate regularly rigs matches then the level of play will be correspondingly dull. Spectators will stay away (or, increasingly, fight in the stands). Until now, this has not mattered: as long as football managers were getting their rake-off from the gambling gangs, then they could tolerate the falling gates. But strict economic accounting could force the all-too-corruptible soccer bosses to think again.

10

Travellers' Tales

Smugglers are on the margin of Western society. Even in the British West Country with its mythology of brandy casks rolled onto beaches at night and of cut-throat struggles with customs men, even there smuggling was a fringe activity to all but the smallest of Cornish fishing communities. The old-fashioned contraband networks survive in the Far East and in the cigarettes gangs of the Neapolitan Camorra, but mainly they have given way to the traffic in heroin, cocaine and weapons. Smuggling is big business that profits from the complusion of addicts or the desperation of countries at war; little romance, no popular acceptance.

In Eastern Europe, smuggling has become an essential factor in everyday life. The coffee in the percolator, the chocolate bar given to a child, the rare orange, the sparking plug, the ink bottle: all these items, available only in semi-legal private markets or heavily priced delicatessen shops, are likely to have been part of a West–East or East–East smuggling chain. Smuggling, of course, makes people rich. It makes holidays affordable. But above all, in the Soviet Bloc, it speaks to each nation's shortages. Contraband provides a snapshot of a country's economic problems . . . And it is the lifeblood of the illegal currency market; some eight hundred million dollars a year enter the black markets of the Bloc through smuggling networks. Smuggling, with its dependence on relatively free or relatively closed travel rules, is also a barometer of the international climate. The opening of an East European tourist industry has made smuggling a national preoccupation, taken it out of the domain of professional criminals. The Hungarian magazine, *Hvg* (a commendable blend of *The Economist* and *Der Spiegel*) estimates that one out of every four thousand East European tourists is a professional smuggler, but amateurs – and the divisions are becoming blurred – make up nearly a thousand more.

Jacek is an exponent of creative tourism. He is a chubby, bearded

young man, the son of a Polish sports writer and his architect wife,
worldly wise. To evade military service he arranged (at a cost of one
hundred and fifty dollars) for a doctor to certify him as a schizophrenic
–and so, in certain sense, he is, living in his parents' roomy apartments
in a Warsaw street still scarred from the War but thinking and dreaming
only of the West, that is the wealthy West, of cruising around Palm
Beach in a white convertible. This is his story.

With two friends he bought fifteen pairs of Rifle jeans from Warsaw
Pewex shops and built a working kitty of hundred dollars. They booked
themselves a berth on a Soviet cruise-liner – deep in the bowels, in the
cheap East European section far away from the dollar-paying First Class
West Germans – departing Odessa for the Black Sea and the
Mediterranean. Business began almost immediately: on the Moscow–
Odessa express, a kind of black market on wheels. In the crowded
corridors, full of rosy-cheeked youngsters on their way to summer camp,
they quickly sold their jeans at thirty roubles a pair. Odessa is a bustling
wheeler-dealer place with a long tradition of dockside bargaining; it
boasts an underworld worthy of Bertold Brecht's *Threepenny Opera*:
sailors, whores, Middle-Eastern, Turkish and Soviet smugglers and
middlemen come together in a noisy, bewildering brew. One Odessa
wholesale black marketeer used, until recently, to hire local policemen
to guard his crates of contraband. Price of the private security service: ten
roubles a day per policeman, payable to the police chief. Jacek and his
friends knew what they were looking for – Black and Decker drills,
unusually cheap in the Soviet Union, and strips of silver acetate. Their
empty suitcases began to bulge and they were last on board the liner.

It was never really clear to the rest of the passengers why the three
Poles were first on the gangway when the ship put into port, and last back
again. Conscientious sightseers, perhaps? The first port of call was
Varna in Bulgaria where the gang found a market for the Odessa goods.
The 'value-added' effect was good and they ended up with more
Bulgarian leva than an honest worker would earn in a year. The crucial
point of the cruise came next, in Turkey. In Istanbul, on the Goldern
Horn, it is possible to buy most things: faked passports, real passports,
currencies of all denominations. It is the only place in the world with a
booming currency market in Bulgarian leva – Turks wanting to send
financial assistance to ethnic Turks in Bulgaria buy their currency there in
the seedy Aksenay district. Jacek converted his otherwise useless Bulgarian
leva into Turkish lira and made the most important transition from a soft to
a hard currency. Not too hard though, so the sum was used to buy

cheap leather coats, small mountains of them, in the so-called Little Bazaar. The ship edged its way into the Mediterrenean. On the upper decks, friendships were struck, passengers fell in love, Germans exercised and the women pressed their dresses for the evening ball. 'We were the only ones who didn't get a tan,' recalls Jacek. 'You have no idea how much planning this kind of business trip needs. There's not much time ashore and you have to make your contacts, get your exchange rates straight, and if they don't have what you want you may have to cross town. By the time we reached Greece, I was completely exhausted.' In Greece, they held on to the leather and used some of their dollars to buy angora wool. In Naples ('It's incredibly easy to do business with the Camorra') they converted leather and wool into dollars. 'They tried lire first but that's more trouble than it's worth and it's too easy for them to fool you, all those hundreds of thousands. We stick to the money we know best.'

Their profits now amounted to a few thousand dollars and, as the liner wheeled around the Mediterranean, there was a short alcohol-fuelled argument about whether to call it a day. But the risk-taker won through. In Tripoli, Lebanon, the last hard-currency port of call, the Poles shed most of their dollars and invested in a shipment of three thousand University of Nebraska T-shirts. 'We were a bit worried. There's always some KGB people on these Soviet ships and it wasn't so simple getting the crates on board. Anyway, we had a friend on board, a steward, who kept some of the boxes safe for us, and the rest were in the cabin. It was a hell of a mess. The crates, some loose T-shirts, some of the leather coats we couldn't sell, a couple of drills that we had forgotten and a couple of videos that the Lebanese had given us for almost nothing.' In Odessa, the customs had to be bribed. 'They pulled all the tricks. Kept us in separate rooms, talked to us separately, said they would confiscate everything but eventually they got round to talking about a once-off import fee, say twenty dollars a box. Well, we got them down to ten and as part of the deal they put us in touch with a garment dealer who cheated us too. Still, three thousand T-shirts at fifteen roubles each gave us a lot of roubles.'

The penultimate stage of the trip was important if the gamble was to pay off: translating a few thousand dollars into tens of thousands of roubles is a false equation if you are stuck with roubles. In Moscow, behind the wedding-cake structure of the Foreign Ministry on Smolensky Square, there are a few narrow streets, some with wooden houses, a rarity seemingly untouched by the march of progress as

measured by cubic metres of concrete. In this area they have friends who
buy and sell gold, but Jacek and his friends needed gems since they had
two borders still to cross, from the Soviet Union into Poland, and from
Poland into the West. The connections between the Moscow diamond
market and the legitimate traders in Hoveniersstraat in Antwerp are too
intimate to admit cheating. If the Moscow dealer sold fake or flawed
stones and the buyer brought them to Antwerp, the word would soon get
back and then a link in an important chain, the financing of Jewish
emigration for the Soviet Union, would be severed.

The diamonds, and the three friends, moved westwards. In Warsaw
there was a big party ('I could relax at last,' says Jacek, who claims he lost
two kilos during the three-week cruise) and one of the gang was
dispatched to the West to cash in the diamonds. And then: martial law
was declared in Poland, the frontiers were closed, and the stray
accomplice never returned. He was last heard of in Sweden, having
claimed political asylum and bigamously married a Finnish nurse. 'I
reckon he must have got about thirty thousand dollars for the diamonds,
the swine.' Jacek gives me the man's full name, address and telephone
number and asks me to publish it in *The Times*. Later I ring the man. In
Uppsala, we agree to meet the following week but there was a cryptic
cancellation. Nowadays, the number does not reply. As for Jacek, after
some months of record-borrowing, come-and-meet-my-girlfriend
relationship, he arrived on the doorstep one night, announced that he
was going to a drying-out clinic and touched me for eighty dollars ('To
be returned, I swear, next week'). I never saw him again, and heard later
that he had become a short-order chef in Malibu.

Travel, then, broadens the mind. Certainly it develops mathematical
skills. Every year, as the Iron Curtain becomes even more porous, East
Europeans travel to the West as tourists, moonlight there and return to
the East to take up their positions in the ranks of the New Rich. Earn
there, Spend here. It takes somebody of Jacek's skill to Buy there and
Earn here, but this too has become a staple part of the semi-criminalised
existence within the Soviet Bloc. Perhaps the clumsy phrase 'semi-
criminal' is too charitable. These creative tourists after all are breaking
the law in the West – earning while on strictly no-work tourists visas –
smuggling wares and currency back into their countries and then
illegally selling their booty or trading in dollars. Yet this has become so
much a part of normal life that most Poles scarcely blink when they hear
variants of Jacek's story. Most have similar, slightly less compound or

less profitable tales to tell. It is even difficult to get policemen to express any kind of alarm at what is going on; in an obscure way, the amateur and professional traders are serving the national interest, bringing dollars to the motherland. Gorbachev is promising to ease Soviet passport regulations and plainly there will soon be a Russian tourist boom within Eastern Europe. That will have its effect on the domestic second economy, just as the liberalisation of the Polish travel rules inflated Poland's black market. In the 1970s, the Polish party chief Edward Gierek was the first Soviet Bloc leader to 'destalinise' tourism. That is, partly to appease a young relatively affluent generation, partly to act as a safety valve in a society of rapidly rising expectations, partly in the spirit of détente, partly in recognition of the value of the dollar black market, he allowed some one million Poles to travel (and even work illegally) in the West. It is often said that the Poles are more Western-orientated than the Russians, but one does not have to dig deep into history for the reasons; the travellers of the 1970s in many ways modernised and Westernised a generation. By 1990, a remarkable seven and a half million Poles a year were being allowed to travel to the West. No other country in the Bloc can match this but in 1988 Hungary effectively lifted its restrictions on travel to the West. Faced with a higher per-capita debt, Hungary had been reluctant to see an outflow of dollars Westwards, but the pressure for change, and some of the considerations that motivated Gierek, led to a policy review. Nobody in Hungary knows how long the new liberal rules will last, and the result is an extraordinary scramble for passports and visas before the domestic and international climate changes.

For the romantic proponents of Mitteleuropa, the spiritual reconstruction of Central Europe along the lines of the old Hapsburg empire, the Mariahilferstrasse in Vienna must be something of a disappointment. Hungarians and Austrians are being brought together again, but in the crudest way, over a shop counter darkly. Perhaps a hundred shops in the street carry the sign 'Magayarul Beszeluenk' – Hungarian spoken – and the jam of Trabants and Ladas and heavy Ikarus coaches unloads several hundred tourists, and proto-businessmen, a week. 'The people simply don't believe in this peace,' the businesswoman, Andre Bagdadli, told Radio Budapest. 'They are worried that this freedom could all be over again tomorrow. So they come and buy whatever they can as fast as they can. After all, what you've got, you've got.' The only real restraint on these East–West shopping sprees is the amount of money Hungarians can legally take out of the country; in the summer of

1988, as Hungarian pilgrims were allowed to cross by the tens of thousands to see the Pope in Austria (and buy a few videos on the side), most had no more than three thousand forints, two hundred Austrian schillings. That does not buy the kind of goods most sought after in Hungary: video cameras, video recorders, computers, heavy ghetto-blasters. Not only is the Soviet Bloc lagging behind in the high-tech and information revolutions; it also has a huge hunger for the personal technology, even for products that simply look sophisticated, look like the work of scientists. In the second-hand Commission shops in Hungary and elsewhere in the Bloc, videos can fetch seven times the Vienna shop price, even with the customary ten per cent deduction from the shop that gives a handsome and, broadly speaking, legal, profit. More profitable by far is the black market not only in Budapest but in every provincial township (prices rise according to geography – lowest in the towns closest to the Austrian border, highest in the capital and close to the Romania frontier). How, though, to pay for these Western treasures? On Mariahilferstrasse, they come in with salami, cheese, vodka, Crimean champagne, Marlboro cigarettes made cheaply under licence in Eastern Europe, large jars of Beluga caviar: expensive, but easily available, Hungarian goods. The computer shops accept the foostuffs in part payment and the atmosphere resembles a village market, as cows might be bartered for a sheep and a goat. The demands of the Soviet-Bloc black market have thus spawned a grey market in the West. The cut-price electronics shops in Vienna are striking up deals with restaurants for the delivery of caviar and salami, and plainly nobody is paying tax on the transactions.

It takes Poles, of course, to perfect this form of bartering. The best smugglers rarely cross frontiers, do not so much break the law as out-manoeuvre it. Near a big shop specialising in detergents on Bracka Street in Warsaw, there is a man with a telex. Little else, apart from the price lists plugged onto the wall with what looks like chewing gum, and a G-plan desk, neatly organised. There is a constant stream of visitors since few trust the telephone. The customers – investors, rather – hand the man one thousand, five hundred or two thousand dollars and sign a form requesting the import of a personal computer as a present for a close relative. The telex chatters. A wholesale computer cash transfer is through. The telex talks again. A Polish textile company needs a personal computer which it is willing to buy for seven million zloties, delivery date to be agreed. Transaction complete. The Polish economy is being forced to modernise but the state cannot afford to purchase computers for dollars and the Russian and home-made brands are inadequate. Polish factories, farms and research institutes, benefiting from the great freedom permitted under the economic reforms, can buy in their own computers, though not with dollars. They are willing to put up small fortunes for the machines providing all the documents are clean and the computers arrive promptly. The electronics wholesalers of the Far East are only too keen to offload their PCs, some of which are already outdated. And the ordinary Pole who put up the dollars gets a return of over twice the black-market rate – in return for a short-term investment and a small lie (computers imported as gifts to relatives carry only minimal duty). The man on the telex skims his profits from everybody, and is on the way to becoming very rich. Somehow he is breaking the law – how can such deals be possible in a Communist society? – but the authorities have not yet worked out a way of prosecuting him. It appears to be a form of smuggling but, as one troubled customs officer admitted, new laws will have to be invented to cope with this form of cross-frontier private enterprise. The Gorbachev revolution, it seems to me, can be deemed successful at the point where the man with the telex is not only tolerated but officially recognised and encouraged.

The charm of smuggling compared to other crimes is that though many are cheated, nobody loses. In the computer scam, the Polish state is denied customs duties and sale tax, but it gains a more efficient factory. Most of the individual tourists smuggling within the Soviet Bloc – now a large, thriving business with an impact on international relations – fall into this category. Cheating a state which fails in its fundamental obligation to manage the economy in a way that feeds and clothes its citizens does not seem such a heinous crime. The degree of criminality increases, the more precisely one can identify winners and losers. Nobody, not even his two expensive defence counsel, could argue that Kyril Rashkov was simply improving the flows of goods between countries in short supply. Rashkov was a crook who exploited the East–West marketplace for the enrichment of his family. His one real innovation was to bring organised crime, in the sense of the Sicilian mafia, to Bulgaria.

Even in the courtroom, Kyril Rashkov looked the part: a pampered godfather, a padrone, used to obedience and respect. At forty-five, he was the scion of a criminal dynasty. The criminal records of the family date back to pre-war times: a Rashkov was jailed in Plovdiv in 1937. Nearly all of the adult family members have served time; Kyril's sister,

Dashka, for example, has been sentenced twenty times. The Rashkovs are of gypsy origin and originate from the village of Katunica in Yugoslavia. They only become wealthy after settling in Bulgaria. Kyril's father was almost illiterate but he had a great love of gold and a great talent for crime. He gave Kyril the very best education, teaching him pickpocketing skills, how to steal, respray and sell cars, and the various arts of cross-border trading. Georgi developed an international network, based on 'agreements of trust' between gypsy families in Yugoslavia and Romania. Kyril travelled everywhere with his father, sat in on negotiations, fixed prices with him, bought and sold gold. When Georgi died, the funeral lasted four days and four nights and Kyril was crowned head of the Rashkov family. Unfortunately, he was jailed shortly afterwards for a petty crime and so could not undertake big operations until 1983. Kyril made up for lost time, developing the biggest Balkan smuggling racket in Bulgarian criminal records. His network spanned, indeed spans, Yugoslavia, Turkey, Greece, Bulgaria and parts of Romania. The staple contraband were electronic watches and gold jewellery, with sidelines in video recorders, cassettes and silver.

While in prison in the 1980s, Kyril borrowed one hundred and eighty thousand leva as start-up capital from a fellow prisone, a one-eyed banker called Christiv. The loan was secured by four kilos of his father's gold. The cheap quartz watches were snapped up throughout his main trading area, Yugoslavia, Bulgaria and Romania; they looked Western, chic, were easy to run (Rashkov smuggled the batteries too), and above all more interesting than the heavy Russian watches which had dominated the Balkan market since the War. After a while Rashkov's foreign partner demanded payment in precious metal – preferably platinum or silver – rather than Bulgarian leva, which can only be offloaded in Istanbul. Rashkov found the answer: electronics factories in Plovdiv and Asenovgrad where the silver was being routinely used in production. Silver and gold are still under-priced in the Soviet Bloc; it would be impossible to demand that factories pay world-market prices for industrial silver since that would throw the whole economic plan out of kilter. Security is weak – since the silver was bought cheaply it was not regarded as deserving of high security – and Rashkov found no difficulty in penetrating the factories. Within two years his placemen had stolen several kilos of silver. The thieves were paid generously, their families were guaranteed a monthly income should the thieves be caught, and Rashkov's defence lawyers were always at the disposal of gang members who were arrested.

Shortly before Rashkov was himself arrested for the second and perhaps final time, the Bulgarian police had intercepted seventeen cases of contraband weighing fifty kilos coming from Hong Kong. The delivery was supposed to made by a foreign TIR truck from Vienna to Rashkov's Plovdiv villa. One of the cases contained ten thousand quartz watches.

It was a complicated case to follow. Rashkov, well tailored but without a necktie, occasionally rubbed his wrists – the handcuffs had been too tight – and constantly conferred with his counsel. In the dock with him (not all present on the day I was there) were forty-five members of the gang, most with some form of family kinship. Another hundred were due to face trial. The Bulgarians were treating the trial not only as a big smuggling case but also as an attempt to break the back of organised crime in the Balkans. It was the East European equivalent of the Palermo *maxi-processo* in the same year, a legal assault on the Mafia that shocked by the sheer numbers of defendants. Like the Sicilian Greco family, the Rashkov family was undone by a *pentito*, a turncoat. In Rashkov's case, two: Ivan Kostov, who had cheated the padrone by selling him three litres of rosewater (a valuable Bulgarian contraband unit since it is prized in the West) that turned out to be sunflower oil, and Stanko Stanchev, a minor gang member who was probably a police informer all along. Rashkov took out contracts on both men; a burly, tattooed former fellow-prisoner was to take them out for thirty thousand leva each. The targets heard of the contracts and turned to the police at a time when it seemed that Rashkov's political protection was weakening in Plovdiv.

The defence ploy was to discredit the informers, and this entailed long, obscuring sagas in which more dirt was poured on the hapless Kostov than on Rashkov. But the testimony gave a startling glimpse of the Balkan smuggling underworld. Tribute had to be paid to Rashkov by all and sundry, including, it seems, politicians, and an appointment with the forty-five year old godfather was almost impossible to obtain. The interviewee had to be vetted, to offer references and to bring gifts. Rashkov had a personal bodyguard armed with an automatic pistol. The inner circle boasted ten guns, including an old Sten machine-gun. Above all, the Rashkov family had an eleborate information net. When the police arrived at his three-storey villa (each floor equipped with a television and video recorder and Persian carpets) Rashkov was expecting them and had coffee on the brew.

He was jailed, in 1987, for fifteen years. Half his property has been confiscated, though that still leaves him one of the richest men in Bulgaria, certainly its richest prisoner. The latest reports (from the head of Sofia CID, Georgi Dilov) is that the Rashkov family is still in business and that the titular head of the mafia is a seventeen-year-old Rashkov with a record of pickpocketing.

Gypsy families have an inherent advantage in the Soviet-Bloc black marketeering. They come with ready-made international connections and are not intimidated by frontiers. Not all family members are registered and so can by-pass laws (in the Soviet Union, Romania and Poland) that make it obligatory to have a job. And they have long experience in dealing with gold. Gypsy gangs are an important link in many smuggling chains. There is for example the Warsaw–Lvov–Bucharest express. A Polish-Russian partnership runs sought-after Polish soaps, perfumes and shampoos as well as the obligatory jeans into the Soviet Union, trades the jeans on the way to Lvov (a forward garrison for the Soviet army) receiving gold and jewellery in return, pulls the emergency brake at Gorodok, disposes of the scented contraband, and is met by a happy gypsy in Bucharest who buys the precious metal and sells yet more jeans. On the return journey, the jeans are sold on Soviet territory, again for gold. The Pole later sells the gold in West Berlin. That is a somewhat telescoped account: there are important national price differentials involved, bribes for customs officials and much advance bargaining to save time. The most remarkable aspect, though is the permeability of the Soviet Bloc. Lvov is out of bounds for Western journalists, so sensitive is its troop concentration, while Ceausescu's Romania did everything in its power to scare away visitors from other East European countries (*Polityka*, the Polish weekly, warned in 1987: 'If you can avoid travelling to Romania, do so'). Yet the black market penetrates these borders with the ease of a spoon through blancmange.

The other breed of traditional smugglers are the mountain people; families who have lived for centuries in the Tatras or the Carpathians and who know every path. Mountain frontiers are notoriously difficult to patrol; there are no minefields or watchtowers, only wooden huts, a straggly fence, and dogs that bark in the night. The anti-Nazi underground often sent their couriers through the passes, and for years Czechoslovaks and Poles have been smuggling horses across the frontier. Nowadays the mountains are one of the best routes to bring precious metal to the West. Interpol has an open file on an international gang that gathered at least five tonnes of silver (over several years) and took it through the mountains of Czechoslovakia and from thence into

Austria and world markets. The thieves scoured every industrial plant in southern Poland, ripping silver out of electric contacts (and thus frequently immobilising cranes for a fortnight or more) and putting it together with silver stolen from homes or churches. The heavier silver was melted down and moulded into rods or bars and then, in loads of twenty or fifty kilos, carried across the border and dropped in the Slovak villages of Witanowa, Zuberec and Hladowka. The Poles made about ten crossings a year and received about three hundred dollars a kilo, payable in two instalments. On the way back, the Poles would smuggle in Socialist currencies. In Czechoslovakia the local farmers would transport the silver with their normal market fare to Bratislava. Austrian TIR trucks picked up the loot and stashed it in hidden panels. Some of the group have already been arrested and sentenced, the Austrian dealers received three to four years, the Slovaks between seven and eight years. But key figures in the racket are still being sought including (almost too good to be true) a blonde woman whose criminal trademark was a set of immaculately manicured nails, painted silver (*Przeglad Tygodniowy*, 24 August 1986).

The real fear of the authorites is that the international co-operation between criminals in the West and the black marketeers and smugglers of the East will lead sooner or later to a major drug-trafficking network. It was noticeable, when I lived in Moscow in 1976–77, that the Soviet police were trying to block the use of Moscow as as a transit stop for drug transport into the West. Big-time operators were (and are) commissioning down-and-out or adventurous young tourists to take cheap Aeroflot flights from Bangkok and New Delhi to the West. After a dozen arrests, and stiff jail sentences, the Moscow Connection died down. But the customs set up a specialist anti-narcotics unit within the Customs service and stationed officers at Sheremetyevo. There is still no on-the-spot laboratory testing and so suspects are almost always doomed to miss their flight while un-explained white powder is sent to the police or KGB laboratories in the centre of the capital. But the worry extends beyond Moscow as a transit route. Both the Soviet Union and Poland have large and uncontrolled poppy crops and are major producers for morphine for domestic pharmaceutical use. In Poland this has already led to problems, with private farmers selling crops directly to syndicates of domestic drug dealers. So far the crop ends up mainly as a potent, injectable brew known as *kompott*, with no international implications. But some Polish heroin had been finding its way to West Germany. Clearly the Soviet

and Polish fields do not compare with the rich pickings in Turkey and
the Golden Triangle, but as drug addiction has grown (in the Soviet
Union especially after the Afghanistan war, which introduced many
young soldiers to naroctics) so the potential for large scale cross-border
trafficking arises.

An intriguing (though, in the style of early glasnost vintage 1988,
rather highly coloured) documentary film outlined the drug traffic
between Afghanistan and Soviet Turkmenistan. The fact is that the
Soviet authorities are as afraid of organised crime, *alla* Siciliana, as
they are of drug addiction. The restricted-circulation magazines published for the KGB border troops are full of horror stories about the mafia
which, in the mind of the simple customs officer, must now appear to be
one of the major forces in Western policy. The idea of a criminal
organisation that embraces the production, refining and distribution of
drugs, that recycles the profits through friendly banks, that has scores of
sidelines and that thinks nothing of buying up customs officers,
confirms every prejudice of the KGB soldiers on the borders; on the
other side of the fence there is a vast corrupt conspiracy, an infection
that has to be guarded against. Yet in so far as organised crime is
functioning within the Soviet frontiers, it is operating under their noses.
The diplomatic bags out of Moscow (untouchable) are probably among
the most abused in the world. It is impossible to cofirm this, of course,
though each embassy claims its own purity and nods discreetly towards a
neighbouring mission. Yet valuable icons and antique jewellery have
been passing out of Moscow since 1917, finding their way into private
collections, into galleries in West Berlin that ask few questions, and into
auction houses. Those who deal in such things know that diplomats are
good and sometimes gullible customers.

Tourist Wars

There is no such thing as a 'leisure industry' in the Soviet Bloc. State
travel agencies exist, and there is even a degree of competition, but as
long as the status of 'travel' is uncertain, so too is the planning of
holidays. East Europeans, with the exception of those enjoying political
protection, worry until the last minute whether they will be granted a
passport or visa. Yet tickets, unless bought with money converted on the
black market, entail years of saving. Hotel reservations can be switched
or cancelled at whim; truly it is a journey without maps.

Little wonder that the aspiring tourist wants to minimise the risk of disappointment. It is obviously easier for an East German or a Czech or a Russian to obtain a passport to visit a Black Sea resort in Bulgaria than a Mediterranean resort in Spain. No visa is needed and it is far cheaper. Even so travel, any kind of travel, is a luxury, and luxuries have to be paid for. The result is a rapid rise in intra-Bloc smuggling by individuals rather than organised gangs. The volume of tourist smuggling is now so large that it can virtually count as a separate 'service' sector within the Comecon.

The essence of good holidays is consumer intelligence. You are Bulgarian, travelling to friends in Soviet Moldavia: buy rosewater, Polish cosmetics and meat preserves before departure, sell them in the Soviet Union and buy caviar, in Sofia sell the caviar and pay for a week of your holiday. You are East German and desperate to travel anywhere. You settle on Czechoslovia. You take four bicycles, one for each family member and sell three. You buy a tent, hammock and a car-boot load of sports equipment. At home you sell at a profit. You are Polish and go anywhere: take cheap clothing, a fox-fur coat and Western cigarettes, you sell and buy anything.

Shopping raids have been part of East European cross-border traffic since the Second World War, a natural, spontaneous way of solving domestic consumer shortages. With the exception of a Polish–East German flare-up in the 1970s, they were broadly tolerated. But as consumer supplies worsened, as the Soviet-Bloc debt crisis deepened and the priority was placed on earning dollars rather than satisfying the housewife and the worker, so the regulations were tightened. The southern food producers complained about the plunderers from the north, and the East Germans complained again about Poles, some of them sporting Solidarity badges, who stood in the middle of city shopping centres selling hard-to-get Russian hand-drills; the Czechs revealed a streak of nastiness, the Yugoslavs moved into Poland, and the Hungarians, with their full shops, protested about the way that the forint was becoming the premier Communist black-market currency.

The first shot in a tourist onslaught that culminated in the tourist war of the late 1980s, began in August 1979 when Romania insisted on tourists from other Comecon countries paying in dollars for petrol used during holidays there. The Romanian logic was simple: since it had to pay hard currency for its energy imports, Soviet-Bloc tourists should help balance the books. It was not an unreasonable demand, and East Germany and Czechoslovakia swiftly reached reciprocal agreements with Bucharest. Soon afterwards East Germany, followed by other

Comecon countries, made it compulsory for Socialist tourists to buy
petrol coupons in advance. By 1980, the Solidarity crisis in Poland was
influencing customs behaviour throughout the Bloc. Scared not only
that their shops woud be emptied by panic-buying Poles but also that the
Solidarity bacillus would be brought along in the shopping bag, East
Germany and Czechoslavkia imposed visa and currency regulations
that effectively sealed the borders. In November 1981, Hungary
imposed a general ban on the 'personal export' of a wide range of
consumer goods and soon afterwards Hungary, Bulgaria and Romania
put a strict limit on the value of food taken out of the country by tourists.
Martial law, declared on 13 December 1981, put a temporary end to the
Polish looting of neighbouring countries, but by the mid-1980s, they
were on the road again, truffling out the market shortages and surpluses
in every Comecon country. Only East Germany maintained a
fundamentally hostile approach. Poles travelling to West Berin – close
by and not needing a visa – were treated uniformly as smugglers when
they crossed East German territory. In 1979, three and a half million
East Germans visited Poland, and five and a half million Poles returned
the visit. By 1987, the figures were down to twenty-five thousand East
Germans and forty-five thousand Poles; a shameful figure for two
neighbours, in the same alliance, sharing an intricate history.

By 1989, the frictions between different countries had become
intolerable. A traveller crossing the Hungarian–Yugoslav border in that
year told me of a scene at the beginning of the holiday season. 'The
customs guard came into the compartment and asked which luggage
belonged to whom. He didn't look inside and just went by the size of the
case – thirty dollars for that one, fifty dollars for that, a hundred – yes, a
hundred dollars – for the trunk.' That appears to have been a
misunderstanding (though there have been many such incidents) by a
corrupt officer who thought he was dealing with professional smugglers
rather than hapless tourists. But in the same hot summer the
Hungarians demanded a thirty per cent deposit on the value of goods
bought in by East European tourists. The sum moreover had to be paid
in dollars – at a time when most Soviet-Bloc countries imposed strict
dollar export rules – and the money would be returned, less a two per
cent administration fee, at the end of the visit. The Hungarians did not
inform their neighbours before imposing the rules at the beginning of
the season and thus effectively destroyed many holidays since most
tourists did not have enough cash to continue. The same rules came
into force in Romania the year before. The Romanians, as ever, offered

an exotic alternative: those who did not have enough dollars for a deposit could leave half of their luggage in a specially sealed railway carriage. In practice the railway carriage ended up at the other end of the country and the luggage was lost, since if it was not reclaimed within ninety days it was automatically ceded to Romania. Poles, accustomed to trading openly in Yugoslavia and making a decent profit there, came up against similar, not quite so tough, rules at the main border points. This was by way of retribution against Polish customs who had been imposing informal fines on Yugoslav tourists. The enterprising Yugoslavs have been buying cheap tours to Warsaw, converting their dinar on the black market and (and there is no fooling a Serb on the current exchange rates) buying up suits, underwear, luggage and car spare parts. The customs officers moved through the buses, taking several hours to see if Polish labels had been unstitched and imposing hefty fines.

Each country has been expanding its list of forbidden goods. The East German customs guard, a particularly self-righteous breed, strides into a compartment and barks out, 'Any weapons, cameras, electric equipment, newspapers, coffee, medicines, video cassettes?' He (or she – on one frontier post there is a set of menacing twins who resemble Rosa Kleb) is reciting only a small fraction of the list. The catalogue of prohibited goods for each State, constantly updated, fills whole pages of newspapers, or would if they were publicised. The rule of thumb is: don't take out anything for which there is a demand at your destination. Thus the Hungarians have added lavatory paper to their list of prohibited goods but enforce the ban only for Poles and Romanians (where there is a shortage), and not for Britons or Americans. By the same token, the Czechs forbid the personal export of cuddly toys, and are capable of snatching them from the arms of children, the East Germans ban the export of wallpaper, the Russians prohibit the export by tourists of anything pre-1945, and (useful tip, this) Siberian moose antlers. These rules, which deflect from the real anxieties of the State – the smuggling of drugs, weapons and precious metals or stones – effectively make a smuggler out of every traveller. With sufficient manpower and political will, Soviet-Bloc customs could without much ado arrest every second traveller. It boils down to a question of national temperament, ideological training, political will and manpower. The East Germans have more customs officers per capita than any other Comecon country and only a narrow strip of national territory to patrol. The personal element is decisive, though; in 1986, relations were soured between Prague and Warsaw by an insensitive customs officer striking a

blow in the tourist war. Czechoslavak officials, briefed to stop the
personal export of shoes, ordered a nine-year-old girl to remove her
shoes, bought in Bratislava. The mother did not have a spare pair – she
had presumably thrown away the old Polish pair on buying the new ones
–and so the girl crossed the frontier barefoot. The mother told the Polish
customs post, which stopped the next Czech-registered car. They
demanded to see a sales receipt for the cars's new tyres and, dissatisfied
with the result, they removed all four wheels and jacked up the car for
the Czechs to see. The incident was proudly recorded in all major Polish
newspapers.

They are an odd collection, Soviet-Bloc customs men. Underpaid,
working unpleasant shifts, as beloved as gamekeepers, they are the most
dogmatic of all officialdom. When the Polish authorities had to find a
new job for a discredited secret-service general, Wladyslaw Ciaston –
deeply implicated in the murder of the Solidarity priest, Father Jerzy
Popieluszko – the first natural choice was as head of the customs service.
(As it turned out, he was sent to the Polish mission in Albania, where he
feels comfortable enough.) The customs service has to believe in the
Class Enemy; long after the Soviet Army ended its primitive stereo-
typing in political education classes, KGB border troops were being
trained to resist Capitalist subversion; one key lesson is how to cope with
British commandos parachuted into the Ukraine to blow up railway
lines. Times are changing in the Soviet Bloc, but the customs men are
the last uniformed outpost against Gorbachevism. They are the
Lefèbvrists of the Socialist Church.

Still, Jozef O., head of the Customs 'Black Brigades' on the Polish
Baltic, was amiable enough. I wanted to find out how the Gdansk black
market had become so large and comprehensive that it rivalled Odessa
as the Communist world's illicit trading centre. He was phlegmatic, and
he had been carefully briefed. Everything was under control – Gdansk,
the black market, the internal situation, his facial features, his fists so
tightly clenched that they had to be stuffed in his pockets. 'We are called
the Black Brigade because our officers used to get smeared with oil when
they inspected coal carriers some years back. That was how spirits were
usually smuggled in. Sometimes the sailors would break a bottle of
booze over a pile of coal to get us to search in the wrong place. The real
bottles were hidden somewhere else of course.' All fine nowadays. In
1981 – 'when there was political chaos here,' 'Solidarity?' 'The anti-
Socialist attack on our state' Ah, yes, then – the customs had intercepted
fifty kilos of heroin on the Wladyslawowo. Nothing much since then. It

was difficult to search a ship – 'The sailors know the design of the ship intimately and if we find something hidden they can always deny that it's theirs' – but the trend was away from the professional maritime smugglers towards the passengers, tourists-cum-businessmen. That had the greatest impact on the Gdansk black market. Sailors intended to smuggle dollars; their trading had been carried out en route (using their hard-currency allowances to buy pornographic videos in Hamburg and trading up at each port until they could buy computers in Singapore, selling at a profit in the last Western port before Gdansk). Nowadays, sailors tended to be customers rather than suppliers to the black market. We drank each other's health, a happy stay in Poland, a long life, Peace, Progress, Friendship. We left, he to work, I to rest in a darkened room. 'Tell me', he said clutching my upper arm for the last time, suddenly as cold sober as marble, 'how long have you been working for the CIA?'

11

The Price of a Drink

At midnight the Kristal restaurant in Ulica Marszalkowska has closed, even on the nights that Kasia, a moonlighting ballet student, is supposed to perform a striptease. The street, once Warsaw's proudest boulevard, is empty, yields little to the night-lizards, nothing at all to the thirsty. But a few paces away there is Salvation Square, with its fine double-spired church. During the day, shoppers queue with the discipline of legionaries for fish, for brassières and slippers, for prams, even for second-hand books. The clatter of the trams washes the square. At night, behind the colonnades, Salvation Square offers alcoholic damnation. Dealers, muffled against the cold, present their wares: straightforward vodka (or rather *wodka*) Wyborowa at a huge mark-up on the hard-currency store price, fruit vodkas (even one concocted from cactus) and, for the really desperate, pure spirit. It resembles, in principle at least, a British off-licence; there is none of the normal bargaining of a black bazaar. The clientele include drunks and alcoholics, but also a great many Poles who simply want to extend their evenings and oil their leisure. The police do not interfere, or rather, they pace their patrols at such regular times that the drink dealers can melt away into the corridors of nearby apartment houses.

The black market in alcohol is a huge criminal empire within the Soviet Bloc. In the Soviet Union and Poland the price of vodka is a key dictator of the black-market currency exchange. Raise the official price of Wyborowa in Warsaw, and up goes the unofficial value of the dollar; in this way, the communist authorities can manipulate the illegal markets. The alcohol business both supports and undermines the regime, and therein lies a conundrum from those of the Gorbachev leadership generation who want to use market-orientated reform to create a New Socialist Man. Drinking, hard systematic drinking, is a tradition in Eastern Europe, especially the northern tier of the Soviet Union, Poland and East Germany. Each country has of course evolved its own preferences: the northern countries favour vodka and schnapps, the Romanians potent plum brandy, the Czechs beer. The Marquis de Custine, travelling through Russia in 1839, remarked that 'the greatest pleasures of these people is drunkenness, or, in other words, oblivion.' Accounts of drinking orgies feature in many of the great Russian and Polish classics (see Wsypianki's epic poem *The Wedding*) and the Romanians can date their drinking problem from their distant ancestors, the Getae. Their King, Burebista, ordered the uprooting of all vines to cure the people's addiction to wine. There is thus not only a strong demand for alcohol, but also a long-established pattern of repression. To attend a wedding feast in the Polish countryside, on the second or third day of drinking, is to witness scenes direct from Breughel; the brawls of the early festivities have given way to an extraordinary stupor. Modern Mercedes-owning farmers stagger in slow motion across the field; grown men, who at harvest and sowing time will argue cogently with the hard-baked officials from the state procurement centre, are comatose, dribbling like babies. In short, nothing has changed in four centuries, the quality of excess remains the same.

But there are also more recent contributing factors. The tedium of assembly-line work, the new housing estates, the so-called 'peasantisa-tion' of the proletariat (that is, habits that were imported when young farmers left their land for well-paid jobs in post-war heavy industry): all these aspects of the modern (not necessarily Communist) world have increased an already high alcohol consumption. The Brezhnev era, from the mid-1960s to the early 1980s, saw a rapid rise in worker drunkenness and alcoholism. Wages were pumped up but ways of spending the money – a straightforward leisure or entertainment industry – were lacking. The result: alcohol consumption is five times higher in the Soviet Union now than in 1940. In individual republics, such as Georgia, alcohol intake increased 150 per cent during the Brezhnev years. Average per capita consumption is now over 8 litres of pure spirits a year in the Soviet Union, among the world's leaders, and even that seriously understates the scope of imbibing.

Gorbachev's first move on taking over power in the Kremlin was to launch his anti-alcohol campaign. It was a logical development of Yuri Andropov's attempts to improve worker discipline, but it was also substantially more than that. Reforming the economy was intended to go beyond the repair of a dysfunctional machine; it was supposed to have a moral dimension. Gorbachev's shorthand for the Brezhnev era, 'the years of stagnation,' implies, in Russian, more than economic decline. Alcoholism and drunkenness had filled a spiritual vacuum depicted most tellingly in the works of Vladimir Rasputin whose book *Pozhar* (The Fire) was an allegory for the Brezhnev period. Drunken village firemen, their sense of duty evaporated, fan rather than quench the flames of a local disaster. The worn joke of the 1970s was that Alcoholism represented the intermediary stage between Socialism and Communism. Gorbachev despised the *laissez-faire* attitude to alcohol abuse and saw it, above all, as a way of diminishing the responsibility of the worker, marinating his conscience.

Yet the economic, as well as social, realities weighed against a crusade. Alcohol sales represent one of the largest sources of revenue for all Communist countries. The demand for drink is such that there is no real upper price margin for vodka; if the price of a litre were doubled tomorrow there might be riots in the Ukraine but, in the end, the workers would pay up and household budgets would show a corresponding hole. Poland, unlike the rest of the Soviet Bloc, regularly publishes a list of the 500 most profitable companies: Polmos, the official producer and distributor of alcohol, is always at the top. In 1986 Poles spent the equivalent of 2.3 billion pounds on alcohol: that is admittedly swollen by an unrealistic exchange rate but it excludes about £80 million spent in hard-currency stores on alcohol and it excludes, too, all moonshine. About 40 per cent of the food budget of the average Polish household is devoted to alcohol. Some of these revenues are supposed to flow back into funding drying-out clinics, but there is not much to show for it. The same proportions hold true for the Soviet Union. At least one estimate puts it higher – one-third of combined family income goes on vodka – but this is mainly guesswork in such an ethnically and culturally mixed country.

What is clear is that the budget balancers of the Soviet Union were unhappy with Gorbachev's compaign. In the autumn of 1988 (27 October) Finance Minister Boris Gostev announced that the budget deficit would reach 36.3 billion roubles (about $59 billion at official rates) in 1989. The main reason was the sharp drop in alcohol revenues. At the start of the Gorbachev years, sales tax on alcohol represented 90 per cent of all the selling price, an effortless money-spinner for a capital-starved government. There were two other important strands of opposition to Gorbachev on alcohol. The first argued that the Gorbachev revolution was about increasing personal freedom through economic reform. In so far as there is a Thatcherite lobby in the Soviet

Bloc, it claims that there is a necessary link between increased economic efficiency, responsibility and initiative, and a freedom of choice in personal lives. Since Russians cannot be given a genuine choice of political party, they can at least be allowed to hear and read opposing or critical views, they can be given a better variety of consumer goods and more control over their individual budgets. Banning, or severely restricting vodka, 'the green snake', does not seem to fit into that equation.

Second, the hardliners plead that an anti-alcohol campaign hits directly at the working class who are already bearing the brunt of economic reform. Certainly, four years after the anti-alcohol crusade was launched it remains one of Gorbachev's most unpopular acts, except, perhaps, with the Soviet housewife. But even she has been hurt: she may see more of her husband's wage-packet on payday but bulk buying of sugar (to produce moonshine) has produced new shortages.

There is a key to understanding the Gorbachev era in all of this. He is not committed to the 'market' except insofar as it solves problems. The battle around Gorbachev is not so much Market *v.* Plan, but in the definition, the setting of the problems to be tackled. Gorbachev sees alcohol abuse as causing serious losses to the economy, debilitating the workforce, raising the crime rate, creating a criminal sub-culture in many Soviet cities and damaging physical health. On the other hand, alcohol revenue keeps the budget in balance and ensures a relatively quiescent working class. Controlling alcohol consumption has never been successful, and attempts to ration or restrain are putting great strain on the uniformed police. Gorbachev studies the pros and cons and settles for intervention. But the negative aspects will be the most immediately visible: the worker disgruntlement, the overcrowded police cells, the budget gap. A *laissez-faire* policy would have avoided these all-too-exploitable difficulties.

Has Gorbachev, then, defined the problem correctly? What are the real losses of alcohol abuse? Alcohol consumption is on the increase in all Soviet-Bloc countries but it has been rising steeply in Western Europe too, a reflection of prosperity, greater disposable income, a wider choice of drinks. The most commonly cited Soviet figure is of a 1 to 3 per cent loss in industrial production due to drunkenness. There are variants: for example, one per cent of Soviet construction workers are reported to be incapacitated through drink every day of the week. Productivity in all Soviet factories is down 12 to 15 per cent on Mondays, or days following festivities – the hangover effect.

Absenteeism, the bane of all Soviet-Bloc industry, is directly linked to drinking. Dr George Kolankiewicz reports Polish survey showing that alcohol interfered with 40 per cent of production in Poland and caused up to 15% of industrial accidents. A sociologist studying the Russian Republic wrote that 'more than half of all fatal accidents in just one year involved people in a state of inebriation. Drunkards caused a quarter of all industrial accidents. The number of accidents and injuries on days off and on holidays increases, and on paydays doubles.' (Quoted by Binyon, *Life in Russia*, 1983).

The case for alcohol rationing is also strengthened by the crime figures. In the Soviet Union, 90 per cent of all murders are committed under the influence of alcohol, 50 per cent of all traffic accidents, two out of five rapes, 63 per cent of all accidental drownings are influenced by alcohol, one-third of all emergency calls made to Moscow hospitals are because of drink-related crises. These figures are both stunningly candid and deliberately misleading. Candid, in the sense that fifteen years ago it was difficult to persuade Soviet authorities to admit even the existence of crime, let alone its connections with alcoholism. Misleading, in that the exact relationship is disguised, partly to strengthen the teetotalitarian cause. And there is a bit of neo-Stalinist voodoo included: since Socialist Man should not be capable of crime, his senses must have been fuddled by alcohol.

On a bitterly cold February night I was given the opportunity to see how the crime–drink equation works. The Polish Interior Minister, General Czeslaw Kiszczak, had decided it was time for some glasnost in the ways of the uniformed police and so granted a long-standing request to accompany a police van on night patrol in Praga, the scabby transpontine suburb of Warsaw. Praga is where the Russians arrived first in their drive to liberate Warsaw; arrived and stayed, while the Germans wiped out the anti-communist resistance on the other side of the Vistula. As a result Praga can still boast the long courtyards, side-streets, quasi-slums, the poor sewage of the 1930s. Across the river, the city, razed by the Germans, had to be rebuilt; Praga remained a low priority. Its criminal centre is the Bazaar Rozyckiego, a permanent open-air market where, as in Harrods, one can buy anything. Here, at a price, it is possible to buy Western pharmaceuticals, East German children's shoes, school textbooks, caviar and Red Army leather belts (traded by the Soviet garrison), exotic fruit.

Captain Hoffman of the main Praga precinct is briefing the patrols. He alerts the fifty policemen, two to a van, that a foreign correspondent is present, as if to say: Play it clean today, boys. The blackboard on stage lists three missing girls, their descriptions, addresses of parents. In a monotone he reads out the previous night's robberies and their booty: a hi-fi set, three BMW tyres, car radios, a set of reproduction furniture, one mink, three fox furs, jewellery. The city's best fences, and the hottest goods, are in Praga. The patrolmen are told to use their eyes. With care (in some cases, with lip-chewing agony) the militia enter the details into their logbooks. The captain moves along the desks, arranged in two factory lines as if in readiness for a school quiz, checking guns.

Sergeant O. and Sergeant Z. have drawn the joker, the foreign correspondent. They do not look very happy about it, though Sergeant Z. is suspiciously bright and later, during the midnight tea-break, suspiciously frank. Sergeant O., like all the confraternity, finds it difficult to say anything without a scatological adjective and so, in a nine-hour shift, prefers to say nothing; he drives well.

'We've got three *milena,*' says Sergeant Z. A '*milena*' is an illegal still. There are perhaps twenty illegal stills on his patch of a dozen streets; potato vodka mainly, but there are many brands. As in Moscow, the alcoholic can tolerate most things: formalin from morgues (urban moonshine-producers frequently work in hospitals where alcohol can be stolen), varnish, wood alcohol, valerian, eau de cologne. Down it goes. But the committed drinker, as opposed to the alcoholic, is more discriminating. There is so much competition that he can afford to pick and choose. The quality of Polish urban moonshine is high.

The patrol, following a random pattern, is supposed to raid at least three stills a night. That's the theory. In practice there are emergency calls, and brawls and a dozen routine tasks (Sergeant Z. starts the night by serving a court summons) that interfere with the pursuit of the alcohol producers. The van crawls around the streets. Sergeant Z. enters new Solidarity slogans, written on walls, into his log-book. They will be painted out within a day.

A brawl in a café; the manager has rung for help. 'He was staring at me, like it was none of his business, so I thought he was going to do something, put one on me, so I put one on him . . .'

'And smashed a bottle on his back.'

'Yeah, but no harm done.' And sure enough, in the half light, everyone seems to be friends again. Three men are on the floor, drunk but not comatose, only sleeping like bears grateful for the warmth. The manager withdraws his complaint.

The patrol checks the back of a supermarket. Two figures have been seen outside. A man and a woman, it emerges, making love on the bonnet of a car. It is minus eight degrees centigrade, and falling.

At a bus-stop, a drunk has lain down on a bench and is now unconscious. An ambulance is called. The man looks blue; the policeman is worried, but not the doctor. There is a short debate about whether to take him to a sobering-up station or to the casualty department. The policemen stamp their feet to keep the blood flowing; it is time for the first raid, if only to get into a warm room.

There are important clues. A neighbour has spotted someone going into the apartment with a sack of sugar; there is a strange smell in the corridor; the son of the house does not have a valid stamp in his work-book – that is, he is unemployed. Everything points to a new still.

The mother is baffled when she opens the door. No, she hasn't seen her son for a day or two, but then he's twenty, a grown-up.

'Can we come in?'

'Do you have to?'

'We can come back later.'

'It's already 10.30. You can't do that. Not without a warrant.' The woman, a true Praga vixen, knows the rules.

'We'd like to come in anyway, now if you don't mind.' The militia men move in; the small hallway is like a crowded lift.

'So your son's not at home?'

'As you see.'

'When's he getting a job?'

'He's looking all the time – it's not easy nowadays. FSO [the car factory] might take him. Who's that?' A jab at the correspondent.

'He's with us. Switch off the television please.' Sergeant Z. moves easily into the kitchen. 'A lot of potatoes.'

'Hungry boy.'

'A lot of sugar.' He is going through the cupboards. 'A very big pan.'

'I like soup. What is all this? If you don't get out soon, I'll call your boss.'

Sergeant Z. fingers a large funnel, meaningfully. Then he bends his knees slightly and looks straight into the woman's eyes and speaks very quickly, very quietly: 'If you know what's good for you, you'll stop playing around and if that son of yours should try it on, if he ever comes back here that is, then he can reckon with a bit more than a fatherly little chat.' There was much more, inaudible. Sergeant Z., until now an apparent graduate of Police Charm School, had shifted from the formal

'*Pani*', the third-person form of address, to the familiar, more menacing, '*ty*'. The woman understood, but was not at all intimidated. The policeman, in the manner of a New York cop, continued to stare hard at the mother, until finally she gave way and with an exasperated wave of the hands declared, 'All right, all right, I'll have a word with Piotrek when he comes back, try to calm him down a bit. Now please get out!'

'Thank you,' says Sergeant Z. with the courtesy of a social worker visiting a client, keeping the casebook up to date. 'Sorry to disturb you.'

In the van, Sergeant Z. makes notes and talks over his shoulder. 'It's quite often like this. To bust a still you've got to catch them red-handed. You know, bottling or carrying bottles out – best of all, catch them selling, money in one fist, bottle in the other.' The driver laughed.

'Somebody probably tipped the boy off. He hasn't had a job for over a year and we could get him under the anti-parasite law. Probably wouldn't stick, but we can at least give him a scare. So he clears out, stays with a mate for a week, and that's about it – we can stop production for a week. Do you know what difference that makes?'

The radio interrupts. A suspected rape. A woman, middle-aged, blonde, drunk, found walking barefoot down the street, is in the Precinct writing a complaint. The van wheels around, lights flashing. An apartment house, pre-war, with wooden slats and staircase: not polished wood, but bare, splintering strips as if the house was waiting for bricklayers to arrive with cement. Ground floor. Opposite the entrance, a madonna shrine and some candle stubs. The apartment bell doesn't work, so Sergeant O. hammers while Sergeant Z. sees if there is a kitchen window. At last, a woman comes to the door. She is 30 and looks 50. Behind her, all is darkness and whispers; the electricity has been cut off. The husband is brought to the door. He is drunk, but not out of his senses. He is, however, very stupid. Another young-old face, but lower down the age spectrum: 35 looking 18. He is wearing pyjamas and muddy shoes.

'When did you get back home?'

'An hour ago, maybe two. Been asleep.'

Sergeant Z. collects a torch from the van and looks inside the apartment. After a while he finds a plastic bag with a pair of good-quality women's shoes.

'These yours?' he asks the wife. She shakes her head until told to stop by her husband. A child has started to whimper in the gloom.

The shoes, it became clear, were those of the raped woman. The man was handcuffed and taken to the Precinct. It was the only arrest of the night but nobody was jubilant; establishing fact out of the alcoholic haze of both the criminal and victim would prove difficult. (The woman later withdrew her complaint.)

Sergeant Z. had to complete the night's log and Sergeant O., having signed in the van, came into the Precinct for tea, relaxed now that the ordeal of accompanying a correspondent was over. We sat quietly, thinking about the night.

'Gets you down after a while,' said Sergeant O., stroking his thick moustache. Then he got up, opened the window with a jolt and spat some phlegm into the courtyard. It was the end of his working day.

The police in a district like Praga are fighting a containment mission. It is unusually tough terrain, like the Bronx, say, or Toxteth, and in that sense does not represent the complete picture. But certain truths emerge. The first is that while everyday life has become criminalised in the Soviet Bloc – that is, it is essential to break the law in order to survive, or to carry out one's normal work – the subterranean world has effectively been de-criminalised. The police are constrained in some cases, such as prostitution which has only erratically been regarded as a crime, but for the most part they have made the conscious decision to tolerate organised criminals. The gambling syndicates, smugglers, money-changers, illegal brewers, who inhabit the netherworld are barely touched. Socialist states have no ideological machinery for coping with organised crime, nor do they have the staff and resources. Criminal detection is a poor cousin to the secret, political police; it is organised opposition rather than organised crime which has always concentrated the minds of the political overlords. And so criminal sub-culture has not just been tolerated, but allowed to flourish. Since the principal objective is control, the police have an interest in maintaining largely criminal quarters like Praga. Where do most stolen goods end up in Poland? In Praga. Where are the most efficient police informers? Where is the engine of the black market? Praga. The Warsaw police have (by Western standards) a good record in the recovery of stolen goods, solely because of their well-developed information network. Other Soviet-Bloc cities – Gdansk in Poland, Minsk, Kiev, Odessa and Moscow in the Soviet Union, Varna and Sofia in Bulgaria, East Berlin – have their tolerated criminal quarters too. It is not that they were established or even encouraged by the police – that would be too cynical and too sophisticated – but rather that the branches have never been pruned.

Now, however, these criminal oases are growing out of control, and the reason is alcohol. As the taste for alcohol has spread, so too has the influence of moonshine producers, who are the biggest and fattest of the black-market princes. To grasp the full powers of the moonshine syndicates, one has to look beyond the alcohol consumption figures and discern the patterns. In 1938 the average Pole consumed 1.5 litres of pure spirit a year, in 1970 5.1 litres, in 1977 8.2 litres and by now close to 10 litres. But, according to the Polish scholar Dr Stanislaw Frankowski, the official figure for the consumption of wine represents only 40 per cent of the real total, because of home production. And organised illegal distilling of spirits adds about 10 per cent to the consumption figure – that is, consumption is well over 11 litres a year. That is a national average. The number of possible drinkers in Poland is about 20 million out of a population of 36 million. About two-thirds of these drink regularly, while one-third abstains or drinks rarely. About two and a half million belong to the so-called group of 'intensive' drinkers, polishing off about 50 per cent of all alcohol on the domestic market. Now we are approaching a serious definition of the problem. Each 'intensive' drinker consumes an average of 60 litres of 100 per cent spirit a year. That, then is the natural constituency for the moonshine syndicates: over two million adults, at least half of whom are workers in state industry. There is no reason to doubt that the proportions are any different in either the Soviet Union or East Germany. In all of these countries, the share of spirits is extremely high; thus, the average East German drinks 15.4 litres of hard schnapps a year, compared to 6.3 litres in West Germany.

Gorbachev's first step towards criminalising alcohol abuse were plotted with Ligachov while Konstantin Chernenko was still in power. Two months after Gorbachev's accession, the new leadership was ready for action. The detailed measures included a ban on drinking in factories and offices, no alcohol to be served at official receptions, restriction on sales to the hours of 14.00–19.00 (to stop workers arriving drunk for the morning shift) the closing of many bars and a drink ban on all building sites, railway stations, cinemas, airports, hospitals, schools and factories. In September 1985 the price of vodka was raised by 30 per cent: an unskilled worker had to fork out three day's wages for a litre bottle.

The model for the Soviet legislation was Poland, which, in 1982, introduced the first comprehensive anti-alcohol law in the Soviet Bloc. Drink sales were banned before 13.00 hours, sales outlets were restricted, tough penalties were imposed on moonshine producers, special control squads were supposed to check the sobriety of workers and the identity cards of those queueing for liquor. First the Soviet Union, then, from 1987, Hungary and Bulgaria caught up. In Budapest you can be fined a month's wages for having a drink in the office. Drinking is banned from the usual places, but also from the parks. Bulgaria, which has too many wine drinkers, cut the production of alcohol for domestic consumption and converted many bars into cafés.

These measures have had some support among what might be called the enlightened middle class of Eastern Europe. Both the Polish Catholic Church and Solidarity supported the anti-alcohol campaign. Solidarity, a self-proclaimed worker's movement, took the alcohol issue seriously from the beginning, banning all vodka during the strikes in Gdansk in August 1980. (The authorities had blamed previous political uprisings, in December 1970, on drunken, 'hooligan elements' as a way of playing down the seriousness of the opposition and explaining away the violence.) Women tended to favour the anti-alcohol campaign and one Gorbachev measure – to transfer the wages of drinking workers straight into a savings bank account, rather than handing them the cash – has helped family budgeting. But overall alcohol consumption has scarcely been dented; after an initial improvement, it was back to the bottle.

The fact is that moonshine producers and distributors have moulded their market in such a way that it prospers best at a time of strict repression. Partly as a result of the anti-alcohol legislation in Poland, per capita consumption had dropped from 8.4 litres in 1980 to 6.3 litres in 1982 – officially. But moonshine production had in fact expanded to take up the slack, maintaining consumption at around 10 litres of pure spirit. What happened then, and what is happening now in the Soviet Union, was that moonshine production shifted from the tradional stills in the countryside into the towns, especially heavy industrial areas. Police records (see *Dzienik Zachodni*, March 1985) show that moonshine production does not expand at a time of stable prices and reasonable supply, but rather reacts to crisis and rising price. In 1973, some 40,000 cases of moonshine production were brought to the courts; but in 1982, when alcohol was rationed and prices higher, police broke up 14,000 illegal stills. The move to the towns has also created a different kind of moonshine merchant.

The new-look distiller is young, usually a worker (since most drinkers of moonshine are workers) or the educated son of a worker. His sales team includes pensioners and women who do not, by law, have to hold down a job and who can therefore avoid police checks. Distillers usually share a network of distributors, and that is where organised crime has crept in; big-time moonshine producers provide the equipment and contract their work out. Moonshine has to be stored. In the countryside that did not represent a problem; an old barn would suffice. But the urban moonshine business needs connections: a warehouse, trucks, perhaps police protection. In the Soviet Union, *samogon* (home-brewed vodka) has always been the dominant element in the black market, but now it is acquiring the organisational sophistication of the Prohibition years. There are gangland fights over who supplies whom and deliberate price-jockeying – buying up, for example, liquor from official stores.

The problem with the alcohol trade, as opposed to the much, much smaller drugs black market, is its deep roots. Heavy drinking habits can be inherited, both within families and within a class or sub-culture. Gorbachev, by trying to repress these alcoholic traditions, has merely added to their appeal. If drinking hard is 'manly', then drinking illegal brews merely adds to that manliness, reinforces a romantic mythology about the power of drink and the cunning and prowess of drinkers. Whereas drug abuse tends to divide generations, alcohol abuse unites them. Alcohol is an initiation rite; in 1925, only 16 per cent of Russians were said to have drunk alcohol before the age of 18; now the figure is 93 per cent. The twinning of intensive drinking habits with working-class or even criminal low-life traditions defines the resistance to Gorbachev on this issue.

Add to that the problems of a highly developed market, and it becomes clear that Gorbachev had no chance of success using conventional instruments of repression. The illegal alcohol market has in fact three divisions: the hard-currency market, distribution and production. Vodka (or in East Germany a bottle of 'Korn') is a unit of currency. One bottle bribes a ticket collector, two a bank manager, three a teacher. It is 'safe' in a country like the Soviet Union where the possession of hard currency is an offence. In a bribery case, it is evidence easily disposed of. To limit vodka officially is merely to increase the value of vodka as a bribe. Moreover, as spirits are on sale in all Soviet-Bloc hard-currency shops, vodka is actually a store of value, a hedge against inflation. An anti-alcohol campaign cannot eradicate this important symbolic function of vodka in the marketplace. The best bet is to emphasize the health hazards of concentrated vodka consumption; not to interfere in the first place with the purchase of the vodka, but to deter people from drinking it.

China is pursuing a 'market' rather than a repressive approach to alcohol sales in an attempt to break the power of the black market. In 1988 the Beijing government gave permission for state-run stores to set the retail price of spirits and cigarettes. The black market, until then, had virtually controlled all sales of spirits; the official fixed price was set so low that drink had disappeared from the shelves of the state shops. Overnight, the price of a bottle of spirits rose 750 per cent. Black-market dealers were indeed put out of business or forced to lower prices to stay competitive. But simply sanctioning price rises has never been an option for Gorbachev. True, he wants to take the alcohol business out of the hands of the *samogon* producers, but he also, fundamentally, wants to change the personality of the Soviet worker. It is the worker's demand for vodka that keeps the problem at such an acute level. Raising vodka prices in the Soviet Bloc merely strengthens the hold of the black market; the point is to shrivel the demand. The ideological journal *Kommunist* (No. 12, 1985), reflecting Gorbachev's thinking, declared that the attempts to reform and update the economy hinged on the success of the fight against alcohol. This would not be the first time that *Kommunist* has had to eat its words. But it explains in part why Gorbachev is not experimenting in his struggle with the Green Snake. The vodka-recovery circle is indeed vicious. The rigidly-enforced central planning system has made a monotone consumer out of the Soviet worker, giving him few choices, few ways of exploiting his higher wages and increased leisure time. So he resorts to the traditional Russian pursuit, as Marquis de Custine observed 150 years ago, the pursuit of oblivion. Yet to change the system, Gorbachev needs a sober, participating worker; reform cannot function without him. There are no financial resources to summon up an alternative world, a consumer paradise of such baffling variety that drink is forgotten. And there is not even the economic or ideological flexibility to play the Chinese card, to give state supermarkets the right to charge what they want for alcohol. And so Gorbachev's first initiative was doomed to become his first failure. Inside the bottle that he uncorked in May 1985 there was a collection of demon spirits that have played mischief with his attempts to make perestroika a moral, as well as economic, reconstruction.

PART IV

Managing The Market

12

A Suit From Burtons

Suddenly the physiognomy of the Party has changed. The statues, of course, were ripped down, Lenin busts were lugged out of factories and universities and locked in storerooms. In Kozlowa, the Zamoyski palace near the Soviet-Polish border, there are a dozen Stalins, a clutch of Marx and Engels, a brace of Feliks Dzerzhinsky, a Fidel Castro. The old revolutionary heroes have to go somewhere, and the stables of a former royal estate seemed an appropriate retirement home. Outside in the unkempt park, there was a seven-metre high Boleslaw Beirut, the Polish Stalin. His right hand, the one he used to sign death sentences, has dropped off. Kids used to jump over the wall and daub slogans on him, so the curator wrapped him in polythene, a strange crumbling chunk of masonic megalomania. As for Iron Feliks Dzerzhinsky, founder of the KGB, his statue was doomed from the moment that Solidarity took power in the summer of 1989. The official pretext for removing him was the need to build a Metro station under his feet. But the demolition workers made it plain, with the quiet menace of unionists throughout the world, that the statue was built from 'fragile concrete' and might just fall apart when it was hoisted from its foundations. It did, amid much glee; a broken idol for the 1990s.

But the living fleshly representatives of Communism are also undergoing a transformation. Since Stalin, a certain body language has been *de rigueur* for party leaders: the stony face, the half-wave, the positioning of favourites, the slight half-turn that signifies political distance from those who have fallen from grace. The gestures are precise and, though few admit it, are directly adapted from Stalin, the very model of strong leadership. Lower in the hierarchy there are distinctive physical types. The ruddy peasant-made-good; hard-drinking, tough as boot-leather. The corpulent, chain-smoking regional boss; beady eyes, stomach as tender and swollen as a cushion. And the pinch-faced men, frenetic corridor creatures. A popular anthropologist would order them as rams, pigs and weasels. Now it is a bit different. Mieczyslaw

Rakowski, Polish Party chief at the time when the Communists surrendered government to Solidarity, goes swimming two or three times a week. He has plenty of time on his hands. Mikos Nemeth, the short-lived Hungarian Prime Minister, visits a gymnasium. The East German interim premier, Hans Modrow, is another swimmer. Fast-lane Politburo men typically confess to a love of sailing or scuba-diving. If you wanted to blacken somebody in the party leadership in the 1990s, you spread stories about his drinking (Egon Krenz, very briefly the East German party leader in 1989, was marked down in this way). A decade earlier, the drinking would have been a sign of a seasoned in-fighter, a brawny negotiator, a real man. There are still alcoholics at the top, but they declare themselves diabetics (nobody is fooled) and they are the first to go for 'health reasons'.

These shifting life-styles are not solely a matter of display, nor a mimicking of Gorbachev. The new political class, the 'reformers' simply feel different from the Partisan generation, and from the careerists of the 1970s. They measure themselves on a different scale. Higher education, rather than Party agitation in the factories, is the route to power in the Gorbachev era. Gorbachev himself is the first Soviet leader since Lenin (a lawyer) with proper intellectual training. A typical recruit to the Rakowski Politburo was Slawomir Wiatr, a graduate in his mid-thirties, son of a liberal communist, Professor Jerzy Wiatr. He spoke English, could handle impromptu interviews, answered his own telephones, wore Western suits, knew his Marx but barely mentioned him, let his hair curl over his ears; a man of the new breed. Trained intellect does not necessarily make for political intuition. Rakowski, a thoroughly Europeanised former journalist who wrote his own speeches, had none of the instinct or edge of Gierek, or Walesa, two classic worker-politicians. Gorbachev, though, had political sensors as well as an inclination to play the CEO, the Chief Executive Officer. As a Capitalist, he would certainly have made the Forbes 500. As a Communist politician, he was completely modern. The modern politician takes risks, has an eye for the dramatic, gambles with rather than defends his reputation. He is mobile, flying to the scene of disasters, and is not bound suffocatingly to his local constituency. His policies can be broken into comprehensible parcels. He understands the limitations as well as the opportunities of television. His advisors are rotated. He despises Party-babble. He is not bound to a 'Socialist' image – the baggy suit, the neglected body – but rather to a vision of crisp professionalism.

This is a discussion of Platonic forms, and few on the contemporary scene conform in every detail. Krenz was a risk-taker – punching holes in the Berlin Wall certainly qualifies – but only out of desperation. He was a creature of the old order and, indeed, was using politdrama to rescue vintage socialism rather than to reform it.

Communism, said the new class, was not dead, merely slumbering. The ungainly shape slumped in the shade was not a corpse but a tired, unemployed drifter with nowhere to go. Give him a haircut, a bath, a suit from Burtons, sober him up, point him in the right direction, and all would be well. And so the party re-discovered Social Democracy. The attraction was obvious. Social Democracy was the packaging which would, in a pluralist society, allow leftist ideas to compete in the political marketplace. Social Democracy had always been the natural ally, and therefore enemy, of ruling Communist parties. The survival of either trend almost always entailed the exclusion of the other. West German Social Democrats had formally to renounce Marxism in 1957 to become electable. Much later, the British Labour party embraced the market to bring it into tune with the sophisticated electorate of the 1990s. The Communist parties of Eastern Europe which had consolidated their power in the 1940s by merging with Socialists or Social Democrats and then crushing them in 'unity' parties, began in the Gorbachev era to talk again of reviving the 'broad parties of the Left', of the splendid diversity (but essential underpinning unity) of Socialism. That, in the ideological classroom, is known as dialectics. The new-look Communist parties, these born-again Social Democrats, could draw on a large, important body of reformist theorising. True, reform Socialists had been repressed or expelled (as 'revisionists' or worse), but their writings survived, ready for discovery by each new generation. Here, on the Communist Index, were the foundations of a market-orientated, Democratic, or at least competitive Socialism.

Down Rakowiecka Street in Warsaw, a few blocks past the secret police headquarters, there lived a wizened old man who could remember every attempt to devise a form of market Socialism. Edward Lipinksi was well into his eighties when we started to meet. There were books everywhere, in small uncertain piles on the floor like the store room of an antiquarian bookshop. On the wall there was a large oil portrait of an aristocratic lady, a Potocka. And, buried gnomically in a period armchair, cocooned in an over-large silk smoking-jacket, there was the Professor. He was by this time, a member of KOR, the dissident committee for the defence of workers, and our relationship could be charted by which of his friends, and which of mine, had been just jailed or just released. We talked obsessively of reform. He and Oscar Lange had been in the vanguard of working out how the Plan could be unplanned, how the market could be mimicked. Lange had proposed as early as 1938 that a planned economy could resemble a market system if state-owned enterprises behaved in a way that maximised profits. The Planners would collect information about proposed demand and supply and adjust prices up and down (mainly up, of course). Economic reform theory had moved on considerably since then, while the practice of central planning had barely changed since the 1930s. Lipinski would croak: 'Profit! Think profit! What does it mean? Who picks it up? How to spend it?' For each of his informal seminars he demanded a bottle of good French cognac from a hard-currency store, the market price.

Lipinski, Lange and other Polish reform Socialists influenced the Soviet economist Yersey Liberman who tried in 1962 to introduce the idea of factories drafting their own plans. Liberman, in turn, helped to shape the early reform movement in East Germany and Czechoslavakia. Both countries had a developed base and were not in any sense comparable to the Soviet Union of the 1920s. The Plan hurt these countries but to reject it openly would have been a political rebellion against Moscow. The search was on for a middle way.

There is thus nothing astonishingly new about the reform socialism preached by the Gorbachev evangelists. It was the traditional way of rejecting the Plan without seeming to reject communism. By 1990, even this subterfuge appeared unnecessary. But the modern element in Gorbachev's formula was the freedom with which economic and political reforms could be combined. It was always plain to Lipinski that economic decentralisation and lifting the reins from private enterprise would entail radical political changes. But Lipinski ended his life as a dissident: a sweet irony, then, to see Alexander Dubcek receive his honary doctorate from Bologna University in 1988. From this platform he launched the second phase of his political career with a speech crafted to show that he and Gorbachev were marching in step. A year or so later, the Czechoslovak leadership that had remained intact since the 1968 Warsaw pact invasion, had crumbled and Dubcek, the retired forester, was again centre-stage. The fear that economic reform would again unbottle uncontrollable demands for political change had paralysed Czech politics since 1968; the Husak (later the Jakes) leadership was not competent enough to synchronise their watches with Gorbachev. In truth, apart from the familiar slogans, including the unfortunate Socialism With A Human Face, there was not much to connect Dubcek and Gorbachev either. Their respective reform policies derived from different roots and were a response to different national conditions. Prague 1968 went much further than Moscow 1989. The Czechs had acknowledged early on that trade unions would have to become stronger, more independent from the Party. Worker Cuncils were conceived as a genuine attempt to integrate workers in management decisions. But the rise of Solidarity in Poland made Gorbachev think twice before taking over this part of the Dubcek agenda. Other sections of the programme do indeed feed the Gorbachev reforms. Ota Sik, director of the Economics Institute of the Academy of Sciences during the Prague Spring, devised what he called the Third Way between Market and Plan. This followed Lipinski's thinking – state factories would become 'independent market agents' controlling their own investment, funding themselves from their own profits and credits – and proposed three tiers of prices including a broad band of free prices. But to achieve the necessary freedom for factories, wrote Sik, one first had to break the power of the bureaucracy. That is how a sensible, if cautious, reform programme for a developed but ailing economy began to resemble a national uprising. The bureaucracy, and therefore the ascendancy, of the Communist party was under direct challenge. Now, after the 1989 revolutions, reform Socialism appears to be a political eunuch. Then in 1968, the engines of the T-54 tanks were already beginning to rev up.

The Prague revolt of 1989 was a direct echo of 1968. The opposition leadership which snatched the Presidency, and some key cabinet positions, in December 1989 was of the Prague spring generation and, in so far as it had clear goals, it was fighting for the same ideals. But did the mass of demonstrating students really want a re-hash of Dubcekian Socialism – or did they want to cut away from Socialism altogether? In Eastern Europe, 1989 was the year that the Fear disappeared. The 1968 generation were sentimental Social Democrats who had grown up devising ways of tricking the secret police and Moscow. The 1989 demonstrators, only some of whom were born in 1968, had no Fear to shed. The Invasion was not a memory, only a matter of photographic record. Moscow no longer had the power to shape Prague's internal policies and the police had different loyalties. Shortly before he was elected President, Vaclav Havel held a meeting with students. 'We want a free country,' shouted a pretty girl in big wire-framed spectacles.

'And what kind of freedom did you have in mind?', said Havel, with his usual amalgam of cynicism, flirtation and seriousness.

'Freedom from Moscow.'

'You already have it.'

'Then let's get out of the Warsaw Pact!'

Havel became serious. It was precisely this demand in 1968 that plunged the country into its long, dark night.

'No,' he said after a while. 'Let's not. Let's wait for the Pact to fall apart by itself.' That was the best he could do, but it did not satisfy the students. To their generation, what counted was a moral cut-off point, an independent decision of an independent country to renounce the membership of an alliance. Two languages were – are – being spoken.

The problem for Gorbachev, as he and his advisers tried to sift out the useful parts of the Prague Spring, was the question of control. Sik and the other 1968 theorists had assumed that Socialist reform would weaken the Party (or deflect the interests of an already weakened party). That was the logical consequence of a modernising, multi-faceted economy: it defied daily political control. That philosophy opens up the option of using demonstrations, strikes and other protests as a lever on a recalcitrant bureaucracy. Hard-line ministers and their placemen can be forced to resign. The politics of the piazza can unseat those opposed to reform. But Gorbachev approached reform Socialism from a different angle. His main economic advisor, Abel Aganbegyan (at least Aganbegyan Mark I) conceived Gorbachev's reform programme as a new-age instrument of control, as a way of restructuring the ideological fortress. Why else did his initial advice to Gorbachev exclude the concept of a labour market? Because an army of unemployed would testify to the failure of the system he was trying to save. By 1990 (Aganbegyan Mark II), Gorbachev's kitchen cabinet had accepted not only unemployment but also a full-blooded rush towards the market. Even then, Gorbachev wanted to keep the Party in the vanguard. But the old 1985–88 policy of borrowing and stealing ideas from Eastern Europe had run its course. Gorbachev was under pressure to come up with his own specifically Soviet market model for the 1990s.

By 1990, it was no longer possible to talk of the Soviet 'Bloc'. Nor was there any sense in dividing Central Eastern Europe into reforming or non-reforming camps. Even Romania had cracked; the Fear was gone, the cement had come unstuck. The important division was between those who regarded themselves as Socialist reformers – Moscow, Sofia and Bucharest – and those who, having pushed the Communists to the margin, were considering adopting a free market in its entirety. That applied to Hungary, but above all to Poland. In these two countries both elements of the new political class, the reform Socialists and the free marketeers, had their own style, but they shared common roots.

There is a holiday snapshot, dating from 1978, taken outside Mieczyslaw Rakowski's dacha in the Mazurian lake district. He was a mere journalist then, editor of the reform Socialist weekly, *Polityka*. Sprawled in front of the house there were three dozen of his friends and contributors. Jerzy Urban (later to be press spokesman of the martial law regime), Wieslaw Gornicki (later political adviser to President Jaruzelski), Andrzej Krysztof Wroblewski (later a commentator on Solidarity-run television), Stefan Bratkowski (on the run under martial law, later an influencial editor under the Solidarity government), Dariusz Fikus (editor of the Solidarity government's official newspaper). And so on. The whole reformist team was split down the middle, first by the rise of the Solidarity Union (should we resign as Communists and join the workers?), then by martial law (those who were arrested, and those who decided to argue for the generals) and ultimately by the accession of the Solidarity government (should the Communists be driven out of political life entirely?).

Reform Socialists and free marketeers in the emerging Eastern Europe of the 1990s were bound not only by common memories and family ties (there were many marriages and divorces between the two camps) but also by a common disregard for the Worker. The centre of Marxist ideology, the beneficiary of wage reforms that pushed manual workers up the social scale, had suddenly become a bit-player in post-Communist politics. The worker, once the hero of the system and its *raison d'être*, was now its victim. 'It is no longer necessary to look and talk like a worker in order to represent them,' drawls one of the younger Polish Politburo members, Leszek Miller. One takes the point. Western aftershave, grammatically correct sentences, that sort of thing. But it goes beyond that. The 1989 revolutions were remarkable for the absence of workers. Strikers made Gierek crumple in 1980, but in the East Germany of 1989 workers went to work in the morning and demon-strated against the govenment in the afternoon so as not to lose their bonuses. They were part of the revolution, but in their capacity as young militants or frustrated consumers. In Poland, both Solidarity and the Communist Party, the two main political forces, had ceased by 1990 to compete for what might be termed the 'worker vote'. Instead the Communists tried to re-define workers as 'Poles'. When Communist politicians went to factories (a rarity by 1990) they addressed their audience not as lathe operators and welders but as Poles justly afraid of foreign competition and infiltration. The line was simple: Solidarity was 'internationalising' the economy by encouraging West German companies to set up in Poland and submitting itself to the dictates of the International Monetary Fund. After four decades of Soviet intervention in the economy and society, the idea that Polish sovereignty could be undermined from a different direction was deeply unsettling to the workers. At the FSO car factory there was real anxiety about the liberalisation of car imports, and the mood resembled Detroit at the time when auto-workers publicly smashed up Japanese cars. The Communists played on the xenophobia and, in the factories and mines of Silesia, had a field day. The Germans had been ejected from Silesia after the war. Poles from the Eastern territories, taken over by Stalin, moved westwards to occupy the houses abandoned by the Germans. Now, in pursuit of economic rejuvenation, the Solidarity government was effectively selling Silesia back to the Germans. The Communists have played the 'nationalist' card at other moments of crisis: in Poland, the party stirred up a venomous anti-Semitic campaign in 1968; in post-Zhivkov Bulgaria, the Communist parties of Eastern Europe entered the 1990s as patriotic-chauvinistic groupings. But, confusingly, they were also committed to a mildly redistributive form of social democracy and mixed economies. And, of course, the new pluralism required them to look attractive and win votes. This was not a happy hybrid; there was a buzz of desperation to the Party men as they pursued every possible populist measure – and smiled and smiled.

Solidarity had the biggest problem. It was a union movement with egalitarian roots yet it was also supplying a government as wedded to the free market as any Thatcher cabinet. How to rule, and simultaneously, oppose? Much depended on the interplay of personalities and all those long-forgotten political virtues of style and technique. Jacek Kuron, a founder-member of KOR, became the link-man between Solidarity-As-Government and Solidarity-As-Union. Every Tuesday, in his new role as Minister of Labour, he would talk, unscripted, on television direct to workers and housewives. Prices were going up daily; yes, he understood, it was difficult especially for the old. But why? Because forty years of Communist planning had dislocated society. The performance was always delivered with great gravel-voiced charm. In a sweater or a T-shirt, wiping his nose with his hand, he converted the painful transition to a market economy – the unemployment, the six hundred per cent inflation – into a fairy tale for adults. Few had Kuron's popular touch; only Boris Yeltsin, Gorbachev's wayward rival, came close. Kuron had served nine years in jail, had been arrested perhaps fifty times in his political career. On his first day as a minister, his neighbour rang to warn him that the secret police were outside waiting in the usual car. The tip-off was routine in his Warsaw-Zoliborz neighbourhood. It gave him time to pack his toothpaste and underclothes before the police took him away. This time, though, the policeman was his chauffeur, calling to take the new minister to work. Half naked – eight o'clock was no time for an ex-dissident to go to the office – he stretched out of the bathroom window and bellowed to the chauffeur that he should get some breakfast and return in an hour. Kuron tried, really tried, to wear a suit but he never got the knack; it was like riding a bicycle, he told friends, you could either do it or you couldn't.

Similar discoveries were made in Czechoslovakia. Jiri Dienstbier, Czech radio and television correspondent in Washington until the 1968 invasion, then for twenty years a manual labourer unloading trucks, stoking boilers, suddenly became Foreign Minister. Vaclav Havel, an old drinking buddy of Kuron when they met secretly in the Tatra mountains, became the Czechoslovakian president. Yet they, and others in the new revolutionary line-ups were singularly unable to talk to workers. At first, this was barely noticed and when it was noticed, was not deemed important. Workers were only thinly represented on the National Salvation Front which replaced Ceausescu, but at factory level, workers were busily organising themselves. At the 23 August Rolling Stock Factory in Bucharest, a bearded electrician, Aurel Dumitrescu, told me that the new role for workers was not in notionally 'worker-parties', since they merely bred parasitic bureaucracies, but in shop-floor control of management. 'First we have to make managers tell the truth. Then we have to make sure that they manage well. If they don't, we will elect our own chiefs. Afterwards, we will see what happens to our products. If we are unhappy with the way the economy is run, and if other workers feel the same way, then we will organise.' Workers in the 1990s then were beating a retreat, going back to Bolshevik roots. Politicians were becoming *bourgeois*, since the whole idea of a parliamentary democracy presupposed middle-class political professionals, a middle-class code. In Poland, Lech Walesa also chose to stay out of government. The workers in effect were saying: we have been co-opted for over forty years – now is the time for distance.

The East European revolutions of 1989 stage-managed by the generation of 1968; the Michniks, the Havels, the earnest peaceniks of East Germany. The move into power was thus a matter of some embarrassment. The new leaders hung on to some talisman or other, just as Abbie Hoffman, the reformed hippy, tied his hair back in a ponytail before travelling to work on Wall Street. Poland's Finance Minister, Leszek Balcerowicz, insisted on carrying his IMF documents in a battered US army surplus bag and he could be heard complaining how thieves had stolen the tyres from his modest Polski Fiat. The Foreign Minister of Poland lived in a bed-sitter with kitchenette in Poznan. Four of the cabinet had been interned under martial law, imposed by the now President, General Jaruzelski. They all felt easier at drinking parties with former political prisoners than at formal gatherings. Leading members of the Solidarity underground became deputy ministers and kept their beards and duffel coats. The first moral crisis of the Solidarity government was whether to drive in sleek Lancias ordered by the previous Communist government. Most of the Cabinet wanted to sell the one hundred and thirty limousines and bicycle to work, saving money for the Treasury. Then Lancia pointed out that the cars had been sold at a discount for promotional purposes. If the ministers were going to sell the cars on the free market, then the government would have to pay back about ten thousand dollars a car – and the budget could not take it. And so Solidarity, clenching its teeth, came to terms with its chauffeurs and cellular car phones.

The new political style was best illustrated by the Solidarity Prime Minister, Tadeusz Mazowiecki, when on 12 September 1989 he delivered his inaugural speech to Parliament. He had been negotiating late into the night for the past fortnight and finally had put together a cabinet which satisfied all parties, even the Communists who retained only four portfolios. It had been tough, and he was tired. He came to the chamber early, to sit and pray before the meeting. Then, the speech, a lugubrious, almost boring address delivered with Mazowiecki's customary ecclesiastical cadence. It did not mention Socialism once. There was no point-scoring against the outgoing Communist administration, just the assumption that Communism was entirely irrelevant to the solution of Poland's problems. After about forty minutes, the Prime Minister's face blanched, his hands clutched the lectern and he swayed dangerously. The ex-journalist was led off to an antechamber and, for a tantalising hour, he disappeared. The medical team found that it did not have an electro-cardiogram machine on the premises and search-

ambulances (a specifically East European invention: ambulances commissioned to speed from hospital to hospital, not bearing patients but in quest of equipment) were dispatched around Warsaw. The deputies and journalists assumed that Mazowiecki was still in Parliament and thronged the lobby waiting for a bulletin. Was he having a stroke? Was the first non-Communist government in the Communist world doomed from the start, destroyed, as in Greek tragedy, by human frailty? In fact, the Prime Minister had slipped out for a walk in the park. The Lazienki Park has the charm of St James, the acreage of Hyde; swans, weeping willows, off-duty soldiers necking with shop assistants. Without bodyguards, virtually unnoticed, Mazowiecki was talking to the birds. In Parliament, two hundred yards away, the gossips were already counting on his death or forced retirement; news agency reporters were scrounging for coins to ring their obituary departments. Mazowiecki, meanwhile, was studying the flowers, his jacket slung over his shoulders like a pre-war officer. Nobody could find him. A crocodile of kindergarten pupils passed on the way to the playground and the teacher said: 'Look, children, our Prime Minister – *nasz Premier.*' Poles have not used the proprietorial *nasz* since the war; leaders were always 'theirs', Communist stooges.

There is, then, none of the arrogance of power about the new post-Communists. Andrei Plesu, a former critic of Ceausescu who took over a Minister of Culture after the Romanian Revolution of 1989, called in his departmental heads before the New Year holidays. 'I want everyone in this meeting to decide whether they really served culture over the past year,' the bearded, open-shirted minister told the officials. 'The older members of this ministry can be pensioned off, the younger ones will be found jobs elsewhere. Please examine your hearts and we will see who is left on 3 January.' Nobody had ever spoken to officials like that before. It was a new language; public appeals to conscience were as rare as Sibiu-salami and one-hundred-Watt lightbulbs in Romania.

The problem facing the post-Communist political class is twofold. First, the collapse of the central planning machine and the death of ideology leaves the new government very few options. They are constrained to follow the same policies that their Communist predecessors would have chosen. The exception to this was manifestly the Romanian revolutionary leadership. Despite its largely Communist background, it could appear radically different simply by turning each of Ceausescu's mad-hat policies upside down. No further bans on abortions, no limits to the use of electricity, freedom for private farmers, the scrapping of big senseless investment projects, a five-day week, the right to travel abroad, to shop in hard-currency stores. It all came tumbling out. The not unreasonable assumption was that the mirror-opposite of Ceausescu was, *a priori*, the basis of a free society. But for most East European states in the post-Communist age it was by no means so straightforward. The dissident-run administrations of 1990 were confronted with the same tasks as the Communist-led governments of 1988 and 1989. Plugging the energy gap, raising productivity, mending the rift between town and country, above all filling the shops: this was the nature of the Communist crisis.

The first measures of the post-Communists – paring down privilege, improving parliamentary controls – were well-meant, but seemed to many to miss the point. Mazowiecki's trip to Moscow reinforced that impression. His first foreign trip had been not to the Soviet Union, but to the Pope to thank him for the support of the Catholic Church. Soon enough, though, he had to travel Eastwards. A few reporters were invited to join him on the plane, at two thousand dollars a head, and we were assured that Solidarity would take Moscow by storm. It was not like that. True, on his free evening, the Prime Minister took his cabinet out on the town. The doorman of the Praha restaurant would not let the Government in at first – 'Anybody can say they're the Polish Government, can't they? Why should I let you in?' – but a few rouble notes cleared the barricades. It was quite a party. The Polish cabinet toasted the black marketeers at neighbouring tables, some drunk asked the blonde, buck-toothed government spokeswoman for a dance. She preferred to take a spin with the Finance Minister who, as befits his calling, is nimble on his feet. Mazowiecki was so proud of this outing, this flash of spontaneity, that he alluded to it several times at press conferences. It was unquestionably a charming moment. Yet the underpinning reality was that Mazowiecki had come, like countless Polish leaders before him, to beg for improved supplies of Soviet oil and gas and the writing-off of Polish debts to the Soviet Union. These are the contours of Poland's policy in the world, and no amount of stylish snubbing, or anti-Soviet films on Polish television, can let the country wriggle free.

The other part of this double bind is the heavy dependence on Communist party members within the Executive. Poland came closest of all the East European states to having an alternative cadre, but even then it needed Party members to run much of the economy, the police, the army. None of the post-Communist states has a Civil Service training college in which future diplomats or bureaucrats can be trained; instruction has been in the hands of the Communists for three generations. The most important of reforms were almost the most long-winded; changing the school curriculum and writing history textbooks took years. In the meantime, many teachers (in school at least) were party members, often of the most bitter kind.

A rolling back of the post-Communist revolution was thus a nagging possibility at the beginning of the 1990s. In Romania, in particular, the executives of the revolution were the very same people who defended and helped the policies of Ceausescu. The impression in those first few weeks after the Christmas Revolution was of being confined in a large marquee of evangelists, surrounded by people who spoke in tongues or found salvation. Sauls turned into Pauls with alarming frequency. The Foreign Ministry functionary who had me banned from Romania for writing rude things about Ceausescu gasped with joy during the Christmas Revolution and pulled me into a Hollywood hug, kissed both cheeks and exclaimed: 'At last, we're free!' *We?*

One should not be cynical, of course. Some accomodation had to be reached with the ancien régime and it was in the nature of Romania that the conversion would be instant and total. Slavic cultures purge, the Latins shoot, kiss and forget . . . It is the same elasticity that allowed Romania, and indeed Italy, to change sides with such alacrity in time of war.

Still, the uncertainty about the East European revolutions, the clumsy juggling with concepts such as Reform Socialism and Market Liberalism, serve the idea that the new governors have only a limited life-span. The region is in a state of transition. The political class that is associated with the post-Communist revolutions is also transitory. Politicians, quite simply, will play a diminished role within the new order. Their importance will be in defending frontiers and the identity and interests of their nations as Europe shifts its weight ('from one buttock to another,' as the playwright Janusz Glowacki puts it). This will be a new age of diplomacy. But, at home, the politician is destined to become a rather trivial figure. The Communist Party has lost its formal claim to preponderance, its constitutionally guaranteed 'leading role'. Now, no single political interest leads East European societies though there are still abundant political passions (social envy and nationalist outrage).

Instead, the two main players of the post-Communist age are likely to be the entrepreneur and the policeman. The rise of a money class, of an entrepreneurial bourgeoisie, is central not only to the revival of the post-Communist economies but also to the evolution of a stable parliamentary democracy. The revolution in eastern Europe is market-driven and so the managers of the market, irrespective of their criminal or shady roots, are pivotal to the future of the region. And it is the policeman, rather than the increasingly hamstrung politician, who will control the pace of change. The police and the various monitoring agencies will define ultimately how much Socialism remains in the Socialist world.

13

The Entrepreneur

Out of the rubble of a destroyed system, new patterns are beginning to emerge. The scene is of an earthquake-stricken community. There are Red Cross tents, makeshift shelters, great misery, the rumble of machinery and the persistent question: shall we destroy what is left and start from scratch? Or can we salvage something from the wreckage? That is the mode of passage between systems; there is nothing painless about the collapse of communist planning, there is nothing ordered about the markets that spring up in the crevices and cracks. Until fundamental decisions are taken – Is socialism structurally sound? Can we put up plateglass skyscrapers on the old foundations? Where, exactly, are the fault-lines? – the managers of the post-communist era have to be improvisers, temporary men who will none the less set the rules for the next generation. The vintage categories have gone: it is no longer helpful to talk of 'hardliners' or 'reformers'. Jacek Kuron, the Polish dissident turned Minister, used to say: 'There is no such thing as a liberal wing of the Communist Party; only the pragmatism of those who want to stay in power.' Now, there is no Party hegemony – throughout Eastern Europe the communists have to share the power in order to survive and even Kuron's analysis seems dated. There are, instead, three active groups colouring the political and economic complexion of society: an entrepreneurial money class; judicial technicians; and a political class that is reshuffling its ideas along Western, or pre-communist lines. The 'Republic of Economics', the market dimension of centrally planned systems, has thrown up its own senators and tribunes. Drawn partly from the depressed markets of everyday life, partly from the criminal underworld, there is now a clearly recognisable entrepreneurial figure: he deals with real needs, real demands, real prices and makes real profits.

Such a man was Ignacy Soszynski, the perfume-king of the Soviet Bloc. For a time at least, he was regarded as the richest private businessman in the region, but to hear him tell it he was a victim, an accidental man bullied and repeatedly pushed under by bureaucrats and dogmatic politicians. He had learned over the years to present himself modestly. There was the lime-green BMW, of course, that he used to commute between Warsaw and Poznan. Two sparsely furnished mansions in Poland, and an art collection that included a Renoir and a Gauguin; sensible investments – simple fare compared to the life-styles of his millionaire contemporaries.

Soszynski was the head of a private Polish company called Inter-Fragrances producing cosmetics for both home consumption and export. Set up in 1980, the company reached a domestic turnover of 22 million sterling (at the official rate of exchange), exported five million dollars worth of cosmetics to Western Europe and four million roubles worth to the Soviet Union and its allies. About fifty per cent of his hard currency earnings were skimmed off by the state and the turnover tax was high, but still Soszynski was a wealthy man. He left school at the age of twelve to help his brothers concoct a simple perfume. His job was to root through the city dustbins for likely-looking bottles, scrub them clean and then stand by as his brothers filtered the latest fragrance.

By 1939 he was already operating his own perfume company. The Germans closed him down. For a while he produced perfume and soap for the black market, but the Gestapo was always on the trail, suspecting links between the black economy and the partisan underground. After the war, he started again but was soon forced to shut his workshop as private business, regarded as creeping capitalism, was stamped on. Soszynski left the country and, at the age of 42, decided to study perfume-making arts in France. 'But the perfume business is a practical field,' recalled the old man, smelling, faintly, of soap. 'You have to experiment, mix and above all research – discover whether women really like what you have produced, or whether men like what you have just put on women. If the response is favourable, then there is only one logical step – to produce as quickly as possible.' And so the perfume student from Poland went into business again, this time in France at the heart of the fragrance industry. He bought bottles and materials cheaply at auction and, with minimal overheads, started to export, reaping profits almost immediately. The French scent manufacturers, however, did not approve. By the time Soszynski's work permit expired, there was pressure to close him down.

The wandering perfumer moved on to Casablanca, quickly captured a quarter of the domestic Moroccan scents market, and made enemies.

The authorities began to make noises about nationalisation and Soszynski was on the road again.

At first the Polish government was delighted at the return of the perfume-prodigal. The economy, bursting out all over like a hopelessly overpacked suitcase, was in terrible shape, and the idea of a wealthy Polish expatriate returning to the motherland to pep up his particular sector represented an attractive propaganda coup: here was a man, declared the news managers, with faith. Nothing of the kind of course; rather some sentimentality and a businessman's feel for market niches –shops were empty, great gaping consumer grottoes – and Eastern Europe was a region with low overheads.

The company was called Inter-Fragrances and was intended to supply Polish, Soviet and other East European housewives with perfume, soap and shampoo. The company was also authorised to turn out food essences for bakers, a profitable sideline. The company started in a hired garage, in the manner of the early Californian computer giants. About 16,000 pounds sterling was ploughed into the firm, some of it on raw materials, some on technology and equipping the factory. By 1982 Inter-Fragrances was beginning to make so much money that it attracted the attention of the Poznan prosecutor, who accused the Communist world's perfumer of 'speculation'. This is a broad legal category but in Soszynski's case it amounted to the charge that he was re-selling somebody else's product under his own name. The charges were dropped for lack of evidence.

But evidently somebody (Soszynski's allies surmise a combination of commercial competitors and the anti-private-industry lobby in the secret police) had it in for the perfumer. Inter-Fragrances was virtually minting money. The colourful Inter-Fragrance shop in Warsaw's Piekna Street regularly draws admirers to its window display and there is still a lively interest in the I-F products, which are superior to state-produced brands and those imported from East Germany, while considerably cheaper than Palmolive and Camay. Soszynski was accused of spending only a small fraction of his original investment on fixed assets: the laws which encourage foreign entrepreneurs to return to Poland stipulate that a large start-up sum has to be devoted to building factory premises and installing state-of-the-art machinery. That way, if the businessman tires of Poland, or has come to the country to make a quick killing, he has left the country something substantial. But Soszynski spent most of his start-up money on importing raw materials. Secondly, he used zloty profits to buy an effectively bankrupt timber concern, a large, doomed, Gierek-era project. Soszynski started to use the timber to build prefabricated bungalows and to meet some of the need for small affordable dachas. Poznan officialdom gave him the freedom of the city for saving the timber company. But this move too proved to be a violation of the regulations: Soszynski should have forked out dollars for the timber. Finally, he was accused of making illicit deals with state companies; he simply repackaged their boring cosmetics and then sold them for hard currency to West Germany. The trick, say the prosecutors – upheld even in the supreme court – was to buy in the basics for soft currency (the zloty of negligible value) and sell at great profit to himself on the capitalist markets.

Put like that it sounds like a scam of the first order. But the fact is that all private industry in Eastern Europe is vulnerable to attack; the rules circumscribing their activities are a jungle of small print. Key phrases are ill-defined and left to the courts to interpret. Talking to Soszynski's colleagues in Poznan industry, in state as well as private enterprise, it is plain that most feel he made a real contribution to the local and the national economies and that, for a millionaire in a communist country, he was surprisingly popular, a quiet philanthropist. To no one's obvious benefit, the scent manufacturer had his realm cut in two and, hurt, he moved to the West. It was the eighth and final time that state authorities squashed one of his perfume companies. For Soszynski *pecunia non olet*, but for the Communist authorities, even in the expansive Gorbachev era, money does smell. Private riches and private success is the last taboo in a society where it is now permitted to denounce Stalin and Brezhnev, historical blunders and official corruption.

The shy bespectacled businessman was crushed by his experiences. Now he, and his ilk, are again in demand. The question is whether the Soviet system has simply entered the next phase in its expansion–contraction, liberalism–repression cycle, or whether the terms have fundamentally changed. Older entrepreneurs like Soszynski have been singed too many times to play the game again, but there are important apertures, and a change of thinking, that will make the young business class essential to the management of the post-communist economy.

An opening for private business occurred at what should have been its funeral: the Bolshevik Revolution. In the chaos of 1918–19, the middle-class professionals were learning how to survive in a barter economy. The bourgeoisie had lost its padding. The fine ladies had parted with their lapdogs, their cooks and some of the bulkier furniture. The Scottish governesses, with a few brave exceptions, had gone home.

There was no bread and no conceivable way that a lawyer or a journalist or an architect or a historian could sell his services for food. And so they sold their pianos. Polished by the servants, tuned every week by a Jewish craftsman, the grand piano became a unit in the Soviet second economy. The Chekist requisition squads were marauding the countryside, confiscating grain and shooting peasant hoarders. But still 60% of the bread eaten in the cities had been bought on the black market. One of the earliest Bolshevik planners, L. Kristman, estimated that in January 1919 only 19% of food in provincial capitals came through official distribution and, over a year later, it was still only 29%. The black marketeer was know as a bag-man, a *meshochnik*. The farmer hid grain from the official procurement patrols, and from the trigger-happy Chekists in their leather jerkins, and then gave sackfuls of the food to the *meshochniki* who, avoiding the city guards, would sell it at a huge mark-up. If necessary, a sack of grain could be bartered for a piano. There is a famous Soviet sketch, based on any number of true incidents: a grand piano is hauled by cart to the peasant's dwelling, but it is too bulky to fit in the door. The door is enlarged but inside there is no room either; barely space for the stove, a table, the relatives. The piano is sawn in half. The keyboard stays at home, the rest is put in the barn. And the lawyer gets his bread.

The government, desperate to get bread to the towns, bent its principles. The bag-men and the speculators were declared legal, at least for the purpose of supplying Moscow and Petrograd. In September 1918, the profiteering *meshochniki* were allowed to transport one and a half poods (54 pounds) of grain from country to town. Illegal profits were declared legal overnight and the bread supply improved fourfold in that month.

These are the historical roots of the second economy in the Soviet Union. It was born out of misery, the collapse of normal distribution channels, the breakdown of trust between peasant and government and the debasement of money. War communism tried to ban private manufacture, to nationalise all industry, to outlaw private trade and to snatch farmers' supplies, but by 1921 Lenin was convinced that there had to be a retreat, ideological and economic, to the market. He was prodded by the fear that peasants' rebellions in different regions would merge into something more menacing; the Kronstadt Sailors' Revolt finally convinced him that War Communism had to be tempered. And so the private entrepreneur was encouraged to ease the Soviet system out of its temporary embarrassment. The confiscation of farmers' supplies was replaced by a food tax. After the peasants had paid the tax they were free to sell the rest of their produce at private markets. But since this did not solve the problem of getting food to the big industrial centres, it was inevitable that trade too would be returned to private hands. The bag-men who bartered between towns were replaced by NEP men, private merchants. Trading companies were set up and slowly some oxygen entered the system; money and goods began to circulate.

The Communists retained control of the banks, foreign trade and heavy industry but it was recognised that small scale trade could be passed again into private hands. By July 1921 every citizen was allowed 'to undertake handicraft production and to organise small-scale enterprises not exceeding 20 workers.' Only a few concerns were actually denationalised, but many shut-down private companies were re-started by their former dispossessed owners or the new class of privateer. By late 1923 there were almost 6,000 leased enterprises, 1,800 in food processing, 1,500 in hides and skins – the furrier was a typical NEP man. By 1922–23, 75% of all retail trade was privately controlled. And the NEP man flourished. Only 3.5% of the private businessmen declared an annual income over 3,000 roubles (that is, five times the average wage) but most were dodging taxes and were, by contemporary standards, immensely wealthy. In many country districts the NEP man was the only seller and even in Moscow had a big stake in the wholesale business, especially textiles and clothes.

The NEP man was typically portrayed as overweight, double-chinned, with gold flashing from his teeth and wrists and a sable collar cradling his neck. The image was later taken up by Soviet cartoonists as the archetypal black marketeer, a man grown fat on famine. Later still he would be given a hooked nose and assigned, in the stilted dialogue of cartoon caption, the name of Blum, Rosenberg or Stein. In fact, though NEP men certainly lived well, and though some did indeed enjoy mistresses and wild parties, they worked harder than their counterparts in the Soviet Bloc today.

Despite clear limits on the number of their workforce, they expanded fast and created a great many well-paid jobs. Private craftsmen numbered over two million in 1925, and those privately employed reached almost 300,000. The most successful NEP men were those who established a strong connection between a regional centre like Kharkov, and the capital, Moscow; the NEP men became the key to survival for provincial state factories who knew nothing about independent trading or making profit. The NEP men in light industry, though, were particularly vulnerable, needing supplies from state factories and leasing their floorspace from the state.

The NEP – and with it, the idea that the Soviet system could entertain a mixed economy – was doomed from 1925. State concerns became more competitive and the Party opposition to the profiteers became more and more obvious. It proved all too easy to obstruct the private entrepreneur. Soviet statistics, which must be taken with more than a pinch of salt, show that the private sector accounted for 54% of national income in 1925–26, but only 9.3% in 1926–32. The squeeze started in earnest in 1926: a heavy surcharge on rail transport of private goods, a tax on super-profits, privately-owned flour mills were closed down, taxes on richer peasants (*kulaks*) were stepped up, the criminal code was changed to allow for three-year jail sentences for profiteers or hoarders (the notorious Article 107 which Stalin was later to use against the *kulaks*). It was not a good year for market forces.

Step-by-step, private enterprise was identified as an essentially criminal activity. NEP men introduced to make the system work were presented as sophisticated saboteurs who were blocking the ultimate victory of nationalised industry. The shrewdest of them started accumalting gold ready for flight. In 1929 Stalin was still denying that he was going to kill NEP. In 1930, private trade had in effect been redefined as the crime of 'speculation', and hiring workers for private profit was outlawed.

The legal private sector never really recovered in the Soviet Union. Instead, the mercantile class went underground. By the 1960s, it was plain that a planned economy actually created shortages: that was its essence. The revival of legal private enterprise, through NEP, could be explained away as a response to the exigencies of war and the chaos of transition. But by the 1960s, even taking into account the human and material losses in the Second World War, there were no more excuses. The leadership could either reform, or conceal. But the price of concealing economic failure was to permit, tacitly, the operation of a black market, and an active relationship between the legal and the hidden economies. For how long could a communist regime tolerate such informal arrangements? Not long, as the 1965–66 Moscow Knitwear trials starkly demonstrated.

The Moskva department store, a huge consumer silo on Lenin Prospekt, the favoured shop of academicians and the military top brass, set up its own knitwear department at the end of the 1950s. The initiative came from the manager, a portly, florid woman called Maria Feorovna Korshilova. She was a Russian who had carved out a career as a business woman and had previously run TSUM, Moscow's largest shop both in terms of turnover and the number of employees. A fast-lane career in Soviet department stores required, then as now, Party support. She was a member of the Plenum of the Moscow City Committee and, more important, a long-time friend of Yelena Furtseva, one of the few women ever to reach a Soviet Politburo. Korshilova had a direct phone line (a 'revolving door' connection) with Furtseva's office; such was her power. High wages, big bonuses, access to foods in short supply, topped up by regular bribes from many salesmen under her command. More: because she was highly articulate (rare in the *Nomenklatura* of the 1960s) she was allowed to travel on delegations abroad.

Korshilova demanded, and received, a dress allowance. More precisely, whenever she was due to travel abroad or receive a foreign delegation, she would have an outfit made up by the fashion department of the store. After the event the dress or coat – invariably lined with sable or ermine – was supposed to be sold, but, of course, stayed in Korshilova's wardrobe. Russians were becoming infatuated with imported clothes, she told the Trade Ministry plaintively, and yet the Russians themselves were capable of producing good-quality off-the-peg garments. Why should the Moskva not set up its own knitwear and textiles manufacturing unit? The Trade Ministry agreed; Korshilova, as usual, had chose the right approach.

As head of the unit, she installed an old friend, a skilled Jewish tailor and businessman, Aleksandr Heifetz. Machinery was delivered, according to the state warrants – and a bit more besides. Materials were supplied under state planning orders – and outside them. Production began, some accounted for, some not. T-shirts and singlets, women's and children's underwear, fashionable nylon shorts began to appear on the counters of the Moskva. They were a modest collection, falling far short of the quality of the brightly coloured imported clothes. But even for these products there was a great demand. Most of the production naturally was destined for the black market. The clothes that arrived in the Moskva merely whetted the appetite. Those shoppers who had been disappointed, who were too far back in the queue, could pay three times the price on the black market. Korshilova picked up most of the profits but she also shared out some of the proceeds; the knitwear workers received far more than they would have earned in a state textile factory. The Moskva unit had in fact become a small factory in its own right, producing thousands more items than were needed for the Moskva. The chief difference between this unit and those which had long existed at the Moscow GUM and TSUM stores was that they only made up the garments, whereas in the Moskva, alongside the sewing section, there was a weaving section which produced textiles from nylon, woollen and half-woollen thread. The head of this section was Boris Reidel, another Jew who came from a long line of textile families. Altogether, the Moskva team managed to net about 2.3 million roubles of profits over five years.

The Moskva was a model of how the second economy can, by cheating, corner-cutting and some judicious theft, support the first economy; it created and satisfied a demand for slightly unconventional home-made clothes. The trial, however, showed plainly the limits of state tolerance. Charged with misappropriating state property, the production managers Heifetz, Reidel and Evgenev – all Jews – were put in the dock. The directors and deputy director of Moscow retail shops – Kozlovski, Reich, Zhitominiski, Tsatskis, Tsudechkis – joined them. They too were Jews. The Queen of the Moskva, Korshilova, was only called as a witness; she denied everything.

Aleksandr Heifetz and Yuri Evgenev were shot by firing squad. Maria Korshilova went on to manage another department store. The Deputy Minister of Trade for the Russian Federation, Semyron Alekseev, used to receive regular pay-offs from the store (as well as having special suits made up for his large frame, and woollen jerseys for his dog) but retired peacefully. The minister's Jewish business manager Isaac Fiorent – who used to collect the pay-off every week and deliver it to the minister – was executed.

Khrushchev's plan, with his tough sentences on black marketeering, was presumably to channel the energy of the second economy into the first, to decapitate the illicit producers and give more zeal to the Plan. It was born out of egalitarian instinct – popular distaste for high black-market prices sometimes spilled into anger. And because he understood the darker currents of Russian populism, he allowed the campaign to be directed against Jews.

The plan, like so many of Khrushchev's, back-fired. It was based too obviously on false premises. It destroyed the Soviet Jews as a mercantile class, and (indeed the only) innovating and versatile part of the Soviet economy. True, Jews still played an important role in some metropolitan black markets (in Odessa, Kishinev) but the old relationship (Russian party member lends protection to Jewish businessman in return for profit-sharing) had collapsed. Instead, slowly, the merchants of Georgia and Armenia started to fund the second economy. The death sentence for economic crimes pushed the submerged economy onto the ocean bed; it took a foolhardy entrepreneur to display his wealth in the late Khrushchev and early Brezhnev years.

The pattern of expansion and contraction has not disappeared. Even in Hungary, which (apart from a brief hiccough in the 1970s) has been steadily broadening the legal space for private enterprise, even in Hungary there are problems. Hungary allows 'economic working associations' – large worker co-operatives – as well as 'working association' within state enterprises. These let state workers group together and, for a price, rent unused machinery, buy materials and lease floorspace in their state factory. Then after hours, they can produce what they want and sell it at a price of their choosing. Typically, workers in a furniture factory turning out standardised bedrooms might choose to make varnished reproduction furniture or free-standing cupboards, for which there is a big demand, in their spare time. Then there are private craftsmen, who since 1981 enjoy full pensions rights and social insurance. They can rent under-used factories. No bribes are involved, no lumpy envelopes passed to the wives of party chiefs. Independent entrepreneurs can also compete for tendered contracts and win service contracts. A more modest version of this is practised in Czechoslovakia where private businessmen are allowed to run laundries, shoe-shining, portering and souvenir and refreshment sales. Such concessions immeasurably improved the running of state-controlled hotels. Moonlighting can thus be perfectly legal. Not everybody, though, is perfectly happy. Although Hungary has been relatively consistent in its market-orientated reforms – certainly more so than its neighbours – there is not a great reservoir of confidence in the authorities. After private industry was pushed underground, the various black-market practitioners adapted to the changed enviroment. Now that they are invited to become legal again, they are not so keen.

Istvan, who runs a still-illegal contraceptive business, pondered with me the merits of becoming a lawful trader. 'What happens if I don't succeed? Then the state can take away my license, declare me bankrupt and confiscate my assets. Fair enough. Now what happens if I am too successful? I can get taxed to the hilt and become a conspicuous target for when there is another policy shift. Will these privatisation measures survive? I don't know. But I do know that the risk of becoming aboveboard is as great as the risk of bing arrested for illegal economic activity.'

Istvan is staying where he is; he is rich enough to afford the luxury of hesitation. But for many there is no choice; they have to become legally registered entrepreneurs because they cannot live on what the state provides.

A friend of mine, an archaeologist, asked the same question of the Minister of Education while putting his case for higher university salaries. Who wants any kind of archaeologist? replied the Minister. The room of turbulent academics fell into a morose silence. 'I suppose he was joking but we entered what you might call a collective depression. He was absolutely right. We have no bargaining power because we are unnecessary to the well-being of the economy. At the same time we have no skills that can marketed in the private sector. Intellectuals are the new under-class.'

Sometimes the answer is to offer a manual service but to use brains to outwit the state competition. A group of Hungarian mountaineers – as in Poland, a popular sport among university teachers and writers – have set up a company to repair factory chimneys. They can undercut the state repair teams by not erecting scaffolding. Watch the obituary columns: it is only a matter of time before a major Hungarian writer dies falling off a chimney-stack in pursuit of profit.

Dentists of course have always been able to turn a coin with private practice, be it legal or criminal. Hungarian dentists find that if they set up practices near the western border or on the main highways they can make a lucrative business treating, at a fraction of the Western price, the teeth of Austrians and West Germans who commute across the border especially to have their cavities filled and molars polished. The private treatment is legal, but they must declare their hard currency earnings to the taxman. Usually they overlook this detail.

The foreign currency rules affect only a small percentage of the Hungarian moonlighters, but there are plenty of other restrictions to keep them in place. In 1985 the corporate tax on small companies was doubled to six per cent, a special 10% sales tax was clamped on goods sold to state companies by private ventures, and in 1987 Hungary became the first communist country to introduce that quirk of capitalism, the value-added tax. One of the saddest men in Budapest was Zoltan Palmai, a chubby engineer in his thirties. When we first met, he was brimming with enthusiasm for his project; to open the first privately-owned hotel in the Soviet Bloc. There are of course members of the international chains scattered throughout communist Europe: a Hilton and an Atrium Hyatt in Budapest, Intercontinentals in Warsaw and Bucharest, a Sheraton in Sofia. But these are essentially corporation hotels, expensive resting-places for the Western businessman who, barring the occasional blocked lavatory and the funny noises on the phone, can pretend he has never crossed the Iron Curtain. Zoltan's idea was different; his would be a three-star hotel with a family atmosphere, clean and efficient, well up to the standards of service of the big international conglomerates, and much, much cheaper. It did not work. The last time I saw him he was standing outside the six-floor Hotel Victoria, talking mournfully to a hall porter who was worried about another less pleasant incursion from the world of capitalism: unemployment. The bureaucrats had told him that he could employ no more than nine people, far fewer than he needed. He had to pay a 65% tax turnover. He had problems advertising for clients abroad. In the end he had a choice: either raise room prices to the unrealistic level of the big international hotels or sell up. He sold up, as it happens, to the trade union federation; there will never be a Palmai Hotel dynasty – at least, not in Budapest. In 1989 a Law of Associations gave private companies more scope; if defined as joint state companies they could employ up to 500 people. But it was all too late for the Hotel Victoria.

Even in Budapest, where the ideological barriers to private enterprise have largely been overcome, it is not easy for the independent business. Inertia, obstruction from middle-ranking bureaucrats, social envy, an uncomprehending police force, all militate against the most radical of changes. Sometimes the rules seem quite nonsensical. Captain Robert Bujdoso retired early from the Budapest police force. He is a fit-looking man with a reputation for detective skills (this in a capital which has always produced alert criminologists and boasts the best fraud specialist in the Soviet Bloc). Bujdoso's idea was to set up as a private eye. This had never been tried before in the Communist world, but there was a clear demand for his services. He handed a few dossiers over his cluttered desk: not a whisky bottle in sight, Bujdoso was no Philip Marlowe. His case book, though, bore some resemblance to that of Chandler's shabby hero. A divorced woman wanted to be protected from a vengeful spouse. There was a mysterious case of industrial theft; a factory robbed blind by somebody on the staff. Theoretically, he said, he should be able to fulfil any of the tasks handled by private Western security companies: escorting payroll deliveries to shops for example, or advising on the installation of an alarm system. But the business was rather too ambitious in a country where the state police claim the monopoly on civic protection. When I returned some months later to see how the agency was faring, the shutters were pulled down. The private eye had gone to ground. The local authorities had told him that collecting information about individuals was a field only handled by 'state organs'. And he was barred from toting a gun. At the age of 51, even Karate skills lose their deterrent force.

But the terms of political calculation have been shifting. The core reform constituency in Eastern Europe – Poland, Hungary and Gorbachev's Soviet Union – now accepts that the second economy is an auxiliary engine of the first. For Moscow especially this is a quantum jump. Whether under Stalin, or Khrushchev the arch de-Staliniser, under a languid Brezhnev or a Cromwellian Andropov, the Soviet Union has always acted against 'speculation' – profitable re-selling – and its acceptance of private enterprisee, as we have seen, ebbs and flows, commuting between tolerance and repression. The idea is Italian. Dr Guiseppe de Rita, of the Censis Institute, regards the second economy as a logical response to political and economic rigidity. In the Italian case, there was the Workers' Statute, which committed the employer to an extraordinary and frequently impossible list of obligations. The 1970s in Italy was a time when the power of the trade unions was at its peak, when state industry had become top-heavy with white-collar workers, when social welfare payments cut into the profit margins of the bosses. Yet it was also a period of modernisation, a time when 'everyone invested in himself and his work.'

The Soviet Union has now reached a similar point. Some form of relationship between work and reward has been restored, yet the institutional structures – the dead weight of central planning, an inflated political and economic bureaucracy – do nothing but frustrate. Out of a honeycomb of alternatives, second, parallel or black-market arrangements, there emerged an Italian pattern that could well be duplicated in the Communist Bloc. It was, De Rita says, 'an unexpected gift for a troubled Italy, an auxiliary engine able to make up for the non-firing cylinders of the regular, institutional economy.' Italy's second economy was the main modernising force, able to provide entrepreneurial flexibility and cohesion at the most basic levels (family enterprises, local community). There was no unifying reformist logic; not simply the exploitation of the more traditional qualities (commerce, design, product renewal) but rather a reliance on grandiose large-scale innovation. The second economy of Italy specialised in textiles, clothing, shoes, leather goods and furniture and did not, of course, plough investment into advanced sectors such as aviation or chemicals.

But in its area of operation, the black economy, with its nifty small businesses, was able to react quickly to market demand.

By the 1980s these elements of the Italian second economy had been absorbed into the mainstream. The submerged and surface economies proved to be two sides of the same economic and social coin, not parallel, untouching economies. Employers, unable to afford the social costs of taking on new staff, hired unofficially. The employees, in turn, avoided tax. Together they contributed to an economic boom which came *in spite of* the institutional structures. Later, the power of the unions was broken and the labour code revised, but the recovery was already well under way. Hungary has been trying to tread a similar path, tolerating a great deal of moonlighting and black activity that is feeding economic growth. There are clear differences between Hungary and the Soviet Union, of attitude as well as scale. The Hungarian working class retains strong links with the villages and so is naturally connected with the private sector. A large majority of Hungarian workers have always derived part of their incomes from 'second-economy' activities. That dilutes the worker opposition to economic reform, and makes them less sensitive to the politics of social envy. In short, Hungary is suitable terrain to beach the submerged economy. The Soviet Union should, at a Republican level, be able to do something similar. The co-operatives are an attempt, but so far, a flimsy one: to approach the kind of dynamism that gripped Italy there has to be a more general political consensus about the efficacy of the market. The second economy not only reacts to the immobilism of the bureaucracy, it also initiates and innovates; it is an actor as well as a reactor.

To make use of these submerged market mechanisms, the Gorbachev leadership has to find a practical formula that may, at times, seem legally inconsistent. Take the Georgians who ferry fruit to Irkutsk at great personal profit as well as some risk and discomfort. If their activities were declared legal – that is, if the crime of 'speculation' was scrapped – and they were taxed, what would happen? First, there might be a drop in supplies. The taxation would probably be more painful to the dealers than the small risk of arrest. Bribes to police and customs officials already oil their way, minimising the risk of capture, but some network of bribery would remain even if the Georgians were delcared legal. Second, legalising the traders might cause ideological friction and social tension. The taxation would be passed on to the consumers in the form of higher prices and there would, one can predict, be loud cries about profiteering. The Georgians, then, almost certainly prefer to continue operating as part of the second, illegal economy rather than come above ground; consumers and even the government probably agree. Bringing the underground economy to the surface has to be a gradual process, with an eye on social attitudes. The experience of legal private enterprises in the Soviet Bloc shows that consumers are more likely to accept high prices from a black-market trader rather than from an officially registered co-operative shop. The private entrepreneur is thus coming into his own but he has to accept a degree of legal ambiguity. The Gorbachev leadership can promise an independent judiciary, but it cannot quickly dismantle a legal architecture that is designed to protect the weak – the unskilled worker, the pensioner – against an exploitative, moneyed class. It therefore agrees quietly to tolerate black-market entrepreneurs – who none the less provide a service to consumers and fuel the economy – alongside a steadily growing number of legal businessmen. As Tatiana Ivanovna, director of forecasting at Gosplan, has shown, this group controls a hefty part of the economy. She estimates the black/private economy of the Soviet Union to have an annual turnover of about 90 billion pounds sterling. 'The shadow economy,' she wrote (*Trud*, 12 August, 1988), 'is the result of the severe shortage of goods on the market, the gap between a huge demand and limited state supply as well as the direct result of command methods of leadership, imperfections in our economic mechanisms and low labour productivity.' According to her figures, about 16 billion roubles are spent on personal and domestic services, a growth of between 300 and 500% since the beginning of the Brezhnev era. About 5 to 6 billion roubles are spent annually on unofficial home repairs (and home building), tailoring, car repairs, and weddings and funerals; 3.5 billion roubles on leisure services; 2.5 billion roubles on private medical services.

There is an immense energy concealed in these figures. Jacek Rostowski ('The Decay of Socialism and the Growth of Private Enterprise in Poland 1988') estimates that up to 45% of personal money income in Poland is derived from private economic activity, while private-sector employment soaks up one-third of the labour force. That, of course, includes a large number of farmers since over 90 per cent of Polish agriculture is in private hands. In Hungary too, private enterprise contributes to, and draws on, a large number (perhaps a third) of household budgets.

The managers of this private realm are set to be the managers of the new era. There is the unresolved issue of control – who sets the limits to the growth of the private sector? The ideological guardians have lost their voice in Poland and Hungary, and are respectfully ignored by the reform socialists in Moscow and East Berlin; instead it is the police – or rather a complex competitive play between all the controlling agencies –that is defining limits and the speed of change. The process of encouraging private business, and then stamping on it, that has characterised policy since the October Revolution certainly forces independent entrepreneurs into a strange symbiosis with the regulators. A surprising number of Polish secret police families have inter-married with the offspring of private manufacturers. But, as in a human body, constant expansion followed by contraction creates physical changes – muscles, even birth. For Poland and Hungary, and even for the more cautious East German and Czechoslovakian regimes, the vagaries of policy on private business have contributed to a learning process. Consumers have come to accept a two-tier economy, paying either cheap, state-subsidised prices (and standing in hour-long queues for the discount), or paying real prices to black marketeers and private entrepreneurs. The private businessman, in these societies, is not exactly a warm figure of sympathy, but neither is he the threat to the system posed by an NEP man. He provides a kind of choice in a society starved of choice. That is a fundamental change in attitude from the 1950s and 1960s, and allows market-oriented reform a great deal more room for manoeuvre.

The real test of this independent managerial class will be how the question of wonership is resolved. The 'ownership card' is the most dangerous weapon in the hands of the anti-privateers. It is the main reason why there is no legal framework for takeovers and mergers and explains the hurdles facing Communist authorities who want to declare a factory bankrupt. There are bankruptcy laws in part of the Bloc, but a protective mantle surrounds ailing enterprises. Neither the local party chief, nor the trade unions, nor the local bank, want to see factories go under. Quite simply, there is no apparatus for absorbing redundant workers. Some can be retrained, but for the most part they become an immediate burden on the local governors. If private entrepreneurs were allowed, and encouraged, to buy up bankrupt state concerns, the first move would be to close down the unprofitable units. Provincial party barons can see only disavantages in this: the businessman becomes richer, his high taxes benefit the central state coffers, but it is the locals who have to cope with the social problems of unemployement that still does not officially exist.

The taboo on individual private ownership clearly has to be revised. There are signs of popular support for a least a form of 'popular capitalism' à la Margaret Thatcher. A comprehensive opinion survey conducted at two big Polish factories by Professors Pawel Bozyk and Marian Guzek produced some revealing results: three-quarters of the workers interviewed were in favour of replacing state property with a new form of ownership, and over half approved of the idea of selling shares in their enterprise to all Poles. The Hungarian bond market has already opened up the possibility of expanding the base of ownership in state factories, and both the Soviet Union and Poland talk of the inevitability of a stock exchange. These are small steps; the fact is that it is easier to give a green light to small private business than to 'privatise' state-owned companies. Every interim possibility has to be explored first. In the Soviet Union, some factories have been allowed to organise a management buyout. The flaking Butovo Building Materials Company, a brick-maker on the verge of bankruptcy, was rescued when the director Mikhail Bocharov decided to lease the plant from the state and run it almost like a private business. Productivity rose by 30%, the losses were plugged. But the workers were still barred from buying the factory outright and the plan enmeshes even this kind of initiative: the state buys 70% of output and makes it easy for Mr Bocharov by giving him access to raw materials, some (though not enough) new equipment and bank credit. The remaining 30% the factory can sell where it wants; the earnings make up the wage-fund and profits will translate into new investment, social bonuses – such as a tennis court for the workers – and higher pay. Some 13% of Soviet factories were said in 1988 to be insolvent and many of them, especially in the services sector, could be treated to a management buyout. In Poland, such buyouts came a step closer to genuine privatisation but even so, attracted suspicious and sceptical scrutiny from Solidarity experts. Igloopol, a state-run agricultural processor, declared itself private and offered ownership shares. The old state management, which had drawn up the terms of the privatisation, then promptly bought a majority of the shares on offer. They became rich men and the management structure remained unchanged. Solidarity naturally saw this manoeuvre as an evil portent; the old Communist Party *nomenklatura*, knowing that its days were numbered under a Solidarity government, was making jobs for itself. Actually, there were worse fates for Igloopol; the new-old management was at least experienced, and presumably committed to making a profit.

Straightforward individual share ownership, as in Britain and France, is probably not the solution to the East European economic malaise. A more complex and variegated answer to property ownership has to be supplied in countries where the state still owns over 95% of productive assets. There is a vast gap between the estimated value of publicly owned enterprises and the resources of the population. Even if, as we have seen, individual cash reserves are high, even if every saver could be mobilised, he could only afford to buy about 4 or 5% of real public assets. In Poland, Solidarity government economists weighed up the possibility for the 1990s. The most radical proposal was that the government should simply give away all state industrial property to the people. This would be done in two steps. First, ownership of state companies would be divided into blocks of shares. Each Polish adult would be allocated identical 'property tickets' which would, in total, equal the equity share on offer. The Poles could then pick their favoured companies, increasing their holding by pooling tickets within the family. A stock exchange and a normally functioning capital market would attach real value to these shares. When the ideas were first kicked around, in the early 1980s, Solidarity was underground; by early 1990s Solidarity was in government and this kind of popular capitalism seemed feasible. There were serious reservations from the leftists in Solidarity who continued to argue for a form of worker-ownership, with registered shares held only by employees. These were open questions, not just about the future economy of Poland, but about the very nature of the state. 'Why are you obsessed by ownership?' a fine, blinkered Bulgarian scholar demanded, stopping just short of prodding me on the chest. 'In Western Europe you have entrepreneurs like Carlo di Benedetti of Olivetti, who has tentacles throughout Europe. His operations are a mix of private and state interests, many are French or Belgian-owned, not Italian, a complete mishmash. Why? Because he understands the exact character of ownership is not important – what is important, the only important thing, is management.' That is the new Marxist line – at least to Western reporters – under the Gorbachev regime. Meeting the scholars in the reformist vanguard (where were they in the 1970s) one wants to prod them back and ask, 'What about the Workers?' The answer, more often than not, is in the mould of enlightened capitalism: workers can get a slice of the profit.

The more realistic of Gorbachev's advisers have this to say: first, law, or at least the law of ownership, has to be separated from ideology. That is, there has to be an intellectual debate drawing demarcation lines between the laws that regulate everyday life and the state's commitment to Marxism-Leninism. When this has been resolved, or at least aired, then new bills can be drafted expanding the basis of ownership. People have to be educated into understanding that the legal existence of private markets does not endanger the survival of communism. For people, read the police, uniformed and secret, who are responsible for implementing the laws. Second, some form of social-welfare safety net has to be created for possible victims of competition. The prospect of mass unemployment is too facile an instrument in the hands of the anti-reformers. Opponents of Gorbachev used to argue that the private sector bred crime and corruption; now, increasingly, they say that privatisation creates unemployment, a disillusioned youth and an impoverished older generation. In the age of glasnost, the Soviet press is full of letters from pensioners complaining about prices and deteriorating standards. Pensioners are a potent force in the Soviet Bloc; they retain political influence long after their retirement. Their scepticism about NEP men has to be soothed. Finally, for private enterprise to have a real impact on ordinary lives, there has to be a change of attitude on the part of petty bureaucrats. Walking around Moscow apartment blocks that I knew in the 1970s, I found little change in the Gorbachev era. There were the same old House Regulations: no cars could be washed in the forecourt, no furniture could be lacquered at home. The rules were enforced by the house supervisor and the effect was to squash individual initiative. They effectively ruled out the possibility of residents repairing cars after hours, excluded home-run furniture renovation. The difference between the two eras, the mid 1970s and the late 1980s is that people were beginning to find the rules stifling. Here, in the homes and courtyards of the underemployed, there was the germ of an enterprise culture. Only the archaic regulations were holding it back.

14

The Policeman

Alexander Malyschov was wearing civilian clothes – a long grey greatcoat, earflaps down on his *schapka* – when he walked home with his mother on the night of 3 January 1988. It was about one o'clock in the morning and they were at Chernakovskaya street, not far from home. Odessa in the summer and in the sun has a raffish Neapolitan charm. In the winter, at night, caught between the sea and the steppes, it is a grim under-lit place, no cars on the street and not a policeman in sight. The police would in any case have been of little help to Captain Malyschov of the Odessa OBKhSS, the police department that investigates economic crime and corruption.

Five young men blocked their passage. Two had scarves around their mouths and another wore a ski mask. He might as well have been confronting Moslem women under the *chador*.

'You Malyschov?'

The captain nodded. His mother gripped his arm.

'So you're the one who wants to bring Moscow to Odessa? Forget it! Get out of Odessa while you still have your skin.'

Then there was a blow to his forehead, a high kick broke against his thigh and Malyschov stumbled to the ground. His mother, a shrewd 64-year-old, yelled 'Sasha, shoot them, use your gun,' knowing full well that her son had left his pistol at home. The youths scattered. Later, at the main Odessa police headquarters, nobody believed the Captain's report and he was dismissed as an hysteric; at worst, ran the patter, it was a failed mugging, nothing to get excited about. At home, the Captain and his mother received odd phone calls asking for a rendezvous. The Captain went into hiding.

The story of Captain Malyschov's breakdown is salutory. It illustrates the venomous rivalry between the agencies that are supposed to be monitoring economic crime in the Soviet Union and how, in the Gorbachev reform era, this infighting has become even more confused. The existence of black and grey markets has always given an important

lever to the police. Since almost everybody has to break the law or resort
to illegal markets to meet the Plan, or indeed simply to survive, the
police have built up an almost unchallengeable power base. The
criminalisation of everyday life gives the police (broadly interpreted,
including the uniformed, plainclothes and secret forces) a hold on
everybody. It would be impossible to pursue every infraction, and so the
powers of discretion are wide. Ordinary policemen can offer sophisticated deals: we will not prosecute you if . . . The 'if' can, and frequently
does, entail a bribe. But the 'if' is also the essence of an informer system:
tell us all you know about X, and we will not pull in your brother for
changing dollars, or padding the books. The worse the state supply
system, the more extensive are illicit markets and the happier is the
policeman's lot. That might be described as the Brezhnev formula
although a similar relationship between the stagnant economy and the
police existed under Khrushchev. It was the Brezhnev era, however,
that made Soviet policemen rich. A typical argument in a Moscow
police station is over the duty roster for the week: everybody wants to
work on Saturday nights because, prowling outside households where
drunken parties are under way, they can extract hefty bribes. A
patrolman can pick up 20 roubles or more in pay-offs on a good party
night; usually he does not even have to take out his breathalyser bag.
The banknotes are slipped into the driving licence. It is difficult to tell
whether that day-to-day police corruption has come to a halt in
Gorbachev's Russia; probably not. But the fundamental relations, the
terms of the Brezhnev formula, are shifting. Under Gorbachev market
forces are, within limits, desirable. Trading that would have been
regarded as an economic crime in the 1970s is now encouraged. The
laws have not completely caught up with the Gorbachev era –
speculation and profiteering are still on the books – so the enforcement
of the rules is more than ever a matter of police discretion. In the 'spirit
of Gorbachev' it behoves an intelligent police commander to ease up on
those crimes related to the market – the private car market say, or
currency dealing, or private repair workshops. In the old days his
tolerance would have been rewarded with a pay-off. Nowadays, the
regional police commanders have to be cautious about going to the
steam baths with patrons from private or state enterprise. The rules of
behaviour are changing and so is the politcal relationship of the
policeman to the outside world. In the Brezhnev years, police chiefs
were part of the regional elite; their children would intermarry; the
rough edges of life – university entrance, a new apartment – would be

smoothed away. But at the same time, they were outside the normal
Party network; orders from Moscow could (though they rarely did) force
police commanders to forget their close family or neighbourhood ties
and make an arrest. The police commander was thus both courted and
feared. Under Gobachev this settled role is under threat. Police
commanders are being rotated more frequently. A post-Brezhnev purge
of the Interior Ministry cleared out officials, and regional police
commands are constantly being weeded. Gorbachev's KGB, first under
General Viktor Chebrikov, then under General Vladimir Kruchkov, is
the main purging organ, though, as it occasionally has to admit, it is far
from pure itself. But the resistance to Gorbachev within the police force
is an extraordinarily complex matter, pitting regional mafias against
Moscow, party and police factions, splintered into innumerable tribes,
against each other, the procurator against the investigator.

Captain Malyschov, the bright young man of OBKhSS, was a
Gorbachevite before the accession of Gorbachev. As the Polish aphorist
Stanislaw Lec writes, those who are ahead of their time often have to live
uncomfortably while they wait for everybody else to catch up. It would
be wrong to regard OBKhSS (Otdel dlya Borby Khishcheniem
Sotsalialisicheskoi Sobstvennosti – Police Department for the Fight
against Theft of Socialist Property) as some kind of Spartan elite. There
have been several cases of bribed OBKhSS officers, and the department
is often hamstrung by official indifference and the political immunity of
their prey. But it does represent one of the better-educated wings of the
Soviet police force, recruiting and rapidly promoting talented economists, lawyers, and engineers. At the age of 28, in 1985, Malyschov was
already a captain. He looked the part; tall, fit, but slightly bookish with a
tendency to stutter under pressure. It was said that he enjoyed good
connections in Kiev and Moscow and so it did not come as a surprise
when he was summoned to the Cadre department of the Interior
Ministry at no. 6 Ogarkov Street in Moscow. 'This is it – the big one!'
said a colleague slapping his back. His interview was not actually in the
Cadre (or personnel) Department, but in an out-of-the-way block. The
desk was clear, the walls bare even of Lenin slogans or portraits. Still, the
atmosphere was warm. The officer, a major, stood with his back to the
open window; August heat, noises of workmen down below. The
ministry was well-satisfied with the captain's work, said the Major,
promotion was a certainty, he should carry on with zeal until the word
came from Moscow. A bit vague, but pleasing. As Malyschov walked
down the stairs from his interview, he bumped into an old colleague

from Odessa, an officer in the Criminal Investigation Bureau. Malyschov stretched out his hand – and was promptly manacled. Seven policemen emerged from above and below him on the staircase. 'Don't say a word, Comrade Captain,' said the colleague from Odessa. Passengers had been thrown off the normal Aeroflot flight and by that evening the up-and-coming Captain was in Odessa Investigative Prison, cell number 13. The next day, 17 August 1985, the state prosecutor told him he was being charged under article 173 – 'the receipt of a bribe in any form by a person in an official position for the purpose of carrying out or not carrying out actions in the interests of the bribe-giver.' Black-market traders and the head of a department store, already in jail, had denounced him. Malyschov was in a state of shock – he was an honest cop who, 24 hours earlier, thought he was about to be promoted for spurning bribe-givers and nabbing black marketeers. Outside, in the police headquarters and the trading centres of Odessa, few people had any doubt about Malyschov's guilt; it was all too probable. At last Gorbachev was cleaning out the stables!

After a depressing day alone, Malyschov was given a cellmate. It was an old trick. The veteran Soviet defence lawyer, Dina Kaminskaya, recalls how two teenage clients, wrongly accused of rape, were put in a cell with hardened cons who urged 'co-operation' (that is, a confession) and who painted a horrific picture of life in the labour camp for uncooperative rapists. Malyschov's plant was just as unsubtle.

'Listen,' he said, 'Goretzki played along and got only five years.' Goretzki too had been an OBKhSS commander in another part of the Odessa region; he too had been accused of taking bribes. The proposal was put more authoritatively by the prosecutor of the Odessa Oblast who visited Malyschov in his cell in early September: either co-operate and pick up a short sentence, or never leave prison.

Malyschov was being primed. By the time his main interrogator got round to details, Malyschov was beyond surprise. The interrogator made it all sound simple. All Malyschov had to do was to make a list of people to whom he passed on the bribe money. That is, the non-existent money. The list should include the deputy prosecutor of the Odessa Oblast, the deputy chairman of internal affairs for the Oblast, the chairman of internal affairs for the city of Odessa, the First Secretary of the Party on the Odessa City Committee and the Head of Administration. Malyschov should not worry his head about all this; false confessions would be arranged. If he co-operated immediately, then his mother could visit within a week, bring some clean underwear and food, and conditions would improve. And if not: new witnesses would be found to testify against him. The charges could be compounded and multiplied to such an extent that the firing squad would be inevitable. The drumbeat of threat-promise, promise-threat, continued for months. 'The man in the cell next door to you, do you know who he is?' This, a typical ploy by the interrogator Bobowski. 'It's an apparatchik from Kiev. He has confessed everything. What he gets, he gets. Nothing can make a difference. All you have to do is say that you brought him cases of cognac to his dacha. You see? No moral dilemma. Good for you, no difference to him.'

The state prosecutor detailed Grigori Pavlovich Schulyatschenko to present the prosecution case. Schulyatschenko, a reliable lawyer without political ambition, studied the indictment and complained to his boss that there was not enough to go on; too many discrepancies, even in the manufactured confessions. Without a confession from Malyschov, it was not a strong case. The state prosecutor fell into a rage and in a three-hour meeting bullied Schulyatschenko into presenting the case in court. 'I realised suddenly,' Schulyatschenko said later, 'that either I said yes, OK, or I would never leave the room.' The lawyer said 'Yes,' spent a sleepless night and the next day, told the court, 'The charges in the Malyschov case do not tally with the facts contained in the indictment.' Such individual acts of bravery do occur in Soviet courts. The cost of courage is settled out of court: Schulyatschenko was fired the same evening.

Malyschov was released some two years later, and Schulyatschenko got his job back. But only after Moscow was drawn into the affair. Reporters from *Literaturnaya Gazeta* and *Pravda* started to stir things up and it became plain that this was a game of high politics. The Odessa party wanted to sweep out Gorbachev-men (or, more precisely, young True Believers who had been inserted by Yuri Andropov), the Odessa police command wanted to protect its pay-off networks and was happy to sacrifice Malyschov, the Odessa KGB, which had planted much of the false evidence, wanted to neuter the anti-corruption squad, the Interior Ministry in Moscow wanted to protect its chums in the Ukraine, and so on, endlessly into the labyrinth. It took a man from Moscow to free Malyschov – the main investigating judge of the Procurator General's office, Anatoly Kondratyev. But Moscow is far away from Odessa. Malyschov has his captain's rank restored but is afraid to cross the street. The purge of the Odessa party continued deep into 1989. Over 400 functionaries lost their jobs. A few were accused of 'ignoring the principles of democracy.'

Malyschov was an honest cop, but that has never been enough in a politically-controlled police force. At a time of rapid change, honesty, in its strict 'bourgeois' sense (telling the truth, pursuing wrongdoers to the best of one's ability) is a handicap since it becomes synonymous with political insensitivity. Malyschov was in tune with the Gorbachev age, but that was more by accident than design. The captain's opponents assumed that his zeal in pursuing corruption cases was inspired politically from Moscow and treated him accordingly as a pawn in a political game; despite a huge genre of 'honest cop' thrillers (notably Julian Semyonov's *Tass is Authorised to Report* . . . which sold 2.5 million in the USSR), it was difficult for the Odessa force to discern Malyschov's main character trait, naivety. The question is: does Gorbachev want a police force full of Malyschovs? Does he need a truly independent police force in the restructuring of the Soviet economy and society? If independence is regarded as important, then there is a job for Malyschov since most autonomous forces can accommodate honest officers (not, say the cynics, too many). But the early indications in the late 1980s, were that Gorbachev's main aim was to purge the police and ensure its commitment to his reform policies. The courts and the judiciary could be given more freedom, but the strict rule of law and neutral law-enforcers were a low priority in the Gorbachev revolution. My last letter to Malyschov, was returned: addressee unknown.

The Gorbachev era poses special problems for the identity of communist police forces and the other agencies of control. First, economic reform is creating new victims and new winners. The old patterns of protection and immunity from prosecution or investigation are crumbling. Because reform is unbottling inflation in a society ill-equipped to deal with it, petty crime is on the rise. That is putting a heavy workload on already under-manned and underpaid police forces. New powers of discretion are required. A factory director breaks the rules to improve the efficiency of his plant. Should he be pursued? A private entrepreneur who is doing a thriving legal business with Austria is recycling some of his profits on the black market. Should he be prosecuted? There are no plain answers; in the Soviet Union, the answer differs from republic to republic, from region to region. By the end of 1988, Gorbachev was beginning to recognise this lack of confidence as a real obstacle to change. The Soviet parliament, the Supreme Soviet, was given more significance (if not real power) and created a legal framework for reform, a set of laws that would protect the factory manager with initiative, that would define the room for manoeuvre for the controllers.

It does not pay, however, to put too much faith in parliaments that have not been properly elected. More important was the role of the KGB in Gorbachev's rise to power. As the ideological heir of Yuri Andropov, Gorbachev inherited a political caucus in the KGB. Andropov was against abuse of privileges by party leaders, inefficiency in factory managements, sloppy worker discipline. He was for the KGB as an instrument of party control, monitoring deficiencies and contributing to improved political and economic conditions. The KGB, it must be said, adapted well enough when Andropov died and Brezhnev's private secretary (and old NKVD hand) Konstantin Chernenko took over. The KGB became less active in domestic policy-making under Chernenko; either its reformers went underground, or its commitment to reform was never that strong in the first place. But as Chernenko weakened, physically and politically, as Gorbachev climbed, so the KGB fought to assert its primacy among controlling agencies. By the time Gorbachev took over in 1985, the KGB was *primes inter pares*: it was the acknowledged vehicle for change, for blackening and outflanking the party opposition (as corrupt Brezhnevites) and for accelerating economic reform. The KGB, which has always enjoyed a close relationship with the Soviet press, became even more intimate with the propaganda machine. The stories that mushroomed in the regional and central press, in the first flush of glasnost, looked suspiciously well researched. KGB files were being opened up and leaked to editors. All well and good: the KGB and other guardians have traditionally contributed to changes in leadership in Soviet-Bloc countries by gathering, sometimes manufacturing, and disclosing information on economic corruption. But Gorbachev was unhappy with his political dowry. First, the KGB, by projecting itself as an agent of change, was putting itself beyond its own organisational reform. Second, Gorbachev wanted to advance much further than Andropov. At the cusp where economic reforms blurs into political reform, Gorbachev encounterd resistance from the KGB under the chairmanship of General Viktor Chebrikov. His replacement on the last weekend of September 1988 heralded a real change of pace: the KGB's immunity to perestroika had been pierced. The contract of 1986–87 –that the KGB will actively support certain economic improvements in return for an acknowledged leading role among the controllers and a veto right on all major political liberalisation – was revoked.

Who then controls the Gorbachev revolution? I use the word in the narrow Slavic sense (as in Lenin: 'Trust is good, control is better') of vigilance (checking, monitoring) rather than command or ownership. The mainspring of the Gorbachev era is profit. The Soviet economy has to become profitable, if all the other plans for the modernisation of society are to work. With a profitable economy, it should eventually be possible to carry out the traditional tasks of a socialist system (protecting the weak, such as pensioners, increasing investment in hospitals, schools, the countryside), the national goals that have evolved since Stalin (the costly development of natural energy resources), maintain the defences of the USSR, preserve its unity (by deploying central funds to make up for regional imbalances) and still get to grips with the Gorbachev agenda. Yet the whole system works against profit. Profitability is suspicious; profit has to be accounted for; profit is an ideological freak (is it not, according to the Good Book, 'exploitation'?). Profit is also difficult to achieve without breaking the rules. It is well-nigh impossible to fulfil the monthly, annual Plan (which in itself does not have much to say about profit) without illegality. Soviet managers, to excuse themselves, sometimes make the useful (though legally meaningless) distinction between *narusheniya* (violations) and *prestupleniya* (crimes). Violations, minor infringements, like concealing a stock of a hundred litres of petrol, or padding the books, are necessary to keep the Plan on course. It is part of the Plan mentality that personal profit, in the form of bonuses for claimed achievements, takes precedence over the profitability of the factory. Managers, as we have seen in earlier chapters, 'store' workers, that is, their existence is camouflaged on the account books in order to provide that extra manpower needed, at the end of the month, to meet all the production and delivery targets. In other words, personal enrichment, the urge to win bonuses, has displaced the productivity of the factory. It is not an economical outlook. (Brezhnev, in his brief 'reform' phases used to tell Russians 'to think economically'. In one sense they did: they kept their thoughts to themselves.) The question of control is therefore a complex one. Plainly, no internal control mechanism can function in a system that has so many in-built distortions. The Soviet economy is indeed a giant, but one with astigmatism. The managers with control functions –accountants, financial chiefs – are part of an elaborate deception machine. The whole ministerial architecture supports this deception. *Sotsialisticheskaya Industriya* (quoted by Nicholas Lampert in *Whistleblowing in the Soviet Union*, Macmillan 1985, p. 39) records an entirely typical case that stretched as far as the Deputy Minister for the Petroleum Industry:

'When the control period was over and it came time to report on what use of the new methods of acting on the petroleum reservoirs had produced, quite encouraging figures showed up in the reports. No, the oil workers did not claim that they had attained the Plan indices. They merely noted, modestly, that they had only just fallen short. However it was only on paper that things were going smoothly. As inspection showed that throughout the five-year plan the ministry had done virtually no serious work . . . the indices given in the report turned out to have been simply invented.'

Note that this report dates from 1981, pre-glasnost, and was by no means a rarity. The awareness that control has to come from outside the factory, industry or ministry, is by no means specific to Gorbachev. The early Bolshevik theologians of the Plan were well aware that they could be bamboozled; that the reporting procedures, the whole structure, could be used by the workers to fool the authorities, or by the authorities to fool the outside world. A hierarchy of external controls has thus been erected. But it is in the nature of these controls that they can be either inert or zealous, according to the energy and commitment of the leadership. Gorbachev's first success has been to convince the Russian people that he cares about control, that he takes it seriously. But if this concern with monitoring is to translate into a more efficient economy, then Gorbachev has to strike a successful balance between the agencies of control.

If one pursues a Brezhnevian policy, then it is enough to blindfold the agencies and take away political support from anybody commissioned to pursue economic mismanagement or political corruption. The police, uniformed and secret, become in this equation the suppressors of political opposition: a traditional, but barely satisfying role. But Gorbachev, if he is to be consistent, needs a flow of authentic information about the economy and the polity: that means taking away the blindfolds. He needs to act on the information from the controllers: that means ensuring an even spread of political support for the different agencies. And he needs to pass on at least some of the information received back to the people.

The legal and administrative changes involved in the Gorbachev revolution have the intricacy of a Swiss clock. The external controllers – the People's Control, the Prosecutor-General, the police, the anti-fraud squad, the KGB – are to be given more credibility. But at the same time they have to be loyal. There is no such thing as a politically neutral police force, least of all in the Soviet Bloc. Gorbachev has to ensure that his controllers provide him with objective intelligence while simultaneously demonstrating their commitment to his reform policies. These aims are difficult to reconcile, but not impossible. The most pressing danger is that a single agency of control, notably the KGB, gains such predominance that Gorbachev is presented with a monotone picture of his country.

Who then are the controllers, the timekeepers of reform? Who controls the controllers, who guards the guardians? And what is their relative strength?

People's Control

The popular element – control by the people for the people – has always been important in the rhetoric of communist supervision. In 1920 Lenin had helped to create two control bodies, the Central Control Commission (CCC) which would monitor Party misconduct and the Worker-Peasant Inspection (WPI) teams that were supposed to mobilise the masses in controlling state bureaucracy and the economy. In fact both were regarded as weapons to put down political opposition. When the two commissions were merged they became one of the major instruments of Stalin's political purges in the 1920s and early 1930s. By 1934, however, the secret police had emerged as the main purging weapon, and the CCC and WPI were split again.

The real Soviet debate about the nature of control came in the Khrushchev years. The control agency had re-emerged after the War as the Ministry of State Control (Goskontrol) and, though it had intimate links with the secret police, it had few powers. It could check on ministries and industries, block funds to factories under investigation, but it could not interrogate suspect officals and had to keep its findings secret. In the Khrushchev era there were three detailed questions. How far should there be mass participation in controlling the economy and the bureaucracy? How far should Goskontrol be the centre of these control operaions? And should Goskontrol staff be recruited because of their skills in detection, or because of their Party credentials?

By 1962, the discussion had crystallised around two opposing schools. The first was that the new post-Stalinist control mechanism should be in the service of the state. It would be run by financial and economic experts who would be able to spot cases of corruption from a hundred metres. They would be backed up by a volunteer force, drawn from the trade unions and the Komsomol youth league. This solution had the advantage of keeping the 'masses' at arm's length and largely de-politicising the battle against mismanagement.

The opposing school favoured control as a party, or rather joint Party-Police agency. It would be staffed entirely by Party zealots. They would report their findings to the police.

The final, inadequate compromise saw the creation of a joint party-state control under the chairmanship of a former KGB chief, Alexander Shelepin. There was confusion from the beginning. Although there were explicit links with the KGB, the new control commission did not have much clout with the police or the prosecutor's office. It could expose corruption or abuse – usually at the level of factory managers, accountants or ministerial bureaucrats – it could make proposals, but it could not follow through. A negligent manager could be publicly reprimanded, but he was to be handed over to the local Party cell for disciplining. If the manager had sufficient political protection he could emerge unscathed. In 1965 the control commission mustered 711,000 'assistance groups' which in turn could call on 4,000,000 members.

Nowadays, essentially the same hybrid structure can call on about 9,000,000 volunteer inspectors. A typical mission would be to check on a complaint that a shop manager is hoarding tights for sale on the black market. The check-up team first informs the police and the local party cell, piles into two cars and arrives at the scene of the complaint. An accountant is collected from trade union headquarters to check the books. With great bustle and vim, the controllers search the store room, question assistants and, if they find little evidence, end up giving the managers a ticking-off. Later an account of the raid will appear, suitably embellished, in the local press or even find its way into *Izvestia*.

Other Soviet-Bloc countries have evolved similar structures of control, accountable to both state and Party, and, in effect, toothless. The Czechoslovak press is particulary bitter about the ineffectivness of the People's Inspectorates. As Prague resisted Moscow's blandishments in the late 1980s to accelerate reform, so it came under increasing pressure to show that its arrangements were working well. This was difficult. People's Inspectorates investigate about 130,000 complaints related to economic crime, but only 11 per cent of the checks actually reveal wrong-doing. This proportion – 11 per cent – has remained stable over the years, despite a steep increase in economic offences.

One priority for Gorbachev must be to establish an effective pattern of control at the factory and industrial level. As the Khrushchev debate showed, this is no easy matter. But Gorbachev carries with him less ideological baggage; there is no obligation to draw on the Komsomol for volunteer inspectors, nor to demonstrate a commitment to the Leninist principles of social control. In fact Lenin's rather scanty writings on the subject have been remodelled so thoroughly by Stalin and Khrushchev that they were no longer a meaningful frame of reference. Two matters have to be resolved if 'People's Control' is to be made an important part of the Gorbachev revolution. First, the acounting skills of the Inspectorate teams have to be improved radically. The padding of factory accounts has become, over the years, an applied, if not a fine art. It is rarely true nowadays that Soviet factories have two sets of accounts, one for Moscow, and the other genuine. In most factories there are no genuine accounts; they are *ad hoc* compilations that tuck away secret assets – extra workers and material – disguise liabilities, and project unrealistic needs on the basis of fictional production and sales figures. The point is that everybody at the top of the factory management ladder understands this, and each department head knows precisely the degree to which his situation has been exaggerated or understated. It is for the People's Inspectorate to unravel this puzzle, as complex as a semiotic novel by Umberto Eco. That needs special skills not usually available to a volunteer force. Of the various Soviet control agencies, only the OBKhSS, Captain Malyshov's employer, has the competence.

The second challenge is to break the powers of protection that surround racketeers within the various industries and economic sectors of the Soviet Bloc. Under the present set-up, People's Controllers have to involve the local police or the local Party before acting against economic criminals. That makes the controllers powerless if the managers are in cahoots with the regional police and party chiefs; cases from Uzbekistan, Armenia, Georgia, Estonia, Slovakia, Silesia and Thuringia have all demonstrated the validity of this simple proposition. The inspectors, underpaid, are easily drawn into this nexus. In Czechoslovakia there have been many instances of inspectors being bribed to stay away from factories where the rules are being broken: the bribe comes from the factory slush funds, but the subsequent report, based on entirely fictional premises, has to be passed by local politicians. Solidarity uncovered the case of a factory that had taken over part of a state poultry farm in Poland. The land was used as a pheasant-shoot by the state inspectors and the factory managers. The outbuildings had been lavishly converted so that the inspectors could be entertained with vodka and girls, paid for from factory accounts which of course remained resolutely uninspected. In Estonia, in the late 1970s, I heard of a factory management that invited the Inspector to its sauna along with the local police chief where they were joined by three girls, one of them under-age. The mother of the youngest found out and tried to make the matter public but faced considerable harassment – her husband had trouble at work, the girl had trouble at school and the police summonsed the mother for a number of fictional offences. Eventually the family left the area, settled with relatives elsewhere in the Republic, and the honour of the factory was preserved.

These kind of scandals are inevitable, given the low pay and prestige of Inspectors, but probably not that widespread. The co-option of the People's Control usually takes less lurid forms; most of the volunteer Inspectors, judging by letters to the Soviet press, are decent unimaginative people. If they are asked by the Party not to rock the boat, then they will not. It is a case not of covering up the facts, but of party discipline: the Inspectorates are there to serve the Party and the People and so one should listen responsively to the voice of the local party chieftain who argues, for example, that a report criticising corrupt management will lead to the closure of a factory and spell disaster for many working people. That is political blackmail at the grass-roots level. Further up the chain of command, there are scores of ministerial bureaucrats, dozens of undersecretaries and Republican ministers, even men in Moscow with an interest in hushing up economic malpractice. A racket at relatively low levels within an industry is usually known about, even if rather vaguely, at the top. Some form of tribute is usually offered to one's boss, and up the ladder to his boss, in return for tolerance. So it was with the Great Caviar Scandal, discovered in 1979. About 200 officials in the Soviet Ministry of Fisheries were packing fine black caviar into tins labelled as smoked herring and then exporting them to the West, or delivering them to the better restaurants in Sochi on the Black Sea. The contents of the tins were re-sold as caviar and the difference in price between herring and caviar was pocketed by the syndicate. The racket ran from the factory level to the top. Unusually, the Deputy Minister of Fisheries, Vladimir Rytov, was put in front of a firing squad because of his involvement, although his role was not that of mastermind. He simply received a generous tribute from the syndicate, paid into an illegal Western bank account. Because of pressure from Sochi residents, the chairman of the local council, Vyacheslav Voronkov, was arrested – he had received bribes from the local restaurants – and was jailed for 13 years. But the normal powers of protection operated for the Party Chief of the Krasnodar region, Sergei

Medanov, who, though fully in the know, was not prosecuted. He was, it emerged, a good friend of Yuri Brezhnev, son of the then Soviet leader, and a deputy minister of foreign trade.

Significantly, the case was not uncovered by People's Controllers, but by a combination of OBKhSS and the KGB. As soon as it became clear that the caviar profits were being channelled into foreign bank accounts, the KGB pulled the case away from the police fraud specialists and set up a special investigation team which reported to Yuri Andropov.

If the People's Controllers, the state inspectors, are to counterbalance the power of the KGB in monitoring economic performance, then Gorbachev must grant them autonomy from both the Party and the government. That is why the Gorbachev team have been studying closely the experiences of the Polish Supreme Chamber of Control (NIK). The Chamber was given legal status in February 1947 (though it took a further two years to prepare executive regulations allowing it to operate) and it was regarded, in theory at least, as independent of the government. It had the same powers as the other Soviet-Bloc control commissions, but it reported to the Council of State, the collective presidency. But in the Stalinist years its paper autonomy was never exploited: the teeth were there, but blunt and rotten from disuse. From 1952 to 1957 NIK lost even this notional independence and was made subject to the government (which re-named it the Ministry of State Control, as in the Soviet Union). The Polish October in 1956, Wladyslaw Gomulka's attempt to de-Stalinise Poland, made NIK subject to parliament. In the future, parliament (known as the Sejm) would be able to monitor government activity with its own investigation body – a sensational move that destroyed some of the traditional patterns of patronage and protection. In fact, much depended on the quality of the parliament itself. Since it was not elected in any Western sense of the word and was dominated by the Communist Party, NIK's copious dossiers about corruption and incompetence were rarely used. As soon as NIK began to look dangerous – under the politically ambitious Mieczyslaw Moczar in the 1970s – Party leader Edward Gierek subordinated the Controllers to the Prime Minister. Since most of NIK's investigations shed light on the incompetence of government – Moczar had accumulated personal corruption dossiers on every cabinet member – it was a time of great frustration. NIK's reports on the impending Polish energy problems, on the debt burden and on the grossly faked economic statistics were simply ignored by the Polish government.

The Procurator's Office

It is difficult to generalise about the effectiveness of the Procuracy as a controller of the economy, or as a political agent in the Gorbachev era. For one thing, the Office is organised on the traditional hierarchical lines, and political allegiance is correspondingly diffuse: a senior Procurator in Kirghizia is a different animal from his counterpart in Estonia. Cerainly a large part of the Procuracy's workload, throughout the Soviet Union and Eastern Europe, has been devoted to economic crime and the abuse of office – embezzlement, falsifying statistics, fraud, bribery and other variants of corruption. The pressure is on to do more. At the end of the 1970s, as Yuri Andropov prepared a bid for the succession to Brezhnev, there was a flood of criticism against the police and the Procuracy for neglecting economic crime and corruption. An important Central Committee resolution of September 1979 urged all legal and controlling agencies to 'establish strict order in record-keeping and storage of valuable materials' and to 'eradicate resolutely mis-management, waste, report-padding and fraud.' The Soviet Procurator's office then passed on the word to local procurators: get tough on economic offenders. This was a scene, a minor one in the lengthy stage drama of Kremlin succession. Since the Procuracy was falling down on the job, the KGB, under Andropov, could assign itself the task as main fighter of economic and political corruption. The Procuracy argued, successfully, for greater legal scope in supervising investigations. But this did not affect its position in relation to the KGB and it had to sit on its hands as corrupt or inefficient Procuracy officials were picked off in Kirghizia, Georgia and Azerbaidjan.

All the Soviet-Bloc countries used this transitional period, in the late 1970s and early 1980s, to ginger up their Procurators. In East Germany there was a campaign to improve the economic and financial expertise of procurators because (in the words of the journal *Neue Justiz*, February 1981) 'It will certainly be necessary to intervene more severely in cases of illegal individual and collectively selfish efforts which by their very nature reflect disregard of total societal needs.' This was as close as the East German press came to denouncing corruption.

In a subsequent article in *Neue Justiz*, the academic laywer Dr Walter Girebe took up the cudgels: 'Crimes against socialist property and also those against personal and private property predominate numerically in the number of crimes reported in the DDR (East Germany). They account for about half of all registered crime, and 50 per cent of all crimes against property are directed against socialist property . . . the damage caused by these crimes and the destructive effects that follow are considerable, diminishing the economic successes achieved by our national economy . . . the struggle against these crimes is therefore always within the purview of the prosecuting organs.' That final comment is important becuse because it demonstrates one of the central flaws of relying on a Procurator's office to monitor corruption. As in the West, there is a constant pressure either to close a case early or to bring a swift and successful prosecution. But most high-level corruption cases involve years of thorough and complicated investigation. A witness often has to incriminate himself and, though the Procurator's office can waive charges, there is no great readiness in oblige – there are too many extra-legal repercussions for someone involved in such a case. To lose a job, a chance of a promotion, the hope of foreign travel – these are bitter punishments and easy ways in which vengeful spirits in the corrupt bureaucracy or factory management can make their displeasure known. Better be silent and wait for the storm to blow over, especially as the internal rivalries between Interior Ministry, secret police and Procurator's office can sometimes lead to a case being dropped. The Procurator's office is hamstrung by its lack of finance – compared to the huge budget of the KGB – by the breath of its activities, by the rivalry of other departments, by its pressure to produce results, by its lack of specialised expertise and sometimes by the legal system itself. Conviction in a corruption case can only follow – given the restraints on the office – from the evidence of an informer in the pay of the authorities or by a disgruntled former accomplice who has been offered immunity. But in Soviet Georgia for example too many deals have been done between underworld entrepreneurs and the local police to make it worthwhile for a former criminal to recant in a way that implicates top operators. When the police and the underworld are in league, those who co-operate with a prosecutor are likely to meet unpleasant accidents.

The criticisms of local Soviet procurators are that they suppress cases, that investigations are superficial, that cases of corruption usually focus on relatively junior officials and that if culprits are brought to book they are often charged under laws that lead to softer punishment. But the Procuracy is not wholly to blame for these shortcomings. If the evidence is somewhat threadbare in a corruption case, then it must work out a formula, usually involving a confession to a minor offence, or drop the case altogether. In that sense, the Procuracy adheres strictly to the law. But it also listens: if political advice from the Central Committee suggests that investigations are probing too deeply, then the office will pull back its investigators and prosecutors. The law becomes subject to political expediency. That does not mean Procurators as a breed are spineless. In the Stalinist era many Procurators were purged for not condoning violations by the secret police. None the less Procurators swim in that strange polluted lake known as Socialist legality. As the Gorbachev revolution proceeds, this term becomes vaguer and vaguer. What is Socialist? Licensed private enterprises? Family farms? Bankruptcy? Factory redundancies? And what is legal? The reforms are running ahead of the legislative process. Guideline or framework laws exist, but the detailed instructions or 'executive regulations' that tell civil servants how to implement the legislation are often missing, or the subject of rearguard political struggle. And what of the marketplace, now officially blessed but still black or grey? The Procurators, in cases of doubt, reach for their telephones and ring their contacts in the Central Committee; even then they probably hear conflicting advice. Even if Gorbachev's legal reforms move in the direction of an independent judiciary, the pace of change will paralyse the Procurator's office.

The Police

MILITIAMAN: 'What we want from our union is to tell society the truth about our earnings, alleged privileges and disavantages of the profession.'

INTERVIEWER: 'You don't need a union to do that.'

MILITIAMAN: 'You are right. But there are also many other affairs to be settled within our professional community. We do not receive any compensation for night shifts, holidays, extra duties. There are also housing problems. I have been working as a militia officer for quite a long time. And yet a new militia officer gets only a fraction less than I do. For several years I have been refused a place for my family in a summer rest house. But there is a lot of room for others . . . in general we want respect for the militia officer's uniform. We want to work in accordance with the rules of law,. If anybody discredits this uniform we will exclude him from our ranks . . .'

The idea of a Soviet-Bloc police union (presented here by an anonymous spokesman in *Ekspress Wieczorny* 1 June 1981) died when martial law was declared in Poland in the winter of 1981. Nowadays one of the founders sells Christmas baubles from a private wooden kiosk; another runs a boutique in Warsaw. In 1990, under a Solidarity government, the idea was revived, but without enthusiasm. The purpose of the union was to restore the depleted prestige of the militia, the uniformed police: opinion polls had put them at the bottom of a league table of most trusted institutions, well below the Church, the Army, Solidarity. The collapse in police authority, most graphically illustrated when the Polish army had to set up its own control teams to monitor corruption in the shops and the countryside, was not unique to Poland. Every Soviet-Bloc country, above all the Soviet Union, saw an erosion of confidence during the 1970s and early 1980s. It was partly a matter of poor pay. The 1970s saw a sharp rise in worker wages in the Soviet Union and elsewhere; living standards improved dramatically. When the state shops could not soak up the cash, the black market stepped in. For the first time since the War, there was mass participation in the black market. It was no longer a question of sharp operators selling to other sharp operators. or a handful of New Rich. Everybody was buying and selling. And the police were left behind. This has always been a problem in police forces.

In 1829, Gray Bennett told the British House of Commons that 'great service, great temptation and little pay' was the policemen's lot. 'The first police officers had only a few guineas a week. They might get an additional allowance indeed at times, if they were employed by individuals or appointed to attend the royal family. But there was no remuneration for danger, no allowance on account of wounds or injury to health, no pension on retirement.' The same speech also highlights the background of 'high constables'. Many had fled from their original parishes to escape creditors and a surprising number had been or still were coal dealers. 'The secret of this was that they supplied with coals the brothels and alehouses, and in return answered for their character or screened them from detection.' This factor in police corruption has continued to the present day both in the West and the East. Operation Countryman in Britain clearly revealed that bribery was widespread especially in the Metropolitan Police and that a new class of criminal 'brokers' had sprung up to put leading crooks in contact with corrupt police.

In relatively closed communities an informal relationship springs up between those who practice crime and those who combat it. When that crime is organised, or when the criminal is politically involved, there will be an attempt to buy off insecurity by bribing police. The more 'respectable' the criminal, the more he wants to minimise the risk of prosecution. But in the Soviet Union the ground rules are different.

When almost every individual entrepreneurial action is illegal and
when the police can, thanks to informers, be aware of the hatching of a
crime at an early stage, then the initiative for bribery need not rest with
the criminal. The Brezhnev era was a time when the police actively
sought out cases that would produce rewards for the subsequent
dropping of investigations. The whole point of investigation became to
expose the maximum weakness of the target and then secure the
maximum gain. The ordinary citizen, left to the mercy of ordinary
criminals, began to feel excluded from this cosy arrangement. It takes
decades for the police to establish trust in a community, only months to
lose it.

Two other factors eroded the position of the Soviet police (the same
endemic corruption never really applied to the Soviet-Bloc neighbours;
rather there were several spotty cases, several scandals, that in a smaller
way tarnished the already dullish prestige). First, there was a sense that it
was easier to drop an economic case than to pursue it to the bitter
end. There is a constant, nagging problem of evidence. How is one to
prove a case of bribery unless either the recipient or the donor confesses?
How is one to extract a confession? There are few witnesses to a bribe
and vast research is required to demonstrate, for example, that school
teacher X promised to give a pass mark to the son of Housing
Department clerk Y, in return for priority on the housing list.
Policemen with a heavy work load (made heavier now by Gorbachev's
anti-alcohol campaign) have no zest for the fight. Even small-scale
enonomic crime – street-trading in foreign currency – carries few
professional rewards.

Inadequate legislation breeds police corruption: it is not possible to
enforce the existing laws effectively so a flawed cameraderie develops
between the two notional adversaries, the policeman and the criminal.
If the cop cannot do his job, he may as well be paid for not doing it: that
is the logic of the underworld which pays its tributes to the law non-
enforcers. The policeman on the beat comes to resent the prosecutor's
office. The office is constantly demanding evidence that cannot be
obtained, threatening to put its own investigators into the field,
complaining about the shortcomings of interrogations and the lack of
legal training of the militia. An odd relationship arises in which the
policeman, who has struggled out of the lower reaches of the working
classes, feels a great social gulf between himself and the university-
trained prosecutors but can understand and even sympathise with the
criminals they are pursuing.

The other element undermining the standing of the police is the competition from the KGB. The KGB is a self-proclaimed elite force; its tasks are less banal, the scope for individual responsibility is larger, the impact on neighbours and family is more satisfying. And yet in some areas, especially tracking down economic crime, the two forces are engaged in exactly the same work. The anti-fraud squad of Captain Malyschov, OBKhSS, is particularly sensitive. The KGB tries to snatch all major OBKhSS investigations and has been marching steadily into OBKhSS territory.

OBKhSS investigations are starved of funds. There have been instances of OBKhSS officials forced to delay an investigation until the following budget period because there was not enough money to pay for a train fare and a week in a provincial hotel. KGB men do not have such problems (or at least, not to the knowledge of Western observers). Local police are obstructive, ministries are reluctant to surrender figures and quite often the final OBKhSS reports are ignored. As some officials are seconded from the Ministry of Finance, there is a solid, academic feel to some of their analyses. Summing up a year's activity, an OBKhSS officer concluded that one-third of all anti-socialist fraud – that is, corruption in state industry – came from: (*a*) extremely high levels of permitted raw material consumption (that means factories are allowed to order more petrol or coal or ore than they need and then resell it, on the black market) (*b*) large tolerances in packing (that is, putting less in and disguising the true weight and quantity of the product) (*c*) in the weighing of the final output. Had OBKhSS the power it needs to combat corruption, stringent checks on raw-material deliveries and needs would have been imposed, limits on packaging enforced and new weighing machines and reliable supervisors installed. The report said that the input of a factory was exaggerated so that material could be resold at a profit, and that output was being exaggerated for the same reason. But nothing happened, in the factories nothing moved.

Not surprisingly, the KGB seems a more attractive career option for the bright economics graduate. And it was the KGB that was to wield the big broom when Andropov decided to clean out the militia. Friction between the militia (more accurately the Interior Ministry, the MVD) and the KGB had been increasing towards the end of Brezhnev's life. In the autumn of 1982 (Brezhnev died in November) the MVD and the KGB were repeatedly at odds about who should handle a number of important cases of economic crime. This was an institutional struggle, but with a political edge: the Interior Minister, Nikolai Shchelokov, was protecting friends and some members of the extended Brezhnev family, while the KGB, determined to oil the Kremlin succession, wanted to push hard against corrupt regional Party mafias. As soon as Brezhnev died, the MVD was put on the defensive. Andropov's first personnel change was to sack Shchelokov, who slid all the way down the pole; expelled from the Party, close to being charged for corruption, he committed suicide. The new man was Andropov's former deputy Vitali Fedorchuk, who had cleaned up dissent in the Ukraine and who, from his time in the army-monitoring department of the KGB, had wide contacts in the military. His task was to use the KGB to purge the MVD. Politically, the point was to neutralise one of the prime power centres of the Brezhnevites. But this was more than a Kremlin game: there was considerable public unease about crime rates, about gang warfare in the urban housing estates, about the laggardly investigation of rapes, about the corruption of shop managers which seemed directly linked to consumer shortages, about the flashy lifestyles of black marketeers and their political cronies. As in the West, law and order is a populist cause. In a Communist society it has even more force because of a nominally egalitarian ideology – why should I obey the rules when my neighbour is getting rich on the sly? – and the pretensions of the State to protect the weak. The Fedorchuk purge was thus rather welcome to the Soviet populace, at least in the initial stages. The Soviet Procurator General, Aleksander Rekunkov, anxious to show that the Procuracy was up with the game – and to distance it from the sloppy policing of the Brezhnev years – wrote a remarkably frank description (*Pravda*, 9 January 1983) of the state of the country. People in many towns and villages were afraid to go out at night, lest they be attacked. Police were tolerating crime, theft at the factory and workplace had reached an unacceptable level, and the militia had become infected by the national malaise. As they jostled for influence, Fedorchuk was quick to point out that the Procuracy carried its share of the blame

The MVD's departments were reshuffled and within city police headquarters a new shift system was introduced. More policemen were put on the beat and, in Moscow at least, foot patrols could be seen stamping their boots in the slush of bus stations and around the main railway stations. There was talk of neighbourhood policing – that is, re-establishing the personal links between the district and its policemen. Computers were brought in to take over some of the paperwork and thus free the police for more visible duties. The Central Committee Administration department drew up a scheme under which Party

commissars were installed – as in the army – to supervise the political life
of the police, thus, notionally, to improve their morale and sense of
civic duty. However the transplanting of the army practice never really
worked; nor has it in Poland where similar moves were made after
policemen murdered the Solidarity priest Father Jerzy Popieluszko.
The professional ethic of the police either excluded the political officers
or co-opted them. All that happened was a weeding-out of incompetent
or outrageously corrupt policemen. 'The personnel of the internal
affairs organs are being purged of backsliders and of those who are
ideologically and morally immature,' said Fedorchuk. New staff were
brought in – some 55,000 Party and or Komsomol members – and
tougher sentences were introduced for embezzlement and black
marketeering. From January 1983 black-market dealers could face up to
10 years in jail and, more importantly, a range of other lesser penalties
were introduced. The aim was to make the law enforceable: harsh
penalties may deter some criminal activity, but they also deter arrests
since no police force wants to be burdened with a major trial for
relatively minor and common offences. Fedorchuk revived one of his
Ukrainian practices and tried to systematise the police informer
network. Local policemen visited every apartment in their neighbourhood to check whether the residents were officially registered. They left
cards bearing the printed phone number and address of the nearest
police station and a list of offences: persistent drunkenness, vandalism,
black market involvement, taking drugs, being out of work. If the
resident should spot his neighbour committing any of the offences, he
could simply underline the category, insert the name of the offender
and, without signing his own name, drop the card in the postbox. This
raised the tradition of denunciation to new, unscaled heights.
Denunciations are usually anonymous and trivial (in Poland the *Donos*
is used to get back at neighbours who play their record players too loud)
and, apart from the most dramatic claims, are ditched by the police. But
Fedorchuk was evidently aiming to restore the trust between the police
and the population by sowing distrust among the people themselves; a
classic KGB approach.

Those who know Fedorchuk describe him as a bully, a man who lives
hard and drives his workers too far too fast; not a comfortable politician.
But he did understand that repression alone was not enough to clean up
either the police or the black market. Draconian laws frighten the
criminal, but they also politicise justice. Romania, for example, had a
body of extraordinarily strict anti-corruption laws, but at the same time

had built-in clauses that discourage their implementaion. The laws were only applied when it served the political interests of the Ceausecu leadership. Typical was the June 1969 law on illegally acquired property that had been framed in such a way as to protect those high politicians who offended against it.

Ceausescu's Minister of Justice, Adrian Dimitriu, explaining the law, made it sound rather a noble creation. Romanians, he said, were entitled to own personal property acquired through labour. But 'the accumulation of belongings paid for out of income acquired through other means than honest labour tends to turn private property into an instrument for the exploitation of other's labour, or for profiteering.' The law concerns properties dishonestly acquired or transferred since 1 January 1962 and can be implemented in the following ways. First, on the basis or written information, signed by an individual or by the management of an enterprise in which the person is working, secondly at the request of a person publicly charged with fraud, thirdly at the request of financial or judicial authorities.

So far, so good, in theory at least. It should be possible for any Romanian under this legislation to denounce a member of the government for having built a villa using state-owned concrete and workers loaned from the local prison or army garrison. The complainant may even have found out that the bathroom fittings have been coated with gold leaf officially purchased by the state trading agency for touching up icons in the Museum of National Art. Under the law, it would suffice, say, to have photographs of the house and some documentary evidence before going to the authorities.

The checking procedures also seem, on paper, to be fairly scrupulous. Investigation commissions attached to the county courts check the information. If the investigation commission decides that the information is correct, it can either turn the case over to a low-level court or refer it to the Prosecutor's Office for criminal action.

Now the sting: if the investigation commission finds that the information supplied by the informant is false or incorrect, then the person concerned is liable to arrest and prosecution under charges of slanderous denunciation which can result in several months or even years imprisonment. So, in the name of stamping out corruption, it is legal for Romanians to complain about the illegal practices of their leaders – or of their neighbours, for that matter. But once the complaint is made, it passes into political hands. Suddenly the complainant is in the dock, suddenly he has to prove his innocence. How did you get your information? How dare you slander leading fighters for Romanian socialism? Long live Doublethink. The law has not been repealed.

Fedorchuk tried to avoid these pitfalls. After a while, he withdrew his denunciation questionnaires, and eased up on private traders. The roar and the rattle of a war against crime and corruption died down; this was trench warfare not *Blitzkrieg*. The public image of Andropov and his man Fedorchuk as moral crusaders lingered on, though. The nervous jokes proliferated. What was the text of Andropov's New Year message to the nation? Happy New 1937.

The results of the militia clean-up were patchy, and for a frenetic year no policeman felt truly safe from the purges. Every force that maintained contacts with local bases of organised crime came in for an internal investigation. Sometimes these purges were symbolic, enough to discourage the others, to encourage more discretion, and sometimes so intensive that chains of suicides broke out throughout the force under investigation. It was rumoured that Fedorchuk, like Caesar, would enter ordinary police stations in disguise to check on low-level corruption.

Heads began to roll: a senior officer in a central Russian farming area was sacked for covering up a car crash – he was the driver – in which several people were killed. In Soviet Georgia, two gang chiefs were brought to trial in early 1983 and their testimony indicated that a large number of policemen were receiving bribes and were even involved in profit-sharing arrangements. Sackings followed; the haul – initiated by the Party chief Edward Shevardnadze apparently to show Andropov what a sterling opponent of corruption and staunch ally he had in Georgia – included a militia officer who had received bribes from the Georgia underworld in return for hushing up the rape of a thirteen-year-old girl, and another who had not only tolerated burglaries but who had actually directed police away from the area where the break-ins were about to take place. March 1983 was a bad month for the police and there are some Kremlinologists who believe that the opposition to Andropov crystallised around the disgruntled police faction in that month. The KGB challenge was too overweening and too comprehensive for the district mafias whose leaders usually included city officials, plant managers of big economic enterprises, and senior policemen. Their discontent, funnelled back through the twisted labyrinth of 'democratic centralism', helped to fuel Central Committee and Politburo opposition to the planned reforms to Andropov. Fighting police corruption had become a popular cause. In

Kirghizia, for example, a public prosecutor was sentenced to death for soliciting bribes from a managers of a town abattoir, some 40,000 roubles ($29,000) in two years. In Krasnodar, whose police district includes the resort of Sochi, nine senior policemen were arrested for corruption. In Odessa a senior militia commander was fired and disciplined for persecuting a Young Communist who tried to expose corruption. Nikolai Rozovaykin, leader of the communist youth league in the training school for the merchant marine, complained about the disappearance of money earned by school cadets: the money had in fact been embezzled by the school board whose members included several local dignitaries. Rozovaykin was expelled from the college and when he continued to protest to the police he was arrested on a fabricated charge of hooliganism, held for 20 months in jail and finally acquitted for lack of evidence. The only job he could find was as a sweeper in the Odessa docks. During the same month, March, the newspapers maintained a battery of criticism against the police for their indifference towards the public and the tendency to concentrate on feathering their own nest. *Pravda* (21 March) sharply attacked the police for the time needed to respond to emergency calls. It cited the case of a drunk who broke into an apartment armed with a knife. The occupant managed to ring the police bureau and was told to wait for a patrol car. She then ran into the street and, distraught, stopped a police vehicle. But the sergeant driving it said he had more important business and the woman was later assaulted by the knife man. The 'important business', it emerged, was the delivery of some official papers from one building to another.

It all had to come to an end, of course. If Fedorchuk's task was to restore the standing of the MVD, then constant exposure of police corruption was no way to do it. If his purpose was to throw out the Brezhnevites (the leader's son-in-law, the barely competent Yuri Churbanov, was deputy minister of the Interior) then that needed not just brute force, but also some subtlety and patience. After six months of Fedorchuk there was not a Soviet policeman alive who would publicly admit to admiring Brezhnev. If the plan was to neuter the Interior Ministry and thus establish the KGB as the dominant investigative force, then that too required more than energetic house-cleaning. In any case, all Soviet leaders since Stalin have required some form of rough balance between the three agencies of legal control – the militia, the Procuracy and the KGB. If the purpose was to destroy the black market, or even the market's relationship to the police, then who ulitimately would benefit? The black market provided services not available elsewhere. It absorbed excess currency. And the Soviet police, even in the worst repressive years, have never been able to destroy the black market. The only reasonable objective is to control the market, and that was best accomplished by close, but disciplined, contacts. In other words, Andropov ran out of steam: there was no moral basis, no compelling reformist philosophy behind a crusade of this order. It had started to bother the people, too. In the cities, it became at best an irritant to have so many police on the streets expressing their neighbourliness by checking documents. Many Russians were living on the cusp of legality and could certainly manage without their guardians. The tightening up (from January 1983) of the worker-parasite laws had given the police power to arrest anybody living on 'unearned income.' That hit at moonlighting plumbers, decorators and car mechanics, at dentists with private practices, and many others. No, the New-look Post-Brezhnev police were not popular.

Under Gorbachev, Fedorchuk-the-zealot lost his job. In early 1986 he was demoted, to the Group of General Inspectors in the Ministry of Defence, and replaced by Alexander Vlasov, a Siberian *apparatchik* who was a friend of Yegor Ligachov, then Number 2 to (and a thorn in the side of) Gorbachev. Fedorchuk had underrated the internal connection between the MVD and the KGB. Though they are rival agencies, though there is resentment and friction between them, they share many common institutional and personal roots. MVD and KGB families inter-marry. Fedorchuk first made enemies in the police, but then the discontent trickled back into the KGB and, eventually, he lost support in both camps. Only the army (that is the military controllers) still remembered him with affection.

The police then survived, and still, survive. The Fedorchuk effect has been to discourage the police and OBKhSS from the pursuit of economic crime. Even since Fedorchuk's demotion, the police have lost the confidence to push hard. It is too easy for a police investigator, in the Criminal Investigation Department or in OBKhSS, to be framed, to be made the subject of a political conspiracy or bribery and corruption. That much is demonstrated by the hapless Odessa investigator, Captain Malyschov. The power has passed to the KGB, the controller of Gorbachev's reform programme.

The KGB and Political Imagination

There is a puzzle about the secret police. If I cannot see them in action does it mean they are inactive? And, if I believe that, am I naive? If I cannot see their traces, does it mean they are supremely professional? And, if I believe that, am I suffering from paranoia?

Most of my encounters with the secret police have been at a regulation distance of 40 metres and yet had a quality of intimacy. There was the Czechoslovak pair who followed me around their capital, from hot-dog bar to wine cellar and finally to Franz Kafka's grave, in the Jewish cemetery; a small family stone at the end of a line of richer Prague families, the Picks and the Loewys. We kicked through autumn leaves together; I looked back and he (his companion was outside the cemetery gates) froze in the pose of a man lighting a cigarette. Round and round the cemetery: ten cigarettes, started and finished. 'What do you want?' I called out at last, shouting down the aisle of graves. He ran, startled by the noise or the sunlight, to his colleague in the patrol car to listen to the warm hum of his radio. In Prague, at least, to be paranoid was to be in possession of all the facts.

There have been approaches, of course, by terribly cultured men and, in restless bachelorhood, by terribly available women. And you can approach them. There is the KGB reception centre in Kuznetszky Most, where (nowadays at least) bright young officers will listen to your problems; there is a waiting-room, an orderly queue of slightly unhinged-looking people. It is a good place to get warm in the winter, if your boots are leaking. In Warsaw, and elsewhere in the Bloc, there is a special post box at secret police headquarters where you can drop in your personal request to the Interior Minister; it is guaranteed (by whom?) that the Minister or his chef du cabinet will read everything in the box. That too is a kind of contact. There has been over the years a gradual process of demystification of communist secret police forces; to be an effective actor in the reform era of Gorbachev the KGB needs to shed many more mysteries, many more veils. But, to the professionals, each new chink in the armour represents a loss of strength and of operational effectiveness. Just as MI5 saw *Spycatcher* as a professional disaster, so the Soviet services fear glasnost in their own ranks; the ability to control exposure, and command secrets, is the essential quality of all spy services.

Secrecy allowed the first Soviet service to extend their powers well beyond the usual scope of intelligence-gathering and internal security. The KGB has a decisive say in nationalities policy, in border control, in the morale of the Soviet army. It has an important influence on Soviet

Europe. The KGB is interested and involved in anything that could be termed political opposition: the licensing of independent clubs, the 'creative associations' (the Writer's Union, the Film-Makers Association and so on), the internal workings of the Orthodox Church, the internal politics of newspapers, the growth of new communications technology (such as satellite television and the import of video recorders), the social habits of the young (drug-taking), all and everything that could contribute to make Soviet society less of a monolith. Although the Soviet parliament has little real power, the sprinkling of KGB delegates does at least show the range of interest in domestic politics: there are KGB men on Supreme Soviet Commissions that draft legislative proposals, define industrial, building and transport policies, that watch over the Youth programme, consumer supplies and technology, that draw up energy and environmental laws. These delegates were elected in 1984 – in 1966 there were 60% fewer KGB commission members. The KGB under Gorbachev is more involved in domestic policy-making than at any time since the Vecheka after the Revolution; even under Andropov, a former KGB chairman, there was not the same direct influence on policy. It has developed a taste for power-broking, and it has declared an interest in reform. Its institutional interest is not that of the leaden party bureaucracy or that of the *nomenklatura*. There is no obstructive passion born from a need to hang on to privileges; the KGB is in that sense a much more secure part of the power machine. However, its relationship to reform is not a straightforward one; there are limits to its allegiance to Gorbachev.

The history of the KGB is the story of how a small administrative security agency became first the instrument then the exponent of secret government. Corruption was a target from the beginning of the KGB's existence but from the beginning too, action was selective. The KGB, and the East European secret services that were later modelled on it, came to be all things to all men: border guard, nextdoor neighbour, political controller, sophisticated diplomat, spy abroad, spy at home, interrogator and, ultimately, executioner. The KGB in its first post-revolutionary manifestation was known as the Cheka (more properly, the Vecheka), the All-Russian Extraordinary Commission for Combating Counter-Revolution and Sabotage. Its purpose was to defend the new revolutionary government, to defend a minority that had seized power and seemed in the winter of 1917 to be hanging only precariously to the ring. The original idea, conceived by Felix Dzerzhinsky, the Polish founder of the Cheka, was that it should be an administrative body, directly responsible to the Communist Party (in the form of the Sovnarkom) with investigative responsibilites. If a case was found to be persuasive it could be passed for trial to revolutionary tribunals for revolutionary justice. Although the Cheka was soon to expand dramatically, its first principles – its ties with the Party rather than government, its links with the courts – were never seriously to be diminished. By the middle of 1921, according to some historians, the Cheka had reached a total strength of over a quarter of a million, a figure that included 30,000 civilian employees, 137,000 internal security troops and 94,000 frontier guards. Others tried to pull away power from this huge body, to transfer some powers to the Revolutionary Courts, to subordinate it to the Commissariat of Justice or to the Central Executive Committee (which included non-communists). The Cheka resisted, and the Cheka won. Repressive legislation always followed two steps behind the actual practice of the Cheka. Thus Chekists killed about a quarter of a million people in the first four years of its existence, both by execution and in suppressing uprisings. Its powers grew and grew. Together with the NKVD, the People's Commissariat for Internal Affairs, the Cheka was officially authorised in 1919 to order administrative (that is, without the mediation of a court) deportation to forced labour camps. Reliable figures about the scope of deaths and incarceration in these camps is not easy to come by, understandably given the chaos of the time and the bias of those who have chronicled the period. By the autumn of 1922 there were certainly 132 camps but the number of inhabitants is uncertain, the best guess being between 60,000 and 70,000.

Eventually with the range of this Red Terror, the Chekists took over responsibility for stamping out 'corruption'. At the end of 1918 the forcible collection of food from the peasants was put under central control and it was Chekists as well as factory commissars who organised groups to prise the grain from the villages. The move led to the most extreme flashes of peasant violence during the civil war, protests that were in turn put down by the Chekists. The evils of the NEP period, some of them imagined, some of them real enough, were used by the Chekists to assert their rights to identify corruption, and stamp out its practitioners with administrative executions. 'Extreme times, extreme measures,' say Soviet officials if and when the subject is raised in polite dinner-party conversation. But though the Cheka changed names and its acronyms several times, first to GPU and eventually settling for KGB, its own assumed right to decide what is and what is not corrupt, what does and what does not threaten the welfare of the Soviet union, has remained unchanged since those early post-Revolutionary days.

The only serious blow to the expansion of the KGB came after the discrediting of Joseph Stalin and his methods of control in 1956. Throughout the wartime years, the slightest form of black marketeering – and every Russian city had illegal markets – could be reshaped into a political charge of sabotage, according to whims of the security police. Corruption nonetheless flourished: looted goods such as furs exchanged hands in Leningrad for immense prices, the rouble having lost its value as a reliable means of acquiring scarce foods. After the war, patterns of corruption bred in the improvised atmosphere of the war, set and solidified in the bureaucracy. Arrests and tortures for political offences continued, but the corrupt liaison either survived intact or was used as a way of implicating a politically suspect person against whom no other evidence could be found. Bribery of officials and market dealing was observed by the secret police, and was documented but not seriously disrupted. In general the black market provided the Soviet secret police with a steady flow of information, of gossip and rumour that gave useful pointers at a time when few people dared to talk in public

The revelation of secret-police abuses in Khrushchev's secret party speech of 1956 and in other East European countries that had suffered purges, notably Czechoslovakia, Hungary and Poland, was a formidable blow to the prestige of the security services. As prisoners returned from the Stalinist Gulags it was inevitable that stories would gain currency about the cruelty of interrogators, of the torturers and warders. There were two responses to this broad discontent: first, rigid control over what was said about the Stalinist period; criticism was correct but muffled in the rhetoric of 'socialist illegality and deviations'. Above all, artists, citizens, or party activists were not permitted to draw any conclusions about the validity of socialism from the horrible murders and confinements of the Stalin age. This meant concentrating political criticism on the perpetrators, the policemen and their heirs. The second response was to scale down the secret police to its bare bones, its Chekist essentials. An organisation swollen from eating too many of the Children of the Revolution was to be brought back into shape with a radical cure. The secret police had very definitely to be subordinated to the Party; no longer should Party activists or generals fear the knock on the door. That, at any rate, was the theory when Khrushchev came to power. The view was perforce shared by the party leaders of Moscow's allies. A generation of secret policemen, many of whom had spent the war in the Soviet Union and who were seen as interlopers, alien keepers of the peace, when they returned, were pensioned off. In Poland, ultra-nationalist groups such as the Grunwald Association were later to use these secret policemen, many of whom were Jewish in origin, as a way of justifying anti-Semitic programmes. But as a rule these men were not killed or even imprisoned; their reputation was well-guarded by a censorship which banned films such as *The Interrogation* by Ryszard Bugajski, a film that portrays the slow dawning of the love of a secret policeman for a woman arrested in error.

In keeping with the scale of the tragedy, the sharpest measures were taken in the Soviet Union. The Gulags, the prison camps, were transferred from KGB control to the Ministry of Public Order. The KGB was forbidden from trying cases. It could make arrests only with the permission of the Prosecutor General though it could still detain, interrogate and investigate people in preparation for court proceedings.

The KGB under Khrushchev was a Committee rather than a wing of a ministry and in that sense returned to its Chekist origins. The important thing for Khrushchev was to re-establish the control of the Soviet leader rather than the Party as a whole and the balance had to be adjusted. To do this, Khrushchev introduced the most important of all changes: he guaranteed the immunity of Communist Party members from arrest by the KGB. The secret police were obliged simply to gather information about a suspect and then present it to the Party control commissions which would then discipline the member according to the long-established grades – first a Party reprimand, then a strong Party reprimand, then a strong Party reprimand with warning, then expulsion. The idea was to prevent the KGB being used as a method of disposing of Party opponents, of using police methods to solve Party disputes. But the immediate effect was to reduce the KGB's powers to investigate corruption and by the same token breed a sense of material privilege in the Party *apparat*. It was in the Khrushchev period that the big intra-Party bribing began. In many republics, the payment of tribute to the First Party Secretary became common practice. The payments were increased if it was felt that the KGB might have a dossier on some political, quasi-legal or business manoeuvre, for the Party Secretary could ignore the evidence at will or, if under pressure, hand out the softest form of Party reprimand. Suddenly, it was worthwhile financially as well as politically to join the Party.

If the Party was to police itself, then, it would have to equip itself with the organisational sophistication of the KGB. What followed was the creation of a Party informer network which provided for fully fledged Party members to tell, as a matter of Socialist duty and not for financial reward, their superiors about the weakness of their colleagues. But their brief extended to non-Party members, to local butchers cheating housewives, to the Orthodox priest who overstepped his priestly duties by holding Sunday-school classes, to the social and sexual habits of the district nurse. Those who remember this time report different experiences: one tells me of a Party informer who regularly received bribes from every shop in the village (in truth, there were only three) but who none the less informed on them. Another, a young girl at the time, recalls that there were few bribes in her Estonian township: the Party informer was seen as incorruptible and the fear that had once been felt of the secret police was now transferred to the Party activist. Lively conversations in the shops or bars transformed themselves into desultory discussions of football as soon as the informer walked in the door. In 1958, Khrushchev dismissed his friend General Ivan Serov (notorious for his deportation of the Crimean Tartars) from the chairmanship of the KGB and replaced him with Aleksander Shelepin, the chief of the Komsomol Young Communist League. The Komsomol effectively took over the running of local KGB offices, the aim being to establish young ideologically loyal communists without any of the stigma of the Stalinist generation. The result: a collapse in expertise, allowing corruption to bloom unchecked in the Party machinery and in factories. The new-look KGB went after teachers who made a slip in the history lesson, after Christians and nationalists and against writers like Andrei Sinyavsky and Yuli Daniel, whose trial, with its botched evidence and faked testimony, represented the high point of a decade of unprofessionalism. 'It is,' Andrei Sakharov, the Nobel prize-winning dissident once told me before he was exiled to Gorky, 'the easiest thing in the world for a secret policeman to manufacture a case against a dissident. He tapes the flat, the telephone, he follows you, your wife, your chldren, he questions who he wants. Eventually he will hear or read or find something he wants: it need only be a word, a foreign banknote, a taped message from a friend abroad. On this note, a world, a complete fictional world can be built. Common criminals can be pressured into corroborating stories – "Yes, that banknote is one of 500 that I was instructed to give Andrei Dmitrivich by my foreign paymasters, by the man with the American accent." This is a decision they can take at any time. The law means nothing, for the agencies that administer that law are themselves in a state of lawlessness. How much easier all this is than uncovering corruption, digging into swindles of everyday life, of life at the top.'

Two elements are essential if one of the Soviet Bloc's official guardians is to pursue a case of high-level corruption: political will and professional expertise. Under Khrushchev, under the KGB heads Serov, Shelepin and Vladimir Semichastny, neither of these qualities was much in evidence. When Andropov took over the organisation in 1967 he set about recreating a sense of professionalism, of establishing too a more legalistic approach to cases. He abolished the Party Informers but at the same time tried to keep a balance between making the KGB more efficient and powerful without presenting a direct challenge to the Party. In this way he earned the loyalty of his own employees, building up their self-image through glorious if improbable James Bond-style accounts of derring-do with super-slick agents throwing themselves out of speedboats adjusting their finely-tuned Russian-made chronometers (the likes of which have never been seen in Moscow shops) and throwing imperialist agents to their rightful fate at the bottom of an abyss. In these stories and films, the CIA agent invariably wears sunglasses, a badly-cut suit and has bad personal habits (picking his teeth in public, spitting on the floor, slapping women's faces), a mirror-image of the Western view of the KGB man abroad. The KGB was not technically in charge of corruption cases. Its brief included the monitoring of all cases involving foreigners, active espionage abroad and counter-espionage at home, dealing with the national minorities, all major state crimes including treason and sabotage, the suppression of political dissidents and offences involving senior Party officials.

Khrushchev had laid some of the legal groundwork. A December 1965 decree specified that in certain offences – currency speculation, misappropriation of state property – the agency that had opened the investigation should pursue it to its conclusion. That gave the KGB the power to move from strictly political cases into economic crime. Gradually the KGB began to argue that economic and political corruption could reach such a pitch that it endangered the state. What did that mean? Nothing much, except that the KGB was marching into the economic front line. Certainly Andropov now had a broad enough brief to move into all of the important corruption rackets in the Soviet Union.

His dossiers on every member of the Brezhnev family smoothed his way to power. His interest in economic reform and the fight against economic crime could be justified under the label of opposing sabotage and the black market. Even his mission to defend the Soviet Union against dissidents could be turned to his advantage in expanding his empire into anti-corruption. Take his speech in 1977, the year that the KGB acted against such dissidents as Anatol Shcharansky, Alexander Ginzburg and Yuri Orlov: 'If they persist in their actions and continue to be so-called "dissidents" and even violate the law, we will treat them quite differently. There are unfortunately a few people like this in our society, just as there are thieves, black-market speculators, those who take bribes and other common criminals. The former and the latter groups damage our society and we treat them accordingly.' (*Izvestia*, 10 September 1977).

Significantly, the KGB found (planted) dollars in the flat of Ginzburg and in subsequent moves against dissidents accused them repeatedly of illegally obtaining foreign currency. The mere suspicion of this was enough to justify searches of apartments and confiscation of any material that could be deemed anti-Soviet. It was Andropov's reign as head of the KGB that created or discovered the connections between high party officials and big-time currency speculators, between the underworld and the peak of the over-world as well as between the underworld and political dissenters. The links thus forged were the products of *Realpolitik* rather than reality but they were none the less ominous.

The KGB reforms under Andropov were designed to restore the standing of the secret police and show that the agency had a role to play in every major sector of Soviet society. That, in a modest way, was also an attempt to make the KGB more accountable, to pull it back into the mainstream of party politics. If it had not been for the modernisation of the service, and the evolution of a kind of economic programme, then Andropov would never have been able to use the KGB as a springboard to power. He had few Party alliances, no regional constituency. But there were KGB men fulfilling their social and patriotic duty everywhere, in the propaganda machine, in the diplomatic service, in the fight against corruption, in the factories and in heavy industry. That was sufficient given the hollow, creaking structures that were now the institutions of Brezhnev's Russia. It was not enough however to push through a radical change of course. And it was not enough to keep the sick man alive. Gorbachev has played the game intelligently. He has inherited the Andropov mantle and, though he wants to go about the problems in a completely different way, he is content for the

Andropovists in the KGB to think that he is carrying out the Andropov agenda.

But he has made subtle alterations; above all, he is positioning the KGB, not the other way around. For two decades the KGB has been defining the nature of dissent in the Soviet Union. But Gorbachev has changed the ground rules. Before his death, Sakharov was regarded as a genial ambassador of the Gorbachev revolution. The Serbsky Institute has gone back to treating rather than creating schizophrenics. In so far as there is discussion about pluralism, it boils down to the old Kadarist slogan : he who is not against us is for us. The KGB has been somewhat wrongfooted by this. But the frame of debate is healthier. 'The Party and the interested organs,' says a respected Soviet commentator, 'must sit down and find a formula for how economic reform can properly relate to political change. We have to agree jointly on where we are going.' The 'interested organ' is, of course, the KGB, which no longer has a monopoly in this area. But it does have an increasing role in controlling the nationalist unrest – from Estonia to Armenia, from Kirghizia to Lithuania – that is not so much the result of perestroika as an anticipation of it. Gorbachev is most vulnerable, in the political struggle, to hardline criticism that his reforms are unravelling the empire. The KGB can thus offer Gorbachev flanking support by putting down these revolts. The skill with which this is accomplished will be a measure of the intentions of the KGB. If police start to fire on demonstrators, it will be a sure sign that Gorbachev has lost control of his controllers.

The KGB was moulded into an economic protagonist by Andropov and is reluctant to abandon this interest in the Gorbachev revolution. But it is also a foreign-policy actor, and in this sphere is much more of a traditionalist. If the KGB has any kind of unifying ethos, it is for a strong Soviet Union. What does the KGB make of a policy that encourages Western borrowing? What does it think of membership in the IMF, or of Polish and Hungarian membership? How does it evalute a Soviet troop withdrawal from Eastern Europe? Under Chebrikov, the KGB was plainly not happy; under his replacement Kryuchkov, it is merely silent. It is conceivable though that the KGB's broad sympathy for reform could be turned around by excessive concessions in foreign policy or by a change in policy towards the Soviet ethnic minorities.

The risk is constantly present because the KGB now embraces so many different functions. Gorbachev has a choice. He can diminish the responsibilities of the KGB, cut back its authority. Or, more safely, he can spread the risk by enhancing the role of other institutions. Giving the other control insititutions – trades unions, the people's and state inspectorates, the cleaned-up militia, a more independent judiciary – more teeth is a step in this direction. Certainly it will be less painful than pulling the teeth of the KGB.

There is an interpretive danger in writing, as a Western outsider, of communist police forces. We assume that the historical tendency of the Gorbachev era is towards Western democratic forms: that is, he wants them to become more like us. That may be the case, but it is not an inescapable conclusion. Unleashing market forces could indeed help create the conditions for a more pluralist society. But market economies function in other kinds of political systems too – in South Korea and Chile. The KGB, coming to terms with a market-orientated reform, might well prefer a Korean model to a Thatcherite. A stifled opposition, attempts to keep increasingly articulate workers separate from mal-contented intellectuals, tight controls on everyday life, government centralisation. yes, the Korean model of economic recovery offers some attractions for a police force unwilling to surrender its authority.

Conclusion

Repair, Reform Or Revolution

The guns that thundered over Tiananmen Square in June 1989 silenced an important debate in China and provided a frightening glimpse of the future for the market reformers of the Soviet Bloc. To the West, the shooting of students by the Peoples Liberation Army was proof positive of the failure of Communism. But the issues were more complex than that. Although the students crowding into the square were demanding political changes, they were driven by the economic and social frustrations of a decade of first cautious then galloping market reform. There was double-digit inflation, persistent consumer shortages, an expanding black market – in 1988 there was a run on the banks, an almost unprecedented event under Communism – and huge income differentials. Students, on fixed incomes, with no economic bargaining power, living in cities remote from food supplies, were natural victims; victims, that is, of a nascent neo-capitalism and the more familiar weaknesses of central planning. Their protest bore comparison with the Polish Solidarity movement of 1980–81; there were the same egalitarian instincts, the contempt for Party privilege, suspicion of rising prices, a common sense of exclusion from black-market forces. The Polish protests also ended with tanks in the streets. Martial Law Warsaw was admittedly a less bloody landscape than Martial Law Peking, but the effect was the same: a freezing of debate. Both General Jaruzelski and the Chinese leadership wanted to reassert that change, even market-oriented change, was not really in question, only its rate of acceleration. The soldiers, then, raised their rifles for the market.

The Chinese student revolt displayed more than the fears of a disadvantaged class; it also showed an awareness that market forces had overtaken political institutions, that the Party was losing control but was not willing to create new openings for the young and radical. Either the system or the leadership had failed. The real breakdown in China had cultural as well as systematic roots. The leadership was unable to open the crucial economic arguments, to define the issues and choices for the opinion-forming classes. Instead, the three main economic schools congealed around political factions and, as one of these factions could claim the loyalty of the army, a military solution became an active possibility.

The closed discussions on the future of China were conducted on the fringes and at the centre of power. Professor Jinglian and Dr Zhou Xiaochuan at the Economic Research Institute worked out an austerity programme, in 1988, at the behest of the Council of State. They were the radical marketeers, arguing that the State should be ousted from the running of the economy and that the priority should be price reform. An end should be put to the wide net of subsidies, a proper market relationship restored to supply and demand. 'As soon as inflation is under control, this is what we must do,' said their report to the Council of State. 'Because of irrational pricing there are shortages and consumer logjams. The result is that the State has to distribute scarce goods and is becoming too involved in daily economic life.' The market radicals, however, were ignored by the Party leadership, which listened rather to the Conservatives at the People's University who argued only for a refinement and tuning of the Central Planning engine. But the most politically important friction was between the market radicals and those who argued for a 'Chinese' solution combining a planned social welfare state with market elements. The latter group, identified with Li Yining of Peking University, said that an austerity budget would put a brake on growth and produce stagflation. Li Yining argues that market reforms cannot work without a change in property rights, above all the right to own the means of production. 'The present system does not offer the slightest room for manoeuvre in re-establishing a price mechanism in the market sense of the word.' There was, of course, a booming private sector, 'but the ownership relationships between government and industry are still so confused and entangled that one often cannot tell where something begins and something else ends.' (*Weltwoche*, Zurich, 25 May 1989). To free prices would trigger a social explosion. 'The East European experience of recent years shows unanimously the catastrophic effects of such policy.' But the radical marketeers say that to sort out a new property law in China would take at least fifteen years: some ten thousand large state concerns and scores of thousands of small businesses would have to be put on some form of new property basis. But a price reform can be imposed immediately.

These seemed, in 1988, to be technical issues constrained only by the relative fear or boldness of the political leadership. But by the spring of

1989, with protest on the streets, the concealed economic issues were being translated into the most lurid of political terms. And by the summer of that year the debate was settled, or at least suspended, at gunpoint. In so far as a coherent economic policy survived those months, it was this: reform must be at a steady rate, the pace dictated from above, not below. Market forces should be introduced with caution in specific problem areas and only then allowed to spread. During this process, the police should batten down the students and ensure there was no link-up between workers and intellectuals. The market transition period, in other words, should be introduced under police-state conditions, as in South Korea or Taiwan, and not as part of a free-ranging Democratic revolution.

Markets have invaded the Communist system, but the response to that invasion is coloured by history and cultural traditions. The acid test of how Communism will survive the twentieth century lies in the individual national response to two groups of problems. First: Where does the market fit into a planned economy; what is the scope of failure of the plan; how compatible are plan and market; at what point in the market's advance does Marxism stop being Marxism? Second: How far do market-orientated changes have to be accompanied by political reform; in what direction should such political changes go; how fast, and in what order?

Although the Hayekian premise – more market, more freedom – needs to be treated with caution, it is clear that market reforms pose problems for authoritarian regimes whatever their complexion. The unrest faced by a Communist system introducing market elements – China, Poland, the Soviet Union, Hungary – can stand comparison with the troubles of Chile or South Korea where fully fledged market economies sit uncomfortably with authoritarian governments. There is obviously no mathematical formula: Chile has more market than Hungary but is it more free? Economic liberalisation does not lead inevitably or directly to a democratic structure. But the market breaks up monolithic rule, creates new apertures and new tensions. These must define the nature of political reform in the Communist world and in Western authoritarian societies.

Market economies demand dispersed decisions. If a government accepts the need for wide and free markets, then it must also accept a loss of power. In a market economy, businessmen, traders, farmers, factory managers and salesmen have more control over their affairs; the decision about what to produce, what to charge, how to supply it, becomes a matter for the individual entrepreneur. So does the risk and reward. An authoritarian regime sees some of its authority ebb. Moreover, this independent segment has a tendency to spread. If a Bulgarian businessman is to be allowed to trade freely – that is, without the mediation of a State agency – then he must travel to the West, collect Western currency (if necessary on the black market), seek customers abroad. He demands from the State the right to travel. But soon enough it emerges that this is a universal right. Even in pragmatic terms, it makes no political sense to stir up envy over the new business class when it is supposed to save the economy and drive the nation. And so, a simple by-product of economic reform translates into a political demand for more liberal travel regulations for all Bulgarians. In the 1970s, the Polish authorities tried to spin a web between the political establishment and the new entrepreneurs. Private businessmen were often brothers or cousins of Ministry officials, sons of police colonels; a licence to trade with the West was a golden prize that was awarded, with due ceremony and kickbacks, by the authorities. Dollars flowed back into the *nomenklatura*; the extended family was never as intact as during the Gierek era. That was one way of minimising the damage of the market, a temporary device to side-step the demands for political change. In the long term, though, those functioning in the marketplace could not continue as coalition partners of politicians in an authoritarian regime.

Markets, then, splinter authority. And, in a centrally governed empire, they create a constant tension between the centre of power and the provinces. Not all of the Soviet Union nationality problems relate directly to the market. The Soviet nationalities policy was ripe for overhaul in the 1990s; semi-tolerant, semi-autonomous under Lenin, heavily centralised under Stalin, the system of authority had been cracking since the 1970s. The 'Russification' of the provinces, Moscow placemen in regional elites, close ties with Moscow through the police, the whole apparatus of a pseudo-federation was beginning to crack under Brezhnev. Plainly, the Soviet Union would be able to solve its national unrest – in Kazakhstan, Uzbekistan, Georgia, Armenia, Azerbaidjan, the Baltic States – only within the framework of a policy that gave new powers to the Republics of the Union and guarantees to the often arbitrarily located unhappy minorities (such as the Armenians within Nagorny Karabach).

That task was beyond a Gorbachev who was simultaneously trying to uphold the legitimacy of the Party while denying its dogma. There was nothing 'market' about the upheaval in Soviet Georgia in the Spring of 1989, nothing specifically Communist about the way it was put down (by poison gas and by troops wielding shovels as weapons). Yet Soviet Georgia had been resisting perestroika, was at best lukewarm about economic reform: market forces were already operating underground and there was no profit for gangland leaders and their political protectors in making the market legal. As in Armenia, Azerbaidjan and Uzbekistan, the reformers in Moscow detected a direct link between anti-reforming, organised crime and national unrest. The effect of the market on ethnic troubles can be more plainly seen in the Baltic Republics and that most uncomfortable of socialist federations, Yugoslavia. In Estonia, which is relatively prosperous thanks to a large, legal private sector, a highly educated work-force, unbroken mercantile traditions and the proximity of Finland, there was talk in the late 1980s and 1990s of developing a separate currency. The rouble was so firmly identified with Russian dominance and the distortion of the local economy, that the Estonians put forward the idea of a rouble-free zone, a Baltic common market that would trade as a separate economic unit with Moscow and the rest of the Soviet Union. Here was a specific example of a successful (albeit limited) market reinforcing national, separatist sentiment. Gorbachev, astonishingly, went some way towards granting the Balts financial autonomy, but the rouble still reigned and there were both clear and unspoken boundaries of action for the Estonians and other Balts: Gorbachev feared that too many concessions would prejudice the future remodelling of a nationalities policy.

In Yugoslavia, the late 1980s saw a merging of two crises: the crisis of national self-assertion and the long time-fuse crisis of the market. The emergence of a virulent nationalist, Slobodan Milosevic, as Serbian leader seemed at first to be a simple historical progression, the rejuvenation of the Serb nation. That these dreams of a Great Serbia were being imposed on a Muslim Kosovo was unpleasant, to say the least, but not unexpected. Yet the rise of Milosevic represented more than the dismantling of Tito's Yugoslavia: it was a response to the spread of market forces that were rapidly making the Party an irrelevancy. Milosevic also claimed to be a marketeer – he promised that ten thousand private businesses would be set up in Serbia – but state-owned heavy industry in Serbia would never survive a true market revolution. Milosevic found a new mission for the Party as the vanguard of a vulgar nationalism. Meanwhile the Yugoslav premier, Ante Markovic, was trying to set up a nation-wide market, accepting implicitly the need to bury the Party – at least as a specifically Yugoslav institution. Milosevic supported a nationwide market economy too, but most Croatians and Slovenians were suspicious. Croatia and Slovenia have the most developed markets in Yugoslavia, are 'European' in look and feel. Perhaps there was a plot, under the guise of setting up a Yugoslav market economy, to funnel profits from Croatia and Slovenia to the poorer inefficient republics like Serbia? A witches' brew. Slovenia was more wedded to the market than any other community in Eastern Europe, yet it was resisting the idea of a national Yugoslav market. Serbia, crippled with ancient industries and in no apparent hurry to change, was espousing such a market. The main market proponent was a man set on re-establishing the control of the Party in a stridently nationalistic manner. It was all very strange to the outsider but entirely consistent within the closed logic of the Yugoslav federation. Markets were about losing political power; the game was played accordingly. By June 1989, Slovenia was talking seriously about leaving the federation. Milan Kucan, the Slovenian Party leader, told a rally in Ljubljana that 'Slovenia would not continue to be part of Yugoslavia if it were subject to political and national domination.' The pivotal phrase, referring to Serbia and presaging the break-up of Yugoslavia, was: 'the unitary ideas among big nations are actually separatist in intent.' In Yugoslavia, as in the more straightforward case of Estonia, the spread of the market (and the accompanying economic self-confidence) led to a suspicion of 'bigness'. Calls for national unity and discipline were historically to be interpreted as codewords for more central control and for the stamping out of local initiative and cultural autonomy.

Although in some ways Eastern Europe of the late twentieth century appears to be mimicking the industrialisation patterns of the West in the nineteenth century, there are significant differences. The inevitability of a nationwide market, set in motion by the early Western Capitalists, was not completely accepted by communities in modern Eastern Europe: the market had dispersed and diluted central authority, freeing national sentiment after four decades of ideological corseting; the market was a catalyst for independence-seekers. When Gorbachev talked of releasing broad-based market elements throughout the Soviet Union, he received loud applause from the West but not from the most advanced of the market-reforming Republics in Estonia, Latvia and Lithuania. Their insecurity was understandable. The Baltic Republics were high performers, adaptable, profitable and proud. The evolution of the rest of the Soviet Union into a collection of mixed economies with

strong market elements would produce demands on the Baltic
Republics; Gorbachev's market revolution was not just about profit and
productivity but also about redistribution. The profits from the efficient
would by hook or by crook be siphoned off to benefit those republics in
the south least capable of adjusting to change.

Marx is not much help. If anything, he was rather dismissive of the
Czechs, the Croats and the Serbs who were fighting against the
Austrians and Hungarian rulers during the 1848 Revolution. He was
aware of Nationalism as a problem but was convinced that, like
Capitalism, it would disappear. Even more recent Socialist or Liberal
historians – G. D. H. Cole, E. H. Carr, Hugh Seton-Watson – have
tended to under-rate the force of Nationalism, regarding it as an
'anomaly and anachronism' (Carr), obsolete (Cole) or transitional
(Seton-Watson). The ethnic minorities were tucked away like old socks
in the untidy cupboards of great powers. This twentieth-century
disregard for the interests of small nationalities, this focus on concentrated and centralised power, tended to blur by the 1980s. As Gorbachev
sought out neo-Capitalist solutions, the old assumptions began to
crumble. Gorbachev was trying to reform Socialism; after a few years of
scepticism, this was generally accepted, at least in the West. But reform
in whose interests? Not, evidently, in the immediate interests of the
workers, the supposedly ruling class. Workers from Beijing to Bialystok
were nervous about the market and the loss of subsidised prices, about
unemployment. Conceivably, the marketisation of the Communist
world could benefit their children, but Soviet Bloc families have long
ceased to believe in the 'second-generation bargain', present sacrifice in
return for a better, unspecified future. Nor was reform producing better
living standards for the intelligentsia. Though they thrived in a freer
political climate, the 1970s and 1980s contributed to a dramatic
impoverishment of white-collar workers and indeed of all who fell into
the extremely broad social category of 'intelligentsia': on fixed salaries,
with diminishing political muscle (recalling the aphorism of Stanislaw
Lec 'those without teeth can move their mouths more freely'), they were
the first casualties of inflation. The farmers and the new Money Class
were clear beneficiaries but these were narrow segments of society. The
simple answer was that reform benefited a nation rather than a class. But
what, in the Communist world, was a nation? Who belonged to it? After
four decades of centrally steered denationalising ideology, these were
new questions that popped and sparked in the firmament. It was an early
experience of the multi-national Soviet Union that cultural rights,

though they were constitutionally guaranteed for dozens of communities, became meaningless unless they were given the appropriate political weight. The need to re-adjust the national or ethnic power balance has thus been a feature of every reform phase in the Soviet world. Nationalists enter, more often than not, on the side of the economic or political reformers since they too have an interest in changing the status quo. But there is nothing fixed, or very reassuring, about the coalition between market reformers and those seeking to assert national rights: it is a relationship in flux. Slovak nationalism was an important ingredient in the Prague Spring of 1967–68, contributing to the fall of Novotny and the rise of Dubcek. The Slovaks were determined to rehabilitate fully the Slovak Communists who had been branded 'bourgeois nationalists' in the 1950s; this, in turn, fuelled the anti-Czech resentment and the call for an internal re-adjustment. But sometimes it is easier to contain nationalists who call for autonomy than to meet the demands of economic reformers for social change.

The Slovak grudge was that the Novotny regime had not completed the de-Stalinisation campaign, especially after the April 1963 Central Committee plenum; the plenum conducted only a pallid investigation into the trials of the disgraced 'bourgeois nationalists' and left in its place the main prosecutor of the time, Wilem Siroky. In short, the Prague leadership of Novotny was keeping the Slovaks in their place; it was still a heresy to seek a Slovak road to communism. When the ferment grew, Novotny found it easier to appease the Slovak nationalists than the social reformers. Siroky was sacked, Novotny gave ground. Even after the fall of Novotny, the rise and fall of Dubcek, and the numbing years of 'normalisation' (which equated economic reform with political upheaval and effectively froze society for 30 years) the Slovak national agenda survived. While the post-Dubcek leadership rigorously stamped out any manifestation of pluralism and re-asserted central control, it also gave a much greater voice to the Slovak communist party. The Slovak demands, as far as Moscow was concerned, were the acceptable face of reform since they had clearly defined limits and did not challenge the communist system.

National unrest in the Gorbachev era was also seen benignly – at first. Just as the Brezhnev leadership had tolerated the Slovak demands, so the Gorbachev team was sympathetic to the early problems expressed by nationalist protesters. National unrest was a rite of passage. Grievances felt by the peoples of Kazakhstan, of the Baltic States, of Armenia, Azerbaidjan, Georgia, Uzbekistan, Turkmenistan, by the uprooted

Crimean Tartars, had been bottled up by the Brezhnev era and were due for release. One Gorbachev approach was that demonstrators were protesting against the surviving pro-Brezhnev anti-reformist regional leaderships. Often, as in Kazakhstan and Uzbekistan, there were indeed corrupt, underworld connections between the party in the provinces and Moscow. Ethnic unrest thus had both a *moral* and *political* basis; to demonstrate under those circumstances was a vote for Gorbachev, a way of signifying that one was part of his consituency. Sometimes, even with the astonishing sleight-of-hand of Gorbachev's crisis managers, it was impossible to assign such charitable aims to the demonstrators. Sometimes, it was plain, the demonstrators were implicitly attacking Gorbachev. In such cases, the Moscow team (in Washington they would be called 'spin-managers') decided that the demonstrators were simple, ethnic working folk being manipulated by corrupt regional hierarchies. Both explanations gave the Gorbachevites an excuse to purge regional leaders and install sympathetic figures. At no time has Gorbachev responded to popular cries for de-centralisation or separatism with a promise of greater autonomy. He is a centraliser when it comes to nationalities policy; he has no other approach than to accumulate power, that sits uneasily with an avowed market-orientated reform. It is only one of Gorbachev's many contradictions, but it will be the fatal one. By July 1989, national unrest had a specifically anti-Gorbachev edge. He responded with a dramatic televised speech warning of the impending collapse of perestroika if ethnic troubles persisted. But there was no halting the separatist wave. Riots had become a way, perhaps the only way, of bargaining with Moscow. The Foreign Minister flew to his native Georgia in 1988, the PM put out fires elsewhere; Gorbachev became increasingly irritated, for it exposed the imperial frailties he had preferred to ignore. His book *Perestroika* is a blueprint for a modern Socialist Society in transition; society has problems, they should be acknowledged and, borrowing from more successful societies, the Soviet Union should re-structure, up-date and invigorate itself. He argued, moreover, that this 'borrowing', this neo-capitalism, need not compromise the essential ideological roots of the October Revolution, nor diminish the ultimate goal of establishing a communist society. The key phrase is: *Revolyutsiya Prodolzhaetsya* – the Revolution is continuing. But Gorbachev must have become aware, some time in 1989 when his book was into its third or fourth Western printing, of the self-deception at the heart of his work. Much of the Soviet Union is still at the so-called Asian level of production. A nation like Uzbekistan, with its cotton barons and gangs of slaves, is still in the feudal era. Half of the great territories of the Soviet Union, now in turmoil, have never really become Socialist; instead they are governed by complex system of tribute and obligation. Once that has been dismantled, there is nothing. The mechanics of reform are as remote as the engine of a space launch vehicle in Baikonur. The rhetoric of reform can be mastered of course, like all previous texts, as a way of keeping the peace. *Perestroika* was a best seller in Alma-Ata and Düsseldorf yet it was understood, one suspects, in neither city.

The 'conservatives' always understood the national dimension. The 'conservative' label misleads since it links, under one inadequate banner, the radical free-marketeers of Britain (who are, of course, more truly economic liberals) with the anti-marketeers of the Soviet Bloc. But conservative they are, concerned with heritage. A Soviet conservative argues that Gorbachev is sewing dragon's teeth throughout the Empire. Markets disperse authority and, in so doing, they betray the historical heritage of Russia. The legitimacy of the Party has been questioned by the Party leader: he talks of the need for political competition, yet permitting this, contemplating the sharing of power, is a sign of weakness. That, at any rate, is how it is perceived in the Soviet provinces where opposition is smashed or bought off, but never openly acknowledged. Conservatives against market reform could be found in the late 1980s at the meetings of the Russian populist 'Pamyat' group. But mainly they were on tour, honoured guests in Baku and Bokhara. Gorbachev tried to destroy the power of the barons in the Central Committee and, having achieved only limited success, moved the focus of reform to a newly active Party-dominated but free-spoken parliament. He won notable victories: there was no longer any discussion for and against reform, only controlled debates about the *pace* of change: there was broad agreement on the economic problems and their causes. After three or four years, Gorbachev had set the tone of political life. Yet the conservatives had simply withdrawn from the debate, they had not been dissuaded. For them, it was a question of power, of forming the coalitions that would make an alternative to Gorbachev when reform policies finally cracked. One looked in vain, in the Moscow of the 1980s, for a subterranean think-tank, for shadow talk. The conservatives, battered by glasnost, had moved beyond talk, pro or contra market, into conspiracy.

And, of course, the conservatives were right. Gorbachev was presenting a false option. He encouraged the idea of a historic alternative within socialism: a continuation of the over-centralised, incompetent Brezhnevian rule that would drag the Soviet Union into terminal decline; or a radical NEP-style programme, introducing competition, efficiency and new blood at the top. Yet NEP, in the 1920s, was never a 'choice'; it was a retreat, a diversion, a short cut and, above all, an acknowledgement that War Communism had failed. The only real turning-point was in 1929 when NEP was already in tatters. 1929, as it is presented in the Soviet Union today, was the year of epoch-making opportunity. The decision: whether the country should embrace the 'gradualist' human-socialism of Bukharin, or the forced industralisation and collectivisation programme of Stalin.

Gorbachev introduced himself as the heir to Bukharin (now rehabilitated) since it established a direct link with Lenin that bypassed Stalin. Bukharin, in that sense, has been re-invented to serve as the grandfather of perestroika. Yet the choices then were never as stark as they are now packaged by Soviet historians. And 1929 is not 1989. Stalin, in supporting heavy industrialisation, was making a rational development choice. The failure of revolution abroad, especially Germany, the reasonable (as opposed to the later paranoid) perception of an invasion threat from the capitalist West, the Wall Street collapse and the Western recession all framed the decision. Second, the nationalisation of the country's resources took into account the recent negative experience with limited markets. The Bolsheviks learned from the years 1917 to 1921 that peasants would only sell food and raw materials to cities and industry, under commerical market arrangements, if the cash could be spent on manufactured goods. (Poland which retains an overwhelmingly private farming sector is encumbered with this problem even in the 1990s). And so, it was reasoned, agriculture should be collectivised, in step with industrialisation. Collectivisation gave the government control over the distribution of farm produce; spared the authorities the need to divert light industrial goods to the countryside, and created a form for the mechanisation of the farms. To industrialise rapidly – under capitalist or communist conditions – requires huge investment (perhaps a quarter or a third of national output) in machines, in schooling, in construction, mining and transport. An element of compulsion was built into the running of the Soviet economy from the start. Bukharin's concept of NEP (at least, as portrayed by his biographer Stephen Cohen) was a sound, structured critique of Stalinism. But could it really have achieved the same speed of development? Could market forces, in the primitive conditions of 1920s

Russia, really have produced a similar, or adequate modernisation? That is how the conservatives argue. Of course (even they concede) there were mistakes, though they still quibble over figures just as neo-Nazis question the death toll in Auschwitz. They admit the failings (the slaughtering of *kulaks*, the purging of the officer corps) but deny the consequences (mass famine, and a disastrous response to German invasion). Yet the bloody hands of Stalin, do not make Bukharin right. The Bukharin road to socialism was never that; it was an approach, a style but not an alternative. Lenin had already structured the choices and had, in Zbigniew Brzezinski's words, 'de-Westernised' Marxism. Lenin's emphasis on 'dogmatic belief, on violence, on conspiratorial activity, and in the almost total subordination of the individual to the Party, as well as his intolerance of dissent and his paranoid suspicious-ness, both reflected and extended the brutal autocratic tradition in which he operated' (Brzezinski; *Between Two Ages*, 1970). Lenin had steered Marxism into an oriental despotic mode and away from occidental democratic tendencies. These are old debates, well rehearsed by Western scholars and, increasingly, by Soviet academics. But this much is plain; a 'human face' socialism, a reformist option, did not really exist in 1929. Gorbachev, in tracing the roots of perestroika back via Bukharin to Lenin, is playing the same game as Dallas businessmen who claim to be descended from King Henry VIII: seeking legitimacy with cooked genealogical charts.

If anything, Gorbachev's choices have narrowed from those available in 1929. Communism has failed as an economic system. Central planning generates consumer shortages and mediocre growth. It has outlived its primary function, which was to convert the Soviet Union into an industrial power. The Plan has also abandoned its primacy as an ideological device, as a just distributor of goods and services, of rewards and punishment. Yet so much of the system of belief still hinges on the Plan, as a vehicle of social justice. Gorbachev cannot completely jettison the Plan and embrace the market since this would effectively leave the Soviet Union without a ruling ideology. His radical advisers say: we do not need a 'ruling ideology' in the economy, we need efficiency. But if the Party is divorced from the economy, ousted by the market, where can it assert its presence? The other pillars of belief are already crumbling. The 'leading role of the Party' – its undisputed right to occupy the key seats in political, economic and social life – was detached by Poland in 1989. Solidarity became an authorised opposi-tion with a large block of seats in parliament, and then won the premiership. Now, no major decisions in Poland can be made without the approval of the formerly banned trade union. Coinciding with the collapse of Party morale, all social initiative has now passed into Solidarity hands. Hungary has embarked on a multi-party system, so has the Yugoslav republic of Slovenia. Discussion clubs in Estonia and other Baltic republics are, in effect, embryo parties. Gorbachev aims to restore the standing of the Communist Party by making it the helmsman of a newly strong and competently managed economy. But he cannot achieve an economic miracle within the stifling confines of the Plan. He reaches for half-way formulae – for lease-back schemes, share ownership, co-operatives, private enterprise with soft edges – and in certain controlled areas, the market. Yet by driving Lenin out of the factories, by de-ideologising the industrial economy, by assessing managers on competence rather than political loyalty, he is destroying the last (the police and army excepted) major base of authority of the Party; he has condemned the Party of Lenin to social irrelevance. He does so at a time when he is asking the Soviet people to take on new burdens. Already saddled with the queues and backbreaking futility of a shortage economy, the Soviet consumer now has to accept rapidly rising prices as a permanent feature of his existence. 'If there were oranges in the shops,' was a typical lament of the late 1980s, 'we would pay more for them, pay a market price.' But there were no oranges and the alternative fruit was becoming impossibly expensive. Gorbachev's Party, in the era of the market, still carries the responsibility for the economy, but does not have the power; the standing of the Communist Party, never high, tumbled; more important, its self-esteem fell too. In the early 1990s Gorbachev's survival was dependent on two things: on distancing himself from the Party that he had himself helped to discredit but which he none the less led, and on the creation of alternative political and social outlets for the Soviet people, perhaps in the form of a cautious multi-party system. It was plain then that the original aim of the Gorbachev programme was doomed. He had set out to restructure the Party but succeeded only in smashing the old certainties. He had wanted to stop the economic and social decline of the country, but had succeeded only in dragging more people towards the survival minimum.

Yet this bleak picture of Gorbachev's prospects should not invalidate the idea of 'market socialism.' It is not (as the New Left, such as Hillel Ticktin argue) a contradiction in terms; it has real meaning. In this book I have tried to show how markets already function within socialism, legally and illegally, and how separate social problems can be treated with market forces. I maintain that in the developed countries of Eastern Europe, market socialism is feasible. It is dependent, of course, on the goodwill of the Soviet Union; tanks destroyed the market socialism of Prague in 1968 and, under a new Soviet leadership, it is conceivable that Moscow would again try to assert its control over the pace of change. Here then is a paradox. As long as the Soviet Union retains an imperial structure, the idea of Soviet market socialism will be impossible to implement. The centre has to have the authority, the legitimacy to re-distribute from the richer to the poorer of its dependencies and, at the same time, maintain social order. Every known aspect of the market undermines this mission. Yet the success of East European market socialism is dependent on the Soviet Union believing, probably erroneously that it can introduce market socialism in its own territory. Soviet reformers travel to the neighbours and pick up ideas – the Kombinate of East Germany, efficient collective farms in Hungary, political innovations from Poland – and East European economists are continuously quizzed in Moscow. But there is a willing deception, not the first in Soviet–East European relations. For years Soviet-Bloc leaderships have bamboozled Moscow into supplying artificially cheap oil, gas and raw materials. Moscow allowed itself to believe that this was an obscure imperial obligation, but the reality was that the small Soviet allies were treating the Big Brother, for so long the apotheosis of totalitarian domination, as a colony. The Bulgarians sucked up Soviet oil and in return supplied strawberry jam in much the same way as the British drained their colonies and off-loaded unwanted, or uncompetitive goods. Fraud, then, has always been at the heart of the relationship between Moscow and its allies. Now, this fraud is about reform. It is necessary for the East Europeans to convince Gorbachev that he can succeed in order for them to succeed themselves. Yet few think it possible that Gorbachev's broad market reforms will last the 1990s. Hungarians and Poles, who have most to lose from the fall of Gorbachev, were saying in 1990 that the Soviet leader would have to steal more and more clothes from the conservatives to fend off his domestic critics. Reform will slow down, and though newly legal markets might survive in the crevices of the economy, the Plan, the Planners and their bureaucratic supporters would win the day. Gorbachev was still operating within the Leninist framework, which virtually rules out revolution from above or below. And a gradualist approach, as Mrs Thatcher found in the much smaller task of using the market to turn around the British economy, was never going to work. In Budapest at the dawn of the 1990s the harsh verdict on Gorbachev was that he was talking too much and letting the reformist impetus slip away.

Yet there are ways of successfully introducing market forms into closed societies and even in the Soviet Union – albeit a USSR less burdened with imperial duties, less troubled by the loss of its ideological identity – there is some hope. The hope may have to be deferred to the post-Gorbachev era, but it is there, glowing like a night-light in a hospital ward.

The first step must surely be to agree on a minimal definition of a socialist economy. Perhaps the most useful proposition comes from Wlodzimierz Brus, once a Party heretic in Warsaw, now an Oxford academic whose ideas are in the mainstream (even a little conservative) of the East European reform movement. He thinks (*Socialist Ownership and Political Systems*, 1976) that an economic system remains socialist when it fulfils two fundamental criteria. First, the means of production should be used in the interests of society, in the 'social interest'. Second, society must have effective disposition over the means of production it owns. It need hardly be said that this is a commendable dilution of Marx ('the national centralisation of the means of production will become the national base for society' . . . etc). Marketeers can demonstrate easily enough that the planned economy is not being used efficiently in the interests of society; that market forces serve the people better. The mere transfer of a factory from private ownership into state hands no longer guarantees improvement for the workers or consumers, or whoever is regarded as representing the interests of society. The people of Eastern Europe grasped this three decades ago; the British Labour Party in 1989. The second criterion also ensures a substantial place for the market. As the credibility of the Party has collapsed, so the idea that it truly represents the broad interests of society has disappeared. Instead the Party is now generally regarded in terms of the *nomenklatura*, a self-appointed group monopolising state functions, operating without effective controls and, in the absence of a market, manipulating information. That, at any rate, is the popular view in Poland, where the Party was humiliated in the June 1989 elections. The Party was at a similarly low ebb in the rest of the Bloc. Certainly, Brus's criterion – 'society must have effective disposition over the means of production' – no longer translates into Communist control, since there is no identity between Party and State. Yet Brus sees the market as a way of improving on planning, not substituting for it. In his view, the central planners must continue to determine the main areas of investment and they should be able to affect the growth of production. Planners should have some say over the wage funds of factories. Manufacturers should be free to encourage good-quality market-orientated production, but at the same time the state should have the power to halt wage inflation. The state should retain some control over prices and act to satisfy important social needs, such as health, education and defence. Many Soviet and East European reformists, moved by the spirit of the free market, would go much further than Brus. Are private hospitals and private schools to be excluded (there are already moves in this direction in Poland) or is it just a matter of degree? And who decides the limits? For many of the vanguard economists Brus gives too much interventionist power to the state and in so doing restricts the freedom of entrepreneurs. For the political radicals, Brus offers too many platforms for the Party; the Party is on the retreat but Brus offers it some shelter.

My feeling though is that the Brus model broadly accords with popular, rather than academic, sentiment. After four decades (seven in the Soviet Union) of Socialism, certain values – a gut egalitarianism, a commitment to protecting the lower paid – are part of the social fabric. So too are less noble prejudices. Envy of success or individual progress is widespread; there is an overweening desire to profit from the subsidised economy. Why, after all, are there 15-year queues for apartments in Poland? The queue is for *cheap* housing; at a price, apartments are available. Market socialism, if it is to work, has to be socialist enough to meet expectations of fair play, market enough to end the distrust of money and true economic values. That is why a political calculation must enter the overall formula. It is not just a question of the market robbing the Party of power. There has to be a wholesale redistribution of influence, a new system of values and a long period of re-education; half a century of collectivism cannot be undone in a few flushed years. How is this complex balance to be achieved and more important, how, is it to be maintained over time? There are a number of broad strategies available: the police state, the auction, parliament or populism.

The police state model. The shooting on Tiananmen Square happened in the same month as Poland held its astonishing elections. The Polish vote, a humiliating defeat for the Communist Party, was essentially a negative vote; a poll against communist rule that had never been remotely popular, but a poll too on the Party line-up that had imposed martial law in the winter of 1981. The Chinese and Polish cases can bear comparison. In China, economic market reforms had advanced much further than in Poland but, as discussed earlier in this chapter, had reached an impasse. There was a failure of political will, a reluctance, because of an emerging succession crisis, to take difficult economic decision. But the decisions were always seen as just that, *economic*, a choice between painful or gradualist reform, a choice of priorities between growth and combating inflation. Of course there were several condemnations, even the possibility of unrest, but they were mere footnotes in the discussion documents of the Central Committee. The students, by crowding into the centre of Beijing, put politics on the agenda just as surely as had the striking dockworkers in Gdansk: to a leadership generation rattled by the Cultural Revolution, this stirred up real fears. In China, politics can be made on the piazza. What did the students want? A political outlet for the anxieties generated by rapid change. In so far as those changes were prompted by the market, the demonstrators were anti-market; as with the Solidarity protests of 1980, there was a strong egalitarian aspect to their movement. Anti-market, but pro-democracy. Later, the Chinese authorities said the students wanted to introduce capitalism, that it was the germ of a counter-revolution. But the point of that and the many other comments was to frighten young workers away from supporting the students: capitalism is a boo-word if you work in a state factory, without access to hard currency or time to moonlight. It means simply higher prices, harder work.

The Chinese decision to fire on demonstrators and later to lock up thousands, had clear precedents in Eastern Europe: Hungary 1956, Czechoslovakia 1968, the beating of students in Poland in 1968, the shooting of workers on the Baltic Coast in 1970. But the similarities with martial-law Poland are most obvious. Both used force to keep control over the pace of change. Reform was the programme, but reform meant in the first, even second, place, austerity. The Party lacked the language to persuade the people of the need for sustained sacrifice, lacked that authority. And so the expectations of the people, galloping ahead of the system's ability to deliver, had to be battened down. If reform is perceived, within leadership groups, as a *revolution* then the reformist clichés of 'social partnerships', or contracts between leaders and led, are rendered irrelevant. Revolutions are about control; who steers, who emerges stronger and – an afterthought – who benefits. Both the Chinese and the Polish parties decided that a market-orientated revolution should be imposed from above; to let students or Solidarity set the pace would destroy the Party, or play into the hands of the conservative non-reformist factions. Jaruzelski in December 1981 had two major aims; to crush Solidarity as a competitive spokesman for the working class (this was supposed to be the Party's role) and to clean out the anti-reformers in the Party. To bring in reform at the point of a bayonet. A third possibility exists, the official justification that the Soviet Union was preparing to invade Poland. Few people can test the validity of that thesis. It will remain a blank spot in modern Communist history, even in the glasnost era, since one of the members of the Soviet politburo at the time was Mikhail Sergeyevitch Gorbachev, who, in the summer of 1989, declared his readiness to meet a Polish Prime Minister selected from the ranks of newly elected Solidarity parliamentarians.

Jaruzelski, in imposing martial law, was following bad advice. First, by jailing Solidarity and by pursuing an ambiguous attitude towards its underground wing (chasing, jailing, beating – but also tolerating, penetrating, splitting), he helped create a unity of opposition that had never existed previously. Workers and students, even farmers, were fused in their resentment of the General and his regime. Second, by using the military to solve a political problem, he broke the spine of the Party. True reforming communists, and their hard-line opponents, were shuffled off into exile as diplomats, or thrown out of the Party. What remained was a cowed, defensive Party committed opportunistically to a programme of mild reform. Some Solidarity-inspired legislation – a factory self-management act – was passed into law, other relatively liberal measures (a potentially useful trade union law) also stumbled through parliament. A strange precursor of glasnost came into operation with rationed candour at government news conferences and within the government-controlled press (the small Catholic press, by contrast, was mauled by censorship). But the machinery of power overwhelmed what was left of the reform programme and made martial law an expensive futility.

Jaruzelski thought that he had been, would be, the saviour of the nation, yet the nation wanted change, above all higher living standards, not salvation-by-numbers. Caught in a shrinking circle of advisers, incapable by temperament of seizing a populist initiative, Jaruzelski was only saved by Gorbachev, but the Kremlin leader's support (and undoubted popularity, even in Poland) was unable to prevent an electoral disaster in 1989. Gorbachev freed Jaruzelski from the Black Spot, the memory of his time as a young Minister of Defence co-responsible for planning the invasion of Czechoslovakia. The limits of reform were clearly defined in 1968 and they still frightened the government – indeed, the whole of the Czechoslovak leadership – two decades later; Gorbachev blurred those frontiers and eventually abandoned the Brezhnev Doctrine, declaring for example at the Warsaw Pact Summit in Bucharest (July 1989) that there was no one, true road to socialism. As Gorbachev grew stronger politically, so too did the Polish government's willingness to consider genuine political reform.

If there was a failure of courage, it was in the realm of economics. What level of bankruptcy, of unemployment, of wage inflation was tolerable? The Chinese feared the political card most of all; the Deng leadership was a quiet, mild bunch, intent above all on avoiding Maoist extremism. Most of the key Politburo members had suffered politically in the Cultural Revolution; some had children who had been beaten up by the Red Guards; all knew people whose sons had been thrown out of windows or lamed with lead piping. Their 'police state' answer to reform was partly borrowed from Poland: after the crippling of the student revolt, the arrests and the martial law courts, there was, as in Poland, widespread 'verification', vetting of political beliefs in the media, judiciary and other institutions. But it was also in the Asian tradition. South Korea and Taiwan had successfully developed market economies while keeping the screws down on their people. Yet martial law or police-conducted reform requires a high degree of isolation, to guard against infection. The first act of the Polish Government on 13 December 1981 was to cut telecommunications with the outside world and impose strict censorship. Solidarity's survival in the martial-law years was to a large degree because it broke through that isolation: Western radio stations beaming into Eastern Europe, Western money and equipment (though Solidarity, for obvious political reasons, still plays down this factor) and Western press coverage helped to sustain the idea of Solidarity and even create the illusion of a mass underground organisation.

South Korea began to head for political trouble when, in search of new technical skills, it sent an increasing number of students abroad for training. They returned and immediately put pressure on the inflexible whalebone structure of the political system. To introduce market reforms is to enter competitive world markets, and that means an end not only to protected industry but also protected politics. By 1987 China had signed 10,000 contracts for foreign-funded investments and that year there were 20,000 students from China studying at US Universities. South Korea and Taiwan have similar numbers. Markets abhor isolation; technological change has made the ancient physical barriers, such as the Iron Curtain, irrelevant. Increasingly too, markets undermine the act of governing through physical force. Could martial law be a shield for reform in the Soviet Union? The use of troops and poison gas against demonstrators in Tbilisi in 1989 suggested that there might be some form of dress rehearsal under way. It is not difficult to isolate individual Soviet republics at the moment. As reform takes hold, it will be more complex. Jaruzelski's and the Chinese leadership's decisions to use force in the name of reform both indicate considerable political naivety. The Polish generals were genuinely taken aback when the nation turned against them: they were blinded by a perverse patriotism and the months of intricate planning. Martial law is, at its inception, a conspiracy, it feeds a closed conspiratorial psychology, cuts the conspirators off from changing political realities. So it was that Chinese Prime Minister Li Peng could defend the use of live ammunition against the Beijing students by saying that the army had unfortunately been short of tear gas and rubber bullets: 'the soldiers did not want any bloodshed – they wanted peace.' This remoteness from the truth, verging on the ludicrous, is a dangerous feature of all reform leaderships. Take Nikolai Schmelyov, the most radical of Gorbachev's kitchen cabinet. Brave, of course: 'There is no alternative to a manageable market. We've tried everything else, including concentration camps. All proved inefficient. Establishing the market is a matter of survival for us' (*International Herald Tribune*, July 1989). There is some political confusion concealed in this entirely typical, outspoken interview. The gulags – inefficient? Is that not rather missing the point? Soon enough it emerges that Schmelyov, like many other Gorbachev advisers, like Jaruzelski's team (journalists and soldiers) is a naif. What, he is asked (by the redoubtable Flora Lewis) of the nationalities problem? 'It was quite unexpected. Everything was so calm.' This, from a man who wants to introduce an integrated, nationwide market economy. The idea of economic reform comes from outside, or the outer fringes of, the Party; its supporters are similarly out of the machine. There is an *unpolitical* quality to them that gives the idea energy and impetus. (It is easy to imagine the journalists of the Jaruzelski circle – Urban, Gornicki, Rakowski, Kwiatkowski – sitting around a table and discussing how to improve Poland's image abroad. 'How about a weekly press conference that tells most of the truth?' 'Brilliant, Jurek!')

But it also contains the seeds of disaster. The advisers, unschooled in the normal back-door, smoke-filled room strategies, reach too easily for the shocking, the extraneous solution: Martial-law reform protected by soldiers must have seemed like a brainwave. It was not.

Governments that can no longer rule by force must rule by consent. But the knitting of consensus requires immense political sophistication, and the threads unravel all too easily. Hungary in its slow march towards economic reform showed this plainly. Janos Kadar's Hungary was, for over two decades a tightly regulated place. There were artfully constructed breathing-spaces, enough oxygen entered the system to heal the wounds of 1956. The collective memory of the Soviet tanks created, for a generation, a self-limiting, self-censoring approach to politics. The Kadar policy – 'those not against us, are with us' – of social inclusion helped to scratch back some of the trust forfeited by the Party (and by Kadar himself) in 1956. And, from 1968 with a brief hiccough in the 1970s, the economy was treated to useful injections of market competition. Private entrepreneurs flourished, within agreed limits, moonlighting was legalised, the underground economy merged seamlessly with the official economy. In the early 1980 it was common enough for Western journalists, dazzled by the fine shops of Budapest, to declare that the Communists of Hungary would be the only Party in the Bloc to win an election. Free elections, in those days, were pure fancy. Others talked of Kadar as a kind of benign but absolute monarch who had steered the country back to a form of self-respect. Yet by 1987, Kadar's popularity was flaking, by 1988 there was talk of stagnation, of growing social problems (poverty, above all) that had been shelved under Kadar. By the time his successor, Karoly Grosz, was in the saddle, the Kadarite consensus had collapsed. New parties – for the most part intellectual talking-shops, but still significant – were sprouting up everywhere. Even then, it was not enough for Grosz to hang on: the huge reservoir of political discontent had swollen too dramatically. Naturally the process of modernising politics had been accelerated by the accession, and survival, of Gorbachev in Moscow. But the main point was that the Kadar formula, economic reforms kept in check by a mild party-police state with a popular patriot at its head, could not hold up over time. The economy had become too vulnerable to the vagaries of the world economy; a Western recession, higher oil prices, all demonstrated that the authorities had ceded some vital element of control to the market. Government by consensus, in a half-closed system, is a matter of almost constant negotiation. The reform constituency of the Soviet Bloc – Gorbachev's Russia, Poland, Hungary – spent the late 1980s finding partners for a dialogue, people outside the Party system, with whom one could do a deal. It had not seemed necessary before. The police-state mentality survived, but only among the anti-reformers like Romania and East Germany, or those, like Czechoslovakia and Bulgaria, where reform was creeping ahead so slowly it was barely visible.

The auction model. When monolithic rule begins to crack – and when the cracking is due to an economic crisis – then the pursuit of political and economic freedom begins to resemble an auction. There are several points at which an economic freedom entails the restriction of a political freedom; lobbyists emerge, politics bids against economics. Poland, it was said, had efficient political bidders: Solidarity had won active participation in a multi-party parliament and the promise of much else besides. But the economic bidding was at a much lower level: where were the new guarantees for private businessmen, where was the dismantling of smokestack industry? Not all of this was because of retrenchment by Party hard-liners. The contradictions were contained in Solidarity itself. Few in Solidarity could contemplate the shutting down of the manifestly inefficent Lenin shipyard in Gdansk: it was the symbol of Solidarity's alignment with industrial workers (and, of course, the birthplace of Solidarity itself) yet it was also a prime candidate for bankruptcy. So, it followed, Solidarity felt on safer ground bidding in political than in economic auctions. Even between the reforming countries, there is a form of bidding and counter-bidding, since countries like Hungary and Poland are competing for Western loans. Hungary, its spokesmen will say, is far ahead of Poland in providing opportunities for joint ventures. Suddenly Poland will come up with new joint-venture rules that give it an edge over Hungary. Poland's political liberalisation, the result of a decade of pressure and four decades of weak, low-credibility Communist rule, is touted as an attraction for foreign investors while a parliamentary semi-democracy vouches for stability. The opposition in Hungary promptly steps up its own demands: the Poles have this, why can't we?

Yet bidding up freedom poses some new philosophical problems, New, that is, for the Communist world. There is the familiar dilemma, of course, namely, who sets the limits, who draws up the rules, if the Party no longer has monopoly rights on political life. The problem at the kernel, though, is about freedom itself. In concrete terms, one can ask:

What is freedom for Hungary or Poland today? There are an accumulation of desirable and attainable freedoms. The freedom to explore the historical past, to question Soviet interference, the freedom to expose police or institutional abuse, the freedom to change one's job, the 'bourgeois' freedoms – to worship, to public expression – the 'socialist' freedoms – to job security, to housing and the freedom to drop out. The broad-brush demand might well be for neutrality on the Austrian model. But neutrality on the basis of a sick economy does not translate easily into 'freedom', only into a more intricate network of dependencies. Freedom, say the neo-liberals in Solidarity like Aleksander Malachowski, is quite simply the market. Planning is the negation of freedom. It assumes omniscience, priorities have to be ordered taking into account all available information. Yet priorities change, information, as gathered by the centre, is incomplete and out of date and so the planner must perforce make arbitrary and partially uninformed decisions, nominally in the interests of society but actually in the interests of a controlling group. This tends, inevitably towards authoritarian rule; coercion is part of the planning machine. The market, ever sensitive to individual wishes, is the only true arbiter of freedom. Expanding the market increases the scope for freedom. That is the Hayekian thesis. Simply, there is no middle way if political freedoms are to grow. Planning constrains, dictates and, ultimately, is the 'road to serfdom'. Some political bidders are thus going all-out for the abolition of communism and central planning and for the introduction of the market, in the hope that a fully realised, integrated market will lead to political independence. The Plan is the glue of the Warsaw Pact. Already by the summer of 1989, at the Bucharest summit, it was clear that the Soviet Bloc no longer existed as a Bloc; it was divided into a market-reforming constituency and a variegated anti-reform rump.

But in the think-tanks of Moscow, Beijing, Budapest and Warsaw, neo-liberals are still a minority, albeit influential. What, ask their critics, does Hayek mean by freedom? If we accept that the Plan is serfdom, will abolishing it really bring freedom, or merely the absence of chains? The market reformers go some way with Hayek. They accept, for the first time, that freedom is not conditional on equality. That truly marks the death of an ideology. But they do not want to abandon all claims to egalitarianism – even Hayek urges equality before the law – and that pre-supposes a measure of coercion. Resources have to be coercively redistributed against the free play of the market. The state has to retain some responsibilities and some coercive power in order to act in the interests of society as a whole. These are ancient arguments, a continuation of the Great Debate of the 1930s. Hayek, Ludwig von Mises and the Austrian School, regarding with horror the Stalinist development of the Soviet Union, were quite definite about the incompatibility of Plan and Market. Von Mises argued that the market mechanism was linked inseparably with private property, because market forces were about maximising profit. The quest for private profit compels entrepreneurs to limit their costs and efficiency and match supply with demand, and at the same time provides their individual motivation. Take it away, and one is left with 'the senseless output of an absurd apparatus. The wheels will turn, but will run to no effect.' In other words, political reformers in the communist world are doomed to be counter-revolutionaries: nothing less than the return of capitalism is consistent with political freedom. Is that what Hayekian pupils – the Thatcher, Reagan, Bush administrations – believed? Almost certainly not, since they themselves, while freeing market forces, chose not to abandon strong state control. It is now acknowledged, even by marketeers, that the introduction of market forces is profoundly destabilising politically. The leaders of the West are seeking to stimulate market change in the 1990s and at the same time to maintain stability. It was they, rather than the reformist socialists of the East, who were trying to square the circle. (An oddity; Mrs Thatcher, who came to power in 1979 committed to ousting corporatist politics, found herself ten years later pumping aid into a Poland that was attempting to salvage a corporatist strategy from the wreckage of communism.)

The working definition of freedom shaped by the moderate reformers includes four essential features. The aim is to produce a mixed system of plan and market, in which the market tends to increase its importance and state intervention tends to be exceptional. The function of the plan is not to order everyday life or provide the framework for totalitarian rule, but to define the social interest and achieve a reasonably equitable redistribution of wealth, to set goals but not methods. Third, the coercive element in central planning should be held in check through democratic institutions which would also protect the individual against the state. All the reforming regimes would subscribe to those goals, just as all would agree to the minimalist definition of socialism outlined by Brus. That, then, gives some indication of where the bidding will stop. Poland cannot become America.

The role of parliament. An active, more or less democratic parliament can help establish goals, identify priorities, protect markets and individual liberties and take away some of the coercive sting of the plan. Deployed intelligently, elected and responsible parliaments are a useful device for reforming systems. They cannot however be a reform-terminus and cannot substitute for an overhaul of institutions, from the judiciary to the police, that were conceived and moulded at a time when the Party enjoyed a monopoly. The hope of Hungary, the Soviet Union and Poland is that parliaments can become the setting for the historic compromise between plan and market, restraining the arbitrary aspects of the plan, but also the arbitrary or socially divisive aspects of the market. But the theorists of the Great Debate were always rather sceptical about the stamina of parliamentary democracy. As the early days of the new Polish parliament showed, there was not much chance of an elected chamber establishing unitary goals for society. In Gorbachev's Soviet Union, the Congress of Deputies assumed a court-jester role, licensed to mock and criticise the vanities and policies of the monarch. Gorbachev, as President, was obliged to sit on the podium and listen to the stridencies of a stenographer from Sverdlovsk. Healthy stuff, an improvement on the rubber-stamp parliaments of the Brezhnev and pre-Brezhnev days, but not a revolution. Gorbachev had his uses for parliament. He could shift the reforming impetus from an obstructive Party to the more malleable state institutions. Since the Party was defending its position, it suited reformist leaders to govern through parliaments (where party power was diluted) rather than Central Committees. It was easier by far to reshuffle a cabinet than a Politburo.

Hayek warns that it is not parliamentary democracy, but the market itself – and the minimal state – which guarantees freedom. Indeed 'it is at least conceivable that under the government of a very homogeneous and doctrinaire majority democratic government might be as oppressive as the worst dictatorship. This may explain Mrs Thatcher's appeal to the likes of Mieczyslaw Rakowski and Karoly Grosz who, as interim leaders of Poland and Hungary, expressed an embarrassing admiration for the British leader. Rakowski has undergone several conversions in his life as a party journalist-turned-politician. He supported, and later abandoned, the three major very different post-war leaders of Polish communism: Boleslaw Beirut, Wladyslaw Gomulka, Edward Gierek. After Jaruzelski became premier in February 1981 Rakowski's political career began in earnest: as deputy premier in charge of negotiating with Solidarity and, after a few ups and downs, Prime Minister in 1989. By 1990, he was writing his memoirs. His critics regard his career as one of model opportunism, his friends detect an active, if sometimes delayed conscience. But more significant are his changing visions of Poland. Tracking through his articles since the 1960s, he appears to have been a passionate fan of Janos Kadar's Hungary, of the West German social democratic party, Sweden, and latterly Ludwig Erhard and Margaret Thatcher. Each of these have presented models for Poland, seen through a reformer's eyes. The discovery of Erhard marks his conversion to the social market, the *Sozialmarkt*. His discovery of Thatcher suggest that he has discarded the *Sozial* in the *Sozialmarkt*. But the charm of Mrs Thatcher, for a communist politician, is rooted in more than the way she has crushed the trades unions and closed down lame-duck factories. The attraction is her absolute parliamentary majority. An electoral system that simulates social consensus to such a degree that a leader can for 10 years introduce unpopular but partly successful market-fostering legislation – that, surely, is the envy of the Communist reformer. The elections of June 1989 put an end to his hopes that discredited Party-dictatorship could somehow be replaced by a working reformist majority in parliament. While, unquestionably, the majority of Communist and Solidarity deputies were committed to reform, their ideas were far apart. The Polish Communists ceased to think of themselves as communists and, like their Italian comrades, they regarded their mission as an essentially social-democratic one. Solidarity ceased to think of itself as a monolith, and its members began to talk like Christian Democrats, Hayekian neo-Liberals, Social Democrats of the Swedish school, Catholic Radicals. Parliament magnified the differences, accelerated the splintering. This was the parliamentary pluralism they had fought for, bargained for, but it did not bring Poland any closer to a coherent version of market socialism. Hungary, perhaps too willing to follow the Polish lead in political change, prepared for a similar parliament. In the Soviet Union, the provincial deputies became ruder and ruder about Mikhail Gorbachev. And still, the market shimmered enticingly, always close yet unattainable.

The populist temptation. It is easy to throw a few jibes at politicians like Rakowski: regular converts always attract suspicion. But his sequential dream of Poland – from Kadarist Hungary to Erhard's West Germany to Thatcherite Britain – is moving in the right direction. It shows that he, like his political class, is coming to terms not just with the market, but with market disciplines. The prime economic problem facing the reforming Russians and East Europeans was monetary overhang. Any resort to the free market sent prices shooting through the roof. Schmelyov estimated in 1989 that there were some $225 billion worth of 'loose roubles' in the Soviet economy that could trigger Latin-American-style inflation (on top of the existing 10 or 11 per cent) when prices were freed. Schmelyov's solution was to increase consumer imports. But the real economic solution is currency reform – on the Erhard model – that will, among other things, wipe out savings. The political solution, bearing in mind the tensions of the pluralism, is more complex. Can Solidarity, still the voice of the industrial working class, resist the temptation to play the populist card? Can it share in decisions that directly hit the pockets of workers? It is easy to see how the market revolution might dissipate into Argentina-style chaos, with Solidarity, endeavouring to keep faith with its traditional constituency, running a weak coalition in creating new half-jobs, raising wages and buying a few years of pseudo-prosperity. Argentina, shifting from corrupt generals towards democracy, elected a democratic president, Raoul Alfonsin, who was not strong enough to soak up the overhanging money supply. By the time the second presidential elections came round in 1989, inflation was above 6,000 per cent a year and the Argentines were ready to vote in a Peronist who was promising a broad range of populist, and potentially disastrous measures. Jeffrey Sachs of Harvard ('Social conflict and populist policies in Latin America,' NBER paper no 2897) compared four populist cycles – Argentina 1946–49 under Peron, Chile 1971–73 under Allende, Brazil 1985–88 under Sarney, Peru 1985–88 under Garcia – and came up with clear connections between large income inequalities, social conflict and chaotic, hyper-inflated economies. Political pressures stemming from income inequalities tempt government into fiscal expansion (to tackle poverty, for example) and protected exchange rates to prop up the real wages of industrial workers. Poland, with its heavy debt, its articulate workers and political hybridism, was an ideal candidate for such a dangerous short-cut to popularity. Rakowski, the Solidarity Premier Mazowiecki and others of their generation were aware of the pitfalls; they remember the short-lived popularity of Gierek in the early 1970s, when he imported consumer goods to fill the shops. The sober tones of the establishment (including the top advisers to Solidarity, who were frequently former colleagues or comrades of Rakowski) helped by the unwillingness of the West to throw large sums of money at Poland, steered Poland away from the populist option. But for how long, nobody could judge. In the Soviet Bloc with both the ideology and economy collapsing simultaneously, it remained a potent factor. Boris Yeltsin, who made his mark by demanding the end of Party privileges, and figures in the leadership of the Soviet republics attracted large followings from otherwise politically apathetic people. In Hungary, a tradition of patriotic, slightly racialist, rural romantic politics was reviving, helped by Romania's fanatic campaign against the Hungarian minority. In Poland, KPN (Confederation for Independent Poland) captured the hearts of the resolutely anti-communist, anti-Soviet, conservatives. The imagery of underground struggle was kept alive meanwhile by a militant Solidarity faction, Fighting Solidarity. None of these groups had the sheer mobilising force of Yugoslavia's populist politician, the Serbian party leader Slobodan Milosevic. What united all these groups was a vocabulary anchored in the 1930s, frequently anti-semitic, searching for political roots in a black, pre-communist past. In the Soviet Union the populists go back much further, trying to tap the peasant mysticism of the Czarist days. The more enduring is the limbo between the death of Utopian Marxism and the birth of a new code, the more likely it is that the peoples of Eastern Europe will turn to crowd-pleasing non-solutions. The populists offer passion at a time of fatigue. The worst outcome must surely be this: that communist states, but above all the Soviet Union, will remain permanently embedded in the condition of non-communism and non-capatilism, that no coherent middle zone can be found or staked out, and that each decision has to be improvised. The leaders, unable to grasp the initiative, slump into a kind of muddle-through tinged with corruption and lethargy; the led, in a barely tolerable present, seeing the past betrayed and a future without dreams, emigrate to the West (if given the opportunity) or retreat into a private nether-world.

It need never come to this (though it represents a fairly precise description of contemporary Romania). The way out is to help the cracking communist societies towards a market that is more than an economic arrangement, a market with moral purpose. As the economic structure of socialism enters a period of protracted decline, so capitalism should think more seriously about those ideals of social justice that have never, or only spottily, been applied in the East. Putting markets in a moral framework makes it easier for a dissatisfied communist society to move in that direction. Answers have to be provided to questions such as: who is to take care of the poor? Who guarantees stability when income differentials are growing rapidly? How can we control industrial pollution in a market context? How to prevent the erosion of workers rights while extending entepreneurial freedom? How permanent is unemployment? How deep can a man fall? Why do markets fail? It is the failure of market thinkers and practitioners in the West that they have not adequately tackled those problems which frighten the people of the East steeped for several generations in egalitarian values. It is useful, but not sufficient, to train the emerging business class of the Soviet Bloc. Creating more managers does not in itself establish the universality of market values: the people of Eastern Europe have to be persuaded that the market, as well as improving and modernising the economy, can also uphold certain social values. The market revolution in the Gorbachev era can be seen at home by ordinary Russians in the form of expensively (but rationally) priced co-operative restaurants and the organised criminal gangs running the black market who blend with legitimate businessmen to form the new embyro money-class. Abroad, the market means full shops, but also mass unemployment, the Wall Steet crash, bankruptcy and failure. It is not an encouraging vision. That is why the stainless-steel Welfare Capitalism of Sweden – which actually offers only a fraction of the appropriate solutions to Warsaw, Moscow and Budapest – beckons so attractively East of the Elbe.

The divorce of the market from its moral context is a relatively recent process. Adam Smith was analysing economic issues only with the aim of arguing Social policy. Why is usury a sin? The case for and against mercantilist market controls, the social function of prices. Governments, in Smith's day as in ours, were regarded as inefficient, corrupt and wasteful and so, plainly, the less government spent and the less it interfered with markets the better. But even at the height of *laissez-faire* analysis, there was a spiritual, or metaphysical dimension to economic theorising. Ricardo reduced, or raised, the previously interconnected social and economic problems to arithmetic forms. Yet even twentieth-century neo-liberals like Hayek have never stopped asking questions about individual liberties, although his practising disciples in Britain and elsewhere merge a supposedly value-free market and the competitive pursuit of efficiency, with over-centralised government to override personal rights. Mrs Thatcher began the 1990s by contesting a worker's charter in a future, integrated Europe, fearful that recently opened markets would be endangered by a new era of imported corporatism. Yet the most muscular expansion of industrial capitalism was accompanied by a fundamental extension of worker's rights – worker compensation was enacted in England in 1880 and 1897, in Germany in 1879, in Austria in 1887, in France in 1899; factory inspection was introduced in

England in 1833, in Austria in 1883. None of this represented a socialist conspiracy. Conservative and liberal governments worked on factory legislation in Germany where both Roman Catholics and Social Democrats helped create a network of worker protection; in Austria, the Church was the moving force. The picture of Europe in the 1990s is supposed to twin a robust, integrated Western Europe, with an Eastern Europe emerging from the shambles of defunct ideological rule. Put in slightly different terms, that is the vision of President Gorbachev and President Mitterand, of Chancellor Kohl and Prime Minister Mazowiecki. Yet there can be no real convergence as long as capitalism is displayed in its most brutish (some would say, British) form. From the days of Marx, the denial of workers' rights by capitalists has been the clinching argument for communists.

The market, it must be said, already contains elements that fit into a definition of social justice. That is rarely accepted by East European scholars, even of reformist persuasion; the justice bit, in their view, has to be added on afterwards. But there is, for example, the equity of risk. Each person, in a market economy, is free to chose the level of risk at which he wants to live. A worker who enters a contract with one employer, and who can thus legitimately claim those rights guaranteed to him under employment law, cannot demand as his due a share of the employer's profits since he is chancing nothing. Second, technical progress is no longer in the realm of control of a close, relatively small group. Innovation is diffused through competition, its effects trickle down rapidly. This technical progress, more evenly spread than ever before, improves productivity. Higher productivity gives the chance of higher wages. Because of the interdependency of the economy, the wage increases are not restricted to a few sectors, but spread. In conditions of continually climbing productivity, all active participants in a market economy benefit, irrespective of their personal input. That might be deemed a kind of distributive justice.

It is not enough, of course; these are just pleasing by-products of market forces, accidental justice. It is right, as Professor Brian Griffiths has done, to define certain moral goals that are in accord with a market economy. In his view they are: the legitimacy of wealth creation, the necessity of private property rather than state ownership, the ability of each family to retain a permanent stake in the economy, a mandate on the community to relieve poverty rather than pursue equality, a caution against materialism and the importance of accountability and judgement. Griffith (*Morality and the Market Place*, London 1989) finds a scriptural basis for those criteria that must police the free market. But the reforming states of the Soviet Bloc all have Christian traditions (Poland most ostentatiously so) and, having ditched their ruling dogma, there seems no reason why their governments should not be influenced by a Christian Democratic ethic.

Social envy is not to be under-estimated; it is ugly, and at its angriest it is the only genuinely revolutionary passion left in the Communist World. It brings the shipyard workers out, it guarantees the support of their wives and their priests, it mobilises the supporters of Yeltsin and Milosevic. As the market takes hold, so income differentials will increase. There is nothing intrinsically disruptive about this, but conventional sociology has it that rising expectations and relative deprivation can create a situation where groups, perceiving themselves as slipping down the prosperity ladder, react angrily. The relatively poor realise that they are being blocked from becoming relatively rich – or that they can improve only with disproportionate sacrifice. That is a breeding ground for revolt and condemns the Soviet Bloc to almost permanent instability as it moves from the old to the new order. To make the new order more palatable, the West should be framing policies that make plain the moral purpose of the market.

That means finding a 'market' approach to tackle poverty, to cope with the regiments of the under-class that have been mustered in a decade or more of radical market, or monetarist, policies. An obvious first step is to encourage equality of opportunity and promote social mobility. The connection between a market economy and a merito-cratic society is not automatic. Merit has to be rewarded, not just financially, and to be built into the system. It is already easier for a poor Pole than for a poor Englishman to obtain higher education. More, the quality of education in most (non-ideologically influenced) areas has generally been upheld despite long years of economic crisis. Soviet and Polish doctors are well-trained, Hungarian dentists legendary, Soviet-Bloc engineers thick on the ground. But many nowadays do not seek university education because there is no sense of social progression; dead-end state-sector jobs at the end of the line and frequently lower wages than unskilled workers in heavy industry. In a survival culture, the value of time-consuming higher education is debased. The West must ensure its continuing vitality by unblocking its arteries, easing the movement between classes with high-quality (not just 'higher') educa-tion; that means state intervention and heavy investment, but it is still consistent with a 'self-help' approach to domestic poverty. The East too

has to find a way for its highly educated workforce to deploy its talents.
That is not only a moral obligation, it is also a matter of simple
pragmatism: mass emigration of technicians to the West, and articulate,
disgruntled workers at home, provide no recipe for stability or growth.
The West then has to encourage management schools in the Soviet
Bloc, institutes that challenge the old Plan mentality. It must become
easier for a skilled worker to enter the management hierarchy, and, of
course, the Party must be chased out of management altogether.
Workers, if they are not to be unhinged from the market reform, must
see it as a means of self- as well as national betterment. Factories should
be encouraged to hire successful managers from state or private industry
(even from abroad); there must be a free market for such skills. One of
the shrewdest moves that Mrs Thatcher made in her pivotal dispute with
the miners was the recruitment of a successful businessman, Ian
McGregor, to head the Coal Board. The Soviet Bloc can easily learn
this kind of elasticity, since it involves no more than recognising talent,
buying and deploying it.

For the confused in the East, the issue is this: markets, and a form of
neo-capitalism, offer the best available exit from their economic crisis.
This book has tried to show that some balance between markets and plan
(or even total surrender to the market) can be struck in most sections of
everyday life. But if these developments are to shape a systemic
alternative, then a decision must be made on what brand of capitalism is
most suitable for the countries of the East; capitalism is no more a
monolithic form than communism. The rapid introduction of markets
should not become dogma, neither should they be adrift from a broader
social responsibility that was once the prerogative of communism. The
temptation is to shift from reform socialism into a kind of reform
capitalism – welfare-state capitalism – rather than a hard-edged and not
always exportable variant of Thatcherism. Yet the record of welfare-state
capitalism, at least in Britian, is not good. There is a critical gap between
the goals of the British Labour Party in the 1930s – abolition of poverty
and malnutrition, full employment, minimum income, reduction of
property income, erosion of the class system – and the actual
performance of the Labour government in 1945–50. Nationalisation
was very selective – about a quarter of industry, with full compensation
for shareholders – and included public utilities (gas, telephones,
railways, civil aviation) and a declining industry (mining). Although
this could be said to serve, in the communist sense, the 'social interest',
it built inefficiency into the post-war economy. The big achievements –

the National Health Service, public housing, old-age pensions, unemployment benefit – successfully transformed the social profile of Britain and helped diminish the crasser class differences. Yet these institutions were put into place without any concept for modernisation or change. What if demographic trends put too much stress on hospitals? What should be the desirable level of medical care? How, in the long run, was it all to be financed? The Welfare State entered a budgetary and strategic crisis in the 1980s. Nationalised enterprises were dismantled, individual stock ownership – a primitive democratic capitalism – was increased and markets arose in health and education. These are the options facing the Soviet Bloc as its own public-sector rule breaks on the rocks: it too must consider privatisation and share-ownership, while markets have crept into every crevice. Capitalism at its most socially concerned, at the height of the Welfare State, was something of a failure and cannot offer Eastern Europe much solace. Yet both the capitalist West and the Communist East are confronted with a similar dilemma. Can markets expand at liberty in the health and social services? If not, where are the limits and who defines them?

Efficiency is fine. But what are the values that we are seeking to uphold, where is the 'social interest'? As I write this, at the onset of the 1990s, it is plain that neither Western parties labelled 'conservative' nor Eastern governments tagged 'reformist' have been able to determine what should be conserved and what can be reformed. In sympathy with whatever policies can better the human lot of those who live under defunct-communism, I nonetheless despair of reformers whose per-spectives stretch no further than the next Party congress. And their friends in the West must think carefully before advocating a naked market as a substitute for the declining, but still potent, egalitarian creed. The 1990s can stand with the mid-19th century when the first wave of industrial capitalism was crashing on the shores of Europe. Then, the new Money Class seemed to be the standard-bearers of the future, bringing with them the new technologies of steam, rail and telegraph that appeared to be unify Europe and nations in an era of peace and prosperity. Within a generation, wars and revolutions shattered the bourgeois world. The new capitalism in West and East contains similar seed. It is foolhardy to expect the collapse of an ideology, 20th-century Marxism, to bring nothing but tranquillity.

Index